MW00838114

Healing the Heart of Trauma and Dissociation

Carol Forgash, LCSW, BCD, is a psychotherapist in private practice in Smithtown, New York, specializing in EMDR and ego state therapy. She is an EMDR Institute facilitator and an EMDRIA Approved Consultant. She presents at psychotherapy conferences and at workshops in the United States and internationally on the integration of EMDR with ego state therapy and psychodynamic treatment, the treatment of complex posttraumatic stress and dissociative disorders, and the treatment of the complex health issues of sexual abuse survivors. She is the board president of EMDR Humanitarian Assistance Programs.

Margaret Copeley, MEd, is a freelance editor specializing in the mental health fields.

Healing the Heart of Trauma and Dissociation

With EMDR and Ego State Therapy

Carol Forgash, LCSW, BCD
and
Margaret Copeley, MEd
Editors

SPRINGER PUBLISHING COMPANY

New York

Springer Publishing Company, LLC
11 West 42nd Street
New York, NY 10036
www.springerpub.com

Acquisitions Editor: Sheri W. Sussman
Project Manager: Julia Rosen
Cover design: Margaret Copeley
Composition: Apex Publishing, LLC

11   12   13/ 8   7   6   5

Library of Congress Cataloging-in-Publication Data

Healing the heart of trauma and dissociation: With EMDR and ego state therapy / edited by Carol Forgash, Margaret Copeley.
    p. cm.
   Includes bibliographical references and index.
   ISBN-13: 978-0-8261-4696-0 (alk. paper)
   ISBN-10: 0-8261-4696-1 (alk. paper)
  1. Psychic trauma—Treatment. 2. Dissociative disorders—Treatment.
3. Eye movement desensitization and reprocessing 4. Hypnotism—Therapeutic use. 5. Dissociation (Psychology) 6. Ego (Psychology)
I. Forgash, Carol. II. Copeley, Margaret.
   [DNLM: 1. Stress Disorders, Post-Traumatic—therapy—Case Reports.
2. Dissociative Disorders—therapy—Case Reports. 3. Ego—Case Reports.
4. Eye Movements—Case Reports. 5. Hypnosis—Case Reports.
6. Psychotherapy—methods—Case Reports. WM 170 H4333 2008]
   RC552.T7H43 2008
   616.85'2106—dc22   2007035619

Printed in the United States of America by Gasch Printing.

With gratitude to my husband, Hank Glaser, for his
enduring love and support.

—*Carol Forgash*

For Marco Boscolo, who taught me about the life journey
and accompanied me across the threshold.

And for Kevin, who showed me where to find the Best Self.

—*Margaret Copeley*

Contents

Contributors

Uri Bergmann, PhD, is in full-time private practice in Commack and Bellmore, New York. He is an EMDR Institute Senior Facilitator and Specialty Presenter as well as an EMDR International Association Approved Trainer and Consultant in EMDR. He is a lecturer and consultant on EMDR, the neurobiology of EMDR, and the integration of EMDR with psychodynamic and ego state treatment. He has authored and published articles on the neurobiology of EMDR in peer-reviewed journals and has contributed chapters to various books on EMDR.

Jim Knipe, PhD, has been a psychologist in independent practice since 1994. He is currently the Colorado Springs regional coordinator for the EMDR International Association and an instructor at the Colorado School of Professional Psychology. Since 1995, he has been involved in humanitarian EMDR training projects in Oklahoma City, Turkey, Indonesia, and the Middle East. In addition, he has written on the use of EMDR with complex cases.

Barry K. Litt, MFT, studied contextual therapy with its founder, Ivan Boszormenyi-Nagy. He is in private practice in Concord, New Hampshire and serves on the New Hampshire Board of Examiners. He is an AAMFT Approved Supervisor and an EMDRIA Approved Consultant. He has presented numerous workshops to international audiences on contextual theory, couples therapy, dissociation, and EMDR. He is a regular presenter at ISSD and EMDRIA annual conferences.

Michael C. Paterson, PhD, DClinPsych, is a chartered clinical psychologist based in Belfast, Northern Ireland, where he specializes in the treatment of traumatic stress and dissociative disorders. He is an EMDR Institute trainer and trains mental health professionals in the use of EMDR. He teaches traumatology and ego state therapy to postgraduate students at the Queens University of Belfast. He has published articles on stress and on trauma in the emergency services and has presented at international conferences.

Sandra Paulsen, PhD, cofounded the Bainbridge, Washington, Institute for Integrative Psychology to integrate EMDR, ego state therapy, and somatic psychotherapies with ancient healing practices from indigenous cultures. She has made numerous conference presentations, written articles and book chapters, and consulted widely on the combination of EMDR and ego state therapy. She developed the first protocol for the use of EMDR with dissociative clients and she teaches advanced specialty trainings in dissociation for the EMDR Institute and is an EMDRIA certified consultant in EMDR.

Maggie Phillips, PhD, is a clinical psychologist in Oakland specializing in the treatment of stress and pain disorders. She has lectured around the world on hypnosis, EMDR, behavioral medicine, ego state therapy, and energy psychology. She is the author of *Finding the Energy to Heal: How EMDR, Hypnosis, TFT, Imagery and Body-Focused Therapy Can Help Restore Mind-body Health* (2000) and coauthor of *Healing the Divided Self: Clinical and Ericksonian Hypnotherapy for Posttraumatic and Dissociative Conditions* (1995). Her latest book is *Reversing Chronic Pain* (2007).

Richard C. Schwartz, PhD, is the developer of the Internal Family Systems Model and president of the Center for Self Leadership in Oak Park, Illinois (www.selfleadership.org). Formerly he was an associate professor in the Department of Psychiatry at the University of Illinois at Chicago and at Northwestern University. He has authored or coauthored six books and over fifty articles.

Joanne H. Twombly, MSW, LICSW, is in private practice in Waltham, Massachusetts, specializing in complex trauma and dissociative disorders. She also provides consultation in EMDR, hypnosis, and Internal Family Systems. She has given many workshops on diagnosis and treatment of dissociative disorders, on EMDR and dissociation, and on complex PTSD. She is a director on the International Society for the Study of Trauma and Dissociation's Executive Council and a facilitator for the EMDR Humanitarian Assistance Programs. She is an EMDRIA Certified Consultant and an American Society of Clinical Hypnosis Certified Consultant.

John G. Watkins, PhD, practiced as a consulting and clinical psychologist. He is a professor emeritus at the University of Montana and is the author of *Adventures in Human Understanding: Stories for Exploring the Self* (2001). His numerous papers and book chapters are widely published. John and his wife, Helen Watkins, MA, are the authors of *Ego States: Theory and Therapy* (1997). He has presented workshops on ego state therapy at international conferences throughout his long career.

Foreword

Since earliest recorded history we humans have been interested in studying ourselves and others. We want to understand our physical and mental processes, and find out what to do if they are malfunctioning.

There are two general approaches to this endeavor. In one, we use our perceptual skills to observe the behavior of other people. This is empiricism. It is the way natural sciences operate. In recent years, facts ascertained thereby have been valued as more real, more dependable. This is because they are subject to validation through comparison with the observations of others. The empirical approach has brought us great advances in health, welfare, and our ability to treat human ills, such as pain and physical disturbances. In fact, the science and art of medical practice has emanated primarily from empirical methods.

However, there is another approach that has yielded dividends in human understanding and has improved our ability to deal with mental ills, namely, rationalism. Here one focuses perceptual and sensory skills upon one's own behavior and internal processes. This process is called "introspection." One's own thoughts become the "search engine." In this area lie the beliefs and understandings of philosophy, religion, and the humanistic disciplines. Its weakness is that its discoveries cannot be validated by others. Its strength inheres in that we can directly experience its data within our own selves.

Many of the greatest advances of humankind have come about through an integration of the two, when the external observations of other people have been combined with one's internal experiences.

Psychotherapy, the psychological treatment of maladjustment, has been long practiced. In the historical period of Aristotle and Plato, wounded warriors would lie on a stone couch and recount their sufferings to a listening priest, who would then intervene with healing words of suggestion and understanding. He practiced both of what would, centuries later, be called the "directive/suggestive" and "psychodynamic" approaches to therapy. He therefore combined empirical methods (Aristotle) with rational ones (Plato).

Centuries later, Sigmund Freud developed the psychodynamic method into a form called "psychoanalysis," a system that dominated psychological treatment for many decades. Its adherents claimed that this approach got more permanent results than the directive/suggestive ones. However, these results were achieved slowly and inefficiently. Therapists needed to accomplish psychodynamic understanding more rapidly.

Hypnosis offered promise, since it could facilitate both direct suggestion and inner exploration. But it had limitations. We did not understand what happened when a hypnotic trance was induced, and there was wide variation with different therapists and different patients. Some of these therapists achieved better results by combining psychoanalytic and hypnotic methodologies to form Hypnoanalysis. The search for a better therapy continued.

In 1987 a cognitive psychologist, Francine Shapiro, while seeking solutions to a potentially fatal illness, cancer, focused her own introspections on the interplay between mind and external stressors. She discovered that the uncovering of memories seemed to be accompanied by rapid eye movements. From this observation she developed a system of therapy that she called "EMDR" (Eye Movement Desensitization and Reprocessing).

Although the neurological mechanisms underlying this approach have only been hypothesized, EMDR therapy was found empirically to produce excellent therapeutic results, and in a relatively short time. EMDR therapeutic procedures have since been adopted by thousands of practitioners. They seem to involve a special kind of focusing.

Humans develop through *differentiation* and *integration*, that is, by separating (taking apart) and combining (putting together). Focusing involves differentiation; insight and understanding involve integration. In psychodynamic therapies both procedures are used (probing and interpreting).

The term "ego states" refers to segments of personality that function with more or less autonomy from each other. An analogy is the various political segments, nations, principalities, forest districts, counties, and so on. Ego states apparently lie on a continuum and manifest at one end as moods and at the other end as the isolated "alters" of dissociative identity disorder, true multiple personalities. In between, we prefer the term "differentiated" entities rather than "dissociated states." Dissociation refers to severe pathology in which ego state boundaries are rigid and inflexible.

I and my colleague Helen Watkins, drawing on experience with multiple personalities, discovered that dissociative splitting occurs in relatively normal as well as severely ill individuals. Hypnoanalytic techniques were effectively applied to these inner, less dissociated personality segments (ego states) by hypnotic focusing on their interactions.

Ego state therapy thus relates to the integration of true multiple personalities and to the reconciling of more mildly dissociated states, such as found in neurotic and behavior disorders.

Although ego state therapists have generally isolated individual ego states through hypnosis, the fine focusing afforded in the attention to individual states by EMDR shows that a formally induced hypnosis is not always essential.

However, there are conditions that are so severely dissociated that EMDR by itself is not considered to be completely safe. Furthermore, some clients do not react at all to EMDR techniques. Ego state techniques may make the conditions of many clients more accessible and the treatment safer for EMDR therapists.

Hypnotherapists and psychoanalysts focus on mental processes in treating pathology. Ego state therapy (with or without hypnosis) focuses on the interactions of these differentiated personality segments with each other, with the entire person, and with the external world.

An issue not yet settled is the extent to which EMDR overlaps with hypnotherapy. Dr. Shapiro has argued that EMDR is not hypnosis, since it does not involve formal hypnotic inductions. Indeed, the trancelike state of mind in which the EMDR client often works is not the same as in deep hypnosis, and EMDR therapists do not use hypnotic inductions.

However, incisive therapist comments focusing on single communications (such as "Go with it," "What do you feel?" or "Hold the image") may in time induce a trancelike or hypnoidal condition. This question deserves further study.

Hypnoanalysts and ego state therapists are finding that adding EMDR techniques to their armamentarium can improve therapeutic effectiveness. And many EMDR practitioners are now exploring the integration of ego state therapy with their own procedures.

The significant case studies and discussions in the following chapters advance the cause of improvement in therapy. The contributors are well respected and experienced EMDR therapists who also employ ego state procedures. This book pioneers the integration of EMDR with ego state techniques and opens new and exciting vistas for the practitioners of each.

John G. Watkins

Preface

Ellen came into Carol Forgash's office for her first session in great distress. She had been experiencing serious somatic problems, flashbacks, panic attacks, nightmares, and episodes of dissociation, rages, and suicidal ideation. Her world had come crashing down around her four years earlier, following two major surgeries. At the time, a recovery-room nurse reported that Ellen had screamed, "Louis, don't hurt me! Don't kill me!" as she was coming out of anesthesia. Ellen later identified Louis as an adult neighbor who had molested her and a friend almost daily from the time the girls were four until they were six years old. Her surgery had revived memories of her trauma that were now highly distressing to her.

Ellen was not just a sexual abuse survivor. Both of her parents suffered from depression, and there were many indications that Ellen was a severely neglected child. Her parents were unavailable both physically and emotionally. Financially well-off, they had live-in nannies, but the nannies were physically abusive to Ellen and her siblings. She recalled times as a child when she would retreat into a dissociative fantasy world in an attempt to block out what was happening to her. She said, "I learned how to be somewhere else and to not feel anything."

Not surprisingly, Ellen's constellation of diagnoses included post-traumatic stress disorder, dissociative disorder, and borderline personality disorder. Her psychiatrist referred her to Carol Forgash, an EMDR specialist, for treatment to extricate her from layers of trauma.

Many therapists are confused and even frightened by clients such as Ellen who manifest some of the most serious and intractable symptoms of mental disorder. Under the wrong treatment conditions, these clients can decompensate and the therapy can go catastrophically wrong. They typically migrate from one failed therapy to the next in search of the proper diagnosis and treatment approach.

The practices of the authors of this book have long included many of these most difficult cases, and we are pleased to offer clinicians a new and novel approach that we have discovered to be of tremendous help in treating clients with the most severe trauma-related disorders.

Therapy for clients like Ellen—who have suffered multiple traumas and early attachment disruptions and have a history of conflicting diagnoses and failed treatments—is characteristically the most lengthy, complex, and difficult kind of work, for both clients and therapists. By definition these clients lack the internal cohesion and resources necessary to withstand uncovering and processing traumatic memories. A primary danger of this work is that if trauma memories are accessed before these clients have appropriate coping resources, they may experience blocked processing, flooding, and intense discomfort or severe decompensation.

EMDR as a means of trauma resolution has been available to therapists since its discovery in 1987 by Francine Shapiro and is now a treatment of choice and well supported by a large body of scientific research. But until now, its use with clients with dissociative disorders has been difficult or at times even impossible. This book explains why that is the case and brings to EMDR therapists a unique additional tool that will allow them to successfully treat clients with experiences of severe and prolonged trauma: ego state therapy.

The concept that the personality consists of parts, or ego states, has been a part of the foundation of psychotherapy since its beginnings in the 19th century. When all goes well, the parts of the personality are in close association with each other and work together as a harmonious whole. But in conditions of extreme stress—war, natural disasters, childhood sexual or physical abuse, and so on—the ego states become fractured and dissociated as a means of survival, to protect the mind from becoming overwhelmed by stressors that would disable it.

Extreme stress gives rise to PTSD, dissociative disorders, attachment disorders, and personality disorders. All of those may involve dissociated ego states that get in the way of direct resolution via EMDR treatment. After all, EMDR cannot target all of the ego states simultaneously— especially the ones that are unknown to the client and therapist! The reason for a stalled EMDR treatment with a client like Ellen may be that there are ego states that are unready, unwilling, or unable to safely access and process trauma memories.

For the authors of this book, the connection between EMDR and ego state therapy is a natural one. Ego state therapy focuses on the disjointed internal family system that is a possible outcome of severe trauma. Once that system is stabilized and given new resources, the ego states are able to participate in the desensitization and reprocessing phase of EMDR. Resolution of the trauma with EMDR will further unite and strengthen the ego state system.

The interdisciplinary model that guides this book proposes the careful, individualized expansion of the EMDR protocol to include ego state interventions and phased stabilization strategies to enable these challenging clients to feel safe enough to deal with their traumas. The sophisticated treatment techniques described herein illustrate the connections between EMDR and ego state therapy and are designed to give practitioners trained in each model a more comprehensive approach to the treatment of their clients.

To date, elements of this combined approach have been available in limited venues: at advanced workshops that specialize in EMDR techniques, hypnosis, and ego state therapy, and at international clinical conferences. An integrated EMDR and ego state therapy approach has been presented by some of the psychotherapy field's leading writers, thinkers, and practitioners, but their work has not been assembled in book form until now. The cases presented in the following pages blend these two models and the phased treatment methods of treating dissociation, providing a comprehensive model that can safely promise EMDR treatment to a broader range of challenging clients who would not otherwise be candidates for it.

The nine contributing authors assembled here have taught thousands of professionals how to respond to clients with complex PTSD, personality disorders, and the spectrum of dissociative disorders. Their case studies ground theory in practical application, creatively illustrating treatment techniques.

The initial chapter provides an overview of EMDR, models of ego state therapy, information on trauma and dissociation, and a description of phased treatment. It presents the rationale for this integrative treatment approach, namely, to extend the reach of transformative treatment for trauma and dissociation to often unreachable populations. In subsequent chapters, the authors explain how they combine specific aspects of ego state therapy, EMDR, and other modalities, such as schema-focused work, collaborative therapy, hypnosis, and family therapy. Their approaches target clients with dissociative identity disorder, couples, and those diagnosed with personality disorders. Therapists will learn how to cope with the pitfalls of providing in-depth treatment to this complex group of clients. One chapter is devoted to the speculative neurobiology underlying pathological dissociation.

Throughout the book, techniques are described for identifying, accessing, and stabilizing ego states; resolving ego state conflict; developing self-regulation and affect-management skills; and managing triggers and dissociative symptoms. An appendix includes resources for training in EMDR and courses in ego state therapy, trauma, and dissociation.

A postscript about Ellen:

When Ellen was ready to leave therapy, she reminded Carol Forgash that when the therapist first introduced her to the idea of an internal family, she visualized that she was flying on the back of an eagle, searching high and low for friends to play with. She "flew" during each session, finding no one in the forests below. One day, she looked down and saw a group of children in rags, shivering under the trees. She landed the eagle and asked them who they were. She told them that there was a log cabin nearby with food and clothing and a warm fire. She suggested that they go there.

Then she flew away and did not return for several weeks. During that time this group of children turned the log cabin into a safe place where at last they could offer each other comfort and care in a safe environment, and where they could receive help from the therapist. The children had become Ellen's family, banding together with her in the present to heal her from her traumatic past.

We hope that you will benefit from reading the fruit of the authors' years of refining this integrated approach, finding in it practical ways to help clients like Ellen effectively move beyond the limits of the past—through the immensely creative healing power of the client's mind and your own skilled and humane interventions—to live more fully and freely in the present.

Carol Forgash and Margaret Copeley

Acknowledgments

We would like to acknowledge two special individuals who have made singular contributions to the mental health field: Francine Shapiro, PhD, for the discovery and development of EMDR, and John Watkins, PhD, the founder, with Helen Watkins, MA, of ego state theory and therapy. Their incredible inventiveness has been the inspiration for this book.

We are very grateful to Sheri W. Sussman, our editor at Springer Publishing, for her belief in the importance of our work and her support for our efforts to make it available to the mental health community.

We are extremely indebted to our authors, who have enriched our understanding of the many facets of EMDR and ego state therapy and who have persisted throughout a long process of writing and editing their chapters.

Finally, we pay homage to our clients who have experienced trauma and reached out to us for healing. They have taught us what it is to be fully human, and we are grateful for the privilege of bearing witness to their lives.

CHAPTER 1

Integrating EMDR and Ego State Treatment for Clients with Trauma Disorders

Carol Forgash and Jim Knipe

INTRODUCTION: NEW HELP FOR CLIENTS WITH TRAUMA DISORDERS

Through many collective years of practice, the authors of this book have treated clients with a combination of complex diagnoses, including trauma and posttraumatic stress disorder and attachment, personality, and dissociative disorders. We have found that these clients have borne the most extensive suffering of all those we treat. The intricacy of their internal worlds, their struggles with symptom management, and their problems being in relationship often compel our empathy, our interest, and our horror at what they have experienced. The miracle is in their perseverance to become whole, often in the face of repeated previous treatment failures.

In this chapter, we will introduce what we have termed the "cross-training model," an approach that integrates several lines of psychotherapy theory, practice, and research in order to assist clients with complex presentations. This model consists of EMDR (Eye Movement Desensitization and Reprocessing), ego state therapy, and dissociative disorder treatment methods. We believe that this model will enable therapists to extend the scope of treatment beyond trauma resolution to include the extensive life issues often faced by clients with complex disorders (Wachtel, 2002) and to have the opportunity to develop mastery and competence in treating these challenging clients.

The cross-training model is based on comprehensive information about the nature of trauma and its effects on the human condition, as well as current information regarding dissociation (its predictors and causative factors) and attachment. Understanding the diagnostic conditions that are among the sequelae flowing from experiences of this triad of trauma, dissociation, and attachment problems will provide clinicians with a foundation for understanding the case studies presented in the following chapters. These conditions include simple posttraumatic stress disorder (PTSD), complex PTSD—also known as disorders of extreme stress (DESNOS)—and the dissociative and personality disorders.

In the past eighteen years, therapists dealing with traumatized clients have found that EMDR has filled a long-standing need in their treatment approaches. Previously, many traumatized clients, even those who had obtained insight into their difficulties after years of therapy, were still suffering from unwanted emotions, body sensations, and PTSD flashbacks. EMDR has provided a tool that was previously missing: a way to rapidly resolve the underlying troubled feelings associated with traumatic life experiences. EMDR has met this need of resolving not only the symptoms of PTSD but the underlying unhappiness and intrapsychic and interpersonal issues in a way that brings insight and healing to complex human problems. The processing that occurs during EMDR procedures also increases self-esteem, as indicated by increases in the Validity of Cognition (VOC) Scale during the EMDR standard procedures. EMDR has had a profound impact on the lives of many clients and has been shown in more than seventeen published trials to be effective in the treatment of PTSD (Dworkin, 2005; Greenwald, 1999; Lovett, 1999; Manfield, 1998; Maxfield & Hyer, 2002; Parnell, 2007; F. Shapiro, 2001; R. Shapiro, 2005; Silver & Rogers, 2002; Tinker & Wilson, 1999).

However, as Janet (1907) stated over one hundred years ago, for certain clients with complex diagnoses, treatment must provide stabilization prior to uncovering (desensitizing and reprocessing) traumas, and therapists must keep in mind individual needs for extensive stabilization. In part, this involves providing a lengthened preparation phase, often longer than necessary for most clients with single- or recent-incident traumatic events (J. Chu, 1998; Gold, 2000; Herman, 1992). The sequelae of trauma—especially the intrafamilial spectrum of physical, sexual, and emotional abuse and neglect—predict chronic PTSD and other serious problems (Moran, 2007). Additionally, the preconditions to trauma, common for children from abusive and neglectful families, include chaos and disorganized attachment styles, as well as lack of nurturing and guidance from parents who have limited parenting skills (Gold, 2000; Schore, 1994; Siegel, 1999). This often means that multitraumatized clients may be lacking in social and life skills development, have problems with attachment as adults, and have many of the defenses and issues associated with dissociative disorders and Axis II personality disorders (A. Chu & De Prince, 2006; Gold, 2000; Lacter, 2007; Liotti, 1999, 2004, 2006).

These clients are especially vulnerable to trauma in adult life, such as partner battering, and self-harming behavior. Such early-childhood history also indicates that these clients may have difficulty dealing with intense emotions and managing dissociative symptoms as well as enduring problems with trust. Therefore they may be hindered in their development and maintenance of adult relationships, including the therapeutic relationship (Bergmann & Forgash, 1998; Dworkin, 2005; Forgash & Knipe, 2001; van der Hart, Nijenhuis, & Steele, 2006; van der Kolk, McFarlane, & Weisaeth, 1996). They may be unable to move beyond present symptomatology and become stuck in impasses, resistance, increase in symptoms, and frustration with therapy. They also may have great difficulty managing the normal stresses of adult life, suffer with ill health, and have few life supports (Felitti et al., 1998; Forgash & Monahan, 2000).

Additionally, many clients with trauma histories will dissociate or have destabilizing abreactions in treatment if stabilization and skills training in managing affect, dissociative symptoms, and stress is not provided. These clients are often low responders (Bergmann & Forgash, 1998) who cannot complete treatment and have very incomplete and frustrating therapy journeys.

A PRELIMINARY NOTE TO THERAPISTS

While we will provide an extensive description of this interdisciplinary model, we want to say at the outset that this book is not an adequate substitute for basic EMDR training or a comprehensive course in the study of trauma and dissociation. In this introductory chapter, we will outline the standard EMDR protocol and the methods for incorporating EMDR, ego state work, and stabilization strategies for working with dissociative clients within a treatment plan for treating complex conditions. Readers who are trained in EMDR will be well able to integrate the dissociative treatment strategies and ego state work into their clinical practice. Those who are not EMDR trained will find the information on the phased treatment approach invaluable in their work with challenging clients. The situation for therapists who are new to EMDR or to work with dissociation is analogous to that of the novice driver who must practice on side streets before attempting the interstate. That is, practice and experience in using these protocols is a prerequisite for advanced applications, such as combining these approaches. On the other hand, readers trained in EMDR and familiar with dissociative treatment strategies will clearly understand the rationale for adding ego state work to EMDR. We also hope that those who are not EMDR trained will find the information on the phased treatment approach very useful in their work with challenging clients.

For readers who are interested in expanding their clinical knowledge and skills in these areas, the appendix lists resources for training in the EMDR method, the treatment of trauma and dissociation, and ego state therapy.

THE NATURE AND SEQUELAE OF TRAUMA

What Is Trauma?

We can begin our understanding of trauma with the *DSM–IV* (American Psychiatric Association, 1994) definition of it as an event that is outside normal human experience and is life threatening (Herman, 1992; van der Kolk et al., 1996). According to the *DSM–IV*, a traumatic event occurs when a person experiences or witnesses physical threat of injury and has a response of fear and helplessness (Herman, 1992; van der Kolk et al., 1996). However, this definition does not sufficiently account for the many ways people can be adversely affected by negative life experiences.

Recent authors in the field have addressed the ways this definition is both too inclusive and not inclusive enough (A. Chu & De Prince, 2006; Classen, Pain, Field, & Woods, 2006). First, the same event may be traumatizing to one person but more, less, or not traumatizing to another. Therefore, it is useful to define trauma not in terms of the horribleness of the event, but in terms of the effects on the individual: Was the person's sense of self damaged by the event? Are memories of the event held as re-experiencings rather than narrative memories? These descriptions of the responses to trauma are helpful to understand clients who are haunted by the residue of the past, and are never quite fully in the present.

Moreover, the *DSM–IV* definition of PTSD is focused on the single traumatic incident, whereas many clients have a damaging traumatic history that extends over repeated events, or over long periods of time during childhood. Van der Kolk, Roth, Pelcovitz, Sunday, and Spinazzola (2005) have proposed a new *DSM* category that they term *developmental trauma* to address this type of pervasive trauma. Single-incident trauma is the norm in the population at large: lifetime exposure data show an incidence of 60.7% for men and 51.2% for women (Bride, 2007). However,

19.7% of men and 11.4% of women have reported exposure to more than three traumas, and these individuals may be more likely to seek therapy and have complex presentations.

The sequelae of trauma occur on many levels, often negatively impacting physical and mental health, relationships, and even employment and personal development. Thus when assessing the effect of trauma it is necessary to put into perspective the overwhelming nature of the experience, the context in which it was experienced, and whether it was interpersonal (relational trauma versus a situational trauma such as a natural disaster). Were support and protection available? Was the trauma pervasive and repeated? Did it occur in a family setting?

Severe traumas such as overt physical or sexual abuse in childhood, as well the many life events generally recognized as traumatic (natural disasters, war, violent crimes, and so on), are referred to as "big-T" traumas (F. Shapiro, 2001). In some cases a child may have an overall perception of neglect, deprivation, shaming, exclusion, or lack of appropriate parental response, as opposed to discrete traumatic occurrences (Gold, 2000; Lyons-Ruth, Dutra, Schuder, & Bianchi, 2006). Events of this kind are called "small-t" traumas. They do not match the *DSM–IV* definition of PTSD but nevertheless can be highly damaging to the person. Clusters of small-t traumas may also cause major problems for clients' self-esteem (F. Shapiro, 2001). For the client who is looking for deep resolution of problems, treating the small-t traumas will typically be a necessary component of treatment.

Posttraumatic Stress Disorders

Traumatized clients (even those with single-incident or small-t trauma) may show some or all of the following symptoms of *simple PTSD*: intrusive recollections of the trauma, a sense of reliving traumatic events, hypervigilance, exaggerated startle response, flashbacks, nightmares, night terrors, sleep disorders, irritability, or agitated behavior. They may also describe difficulty concentrating, anger dyscontrol, avoidance of people and triggers that are reminders of the trauma, a range of dissociative symptoms, numbing, flat affect, anhedonia, distress following internal or external triggers, feelings of isolation, detachment, and lack of trust.

Where there has been repeated and prolonged trauma, we often find that the client has traumatic responses that include more than the typical PTSD symptoms. Herman (1992) writes that these posttraumatic response patterns "are best understood as a spectrum of conditions rather than as a single disorder" (p. 119). She calls this spectrum *complex posttraumatic stress disorder*, also known as disorders of extreme stress (DESNOS). Complex PTSD includes a set of additional problems that constitute "profound systemic alterations" (Herman, 1992, p. 121), including alterations in affect regulation, consciousness, systems of meaning, relations with others, and perceptions of the self and perpetrator (van der Kolk et al., 1996).

Clients with complex PTSD often present with intricate layers of symptoms that are daunting to therapists. In order to understand the underpinnings of these complex disorders one must pay attention to the complex ways that family attachment styles and family relationships interact with the kinds of trauma, as well as the duration of traumatic occurrences.

ATTACHMENT DISORDERS AND THEIR RELATION TO AFFECT REGULATION AND DISSOCIATION

In addition to overt trauma, negative family attachment style issues are prime predictors of dissociation and emotional dysfunction in both children and adults (Gold, 2000; Liotti, 2006). Dissociation in a parent is highly correlated with both disorganized, disoriented attachment style in the child and dissociative symptoms in the adult (Barach & Comstock, 1996; Classen et al., 2006; Gold, 2000; Liotti, 2006; Lyons-Ruth et al., 2006). The problems of the parent can become the problems of the child.

Children are born into the world ready to attach. In a "good enough" family environment, parents and children will attach naturally (van der Hart et al., 2006). However, if caretakers are emotionally unavailable, or family interaction patterns are overly conditional (for example, "You are only acceptable if you never bother us" or "Never show anger," and so on), the child may be deprived of the opportunity to learn attitudes of interpersonal trust and comfort that are part of appropriate attachment. If the child's primary caretaker (the mother, in most cultures) is unavailable due to illness, depression, feelings of inadequacy and fear regarding parental responsibilities, narcissism, addiction, or other problems, the bonding process may be impaired and the child, during times of distress, will learn to numb uncomfortably high arousal (sympathetic activation) with simultaneous parasympathetic activation. This pattern, if repeated, may in turn create the template for the later occurrence of shame and dissociation as a highly potentiated response to stress (Schore, 1994, 2000a). Also, inadequate attachment impairs the child's ability to learn to regulate affect (Schore, 2000b; Siegel, 1999). Thus, all of the subsequent developmental stages are impeded by early relational dysfunction.

For older children in similar circumstances of emotional neglect—in which their inner experience was not lovingly acknowledged and validated by a caretaker—the problem can be similar. This lack of validation of inner experience is hypothesized (Linehan, 1993) to contribute to the emotional pathology of adults who are diagnosed with borderline personality disorder and related conditions.

Attachment issues, then, form the background for the effects of overt trauma. If a potentially traumatic event occurs in the life of a child, it is very important that the child's inner experience and distress be compassionately witnessed by the loving eyes of the caregivers. If that is absent, the child may become vulnerable to dissociation. If the family responds to the child's trauma with rejection, ignoring, or chaos and instability, dissociation may be the child's only available adaptive response—which may in turn lead to a split in sense of self and feelings of emptiness (Schore, 2000a; Siegel, 1999). Also, since identity is initially formed as the child sees the characteristics of the self reflected in the eyes of a caretaker (Gold, 2000), a negative self-identity may develop if the caretaker is afraid of the child, disgusted, exploitive, hypercritical, and so on.

Traumas of omission—neglect, parental withdrawal, and lack of attunement to the child—may also have damaging sequelae much the same as more overt traumas and abuse. In situations of repeated severe trauma such as the parent abusing and terrifying the child, or even in situations of repeated verbal abuse or witnessing of conflict (Teicher, Samson, Polcari, & McGreenery, 2006), networks of dissociated ego states may form. In these instances, the traumatic material is partially or wholly removed from consciousness and held in disconnected neural networks in order to contain the unresolved affect. However, this self-protective response also means that much life experience is less available for healthy and adaptive information processing. Moreover, if affect-regulation skills were not adequately learned during earlier attachment experiences, the person will be much less able to close down emotional disturbances. Thus, for clients who have both disrupted attachment and overt trauma in their histories, many natural processes and developmental stages are likely to become disrupted and delayed (Gold, 2000; Liotti, 2006; Moran, 2007).

Axis II disorders and anxiety and mood disorders are frequently comorbid with dissociation. As is the case with trauma, the definition of borderline personality disorder (BPD) is currently undergoing reevaluation (Classen et al., 2006). Current thinking posits a strong relationship between disorganized attachment, relational trauma, dissociation, and the development of BPD. The comorbidity of PTSD and BPD is high: 56% of BPD patients have PTSD, and 68% of PTSD patients have BPD (Classen et al., 2006; Lacter, 2007). Like those with complex PTSD and dissociative disorders, clients with BPD require a phased treatment approach to help develop coping skills and inner stability, resolve internal conflict, and deal with often severe dissociation and attachment issues (Classen et al., 2006; Liotti, 2006).

DISSOCIATION

During the past fifty years, there have been two separate psychotherapy traditions that have addressed issues of personality fragmentation: the tradition of treating the dissociative symptoms that result from trauma, and the tradition of ego state therapies, which have focused on resolving conflicts between separate states of mind but did not have a particular emphasis on dissociation. In the sections below, we will pull together these psychotherapeutic threads and show how the healing power of each can be enhanced by the addition of the other.

What Is Dissociation?

Janet, beginning in the 1870s (van der Kolk et al., 1996), was the first to use the term "dissociation" to describe a mental structure in which traumatic life events were excluded from conscious awareness, resulting in anxiety, odd avoidance behaviors, and conversion symptoms such as psychogenic paralysis. He noted many cases in which symptoms were resolved by bringing these traumas and their accompanying affect into consciousness. Over the past 140 years, knowledge of dissociation within the mental health professions has waxed and waned. Within the past thirty years, there has been a renewed interest in defining dissociative phenomena and identifying effective modes of treatment (Herman, 1992; Terr, 1979), but controversy regarding the very nature of dissociation still exists. Current conceptualizations fall into three categories:

1. The definition of dissociative disorders found in the *DSM–IV* (American Psychiatric Association, 1994)
2. The Subjective/Phenomenological Model, which is derived from observation of symptom patterns in dissociative patients (Dell, 2006)
3. The Sociocognitive Model, which conceptualizes dissociative phenomena as resulting iatrogenically from the expectations of treating therapists (Spanos, 1994)

The *DSM–IV* mentions that dissociated memory material is "usually of a traumatic or stressful nature," but otherwise it does not emphasize dissociation as a posttraumatic condition. Instead, the *DSM–IV* defines dissociation primarily as a phenomenon of separate identities or personality states, with amnesic barriers when an individual switches from one state to another. Dell has pointed out that this model is accurate but incomplete. He observes, from self-report measures, structured interviews, and clinical observations, that in addition to the *DSM–IV* symptoms of switching and separate personality parts, dissociative individuals are also characterized by a variety of intrusive symptoms, primarily "intrusions into executive functioning and sense of self by alter personalities" (American Psychiatric Association, 1994, p. 7).

The frequent occurrence of intrusive symptoms argues not only against the *DSM–IV* definition but also against the Sociocognitive Model, which conceptualizes dissociation as an iatrogenic result of the social expectations of therapists. Within this view, the client's dissociative symptoms result from selective interest on the part of the therapist in client behaviors that fit the diagnosis. If therapists' concepts of dissociation determined and shaped clients' presentations, we would not see intrusive symptoms so frequently in these clients, because neither the *DSM–IV* definition nor the popular conception of dissociation (from books and films) features intrusion.

Intrusion is, however, listed as a Category B symptom cluster within the *DSM–IV* description of posttraumatic stress disorder. As clinicians who work with dissociative individuals can easily attest, clients with PTSD often experience intrusion, accompanied by fear and confusion as their conscious awareness is being invaded by fragments of unresolved memory material. Even with clients who are amnesic for traumatic events, intrusive symptoms of nightmares, auditory hallucinations, and fragmented visual flashbacks often occur. Switching itself can be regarded as a phenomenon that results from the intrusion of traumatic memory material that overwhelms and displaces the person's normal sense of self. Thus, a full definition of dissociation must include not only a structure of separate personality parts and switching between parts, but also intrusive experiences that occur along a spectrum of degrees of amnesia for traumatic events.

Dell (2006) has utilized this spectrum in organizing the most frequently occurring dissociative symptoms, as seen in a group of 220 subjects with dissociative identity disorder (DID). All of these individuals had memory problems, and 83–95% exhibited depersonalization, derealization, posttraumatic flashbacks, somatoform symptoms, and trance behavior. Between 85% and 100% experienced partially dissociated intrusions, such as child voices, persecutory voices, temporary loss of knowledge, and "made" emotions, impulses, and actions (stereotyped patterns of emotional responses that appear unconnected to the person's present situation). Between 61% and 88% of these patients experienced fully dissociated intrusions, that is, amnesia. These included time loss, fugues, finding objects, and learning later of actions.

Dissociative phenomena, of course, are not confined to people with DID. Clients with other conditions often exhibit these symptoms in a less extreme form. Indeed, the emerging evidence from research (van der Hart et al., 2006) and clinical practice (Chefetz, 2006) indicates that some form of dissociation is often present and, indeed, is often a core element within virtually all emotional disorders originating in difficult life experience. Moreover, dissociative symptoms are prevalent worldwide and are clinically similar despite diverse cultural contexts (Sar, 2006).

The Problem of Intrusion and the Structural Dissociation Model

The central role of intrusion in dissociative disorders has important implications for the use of EMDR and other methods of therapy that employ bilateral stimulation to process dysfunctionally stored memory material. Van der Hart et al. (2006) have proposed a new terminology that seems to resonate with clients' understanding of their dissociative experience. These authors hypothesize that a traumatic event splits the pretraumatic personality into characteristic parts: an *apparently normal part* (ANP) that continues to adapt to the demands of daily living and is motivated to appear normal in order to remain connected to others, and an *emotional part* (EP) that holds the sensory perceptions of the trauma in the form of relivings that have a "right now" quality. Intrusive symptoms occur when the reliving experiences of the EP enter into the awareness of the ANP.

The ANP is phobic of the EP's experience and tends to resist, avoid, and dissociate the intrusion of EP experience in order to maintain stability. The EP appears to push for activation or expression. The person has affect and flashback pictures from the EP, and negative self-appraisal ("I must be crazy," "I'm damaged," "I'm unworthy," "I'm stupid") from the ANP. These opposing mental actions each tend to be sparked in a stereotyped way and continually repeat without change in response to internal or external reminders of the trauma. Some degree of this type of inner conflict occurs with most people at some time during life, but if the individual has been through many traumatic experiences, the complexity of this type of conflict between dissociative parts can greatly increase, and identity confusion, anxiety, and dysphoria can result.

The Nature and Origins of Dysfunctional Dissociative Structures

Watkins and Watkins (1997) use the term "ego state" to describe conditions of awareness or states of mind that may be dysfunctionally in conflict. The structural dissociation theorists use the term "dissociative part" to describe the same mental phenomena, with the added connotation of degrees of dissociative inaccessibility between ego states. We will use these terms interchangeably, with the assumption that dissociation may be present or absent to varying degrees within any individual with an ego state dysfunction. The specific ego state therapy approach will be described in greater detail below, but an important contribution of the structuralists is a model for the origins of pathological, conflicted ego state structures (van der Hart et al., 2006).

First of all, structuralists posit that in normal development, nondissociated ego states develop from inborn predispositions for learning—"action systems" (van der Hart et al., 2006)—that are designed to evolve into the elemental mental functions that are necessary to meet basic needs (food, shelter), keep connected with significant others (particularly, during childhood, with caretakers), and engage in tasks of daily living. Van der Hart et al. add that these action systems (such as the need for attachment) interact with the child's environment and take the form that adapts to that environment.

When this occurs normally (with a "good enough" childhood environment), the ego states are co-conscious and relatively well integrated in their functioning. However, when the environment places obstacles in the way of integration, dissociative separation between states will tend to occur. Schwartz (1995) sees the mind as naturally multiple. In his Internal Family Systems Model, problems within the internal system can develop if the external system is out of balance and causes trauma, thus constraining the inner system and its future development.

Boundaries between ego states in the personality system are variable. In a person with a benign history, boundaries are fluid and seamless. A person moves from role to role, or from one task to another, without thinking, "This isn't me." Some clients describe their ego states as parts of themselves but see them as delineated by time dimensions—a five-year-old, teenager, or infant—and others by function, trait, or role, for example, self-hater, nurturer, critic, executive, bratty kid, daredevil, curious, nature lover, parent, grandparent, and so on.

Again, in a "good enough" childhood environment, these different ego states generally develop and function with co-consciousness. Conflicts can exist between ego states in a relatively well-integrated individual, but the individual experiences these conflicts with access to both sides of the internal debate. Often this type of conflict is experienced as simply, "I need to decide what I really want to do."

However, when a person has a trauma history, some boundaries become broad fault lines that determine the dissociative structure that emerges as an adaptation to childhood abuse and neglect. Many individuals with complex PTSD have one ANP that connects with others and engages in the tasks of daily living, and one or more EPs that contain memories of experiences that are originally overwhelming, remain dysfunctionally stored neurologically, and continue to press for activation in conscious experience as relivings.

These EPs have developed from action systems that have an original purpose of protection of the individual against physical pain and emotional pain and loss, and have the characteristics of fight or flight (sympathetic nervous system) or freeze and withdraw (parasympathetic nervous system; van der Hart et al., 2006). Other EPs function as "substitute actions" (van der Hart et al., 2006). We could also refer to these ego states as psychological defenses (Watkins & Watkins, 1997) or as "firefighter" ego states (Schwartz, 1995).

Ego states, whether "apparently normal," defensive, or those reliving trauma, can be construed as networks of the individual's neurology—networks that are functioning at cross-purposes. The inborn action systems will have to develop along different tracks if the childhood environment repeatedly places the child in a situation that is "impossible"—verbal, physical, or sexual abuse, neglect, nonresolvable confusion, or other traumatic experiences. This type of situation will manifest in a variety of ways, as dissociative disorders, complex PSTD, anxiety, depression, neurotic conflicts, and maladaptive behavior patterns.

Child Abuse and Dysfunctional Dissociative Structures

A child who is repeatedly abused by a caretaker is in an "impossible" dilemma. Defensive systems of anger and escape from harm are activated, but at the same time, the child must continue to regard the abusing caretaker as a source of supplies necessary for survival. In these circumstances, a child will often dissociate the memories of the abuse, and in that way deactivate the accompanying anger and need for avoidance of the perpetrator. Or a child might partially dissociate the abuse (only vaguely remember or minimize the importance of the abusive events), and then, to the extent that the anger and feelings of blame are still activated, the child will turn the anger on the self, and frequently have an attitude toward their own abuse ("I deserve this because I'm bad") that reflects (as an introject) the attitudes of the perpetrator in order to continue to maintain the necessary connection with the perpetrator.

The question might be asked, why does this dysfunctional and disturbing dissociated structure of ego states continue in adults long after they have left the abusive and neglectful childhood environments? Some ego states (EPs) are continuing to try to solve problems (such as escape from traumatic events) that in fact were resolved long ago. The individual persists, however, in an inadequate solution (to a long-solved problem) because of the "right now" quality of unresolved traumatic memories. Disturbing elements of the long-ago problem are subjectively experienced as ongoing in the present, and so the inadequate defenses against those elements also persist.

The current conceptualization is that the dissociative structure is maintained by phobias and avoidance defenses within the person's experience: phobias of attachment and attachment loss, of trauma-related mental processes (such as sexual arousal), of actual memory material, and of integration (van der Hart et al., 2006).

Communication within a dissociated internal system may be problematic due to the barriers that form between dissociated parts. Impaired communication prevents resolution of internal conflicts, which in turn continues to impair internal communication. Dissociated parts may partially or totally lack co-consciousness; that is, certain ego states may be ignorant of the existence of other states, or even of the adult personality. The relationships between ego states can be amnesic, hostile, conflicted, indifferent, cooperative, or strongly allied, and these relationships then rigidly define the dissociative structure of the personality.

The Development of Avoidance Defenses

In cases of complex PTSD, a certain type of ego state conflict is often observed. Unresolved reliving memory material from a posttraumatic EP pushes for activation in consciousness. These intrusions may be visual flashbacks, but there are also intrusive feelings without apparent cause, negative self-referencing cognitions, negative cognitions about other people or the world at large, physical sensations, smells, tastes, and so on. These are destabilizing to the ANP, and therefore, with repeated intrusions, neurologically based avoidance responses develop.

These avoidance responses are perhaps initially conscious, but they can quickly become dissociated from consciousness, as occurs with many other automatic behaviors (for example, implicit memory activities like learning to walk, riding a bike, or playing a musical instrument). For clients who are farther out on the dissociative spectrum—for example, those who have dissociative identity disorder (DID)—the boundaries between parts become more rigid and impermeable, so multiple dissociated ego states exist and may even be unknown to each other. Treatment often involves recognizing and working with the client's avoidance responses, so that dissociative boundaries can become permeable and therapeutic accessing and healing of traumas can occur.

TREATMENT GOALS FOR
TRAUMA-DISORDERED CLIENTS

As clinicians, we want to know what kinds of resolution and changes we can expect from treatment. Do we want to merely eliminate symptoms, or is the goal more comprehensive—to help people with these most complicated diagnoses find a way out of suffering and experience satisfaction with their lives? Successful EMDR and ego state treatment integrated within a phased model permits the goals of treatment to become more inclusive of the broader needs and goals of the client. These broader goals include the following:

1. To provide safety and develop stability in treatment and in current life experiences
2. To help clients become affect tolerant and able to regulate emotional responses
3. To help clients discover a whole and integrated sense of who they are in the world and to develop more functional inner boundaries, through the reprocessing of trauma and the elimination of problematic symptoms of PTSD and dissociative disorders
4. To help clients reach their potential in a number of crucial areas, including the ability to meet their own needs more effectively and to become, in effect, parents to themselves—perhaps the parents that they initially needed but did not have
5. To achieve mastery of life skills, to help them move from victim status to able to lead a full life
6. To repair attachment injuries (Barach & Comstock, 1996), stabilizing self/other object representations through facilitation of the development of an internal secure base as well as repairing damage to boundaries and the internal ego state structure
7. To reclaim disowned ego states in clients diagnosed with personality disorders

We as clinicians want to enable the person to develop empathy for the self and the internal family system; to heal internal splits; and to resolve relational and trust issues, attachment breaks and losses, and fears of intimacy. When we work with clients from a position of empathy and understanding of the legacies of trauma, dissociation, loss, and attachment disorders, we can help them resolve their most critical issues and go on to develop and utilize a blueprint for healthy living (Bergmann & Forgash, 2000; Forgash & Knipe, 2001; Wachtel, 2002).

EGO STATE THEORY AND THERAPY

History

Many explorers from Freud, who described the tripartite ego, through Jung, who saw the personality as a multiplicity rather than a unity

(Schwartz, 1995), and continuing to the present have explored and elaborated on the inner dimensions of the personality. Many, such as Assagioli and Perls, have used the lens of psychoanalytic theory through which to develop their theories of ego states (Schwartz, 1995). Janet (1919/1925) first used the term "dissociation" to describe split-off systems of ideas and "covert personality segments." Federn developed a two-energy theory: the ego (perceived as "me") and object (perceived as "not me") cathexis. He saw helping clients develop more ego energy as a primary therapeutic goal and was the first to use the concept of ego states in psychodynamic therapy (Watkins & Watkins, 1997).

John Watkins, later joined by Helen Watkins, developed a psychoanalytic theory that was a further elaboration of Federn's work, combining psychoanalysis with hypnotherapeutic techniques. Their work has produced a comprehensive ego state theory as well as a practical ego state therapy. Ego state therapy has proven to be of great utility in working with clients in broad diagnostic categories, including the dissociative disorders (Bergmann & Forgash, 1998; Knipe, 2005; Phillips, 1993), and has been successfully used in conjunction with EMDR (Forgash, 2005; Paulsen, 1995).

John Watkins and Helen Watkins (1979–1980, 1997), as well as Hilgard (1977), expanded on the concept of covert ego states in the normal personality and overt ego states found in those with DID. Watkins and Watkins are responsible for therapeutic innovations such as the affect bridge, in which a present feeling links back to the earlier or root experience; the somatic bridge, which uses physical sensations in the same way, working to heal conflict through the ego state system; and the use of ego state therapy with people who do not have pathological dissociation.

Schwartz (1995) also subscribes to a multidimensional view of the personality. His model utilizes family systems theory as well as concepts related to multiplicity of mind. He works through the ego state system to help clients achieve four principles: balance, harmony, leadership, and development.

Ego State Systems

An ego state system may be described as an organized system of behaviors and experiences that have varying boundaries, or as syndromes of behavior and experience that are clustered and organized around some common principle. The states may be organized to enhance adaptability in coping with events or problems.

Watkins and Watkins (1979, 1997) describe three pathways to the formation of ego states in childhood: normal differentiation, introjection of significant others, and reactions to trauma that include dissociation.

Ego states may have normative functions geared toward protection and adaptation, and imaginal creative functions, such as daydreaming.

However, ego states formed in childhood trauma may function maladaptively in present life situations. They may seek to protect their existence and roles and the internal system even if these methods are counterproductive now. This is similar to organizational maintenance theory: no corporation willingly goes out of business. Ego states want to continue to exist in the present and sometimes wish to annihilate other ego states, and some fear being expelled or "killed." The following poem by Jessy Randall, "The Seductiveness of the Memory Hole" (2004), illustrates the common wish of an ANP that fears the destabilizing effects of an EP.

> We have an invention. We
> Invented it. What you do is,
> You email us the thing
> That you want to forget.
> You list every detail. You
> Describe in full. When we
> Get the email, we delete it.
> We don't just delete the email.
> We delete the thing. The thing
> Never happened. No one involved
> Will remember it; no one
> Who heard the story will
> Repeat it; even you yourself
> Will forget it.
> We have done it already.
> We are doing it right now.

Ego State Therapy

Ego state therapy utilizes individual, family, and group therapy techniques to access and connect ego states for the purpose of relieving symptoms and healing conflicts among the ego state system (Watkins & Watkins, 1979, 1997). One goal of combining ego state therapy with EMDR and interventions for dissociative disorders is to meet the adaptational needs of the present and to undo the dissociative quagmires. There is a strong emphasis on teaching the client to understand the self and the internal system and to deal with conflict resolution. Ego state therapy, by helping clients develop a connection with the internal system, aids in establishing a connection of felt empathy with the therapist (which often is a major unmet need from childhood) and increases individual and systemic co-consciousness. Ego state therapy has often been combined with other therapy models: supportive, behavioral, psychoanalytic, cognitive, existential, and humanistic, often in conjunction with hypnosis (Phillips, 1993).

The ego state system of each client is unique, requiring the list of therapy tasks to be approached flexibly. It is primary in the early stages of therapy with a dissociative or personality-disordered client to stay fairly close to the client's felt need for relief for immediately experienced symptoms. Many clients will not reveal the whole system until trust in the therapist has been established (that is, phobia of attachment has been overcome) or a part of the system has experienced some relief in therapy.

Sometimes ego state work can be approached and initiated informally. If a client doesn't appear to be highly dissociated, trauma work can proceed after a shorter initial preparation phase. If indicated by a level of client distress that occurs during trauma processing, stabilization and ego state interventions can be provided at that time.

It is the experience of many therapists trained in ego state therapy that utilizing ego state strategies with people who do not have these complex diagnoses provides richness to the therapeutic work. With all categories of clients, the addition of EMDR treatment has frequently led to successful achievement of treatment goals.

INTRODUCTION TO EMDR

The Adaptive Information Processing Model

Why does posttraumatic memory material, held in the EP, push for activation into conscious awareness? F. Shapiro's (2001) Adaptive Information Processing model provides a theoretical explanation, and also a solution. This model, which is the basis for the EMDR therapy method, hypothesizes the existence of an intrinsic neurologically based information processing system that functions to transform disturbing life experiences into narrative memories that are no longer disturbing. For example, a person might see an accident on the road, with gruesome images. Ten minutes later, those images might still be flashing in the person's mind, but then, as the individual continues to think about the accident, talk about it with an attentive other person, and perhaps have a dream about it, the disturbing images fade, so that a week later, while driving once again by the scene of the accident, there is little or no disturbance. The person may retain only a narrative memory of the event, and perhaps also keep some new, adaptive learning ("I will drive more carefully over this part of the road").

Over seventy years ago, Gestalt learning theorists in Germany (Koffka, 1935) postulated neurological mechanisms that seek completion of incomplete perceptions. For example, points in a row are perceived as a line, and a familiar song that is interrupted will continue mentally to completion. There are many examples of how the human brain intrinsically seeks and creates gestalts, whole and completed experiences from incomplete parts. Thus, we can surmise that the push for expression of EP memory material is an example of a neurological impulse toward completion—an impulse that is part of the activation of the intrinsic information processing system of the brain, an EP reliving trauma and seeking completion as a normal narrative memory.

Goals and Mechanism

The EMDR eight-phase treatment method (F. Shapiro, 2001) is designed to resolve the posttraumatic split in sense of self, transform the disturbing trauma memory into a normal narrative memory, and enhance whatever potential exists for positive, adaptive learning as a result of the experience. Francine Shapiro postulated that an essential element of the EMDR method is dual attention, or co-consciousness, between safety, present orientation, and a sense of mastery, on the one hand, and traumatic reliving on the other. If an individual can simultaneously activate the traumatic memory while maintaining an orientation to the safety of the present, and then engage in bilateral, right-left sensory stimulation, adaptive processing of that memory material is greatly facilitated.

EMDR has been shown in over seventeen peer-reviewed clinical trials to be highly effective in rapidly resolving symptoms of PTSD (Maxfield & Hyer, 2002). Significantly, it also has been demonstrated that EMDR can resolve small-t traumatic memories with the same effectiveness (Wilson, Becker, & Tinker, 1995, 1997). This is an important finding for the therapist with a varied practice, since troubling memories are part of the clinical picture for nearly all *DSM–IV* diagnostic categories.

THE EIGHT TREATMENT PHASES OF EMDR

The EMDR eight-phase method can be broadly applied to many conditions that originate in disturbing life experience. A general overview of the EMDR phases follows.

Phase 1: History Taking and Treatment Planning. This phase includes not only the usual procedures of a psychotherapy intake (establishing rapport, identifying client goals, performing a mental status exam, assessing client defenses and object relations patterns), but also an appraisal of the client's readiness for EMDR therapy and a specific identification of events in the client's past, present, and anticipated future that will be the focus of therapy.

Phase 2: Preparation. This phase is of crucial importance in the treatment of clients with dissociated ego states. In the development of readiness for trauma processing with clients who do not have internal resources or ego strengths or who cannot identify emotions and body sensations, the use of the full EMDR trauma protocol without preparation may trigger traumatic memories, destabilize the client, or produce feelings of failure, frustration, and regression. Alternate strategies are often needed to stabilize and develop readiness in such clients. Many of these clients already experience themselves as "treatment failures" and may prematurely leave treatment.

For all clients, there are several aspects of preparation that the therapist needs to address, including (1) ensuring that the client trusts the therapist and can in turn be trusted to truthfully discuss the issues that arise in therapy, (2) giving the client a conceptual framework for understanding the EMDR process, including certain metaphors that can aid in client understanding, and (3) familiarizing the client with the different forms of bilateral stimulation.

In addition, during the preparation phase, clients are taught a hand signal for "stop." Many clients never use this hand signal, but the message from the therapist that they can do so is empowering and gives them control over the therapy process. Similarly, clients may be taught a "keep going" hand signal, for those situations when the client is aware of ongoing productive processing that is not apparent to the therapist.

Clients who are in therapy for single-incident trauma and are not particularly vulnerable to dissociation are generally able to complete these preparation procedures in only one or two sessions. In contrast, though, clients who come to therapy with histories of severe traumatization and a dissociated ego state structure will often need months, and in some cases, more than a year of preparation for EMDR processing. *The most important aspect of this preparation phase is ensuring that the client has sufficient affect-regulation skills to be able to access traumatic material while still maintaining an orientation to present safety, that is, "dual attention" to both the past and the present.*

This ability to manage emotions, and an accompanying sense of mastery over those emotions, are very important elements in the client's ability to sustain simultaneous awareness of the safety of the present and the unresolved traumatic material from the past. Since this is the exact skill that many dissociative clients lack, it is necessary with such clients to work in an extended way on this, perhaps over a relatively long period of time. Procedures for assisting dissociative clients in this way are described throughout the chapters of this book.

Phase 3: Assessment. Once the client is able to maintain a sufficient dual-attention focus, assessment can begin. In this phase, the experiential components (a representative visual image and associated sounds, emotions, physical sensations, and cognitions) of a particular disturbing memory or issue are identified and baseline measurements are taken to provide a basis for examining the effectiveness of the therapy. As part of this assessment phase, the client identifies a negative cognition (NC), which is a self-referencing negative thought, belief, or attitude that is associated with the worst part of a traumatic experience. A positive cognition (PC), also identified during this phase, is the self-referencing belief that would be preferred by the client at the conclusion of successful therapy for the particular trauma.

One of Francine Shapiro's unique contributions was the Validity of Cognition (VOC) Scale, which is a 1–7 semantic differential rating by the client of the "felt truth" of the PC, while the traumatic memory is being consciously accessed.

Also during this phase, the client is asked to report degree of emotional disturbance using the Subjective Units of Disturbance (SUD) Scale. Usually the goal is to have a SUD score of 0 at the end of processing a traumatic experience. The VOC and SUD procedures provide an initial baseline for the client's problem, and then can be used as ongoing process measures of the effectiveness of the therapy.

Phase 4: Desensitization. This is the part of the therapy when all the elements of the dysfunctionally stored trauma memory—not just negative affect—are accessed and combined using sets of bilateral stimulation (eye movements, alternating sounds, alternating hand taps), resulting in the transformation of the trauma memory into a normal narrative memory that is no longer disturbing. Thus this is also the reprocessing phase.

Phase 5: Installation. Installation occurs after the trauma disturbance is satisfactorily resolved. It involves the use of bilateral stimulation to continue the healing work by strengthening the "felt truth" of specific positive cognitions related to the issues the client has associated with the traumatic event.

Phase 6: Body Scan. A body scan is used as a way to ensure that all physical resonance from the trauma has been reprocessed.

Phase 7: Closure. The closure phase occurs at the end of every EMDR session. It includes procedures to ensure that the client will continue to experience the EMDR work positively, even after the session has been completed, regardless of whether the particular traumatic memory was fully processed in that session.

Phase 8: Reevaluation. This final step occurs during the session following the previous seven phases. Its purpose is to assess whether progress has been maintained and to determine whether additional disturbing information has emerged between sessions that may now be a focus of processing. Reevaluation then continues throughout the person's course of therapy; that is, the therapist periodically checks to ensure that previously processed traumas have remained resolved. A full course of EMDR treatment involves not only resolving the traumatic events of the past that are the origin of the client's problem, but also targeting present triggers and anticipated future events, so that the individual is empowered to go forward in life free from the symptoms that initially led the client to seek therapy.

POTENTIAL PROBLEMS WITH USING EMDR WITH DISSOCIATIVE CLIENTS

As indicated above, for clients who are vulnerable to dissociation, there are potential problems that can arise if the standard EMDR procedures are used without additional measures. The most frequent problem is that the processing is blocked and the client reports, "Nothing is different. This isn't helping." This result, which can be discouraging to the client, may be an indication that one ego state opposes the processing that is being attempted by another.

This opposition may be due to a difference—an internal disagreement—regarding the identified goals of therapy. For example, one part of the personality may want to learn to be more assertive, while another may oppose this goal because of fear that assertion would lead to potential loss of a relationship. To give another example, a common conflict with individuals with addictive disorders is ambivalence regarding sobriety. Often this conflict is between an ego state that wishes to quit and another that has strong urges to continue the addictive behavior. A very dangerous conflict that frequently occurs in clients with DID is between states that wish to live and learn to enjoy life and states that are suicidal.

For all of these situations, the therapist and client must carefully define overall therapy goals and, when needed, establish separate contracts with different ego states. In all instances, of course, suicidal ego states must agree to contain their self-destructive urges, or submit to the control of other ego states that will monitor the suicidal state to insure safety.

Another significant concern is that dissociative clients are more likely to experience dissociative abreaction, that is, an intrusion of EP affect that is so intense that the reality orientation of the ANP is impaired or lost. Following the catastrophic earthquake in Marmara, Turkey, in 1999, EMDR HAP (Humanitarian Assistance Programs), a nonprofit volunteer organization sent a team of EMDR-trained therapists, including Jim Knipe, to establish clinics on site and to provide training to Turkish therapists who were treating victims. A woman who had experienced the earthquake reported that she was highly distressed by her memories of the moments immediately before the earthquake began and immediately after, but she was totally amnesic for the earthquake itself. She stated at the start of therapy, "The earthquake is forty-three seconds that are missing from my life." In spite of this dissociative symptom, the EMDR standard procedures were used with the remembered images prior to the quake, and over the course of about forty-five minutes her affect went from a level 10 (most disturbance) to a level 1. At that point, she was asked a standard EMDR question—"What keeps it from being a zero?"—and she remembered the entire earthquake. Her disturbance went back up to level 10, but she was able to maintain her orientation to the safety of the therapy office and continue the processing procedures until her disturbance went to 0. She was very happy with this result, but this is not the way the clinician wants it to go—we hope that the distress will fall steadily during the treatment, but it is possible that it will actually rise.

Therefore, it is necessary with clients who show dissociative symptoms to discuss in advance the possibility of high levels of affect and establish appropriate safeguards. Specifically, it is necessary prior to trauma work to strengthen the client's present orientation and sense of safety and mastery in the face of the threatening memory. This is usually accomplished through an extended preparation phase and through additional procedures to maintain emotional safety during the desensitization phase.

UNIQUE CHALLENGES OF WORKING WITH CLIENTS WITH COMPLEX TRAUMA

Accessing Isolated Ego States and Fragmented Memories

Ego states—both those that constitute the apparently normal part of the personality and those that originate in traumatic experience—can be conceptualized as neurological networks that actually have a physically separate existence (Paulsen, 1995). Supporting this view, it has been shown that people with diagnosed DID have different patterns of neurological activation (as shown in Positron Emission Tomography displays) when accessing a trauma memory (that is, listening to a trauma script) when those individuals are in the ANP, as opposed to the EP related to that trauma (Simone Reinders et al., 2006; van der Hart et al., 2006).

We can surmise that this separation of different locations of memory storage has occurred for an adaptive reason—to protect the person, through fragmentation of awareness, from the horror of overwhelming affect and complete cognitive disorganization. One client in the later stages of therapy described it this way: "I had the choice: either reject my own feelings and try to look normal, or go completely crazy. I learned to leave my body and go up to the ceiling so I wouldn't have to go crazy." If pathological dissociation begins in this way, and if traumatic stress continues in the child's environment, continued fragmentation of consciousness then becomes more and more potentiated. In the extreme, this process results in distinct personality parts that are isolated and inaccessible to each other.

The specific neurological mechanisms of dissociation are not yet clear, and more than one process may be involved in the separation of traumatic memory material into dysfunctionally stored fragments. Traditionally, dissociation has been conceptualized as a passive, "horizontal" process (Hilgard, 1977) in which the person's attention is simply overwhelmed, with resulting confusion and disorientation. In contrast, repression is thought of as an active "vertical" process of removing from consciousness memory material that is somehow threatening to the self.

Anderson et al. (2004) have provided evidence for the validity of the repression model. Their results, using functional magnetic resonance imaging with a nonclinical population, indicate that social influence to forget a previously learned memory task can be associated with a neurological pattern of increased activation in prefrontal cortical regions and a decrease in hippocampal activity. Moreover, subjects who were given the forgetting instruction actually showed a significant loss of memory retrieval relative to controls when tested at a later time.

It seems intuitively, though, that dissociation exists as a process that is different from active forgetting. We all shine the spotlight of attention on certain aspects of our internal and external environment, and not on other aspects. For example, most people do not have an ongoing awareness of the sensations on the bottoms of their feet, and yet those sensations are easily accessible. It could be that the creation of separate, dissociated ego states is a result of both repression and dissociation processes.

Enhancing Present Safety and Grounding

When we ask a client to access a disturbing memory, we are requesting that the client reassociate the memory that has been separated, and this can be therapeutic only if the person is able to do so while maintaining dual attention, that is, simultaneous activation of both the neural networks of present orientation and safety and the networks holding the disturbing memory. Initially, for many dissociative clients, this is precisely what they are not able to do, because the positive networks are absent or weak, or the posttraumatic memory network is intrusive and strong. It is for this reason that for these clients, the EMDR preparation phase must be emphasized and carefully implemented in order to enhance the person's access to the resources of present safety, empowerment, and mastery over the memory material.

It is very helpful during preparation to use bilateral stimulation to increase the felt sense of positive affect (Kiessling, 2003; Leeds, 2002) for many aspects of ANP functioning. For some clients (for example, those who have never had the life experience of trusting or feeling safe with another person) this process of preparation may be complex and extend over many sessions of therapy.

Even for those dissociative clients who have been able to establish trust in the therapist, dual attention can sometimes be difficult to achieve. An additional and sometimes crucial element in maintaining emotional safety is to "lead with the cognitive" (Fine, 1995). In other words, a clear cognitive understanding of the anticipated steps in trauma processing is potentially grounding for the client, and it helps if this understanding is both verbal and visual.

Specifically, it is useful for clients to have, to whatever extent possible, a clear sense of the path along which treatment will proceed, and also to create a map of their own dissociative structure. As seen in the client drawings in this chapter, artistic expression often helps clients identify and understand their ego state systems and the traumas they have experienced (see Figures 1.1–1.11, pp. 25–34). The authors keep in their offices paper and colored marking pens so that clients can make drawings of their internal worlds, either generally or within the context of particular traumatic events. Each of these drawings is an initial step in providing an overview of the whole self and thereby reassociating previously disconnected experiences, as well as providing a cognitive structure, and even a language, which then facilitate the safe accessing of traumatic memories. In this way, memories can be more comfortably brought into full association, where they can be fully processed and placed appropriately within the person's life story.

Overcoming Avoidance Defenses

Some clients have strong avoidance urges with regard to memories of traumatic events, in spite of equally intense motivation to heal from the trauma. In these instances, the person's avoidance defense may be the best point of access to the unresolved material (Knipe, 1995, 2005). The therapist can ask questions that focus on the affect maintaining the avoidance, that is, the feelings of relief and containment that occur when the destabilizing effects of the traumatic intrusion are successfully avoided. With this method, the client can maintain avoidance defenses while the underlying traumatic material is processed. This procedure of targeting the positive affect associated with defense can make the healing effects of the EMDR procedures available to a larger population of severely traumatized clients.

FIGURE 1.1 First in a series of eight drawings by Jackie, a woman with complex PTSD who was sexually abused by a number of perpetrators in childhood. This drawing is of a flashback episode showing her father "capturing" the children in order to sexually abuse them. Her mother is fleeing the scene.

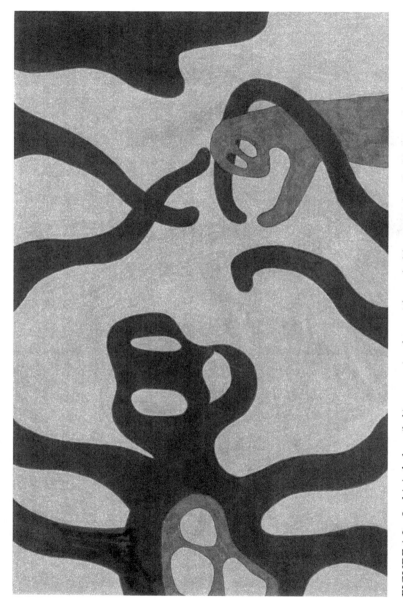

FIGURE 1.2   Jackie's father (left) ensnaring her with snakelike tentacles. Jackie's mother is present as a blind silhouette (far right) who does not see her abuse. The terrified child is left without protection.

FIGURE 1.3 Dysfunctional attachments in Jackie's family. The heart shape represents the family bonds, but in fact they are terrifying and Jackie is entrapped within them. Her father leers at her as once again her mother turns away, not seeing Jackie's abuse. Jackie draws herself dissociating as her only escape.

FIGURE 1.4 Jackie's fragmented internal family. Jackie, represented by the hand (upper left) that reaches out, is unable to connect with her dissociated ego states.

FIGURE 1.5   Jackie trapped in a shell of fear, shame, and aloneness. Her mother (right) and father (left) are walking away from her, leaving her without protection or comfort. This drawing shows Jackie's empathy for her child ego state.

FIGURE 1.6   Jackie's shamed, isolated self. At the core of herself is a black hole, representing her shame. An outer façade covers over the shame. Jackie's eyes are dull with dissociation as she numbs herself against her pain.

FIGURE 1.7   Jackie's depiction of her ego state system in the initial phase of ego state work. She said of her ego states, "I don't want to acknowledge them and they don't want to speak with me." She depicts her internal family very negatively in this drawing, as a tangled, chaotic web that she cannot escape. Her fear of her internal world is clear.

FIGURE 1.8   Jackie's depiction of her ego state system in the second phase of treatment (trauma work). System changes are in evidence: some parts are reaching out, while others are still dissociated. On the right is a mother holding a baby, representing Jackie's feeling of becoming a better parent to her inner parts.

FIGURE 1.9 Ego state drawing by Jennifer, a client with complex PTSD. (One of a series of cartoons with dialogue.) Wee Seamus is trying to reveal an important secret to the therapist. Loony Tune, an absurd clown who alternately protects and abuses Wee Seamus, attempts to prevent Wee Seamus from speaking. The therapist appears disconcerted at the manifestation of the two opposite ego states.

32

FIGURE 1.10   Jennifer's depiction of the outcome of revealing her secret. Loony Tune has given Wee Seamus a black eye for disobeying his directive to conceal the truth.

FIGURE 1.11   Jennifer's drawing of increasing ego unity. Jennifer, as
the central ego state sitting in the middle, is speaking directly with the
therapist and mediating for the other ego states.

PHASED TREATMENT WITH COMBINED
EMDR AND EGO STATE THERAPY

It has long been clinical practice to use a three-part phased model in the treatment of trauma and the dissociative disorders. The development of this triphase model dates back to Janet (1919/1925). Although research on this model is in its infancy, it is the current standard of care because of its efficacy with traumatized and dissociative-disordered clients, particularly those with DID. It is endorsed by the International Society for the Study of Dissociation (ISSD, 2005). Phased treatment is an intrinsic element of the model presented throughout this book, which integrates the EMDR standard protocol and additional components: ego state therapy, attachment theory, and dissociative disorder treatment interventions.

The terminology used to name and describe the three standard phases of treatment varies from author to author. There is general agreement on the tasks central to each phase in spite of the different wording. According to Herman (1992), the task of the first phase is to establish safety; the second-phase tasks concern remembrance and mourning; and the third-phase task is to reconnect the client with life. F. Shapiro's (2001) eight phases of EMDR roughly parallel the three phases described by Herman. We will adopt the terminology used by van der Kolk et al. (1996) to describe the three phases and their tasks:

Phase 1: Stabilization, to help clients control their reactions to the trauma and prepare for trauma work
Phase 2: Identifying and successfully processing the traumatic experiences
Phase 3: Resolution, to clear symptoms, reconnect with self and others, and have efficacy in life domains

In practice, specific therapeutic interventions (working with dissociation and affect management, developing safety and internal stability) sometimes need to be applied in more than one phase (Bergmann & Forgash, 2000; Paulsen, 1995). After Phase 1 skills have been developed, the client may need to return to stabilization and safety interventions during trauma work, even after the reconnecting/resolution or integration phase of treatment.

Clients with trauma histories often have endured years of misdiagnosis and treatment failure prior to reentering treatment. They are in need of a comprehensive and systemic treatment approach. That approach will be described in detail in the remainder of this chapter and the book. The next sections of this chapter present the tasks and interventions of each phase of the treatment.

PHASE 1: STABILIZATION AND SYMPTOM REDUCTION

The important tasks in the first phase of therapy are development of co-consciousness of ego states, providing orientation to the present, and affect management. We help clients gain mastery over their experiences and reduce symptoms, as well as build trust and comfort within the therapy relationship. Another Phase 1 focus is diagnosis and treatment planning, based on extensive history taking and dissociative interviews. Available tools include the Dissociative Experiences Scale (DES; Carlson & Putnam, 1993), the Dissociative Disorders Interview Schedule (DDIS; Ross et al., 1989), the Structured Clinical Interview for (DSM-III-R) Dissociative Disorders (SCID-D; Steinberg, Rounsaville, & Cicchetti, 1990), and the Multidimensional Inventory of Dissociation (MID; Dell, 2006).

EMDR work in Phase 1 includes history taking, preparation, and introduction of EMDR concepts and procedures. The latter will be introduced only when the client is stabilized.

Since life continues while clients are dealing with each phase, it is important to help them avoid being flooded and overwhelmed (in and outside of sessions) and improve current functioning.

An essential goal in this phase is to begin to enhance the evolution of the internal system. One client called this work a "second course in childhood." Part of the legacy of trauma and dissociation is not only the problems with attachment but the missing personal and interpersonal skills. Many of our clients describe trying to function in adult life without the blueprints. Extending the preparation phase allows for time to build up structures that were disabled and broken down by issues such as trauma, loss, or unstable family life.

The ego state work and dissociative disorder interventions presented here should be individually tailored to each client. The client will eventually be able to deal more safely with traumatic material because of the extensive preparation. This can lead to mastery and control in present life.

To be effective teachers, we need to identify the learning style of each individual. Some are visual; others have tactile or auditory preferences; others will have a combination style. The timing of the introduction of specific interventions, ego state concepts, and information about EMDR must be made judiciously.

Psychoeducation

A psychoeducational approach—teaching clients about their symptoms and how they may be resolved—will create the proper environment for stabilization (Bergmann & Forgash, 1998; J. Chu, 1998). Being armed with information will give clients hope for resolution.

We often struggle to find a way to help clients understand what has happened to them. Their PTSD and dissociative symptoms are often terrifying and confusing. Many clients need slow and careful doses of information about trauma and abuse. They are triggered easily. Many wonder, as they hear explanations of their symptoms, "Are you saying I'm a multiple?"

Clients with PTSD and dissociation experience high levels of anxiety. Their anxiety can be lessened and benefits of treatment can be maximized by providing them with information about these aspects of their symptoms and treatment:

- What trauma is and how it impacts the body and mind
- What dissociation is
- How different parts of the personality arise in response to trauma
- Strategies for controlling anxiety
- What the treatment process will be like

It is helpful to use imagery and analogy to normalize problems and symptoms. The concept of ego states can be introduced in visual form such as a map showing the divisions in the personality that result from traumatic experiences. It may help the client to visualize dissociated experiences as held within an egg shell. The shell is never more than semi-impermeable. When an egg is boiled in its shell, bits of material leak out. That image, although not completely technically accurate, helps explain to clients what a flashback and other intrusions feel like.

History Taking

With complex cases, it is not possible to get a full history in one or two sessions. Extended history-taking sessions should be planned around the client's comfort level. History taking needs to be detailed, but structured at the client's pace to be as nontriggering as possible. The therapist's empathy and considerate questioning are extremely important.

History taking should include these aspects of the client's past and present experiences:

1. *Current issues.* Physical and mental health issues—PSTD symptoms, depression, anxiety, and dissociative symptoms in the present; present stressors and triggers; current support from family, friends, coworkers, and clergy.

2. *Developmental history.* Early-childhood and family history that includes family attachment styles and conditions in the home; a complete physical and emotional health history beginning with infancy, for the client as well as family members (for example, the mother's physical and emotional health in pregnancy); compulsive disorders for the client and family; losses in early life.

3. *Trauma history.* Over time, safely explore the trauma history, which can include early losses and other situations that have been experienced as traumatic (including health issues), such as clusters of small-t traumas, interpersonal connections, inability to love, feelings of isolation, fragmentation of self, chronic stress responses, and early reports of dissociative symptoms. Looking for strengths and resources over the client's lifetime is important because clients need to know that they are not just a collection of problems and symptoms. Additionally, the client will be encouraged to draw on these positive attributes during the treatment.

Genograms or timelines to outline or highlight family relationships and critical events are helpful concrete tools in history taking.

Always pace history taking according to the client's ability to stay present. Make it clear that the client is in control of the amount of information the client is willing to contribute during a session. Stress that comfort rather than time is important. Call a time-out when necessary.

Unfortunately, it can be difficult or impossible to elicit a complete history when the client presents with either recent-incident trauma or one major traumatic event (Type 1 trauma). Caution is necessary in this case because the therapist will not be aware of the full extent of the big- and small-T traumas that influence growth and development. With clients with multiple trauma events (Type 2 trauma), proceeding to trauma-target selection, desensitization, and so forth without this information may impede processing or be destabilizing. In these circumstances, therapists need to be alert to the emergence of history as therapy proceeds.

Bilateral Stimulation in Phase 1

Sets of bilateral stimulation (BLS) such as eye movements, tapping, and audio stimulation may be introduced during this phase to support stabilization activities. The decision to use BLS is always predicated on assessing clients for sufficient stability and grounding. BLS seems to increase focus and reinforce stability and activities related to safe-place development, resource development, ego strengthening, and stress reduction. The research-validated, manualized EMDR standard protocol utilizes discrete sets of alternating stimulation, each set consisting of approximately twenty-four right-left movements, followed by instructions to "let it go," "blank it out," or "take a breath." The break between sets allows the client to rest, restore full orientation to present safety, and verbalize to the therapist "what came up" during the set. Different lengths of sets and types of BLS may be used at different times in the therapy process, in response to client needs or preferences. Sometimes different ego states will have different preferences, and this then may be a subject of negotiation between states during the preparation phase for EMDR.

During both the preparation phase and later phases, BLS should occur in sets, for the reasons given above. An exception to this rule occurs for some clients who indicate a preference for continuous stimulation (CS). Typically, these clients are not vulnerable to dissociative abreaction (that is, they are able to easily maintain a dual attention focus) and find CS more conducive to positive imagery; they may even express irritation at having to interrupt processing at the end of each set. The use of CS is possibly indicated for clients who frequently give the "keep going" signal during resource installation or trauma processing. Experienced EMDR-trained therapists can tell when continuous stimulation is helpful, but inexperienced therapists should err on the side of caution and use sets of BLS.

In addition to the above, one study has concluded that BLS in general also has the effect of inviting unresolved posttraumatic material into consciousness (Christman, Garvey, Propper, & Phaneuf, 2003). Since bilateral eye movements enhance the retrieval of episodic memories and other negative material, audio tones or tactile stimulation can be substituted if this retrieval is too intense for the client. For those more fragile, less grounded, or more dissociative clients, BLS will be used only to reinforce readiness activities when it is safe and when necessary—it may be postponed to Phase 2, when trauma targeting takes place.

Initial Ego State Work

The voices or inner conversations described by our clients are those of their internal parts. They sometimes appear to clients to be in a chaotic situation that often echoes their families and childhood homes. What is important for both therapist and client to keep in mind is that ego states also have the capacity to change, combine, grow, and adapt.

Clear explanations about the ego state system and its functioning in the past and in the present continue to give the client a framework for self-understanding. Without being too technical, an explanation that clients can understand is that dissociated ego states are neural networks holding aspects of memory, narrative, and physical sensations. Although the client may be skeptical, provide assurances that there are also healthy ego states that are well-functioning, adaptive resources. Explain that treatment will help the client get to know and understand the ego state system and reconnect with these resourceful, healthy parts.

To normalize ego state concepts it is best to use descriptive vocabulary that fits the client's language—words and phrases such as "states of mind," "fragments," "internal objects," "internal family system," "part selves," and "inner children." The parts can be described as living in the client's mind or brain or having a physical basis as networks of the client's neurology.

Depending on client style, this introduction of ego state concepts may be formal or informal. If the genogram has been used during history taking, state mapping can be described as an internal genogram. Humor helps! A client with years of analysis, when asked about internal parts, said, "Oh, you mean the Committee. You know, Freud was right on target, but why did he stop at three parts?" As they develop curiosity about themselves, clients may bring in ego state cartoons, or begin to draw their ego states. This work marks the beginning of building a functional, internally secure structure.

Accessing the Ego State System

A means must be chosen to facilitate the client's introduction to the ego state system. For some clients, concretizing the ego state system via mapping, listing, drawing pictures of the parts, or creating an internal landscape is helpful. The therapist can also ask, "If the internal family or parts could come into this office now, who might you see?"

The client and the system may know directly or only indirectly of each other's existence and roles. The when and where of meeting the ego state system will be client specific. Some clients may feel as if they are "taking in very abused foster children," as one client expressed it, by even acknowledging the parts.

Clients' attitudes toward their parts vary. We must accurately gauge empathy for the system parts and developmental readiness for this work by listening to the client's language and watching body language. Are the parts described or describing themselves with self-hatred, loathing, loneliness, and isolation? We note if the client's descriptive language is abusive, empathic, distant, or stern. A balance must always be maintained between two important considerations: preserving the stability of the adult ego state that is being asked to access the child or other ego states, and allowing validation and expression of the ego state's unprocessed experience. This is sometimes a thin line to walk.

Clients need to be informed about the ways in which they are likely to be misinterpreted by the ego state system: like actual children, the parts may be listening when clients least expect it. Even if the client is angry at these parts, the client may be able and willing to modify the language used when speaking about the parts. The client is encouraged to criticize the behavior, if necessary, rather than the part.

The therapist should note if there are stern, harsh critics or perfectionists among the states. Bullies can be reframed as once having had a protector role. It is important to tell the client that having an inner critical voice might have prevented punishment from parents in childhood (by reminding the child to stay quiet and invisible).

In helping the client learn about the parts, questioning interweaves may be used: "How old were you when that part had to take on that critical function?" "What was going on in your life?" "What was good about having that part function in that way?"

The Relationship of the Therapist to the Ego States

Through all three phases, it is imperative for the therapist to continue reassuring the ego states that they cannot and will not be expelled, abandoned, or "killed off." Even if the parts change their roles over time, they are necessary to the existence of the ego state system.

The therapist has to form alliances with the ego states during the treatment. This particularly applies to angry, self-hating, destructive, punitive parts. Identifying them and acknowledging their pain, qualities, and roles is crucial to successful treatment. The therapist's consistency in this encourages the client to look at the parts through new lenses.

Creating a Home Base

The home base (Forgash, 2004) is a place where the ego states can find safety, privacy, and relaxation. The creation of a home base is a new idea for many survivors who did not have those things in childhood. The home base has doors and boundaries for some clients who had none, or have lost them.

For some clients and their parts, a home base is impossible in the beginning because no place is yet safe. When the client first develops this space, it may look barren and unprotective, or it may be a lovely structure. In time, the client and the ego state system together invent a beach cottage, a cabin on a lake, a greenhouse with climate and shade controls. Sometimes the home base has to be part of the client's actual home.

Once the home base has been created, some parts want to move in, while others may refuse to go to there initially. Some parts are shunned by others or feared, and may need a separate space or one connected by a hall or breezeway, or they may even live in a separate structure. This usually evolves positively over time. Some activities to build a working relationship with the ego state system involve the client and ego states decorating the house and developing the outside environment.

Choosing and Installing a Workplace for the Ego State System

A workplace, office, or conference room where ego states can be accessed and joint work can take place is also created in this phase. Many types of workplace or conference rooms are suggested in the literature, for example Fraser's (1991, 2003) Dissociative Table Technique, in which the client sits at an oval table and invites ego states to sit in the empty chairs around the table.

Clients may want to include a conference room in their home base. They may wish to use the therapist's office setting or a familiar place for the workplace. The client and ego state system may equip this room with microphones, speakers, a TV, or movie screens to facilitate communication.

Some parts will not want to be visible and will not come readily to the workplace, especially at first. Some will be perceived as "ghosts" and shadows; some will just be sensed. Some will have shape, but no voice. This is to be expected and respected, and states should never be forced to appear. It is not a failure if parts are not seen or heard; it is just a matter of developing readiness and trust.

Orientation to Present Reality

Because EMDR reprocessing of trauma is based on simultaneous attention to past and present, it is important that the client be aware of and have the skill to remain grounded in present reality. Often ego states that experienced trauma in the past—especially child states—may not be oriented to the present. The exercise called Orientation to Present Reality (OPR) (Forgash, 2005; Twombly, 2005) helps the ego states learn about present time and place and can enhance feelings of reality and security and a sense of appropriate caring by the adult.

Parts can use an imaginal screen in their workplace to view images of the therapy office or the adult client and the adult's present age, body, gender, roles, and so on. They can imagine sitting or standing next to the client and noticing the size differences. A video tour of the adult's home, job, present life, family, and so on is helpful.

This sets the stage for an acceptance of current reality and changed conditions. For example, the ego state system may need to learn that perpetrators are dead, that the adult lives independently, and so forth. This information can be shocking. Parts may feel they are being tricked and lied to by the therapist and client.

This OPR work is titrated as needed. OPR generally needs to be repeated many times during treatment, as parts who need orientation or reorientation may appear at any phase.

There is a danger with some clients that they will feel guilty about not "feeling" the realization that the past is over and they are really living in the current year. There may be a history of previous, frustrated therapists getting upset with the client for not realizing, "It's over!!" Being oriented to the present does not imply that any parts will be forced to change their viewpoint.

Constructive Avoidance

Constructive avoidance is a technique for managing current life stressors (Forgash, 2004; Kluft, 1993). The adult client needs to be able to function in life while therapy work is proceeding. The therapist must teach the client not to expose immature or unhealed parts to potentially triggering or frightening events (medical procedures, sexual intimacy) or to situations for which they have no understanding or skills (public speaking, employment interviews, or arguments with spouses).

It is helpful for the client to explain the upcoming situation to the parts—the time and place of the event and what will be happening. The client then encourages the parts to stay in the home base until the adult says, "I'm home" or "It's over." This is very different from what was experienced in the family of origin, where the needs of the child were not considered. Supporting the more vulnerable parts in this manner requires practice in and out of session. Repetition of this work with many different situations fosters mastery and ends the client's past avoidance of necessary situations and life engagement.

Boundaries for Participation in Ego State Work

In working with an ego state system that includes children who experienced trauma, the therapist must establish parameters of respect, consideration, and care that were most likely absent in the childhood home environment.

The pacing of any work is set by the system. Appreciating differences in developmental abilities and readiness among the parts helps therapists time their interventions based on accurate ongoing assessment.

Consent must be obtained from the states prior to any activity. To identify treatment priorities, the therapist can ascertain which ego states are hurting the most and ask the permission of the other states to work with those that most need relief.

Ego states cannot be coerced into participation. Some may not be willing, for example, to listen to important psychoeducation about stabilization. In that case, the skill is taught to the parts who are willing to listen. Not every state has to participate, but all must agree to not sabotage the client or other parts who participate. The therapist must be careful to not impart negative judgment concerning these decisions, which simply can be defined as unreadiness. An activity or exercise can be put off until there is agreement on participation among the states.

Ego state conferences will be used to problem solve these issues. This results in an increase in acceptance of all ego states by opening lines of communication and increasing understanding of their motives and intentions.

The clinician and client can define acceptable participation of the ego states in sessions and set some stable rules for behavior. For example, if one state always gives the client a headache when the client wants to be present in session, the therapist and client have to state why this is not acceptable. This does not occur only in clients with a diagnosis of DID, but with many highly dissociative clients. Respectful engagement should be encouraged. If the part refuses to give up the behavior, the negotiating continues until there is resolution. Sometimes another part is willing to mediate or be helpful.

These old behaviors are framed as once having been adaptive on the part of protective states, but they are not currently helpful. These states are very fearful of change. Contracting for work with a particular part may involve setting very small goals. It will help to acknowledge all ego states' desire to increase the person's chances for survival (even when their strategies appear counterproductive).

Ego-Building Activities

Ego-building activities are designed to increase functioning of the client and of competent ego states in all treatment phases, but particularly in Phase 1. There are many ego-strengthening techniques developed in different therapeutic traditions. In EMDR treatment, Resource Development and Installation strategies (RDI; Korn & Leeds, 2002; Parnell, 2007) are designed so that positive resources, strengths, coping skills, and memories can be accessed and enhanced with the use of BLS. The client is asked to bring up positive skills or memories, internal resources and ego states, conflict-free memories, positive people who have been in their lives, pets, and spiritual figures. Those are then installed as permanent resources with sets of BLS.

It is not unusual for this work to go on for months with some clients, as some cannot grasp the idea of anything positive about them or their life. It is time well spent, as it will enable them to increase awareness of the presence of child ego states with unmet needs. Healing connections are forged between ego states in need and adult states, and the adult states are resourced with skills to meet the needs of the system.

Interventions for Managing Dissociation and Affective Symptoms

Containment. This is both a safety and an affect management technique. We teach the concept of containers for dealing with troubling or overwhelming emotions, thoughts, and sensations. The client is encouraged to imaginally develop containers such as safes, closets, boxes, or bubbles to hold this material temporarily. A room in the home base can be designated to hold the containers. Clients can then imagine letting feelings flow into the container and observe what effect that has on them (reduction of intensity, relaxation). They learn that containment is different from the old behavior of "stuffing," or repressing feelings. This temporarily contained material will be brought back to sessions, not hidden permanently.

Containment can be taught and practiced with some or all parts. It provides a new reality: an awareness that feelings can be put away and that one is not at the continual mercy of emotions (Forgash, 2004; Kluft, 1993).

Affect Regulation. It is common for complex trauma clients to be unable to identify feelings that have been terrifying and overwhelming. Over time, the client and ego state system need to develop the ability to identify feelings and understand their functions. Here is an opportunity to present more information about emotions. Visual activities such as the use of color to express feelings can provide a way of externalizing emotion. Journaling is another helpful technique for distancing, to titrate intensity. When the drawing is complete or the journal is closed, feelings are less intense.

The therapist models how to manage the client's affect through nonjudgmental acceptance, understanding, and validation. The latter element is increasingly important for clients who did not receive adequate feedback and guidance from their original caretakers. They come to acknowledge that processing through emotions results in adaptive resolution.

Constructive distracting and self-soothing activities can be practiced in or out of session. Mindfulness—the ability to have an observing stance in relation to affect, sensations, and temporal reality—can be cultivated through many exercises, including meditation and learning to notice a feeling with its accompanying intensity changes and physical sensations (Turkus & Kahler, 2006).

Self-Soothing. Clients need to learn self-soothing in order to manage affect both during and between sessions. They can take on a parental role by asking the ego states what they need to be comfortable. The response may simply be a blanket or a hug.

Other self-soothing activities include stress-reduction activities, calm- or relaxing-place imagery (Kluft, 1993), progressive-relaxation techniques, breathing and heart-coherence exercises (Servan-Schreiber, 2004), and conscious-distancing techniques. Clients should be reminded to encourage their ego states to remain at the home base in between sessions to avoid dissociation. We encourage clients to develop a check-in system to see how the ego states are faring. Consistent caretaking of the ego states is encouraged, as is dialogue with the parts to problem solve or to discuss internal or external change. These activities help clients develop parental responsibility over time.

Grounding. This involves teaching the skill of understanding the body and self in temporal reality, and being able to stay or return to the present reality. When clients gain the ability to deal with symptoms by using grounding strategies, they gain a sense of safety and control.

These questions will help the client be grounded in the present: "Can you feel the couch behind you? What does that feel like? What are your arms resting on? Can you distinguish between the fabric of the couch and your shirt? Can you feel your feet in your shoes?" The client should be directed to simply notice these feelings.

Grounding procedures are particularly helpful for clients who dissociate (Turkus & Kahler, 2006). They have practical application for stressful situations like driving, where it would be dangerous if dissociation were to occur. While driving, clients need to be able to feel the steering wheel in their hands, or differentiate between different textures and materials in the car. If they cannot, they need to learn to pull off the road until they feel more present. In Phase 2 work, we use grounding exercises when the client appears to be about to dissociate or is too distressed to stay in the present.

Relaxation. Visualization is a powerful strategy for enhancing relaxation. The client can simply be asked to visualize a relaxing or calm place, perhaps a place that they have visited or seen. The client fills in all of the meaningful details—scenery, colors, climate—and finds a comfortable place in the scene, perhaps sitting or lying down. The therapist asks the client to notice the associated emotions and body sensations. This can be enhanced with BLS and then practiced without BLS.

Screen Work and Affect Dial. The affect dial (Forgash, 2005; Kluft, 1993; Krakauer, 2001) is a distancing mechanism that can be imagined as the on/off button on a radio or a television remote control. This dial can be used by the client or by individual ego states to turn off or turn down overwhelming images, thoughts, emotions, colors, or shapes on the TV or movie screen. The size, clarity, or voice volume can be controlled through the dial.

The client starts out by imagining a screen in the conference room or workroom. The client then puts benign images on the screen using a remote-control device that has many buttons or knobs on it—for color and black and white, a fade button, a size and volume knob. This activity is limited only by imagination.

Often this imagery does not work immediately but becomes a useful client tool with practice, if the client is ready for the work. The therapist can give the client some practice in visualization, using nonthreatening images: "Picture an apple. What color is it? What type of apple is it? Make it larger or smaller; fade it out. Turn off the picture."

This helps the client and ego state system develop an ability to distance themselves from difficult, anxiety-provoking material, manipulate images, and imagine different endings or the hoped-for future. Showing past, present, and future events, memories, and activities on the screen is another way for the client and the ego state system to work with and gain skills in this area.

Somatic Work. According to van der Kolk et al. (1996), a central feature of PTSD is a loss of the ability to physiologically modulate stress responses. This can lead to a diminished capacity to utilize bodily signals and may also be responsible for immune system impairment. It is well documented that the chronic PTSD population suffers greatly from a variety of stress-related illnesses and syndromes (Loewenstein & Goodwin, 1999).

EMDR places emphasis on identifying and recognizing body sensations, and this emphasis normalizes the presence of physical sensations that are often troubling to the ego state system. Clients will subsequently be less fearful of processing sensations, symptoms, and the memories to which they are tied.

In the preparation phase there is an emphasis on somatosensory exercises (Levine, 1997) that utilize identification of positive (calm, serene, tension-free, and relaxed) body sensations as resources. This can be enhanced with bilateral stimulation for clients who have difficulty identifying these sensations. The client learns to focus on the most relaxed body part as a positive body resource. The body is felt as a physical safe place, to be returned to whenever necessary. This helps clients master the ability to consciously distance themselves from often overwhelming memories, events, and emotions. In this way, they develop an interior safe space.

This work prevents hyperarousal and numbing episodes and eventually allows clients to stay in their body even when processing difficult material. If practiced regularly, it helps reduce fear, making it easier to process. This work may be enhanced with BLS.

All sessions during Phase 1 end with some debriefing, containment work, relaxation, or somatosensory activity. All of the above interventions and activities can be enhanced with BLS if this is perceived as safe by the system.

Anticipating Problems

If the client refuses to attempt or complete these exercises, the therapist works with the client and the system to understand the resistance or perceived inability. The therapist should identify negative themes and blocking beliefs (being undeserving, lack of worth, self-hatred, and so on) and note them as possible targets for EMDR.

The refusal could be indicative of ego state system problems such as multiple transferences, fear of change, loss of role, or fear of expulsion. It is possible that a part may be listening for the first time and not yet ready to participate.

The client may be testing the therapy alliance for safety. The therapist must be consistent about not imposing authority or a need for excessive control of the work.

There could also be a lack of clarity about the work. In that case the therapist will explore, reassure, provide information, and initiate conferences and dialogues with the client and ego states.

PHASE 2: TRAUMA WORK

Phase 2 of our approach corresponds to EMDR Phases 3 through 8: assessment, desensitization and reprocessing, installation of the positive cognition, body scan, closure, and evaluation.

Prior to beginning EMDR, it is important to assess whether the client has gained the necessary resources and ego strengths to begin trauma processing. If it is found that trauma work has been started prematurely, it will be necessary to return to readiness work and resume processing only when the client is ready.

The expressive therapies are excellent adjuncts to target work in this phase. Drawing the target and using color to express emotion and selecting meaningful music to play during processing are especially helpful.

Choosing Targets

Setting up targets is based on an understanding of the client's issues and the client's preferred sequencing of those. Appropriate targets are selected by learning the main negative cognitions and blocking beliefs of the client and ego state system. Targets are not merely discrete events, but are frequently part of interlocking dissociated memory networks. They represent events, memories, or even images of distorted body parts of the past that are related to present problems and symptoms.

A decision tree is created with the client to determine which targets take precedence. It is preferable to start with the least upsetting situation or event to ensure the least likelihood of dissociation and discomfort. Small-t trauma clusters from earlier times and current life issues rather than large-T traumas may be good first choices.

Targets may be specific to one or more ego states. One client said that her six-year-old ego state requested work on her negative experiences in first grade. Her self belief was "I'm dumb." As she processed the event in the safety of the conference room, she realized that the teacher was old and impatient and that she herself was in fact "okay." Once this was processed successfully, the system that had been watching in the background felt increased safety to go on to more difficult targets.

If the client selects an issue that applies to more than one part, each ego state may require a separate VOC, SUD, and negative and positive cognitions. The client and ego states can develop and view targets together. They may spontaneously combine in a temporary merger for strength and security, leading to the formation of internal alliances.

Ensuring Safety

We stress throughout this book that clients with complex PTSD require special considerations during the trauma treatment. EMDR works best in combination with techniques common to treatment for dissociative disorders when working with these fragile clients. Those techniques—taught during Phase 1—using the screen for distancing and safety, and stopping processing for reorientation and anchoring to the safety of the therapy setting. The work should be fractionated (Fine, 1999; Kluft, 1990a, 1990b)—that is, traumatic experiences should be segmented into small portions that the client can handle—and frequent breaks may be necessary. This is not one- to three-session trauma processing, but long-term work.

The Presence of Ego States

As noted above, the ego state system is informed that all of the parts do not have to be present during processing. They can choose to stay away or not participate. They can stay present, but have speakers and microphones that they can turn off to distance themselves from the processing. The only agreement necessary is that they not sabotage the work taking place. If they cannot commit to this promise, desensitization has to wait until the problem is resolved through negotiation.

Structuring Sessions and Interventions

Actual processing may take only a small amount of session time. It may be typical to begin with a discussion of the client's week between sessions and a safe-place exercise. There will be a short amount of trauma processing in the middle section of the session, and the session will end with debriefing, relaxing, and containing.

The amount of time to be spent on each issue per session is dependent on many factors: degree of dissociation, co-consciousness, the wishes of angry, frightened, or hostile parts present at any given time, and the skills developed by the adult client.

There will be many incomplete sessions due to client fatigue and time constraints. The work is paced by the parts system, which over time grows more competent to tolerate processing and can make use of containment, debriefing, and other management techniques.

Safety techniques are rehearsed whenever necessary. Processing stops to orient new ego states and to solve conflicts, or if overwhelming reactions to trauma material are encountered. The processing work will inevitably be interrupted by crises, transference issues, a need to return to Phase 1 work, as well as the usual issues around illness and vacations.

Using Interweaves for Blocked Processing

When clients become stuck in processing, they will "loop" and continue to repeat the same thought, feeling, or negative cognition. Looping may occur due to the presence of another part who needs to speak. Attention must be paid to that part. Then, if possible, return to the target. Note any future targets that this part may bring up.

An interweave is an intervention used to get the processing restarted when a client is experiencing blocked processing. There are several types of interweaves. A cognitive interweave is a short question or sentence that helps the client see the irrationality of their looping belief. If the client keeps repeating, "I should have stopped him," the therapist can ask, "Who was larger, you or the bully?" There are also body interweaves: "Where are you feeling that in your body?" "Describe the color, shape, and size of that feeling."

To restart processing, the client can also be reminded of existing resources, such as coping skills. Sets of BLS are added, and the client then continues processing. The more dissociated and fragmented a client is, the more interweaves are necessary to maintain therapeutic processing.

Working with the Ego State System

Requesting permission from the ego state system, sometimes at each session, to work on trauma processing is not only respectful, it is also of pragmatic importance, since one ego state may have the power to block processing by other states. Working on continuing to develop benevolent communication and developing (or rediscovering) resources is also necessary, as is exploring conflicts and resolving issues. Clients will continue to explore their ability, resistance, and motivation to work with the ego state system.

Individual and systemwide ego state changes can be expected. As desensitization and processing proceed adaptively, ego states change or merge. They can observe and help the desensitization and reprocessing. Several ego states may watch the session or be supportive. Working with several states simultaneously means that there may be parallel processing of different perspectives of the event. Long-range systemic changes are seen as a result of combined EMDR and ego state treatment. Ego states evolve and change roles. Positive changes for one ego state may create temporary problems for another, necessitating a need for conflict resolution.

Responding to Destabilization

If at any point within trauma processing the client or ego state system becomes overwhelmed by the work, take breaks (unless the client indicates a readiness to continue). Help the client restabilize by returning to Phase 1 work that the client is already familiar with.

If it happens that a client who has not presented as dissociative prior to entering Phase 2 begins to dissociate, stop the work, assess for dissociation, and learn about why this is happening at this time. Inquire about the trigger. The client may have had a flashback or may not realize what has happened. In any case, the therapist must stop the trauma processing and determine what the client needs at this time. It may be necessary to inaugurate work with an ego state appearing for the first time. Do not proceed with Phase 2 work until the client is stabilized.

PHASE 3: RESOLUTION

In this phase, the client is assisted in developing a full degree of reassociation and co-consciousness between previously dissociated ego states. This is now possible because the original purpose of dissociation—to segment and separate potentially overwhelming traumatic material—is no longer necessary. If the posttraumatic images, self-referencing cognitions, emotions, and body sensations are now resolved, the person can proceed to enjoy a unified sense of self, with full adaptive access to memory and positive internal resources.

Maintaining the Momentum of Treatment

The sequence of the treatment phases—preparation, trauma processing, and resolution—dates back to Janet (1919/1925) and also makes intuitive sense. However, in practice, the process of treatment is often not so orderly. Instead, a back-and-forth sequence occurs—of preparation, followed by trauma work, which then requires additional stabilization before additional trauma work can be attempted. During the resolution phase, additional disturbing posttraumatic material that was previously unknown can emerge into awareness, necessitating a return to stabilization procedures and then additional trauma work. It is important for clients during this phase to be informed that "three steps forward, two steps back" is a common occurrence, if not the norm.

Clients at this phase of therapy will usually be able to draw on the positive resource of their previous success in resolving their life traumas and, encouraged in this way, will be able to move more easily through the remaining trauma work. It will be necessary during this phase to examine any areas of dysfunction or disturbance in the client's present life to see if these are connected with previously hidden traumatic experiences in the past. In a similar way, anticipated problems in the future may connect with the past or be signs of deficits in life skills that need to be corrected as part of a comprehensive therapy process.

The client may feel grief and mourning concerning past losses and missed opportunities, and it is often useful for clients to realize that this sadness will process in time, unlike the feelings of anxiety and shame that were previously connected with these losses. These losses may be ego state specific, or the system may process them together (Forgash, 2005). Some clients and the ego state system may want to create ceremonies and rituals to indicate moving forward and reconnecting.

As the resolution phase proceeds, the therapy process tends to gain momentum. The ego states now function with more mutual empathic understanding. The client is enabled to act more independently, try out new solutions as an integrated individual, and in that way, develop a future template for positive behaviors for each situation. Clients may find value in continuing to practice the safety, soothing, and stress-reduction techniques, as well as learning new skills for real-life situations.

Working toward Integration of the Ego States

During this phase, the client and therapist may encounter ego states with a narcissistic investment in separateness and a lack of compassion for other ego states. For example, a client may report, "I go into rages, and then the next day I'm ashamed. When I'm in the rage, I don't care about how I'll feel the next day." Often these points of disconnection are driven by hidden unresolved traumatic material that can be accessed by asking the client to explore the history of this issue.

With a portion of clients with dissociative disorders, the following procedure is sometimes helpful. When there is full agreement within the ego state system regarding a wish for wholeness and resolution, the separate ego states can be asked to "go to the center, occupy the same space, and look out the eyes together" while eye movements (or other BLS) are occurring (Paulsen, 1995). This may at first feel very strange for the client, but typically it will also tend to feel very positive. If the client is unable or unwilling to do this, the presence of hidden unresolved material may be indicated.

During the resolution phase, some clients will want to do a "trial integration" to see if they like it, with the option of going back and forth according to their comfort level. Stress may temporarily bring about a return to dissociative separateness. Typically, a feeling of resolution happens gradually.

Clients report that with increased wholeness, they experience benefits they had not anticipated. They may feel more real—but may also report that "real" also feels "strange" or even "scary," at least initially. But as the process continues, the client is likely to report, "It's better now" or "Life is lighter now than it was." Words like "happiness" and "satisfaction" acquire a personal meaning—they are no longer just words. Some clients report observations like, "The grass and trees are more beautiful, my friends are more interesting." Many describe the changes as helping them become more evolved, self-loving human beings, more connected to others, and interested in living life fully.

THE PERSON OF THE THERAPIST WORKING WITH CHALLENGING CLIENTS

Clients with trauma histories and complex PTSD can have very intense emotions and behaviors. It is virtually impossible to engage with these injured clients and not be impacted by their stories and their suffering. To protect both themselves and the therapeutic process, therapists need to be clearly aware of their personal reactions to their clients.

When a client recounts the details of horrible events, the therapist will then share the client's mental images, possibly leading to secondary traumatization. In fact there is a high incidence of secondary traumatization and PTSD in therapists (Bride, 2007). If the therapist's personal history includes experiences similar to the traumas of the client, this may engender fear and other countertransference reactions in the therapist.

Clients with complex PTSD, dissociative identity disorder, and borderline personality disorder often have dangerous and disturbing behaviors such as risk taking, suicidality, self-injury, severe eating disorders, and acting out. They typically have defensive styles that include rage and projective identification. Dissociation is common. All of those can be unsettling for the therapist who is struggling to stabilize the client.

Therapy, by virtue of its private and confidential nature, lends itself to isolation, which may contribute to therapist vulnerability to secondary traumatization (Figley, 1995; Stamm, 1999) and a sense of helplessness, confusion, or failure. The therapist may become mired in negativity and discomfort and may seek to end the relationship by referring the client to another therapist.

A therapist's discomfort can negatively impact the conduct of the therapy. If therapists experience fear or anxiety when they encounter disturbing material, powerful abreactions, or dissociation in session, they may become avoidant and find themselves overusing stabilization work. Although carefully planned preparation work is critical, moving ahead will be stymied if therapists insist on doing an overly lengthy preparation in order to maintain their own comfort level.

Newly trained EMDR clinicians may be unwilling to use EMDR with difficult clientele because they have not learned to integrate it into their practice style. The EMDR protocol can initially appear to be a more structured therapeutic method than what many psychodynamic therapists are used to. Although it has directive elements, EMDR is primarily directed by the client—therapists are instructed to "stay out of the way" during the processing phase of EMDR. It can be very uncomfortable for experienced therapists to "go back to school" and change their therapeutic style. Additionally, the effects of EMDR can be very powerful, with an immediacy that moves clients at a speed often unfamiliar to the therapist. Therapists need to not only learn, but to give themselves the time to become familiar with these new treatment approaches.

For all of these reasons, it is imperative to learn about trauma and dissociative processes and to understand their effects on clients. In spite of these difficulties, though, it should be noted that the clinician who is confident, comfortable regarding the unfolding of the therapeutic process, and willing to be flexible and innovative in working with this population will be less vulnerable to therapy disruptions. An attitude of ongoing learning as well as regular consultation and, if needed, personal therapy are often essential to help the therapist maintain comfort in the treating role and to avoid becoming traumatized.

CONCLUSION

In this book, ideas and concepts drawn from different therapy traditions have been brought together to make a whole that we hope and believe is greater than the sum of its parts. We have labeled this a "cross-training" model to emphasize an analogy from sports performance training: that skills in one area are often enhanced by training in the skills from another area. Specifically, we have seen that the healing benefits of EMDR can be extended to a much wider population of clients by extending the length and scope of Phase 1 (the stabilization and preparation phase of trauma treatment) and adding EMDR, specific ego state work, and dissociative symptom management interventions to each phase. With enhanced preparation, clients are more easily able to come to an awareness and acceptance of their ego state system and develop the ability to self-soothe and manage dissociative and PTSD symptoms.

Clients with many complex diagnoses who are thus empowered can then deal effectively with their unresolved memory material, looking at their life experience with both compassion and objective understanding. With this integrated treatment model, the internal family system of ego states is recognized for having played purposeful, honorable roles during the earlier times of terror and chaos. With increased internal respect, the processing of long-held traumatic memory material becomes possible. As this occurs, the client and ego state system can increasingly implement a more effective blueprint for living.

The client works successively through themes of responsibility, safety, and life choices and learns in the process how to be spontaneous, appropriate, authentic, and fully human. The client who completes this work is able to say, in all honesty, "I know who I am now. I trust myself. I am a person worthy of my own love and respect."

REFERENCES

American Psychiatric Association. (1994). *Diagnostic and statistical manual of mental disorders* (4th ed.). Washington, DC: Author.

Anderson, M. C., Ochsner, K. N., Kuhl, B., Cooper, J., Robertson, E., Gabrieli, S. W., et al. (2004). Neural systems underlying the suppression of unwanted memories. *Science, 303*(5655), 232–235.

Barach, P. M., & Comstock, C. M. (1996). Psychodynamic psychotherapy of dissociative identity disorder. In L. K. Michelson & W. J. Ray (Eds.), *Handbook of dissociation: Clinical, theoretical and empirical perspectives* (pp. 413–429). New York: Plenum.

Bergmann, U., & Forgash, C. (1998, June). *Working successfully with apparent EMDR non-responders.* Workshop presented at the EMDR International Association Annual Conference, Baltimore.

Bergmann, U., & Forgash, C. (2000, April). *EMDR and ego state treatment of dissociation.* Workshop presented at the International Society for the Study of Dissociation Conference, San Antonio, TX.

Bride, B. E. (2007). Prevalence of secondary traumatic stress among social workers. *Social Work, 52*(1), 63–70.

Carlson, E. B., & Putnam, F. W. (1993). An update on the Dissociative Experiences Scale. *Dissociation, 6,* 16–27.

Chefetz, R. A. (2006). Preface to Dissociative disorders: An expanding window into the psychobiology of the mind. *Psychiatric Clinics of North America, 29*(1), xv.

Christman, S. D., Garvey, K. J., Propper, R. E., & Phaneuf, K. A. (2003). Bilateral eye movements enhance the retrieval of episodic memories. *Neuropsychology, 17*(2), 221–229.

Chu, A., & De Prince, A. (2006). Development of dissociation: Examining the relationship between parenting, maternal trauma and child dissociation. *Journal of Trauma and Dissociation, 7*(4), 75–90.

Chu, J. (1998). *Rebuilding shattered lives.* New York: Wiley.

Classen, C., Pain, C., Field, N. P., & Woods, P. (2006). Posttraumatic personality disorder: A reformulation of complex posttraumatic stress disorder and borderline personality disorder. In R. A. Chefetz (Ed.), Dissociative disorders: An expanding window into the psychobiology of the mind. *Psychiatric Clinics of North America, 29*(1), 87–112.

Dell, P. F. (2006). The Multidimensional Inventory of Dissociation (MID): A comprehensive measure of pathological dissociation. *Journal of Trauma and Dissociation, 7*(2), 77–106.

Dworkin, M. (2005). *EMDR and the relational imperative.* New York: Routledge.

Felitti, V. J., Anda, R. F., Nordenberg, D., Williamson, D. F., Spitz, A. M., Edwards, V., et al. (1998). Relationship of childhood abuse and household dysfunction to many of the leading causes of death in adults. *American Journal of Preventive Medicine, 14*(4), 245–258.

Figley, C. (1995). *Compassion fatigue: Coping with secondary traumatic stress disorders in those who treat the traumatized.* New York: Brunner/Mazel.

Fine, C. (1995, June). *EMDR with dissociative disorders.* Workshop presented at EMDR Network Annual Meeting, San Francisco.

Fine, C. G. (1999). The tactical-integration model for the treatment of dissociative identity disorder and allied dissociative disorders. *American Journal of Psychotherapy, 53*(3), 361–376.

Forgash, C. (2004, May). Treating complex posttraumatic stress disorder with EMDR and ego state therapy. *EMDR Practitioner.* Retrieved July 18, 2007, from http://www.emdr-europe.org/

Forgash, C. (2005, May). *Deepening EMDR treatment effects across the diagnostic spectrum: Integrating EMDR and ego state work.* Two-day workshop presentation, New York. (Available on DVD at www.advancededucationalproductions.com)

Forgash, C., & Knipe, J. (2001, September). *Safety-focused EMDR/ego state treatment of dissociative disorders.* Workshop presented at the EMDR International Association Annual Conference, Austin, TX.

Forgash, C., & Monahan, K. (2000). Enhancing the health care experiences of adult female sexual abuse survivors of childhood sexual abuse. *Women and Health, 30*(4), 27–42.

Fraser, G. A. (1991). The Dissociative Table Technique: A strategy for working with ego states in dissociative disorders and ego state therapy. *Dissociation, 4*(4), 205–213.

Fraser, G. A. (2003). Fraser's "Dissociative Table Technique" revisited, revised: A strategy for working with ego states in dissociative disorders and ego state therapy. *Journal of Trauma and Dissociation, 4*(4), 5–28.

Gold, S. (2000). *Not trauma alone.* Philadelphia: Brunner-Routledge.

Greenwald, R. (1999). *Eye movement desensitization and reprocessing in child and adolescent psychotherapy.* Northvale, NJ: Jason Aronson.

Herman, J. L. (1992). *Trauma and recovery: The aftermath of violence—From domestic abuse to political terror.* New York: Basic Books.

Hilgard, E. R. (1977). *Divided consciousness: Multiple controls in human thought and action.* New York: Wiley.

International Society for the Study of Dissociation. (2005). Guidelines for treating dissociative identity disorder in adults. *Journal of Trauma and Dissociation, 6*(4), 69–150.

Janet, P. (1907). *The major symptoms of hysteria.* London and New York: Macmillan.

Kiessling, R. (2003, September). *Integrating resource installation strategies into your EMDR practice.* Workshop presented at the EMDR International Association Annual Conference, Denver, CO.

Kluft, R. P. (1990a). The fractionated abreactive technique. In D. C. Hammond (Ed.), *Handbook of hypnotic suggestions and metaphors* (pp. 527–528). New York: Norton.

Kluft, R. P. (1990b). The slow leak technique. In D. C. Hammond (Ed.), *Handbook of hypnotic suggestions and metaphors* (pp. 526–527). New York: Norton.

Kluft, R. P. (1993). The initial stages of psychotherapy in the treatment of multiple personality disorder patients. *Dissociation, 6*(2/3), 145–161.

Knipe, J. (1995, Winter). Targeting avoidance and dissociative numbing. *EMDR Network Newsletter, 5*(3), 4–5.

Knipe, J. (2005). Targeting positive affect to clear the pain of unrequited love, codependence, avoidance, and procrastination. In R. Shapiro (Ed.), *EMDR solutions: Pathways to healing* (pp. 189–211). New York: Norton.

Koffka, K. (1935). *Principles of Gestalt psychology.* New York: Ronald Press.

Korn, D. L., & Leeds, A. M. (2002). Preliminary evidence of efficacy for EMDR resource development and installation in the stabilization phase of treatment of complex posttraumatic stress disorder. *Journal of Clinical Psychology, 58*(12), 1465–1487.

Krakauer, S. (2001). *Treating dissociative identity disorder: The power of the collective heart.* Philadelphia: Brunner-Routledge.

Lacter, E. (2007). *Defensive adaptations to the traumatogenic effects of abuse.* Unpublished manuscript.

Leeds, A. (2002). A prototype EMDR protocol for identifying and installing resources. In F. Shapiro (Ed.), *Part two training manual.* Pacific Grove, CA: EMDR Institute.

Levine P. (1997). *Waking the tiger.* Berkeley, CA: North Atlantic Books.

Linehan, M. M. (1993). *Cognitive-behavioral treatment of borderline personality disorder.* New York: Guilford Press.

Liotti, G. (1999). Disorganization of attachment as a model for understanding dissociative psychopathology. In J. Solomon & C. George (Eds.), *Attachment disorganization* (pp. 291–317). New York: Guilford Press.

Liotti, G. (2004). Trauma, dissociation, and disorganized attachment: Three strands of a single braid. *Psychotherapy: Theory, Practice, Research, Training, 41*(4), 55–74.

Liotti, G. (2006). A model of dissociation based on attachment theory. *Journal of Trauma and Dissociation, 7*(4), 55–74.

Loewenstein, R., & Goodwin, J. (1999). Assessment and management of somatoform symptoms in traumatized patients: Conceptual overview and pragmatic guide. In J. Goodwin & R. Attias (Eds.), *Splintered reflections: Images of the body in trauma* (pp. 67–88). New York: Basic Books.

Lovett, J. (1999). *Small wonders: Healing childhood trauma with EMDR.* New York: Free Press.

Lyons-Ruth, K., Dutra, L., Schuder, M., & Bianchi, I. (2006). From attachment disorganization to adult dissociation: Relational adaptations or traumatic experiences?

In R. A. Chefetz (Ed.), Dissociative disorders: An expanding window into the psychobiology of the mind. *Psychiatric Clinics of North America, 29*(1), 63–86.

Manfield, P. (Ed.). (1998). *Extending EMDR.* New York: Norton.

Maxfield, L., & Hyer, L. A. (2002). The relationship between efficacy and methodology in studies investigating EMDR treatment of PTSD. *Journal of Clinical Psychology, 58,* 23–41.

Moran, M. (2007). Developmental trauma merits *DSM* diagnosis, experts say. *Psychiatric News, 42*(3), 20.

Parnell, L. (2007). *A therapist's guide to EMDR.* New York: Norton.

Paulsen, S. (1995). Eye movement desensitization and reprocessing: its cautious use in the dissociative disorders. *Dissociation, 8*(1), 32–44.

Phillips, M. (1993). The use of ego state therapy in the treatment of posttraumatic stress disorder. *American Journal of Clinical Hypnosis, 35*(4), 241–249.

Randall, J. (2004). The seductiveness of the memory hole. In *Slumber party at the aquarium.* Bryan, TX: Unicorn Press, 18.

Ross, C. A., Heber, S., Norton, G. R., Anderson, G., Anderson, B., & Barchet, P. (1989). The dissociative disorders interview schedule: A structured interview. *Dissociation, 2*(3), 169–189.

Sar, V. (2006). The scope of dissociative disorders: An international perspective. In R. A. Chefetz (Ed.), Dissociative disorders: An expanding window into the psychobiology of the mind. *Psychiatric Clinics of North America, 29*(1), 227–244.

Schore, A. N. (1994). *Affect regulation and the origin of the self: The neurobiology of emotional development.* Hillsdale, NJ: Lawrence Erlbaum.

Schore, A. N. (2000a, June). *The psychoneurobiological basis of attachment.* Paper presented at the EMDR International Association Annual Conference, Toronto, Ontario, Canada.

Schore, A. N. (2000b, June). *Traumatic attachment and the development of the right brain.* Paper presented at the EMDR International Association Annual Conference, Toronto, Ontario, Canada.

Schwartz, R. C. (1995). *Internal family systems therapy.* New York: Guilford Press.

Servan-Schreiber, D. (2004). *The instinct to heal: Curing stress, anxiety, and depression without drugs and without talk therapy.* Emmaus, PA: Rodale Press.

Shapiro, F. (2001). *Eye movement desensitization and reprocessing: Basic principles, protocols, and procedures* (2nd ed.). New York: Guilford Press.

Shapiro, R. (2005). *EMDR solutions: Pathways to healing.* New York. Norton.

Siegel, D. J. (1999). *The developing mind: How relationships and the brain interact to shape who we are.* New York: Guilford Press.

Silver, S., & Rogers, S. (2002). *Light in the heart of darkness: EMDR and the treatment of war and terrorism survivors.* New York: Norton.

Simone Reinders, A. A. T., Nijenhuis, E. R. S., Quak, J., Korf, J., Haaksma, J., Paans, A., et al. (2006). Psychobiological characteristics of dissociative identity disorder: A symptom provocation study. *Biological Psychiatry, 60*(7), 730–740.

Spanos, N. P. (1994). Multiple identity enactments and multiple personality disorder: A sociocognitive perspective. *Psychology Bulletin, 116,* 143–165.

Stamm, B. H. (Ed.). (1999). *Secondary traumatic stress: Self-care issues for clinicians, researchers and educators.* Lutherville, MD: Sidran Institute Press.

Steinberg, M., Rounsaville, B., & Cicchetti, D. V. (1990). The Structured Clinical Interview for *DSM–III–R* Dissociative Disorders: Preliminary report on a new diagnostic instrument. *American Journal of Psychiatry, 147,* 76–82.

Teicher, M. H., Samson, J. A., Polcari, A., & McGreenery, C. E. (2006). Sticks, stones, and hurtful words: Relative effects of various forms of childhood maltreatment. *American Journal of Psychiatry, 163,* 993–1000.

Terr, L. C. (1979). Children of Chowchilla: A study of psychic trauma. *Psychoanalytic Study of the Child, 34*, 552–623.

Tinker, R. H., & Wilson, S. A. (1999). *Through the eyes of a child: EMDR with children.* New York: Norton.

Turkus J. A., & Kahler, J. A. (2006). Therapeutic interventions in the treatment of trauma and dissociation. In R. A. Chefetz (Ed.), Dissociative disorders: An expanding window into the psychobiology of the mind. *Psychiatric Clinics of North America, 29*(1), 245–262.

Twombly, J. H. (2005). EMDR Processing with dissociative identity disorder, DDNOS, and ego states. In R. Shapiro (Ed.), *EMDR solutions: Pathways to healing* (pp. 88–120). New York: Norton.

van der Hart, O., Nijenhuis, E. R. S., & Steele, K. (2006). *The haunted self: Structural dissociation and the treatment of chronic traumatization.* New York: Norton.

van der Kolk, B. A., McFarlane A., & Weisaeth, L. (Eds.). (1996). *Traumatic stress.* New York: Guilford Press.

van der Kolk, B. A., Roth, S., Pelcovitz, D., Sunday, S., & Spinazzola, J. (2005). Disorders of extreme stress: The empirical foundation of a complex adaptation to trauma. *Journal of Traumatic Stress, 18*, 389–399.

Wachtel, P. (2002). EMDR and psychoanalysis. In F. Shapiro (Ed.), *EMDR as an integrative psychotherapy approach* (pp. 123–150). Washington, DC: American Psychological Association.

Watkins, J. G., & Watkins, H. H. (1979). The theory and practice of ego state therapy. In H. Grayson (Ed.), *Short-term approaches to psychotherapy* (pp. 176–220). New York: Human Sciences Press.

Watkins, J. G., & Watkins, H. H. (1979–1980). Ego states and hidden observers. *Journal of Consciousness, 5*, 3–18.

Watkins, J. G., & Watkins, H. (1997). *Ego states: Theory and therapy.* New York: Norton.

Wilson, S. A., Becker, L. A., & Tinker, R. H. (1995). Eye movement desensitization and reprocessing (EMDR) for psychologically traumatized individuals. *Journal of Consulting and Clinical Psychology, 63*, 928–937.

Wilson, S. A., Becker, L. A., & Tinker, R. H. (1997). Fifteen-month follow-up of eye movement desensitization and reprocessing (EMDR) treatment for PTSD and psychological trauma. *Journal of Consulting and Clinical Psychology, 65*, 1047–1056.

CHAPTER 2

She's Come Undone

A Neurobiological Exploration of Dissociative Disorders

Uri Bergmann

> Without realizing it, I fought to keep my two worlds separated. Without ever knowing why, I made sure, whenever possible, that nothing passed between the compartmentalization that I had created between the day child and the night child.
> —Marilyn Van Derbur, *Miss America by Day: Lessons Learned from Ultimate Betrayals and Unconditional Love*

> Trauma can be conceptualized as stemming from a failure of the natural physiological activation and hormonal secretions to organize an effective response to threat.... After having been traumatized people often lose the effective use of fight or flight defenses and respond to perceived threat with immobilization.
> —Bessel A. van der Kolk, *Clinical Implications of Neuroscience Research in PTSD*

Life is often an enduring struggle for people who have been chronically traumatized. Their suffering essentially recounts a horrifying and anguished past that haunts them, incessantly. Even as these clients attempt to hide their sorrow beneath a veneer of normality, therapists often feel beleaguered by their many symptoms and never-ending pain. Van der Kolk and McFarlane (1996) note that "experiencing trauma is an essential part of being human; history is written in blood" (p. 3). Centuries of wars, famines, pogroms, holocausts, slavery, dictatorship, and colonization brought every type of horror and abuse into the homes of our ancestors. Some found ways to adapt, but many succumbed to the horror and despair. Despite the capacity of humans to survive and adapt, traumatic experiences tend to alter their biological, psychological, and social equilibrium to such a vast extent that the memory and interpretation of their traumas wash over and taint all other experiences, contaminating the present and future (van der Kolk & McFarlane, 1996).

THE RELATIONSHIP BETWEEN TRAUMA AND DISSOCIATION

The interactive coexistence and relationship between dissociative disorders and trauma has only recently become clear. Van der Hart, Nijenhuis, and Steele (2006) maintain that dissociation is the key concept to understanding traumatization. They view the spectrum of acute posttraumatic stress disorder (PTSD), depersonalization disorder, dissociative amnesia, dissociative fugue, and dissociative identity disorder (DID) as a spectrum of structural dissociation of the personality (Nijenhuis, van der Hart, & Steele, 2004; van der Hart & Nijenhuis, 1998; van der Hart, Nijenhuis, & Steele, 2005; van der Hart, Nijenhuis, Steele, & Brown, 2004). They note that a century of studying psychotraumatology has shown that traumatized individuals tend to alternate between intrusive reexperiencing of, being detached from, or being unaware of their traumas as a result of amnesia. In concert with this shift, the syndrome of psychological problems that have been shown to be frequently associated with histories of prolonged and severe interpersonal abuse has been named complex PTSD or disorders of extreme stress not otherwise specified (DESNOS; Herman, 1992; van der Kolk, Perry, & Herman, 1991). These diagnoses consist of the following six clusters of symptoms that are regularly seen in dissociative disorders (van der Kolk, 2001):

1. Alterations in the regulation of affect and impulses, including difficulties in the modulation of anger and self destructiveness
2. Alterations in attention and consciousness, often leading to amnesias, dissociative episodes, and depersonalizations
3. Alterations in self-perception, such as a chronic sense of guilt, responsibility, and shame
4. Alterations in relationship to others, compromised by the inability to trust and feel intimate
5. Various degrees of somatization disorders and disease processes, in the absence of identifiable mainstream medical explanation

6. Impairment vis-à-vis the integrated functioning of their identity mechanisms

Recently, Classen, Pain, Field, and Woods (2006) proposed the inception of a new diagnostic category, posttraumatic personality disorder (PTPD), to articulate the interrelationship of chronic traumatization, disorganized attachment disorders, dissociative disorders, and borderline personality disorders (BPD). They note that although complex PTSD, or DESNOS, is intended to reflect the consequences of chronic traumatization, the domains that they describe are characterized more accurately as a personality disorder, more specifically, a posttraumatic personality disorder. They propose two types of PTPD: one involving organized attachment and the other involving disorganized attachment, both associated with PTSD. Accordingly, posttraumatic personality disorder/disorganized (PTPD-D) designates the comorbid condition of BPD and DESNOS, while posttraumatic personality disorder/organized (PTPD-O) represents DESNOS without BPD. The researchers posit that understanding the effect of chronic traumatization in the context of either organized or disorganized attachment has specific implications for treatment and further research.

These conceptual changes, informed by decades of clinical experience, appear to indicate that trauma and dissociation do, indeed, coexist and are, evidently, driven by similar evolutionarily based biological systems.

THE EVOLUTION OF BIOLOGICAL ACTION SYSTEMS

This chapter will illustrate the relationship of posttraumatic and dissociative symptoms to biological emotional operating systems (Panksepp, 1998) and functional systems (Fanselow & Lester, 1988). For convenience, these systems will be termed "biological action systems" (Nijenhuis et al., 2004). Panksepp lists six objective neural criteria that define emotional systems (action systems) in the brain. These criteria are as follows:

> The underlying circuits must be genetically predetermined and designed to respond unconditionally to stimuli arising from major life-challenging circumstances; these circuits must organize diverse behaviors by activating or inhibiting motor circuits and concurrent autonomic hormonal changes that have proved to be adaptive in the face of such life-challenging circumstances during the evolutionary history of the species; these emotional circuits must change the sensitivities of sensory systems that

are relevant to the behavioral sequences that have been aroused; the neural activity of these emotional systems must outlast the precipitating circumstances; these emotional circuits must come under the conditional control of emotionally neutral environmental stimuli; and these circuits must have reciprocal interactions with the brain mechanisms that elaborate higher decision-making processes and consciousness. (pp. 48–49)

Therefore, these action systems are self-organizing and self-stabilizing with respect to homeostasis, time, and context of experience. They are also functional systems that have been developed in the course of evolution and are analogous to mammalian biological systems.

Panksepp designates the following emotional operating systems (action systems) as defined primarily by genetically coded neural circuits that generate well-organized behavior sequences, which can be evoked by localized electrical stimulation of the brain:

1. The Seeking system, which mediates interest in and exploration of the environment, food seeking, warmth, and sexual gratification
2. The Fear system, which mediates flight or freeze
3. The Rage system, which mediates fight
4. The Panic system, which mediates distress vocalization and social attachment

These systems, therefore, are the basic elements that shape personality. Ideally, integration occurs within and among these action systems as a result of a nontraumatic developmental course. Over the course of evolution, these primitive action systems have become linked with higher cortical functions, enabling us to engage in complex action tendencies, including complex relationships (van der Hart et al., 2006). Functioning as adults therefore involves a profound complexity of biopsychosocial goals (caring for children, socializing, competing, loving and protecting, and exploring our inner and outer worlds). Meeting these goals involves a deep integration of these action systems. Indeed, most psychological conflicts, from the neurotic to the severely dissociative, involve the difficulty of balancing and integrating these action systems (van der Hart et al., 2006).

Although there is a growing consensus in the fields of traumatology and neurobiology that dissociation appears to be a normative and developmental phenomenon, as well as an outcome of traumatic experiences, this exploration will be conceptualized solely within the context of trauma-related structural dissociation of the personality. The reader is referred to chapter 7, dealing with personality disorders, for a comprehensive exploration of normative, developmentally inherent dissociation.

In order to systematize the varied symptom clusters and syndromes of traumatic and dissociative disorders, this chapter will organize them into aspects of reexperiencing trauma versus detachment from trauma and relate them to the action systems that mediate them. For example, reexperiencing trauma will be associated with the inborn and evolutionarily derived defensive systems of Fear and Rage that are evoked by severe threat. As complex action systems, they encompass various subsystems, such as flight, freeze, and fight. Detachment from trauma will be associated with the action systems of Seeking and Panic, which control functions in daily life (for example, exploration of the environment and energy control), and functions that are dedicated to survival of the species (reproduction and attachment to and caring for offspring; Nijenhuis et al., 2004; van der Hart et al., 2006). In addition, these action systems will also be reviewed in reference to the organizing constructs of primary, secondary, and tertiary dissociation (Nijenhuis et al., 2004; van der Hart et al., 2006; van der Hart, van der Kolk, & Boon, 1996; van der Kolk, van der Hart, & Marmar, 1996).

TYPES OF DISSOCIATION

Primary Dissociation

As defined by van der Hart et al. (1996) and van der Kolk et al. (1996), primary dissociation refers to the inability to integrate the totality of a traumatic event into consciousness, thereby causing the intrusion into awareness of fragmented traumatic memories, primarily in sensory form. These intrusive sensory fragments tend to be visual, olfactory, auditory, kinesthetic, or visceral. Primary dissociation, therefore, is characteristic of PTSD, in which the most dramatic symptoms are expressions of associated traumatic memories, such as intrusive recollections, nightmares, and flashbacks. These phenomenological responses are often associated with psychophysiological arousal, as evidenced by increased heart rate and electrical skin conductance (Frewen & Lanius, 2006; Orr, McNally, & Rosen, 2004). Van der Kolk et al. (1996) write that "this fragmentation is accompanied by ego states that are distinct from the normal state of consciousness" (p. 307). In a more recent conceptualization, called Primary Structural Dissociation of the Personality, these ego states have been designated as the "apparently normal part" of the personality (ANP) and the "emotional part" of the personality (EP), to designate the adult ego state or self and the other dissociated ego states, respectively (Nijenhuis et al., 2004; Steele, van der Hart, & Nijenhuis, 2001). These designations were originally coined by Myers (1940) as the Apparently Normal Personality

(ANP) and the Emotional Personality (EP) and resurrected by van der Hart, Nijenhuis, and Steele in their various writings.

Secondary Dissociation

Van der Hart et al. (1996) and van der Kolk et al. (1996) observe that once an individual is in a traumatic (dissociated) state of mind, further disintegration of personal experience can occur. Derealization and depersonalization tend to manifest: people report experiences of leaving their body at the moment of the trauma and observing the trauma from a distance. Therefore, secondary dissociation allows individuals to observe their traumatic experience as spectators and to limit their pain and distress. Phenomenologically, this produces increased fragmentation and dissociated ego states. Steele et al. (2001) note that in secondary structural dissociation of the personality this increase in fragmentation is observed in increased divisions of the EPs. Diagnostically, this constellation tends to produce the conditions of complex PTSD, DESNOS, depersonalization disorders, dissociative amnesia, and dissociative fugue.

Tertiary Dissociation

Van der Hart et al. (1996) and van der Kolk et al. (1996) write that tertiary dissociation results from the development of "distinct ego states that contain the traumatic experience, consisting of complex identities with distinct cognitive, affective, and behavioral patterns" (van der Kolk et al, p. 308). Phenomenologically, this produces severely chaotic and profoundly dissociated alter identities, often with little or no co-consciousness of each other. Nijenhuis et al. (2004) note that in addition to increased divisions of the EPs, tertiary structural dissociation of the personality also produces further divisions of the ANPs. Diagnostically, this constellation tends to produce the condition of dissociative identity disorder.

Therefore, for example, dissociative self-states will also be articulated as the adult self versus other dissociated self-states or alters, as well as ANPs versus EPs.

THE NEUROBIOLOGY OF PRIMARY DISSOCIATION

With respect to the context of traumatic experiences, I concur that severe threat provokes a structural dissociation of the personality (Nijenhuis et al., 2004; van der Hart, 2000; van der Hart et al., 2006). In its primary form, this dissociation is conceptualized as existing between the defensive action systems on the one hand, and the action systems that involve managing daily life and survival of the species on the other hand (Nijenhuis et al., 2004).

In the past twenty years a great deal of light has been shed on the area of neurobiology. Much of the research has focused on the components that mediate our emotional state of mind. In particular, the interrelationship between the structure and function of the amygdala, thalamus, left dorsolateral prefrontal cortex, anterior cingulate gyrus, and hippocampus has been articulated with increasing clarity. In order to understand the malfunctioning of these structures in PTSD, a brief description of their functional characteristics is required.

Descriptive and Functional Anatomy

The amygdala is an almond-shaped cluster of interconnected structures perched above the brainstem. It is composed of two structures nestled in the temporal lobe, in the right and left hemispheres. The corticomedial amygdala, in the right hemisphere, is connected primarily with the olfactory bulb, the hypothalamus, and the visceral nuclei of the brain stem. The basolateral amygdala, in the left hemisphere, is connected with the thalamus and parts of the cerebral cortex. The hippocampus is also located in the temporal lobe (see Figure 2.1).

The thalamus is situated in the temporal lobe on each side of the third ventricle. The thalamus is composed of many smaller nuclei and is a relay station for almost all information transmitted from the lower parts of the central nervous system to the cerebral cortex. Below the thalamus, also in the temporal lobe, lies the hypothalamus, which is primarily involved with the central control of the autonomic nervous system (P. Brodal, 1992).

Partially encircling these structures is the cingulate gyrus. Its anterior cortex appears to be involved in conditioned emotional learning, assigning emotional valence to internal and external stimuli, and facilitating a more realistic differentiation between real and perceived threat (Devinsky, Morrell, & Vogt, 1995).

The hippocampus and the amygdala were the two key parts of the primitive "nose brain" (rhinencephalon) that evolved and gave rise to the cortex and then to the neocortex (P. Brodal, 1992; Goleman, 1995). These limbic structures are necessary for the onset of learning and remembering (A. Brodal, 1980; P. Brodal, 1992; Goleman, 1995; LeDoux, 1986, 1992, 1994; Walsh, 1987).

The amygdala provides the central crossroads junction where information from all senses is tied together and endowed with emotional

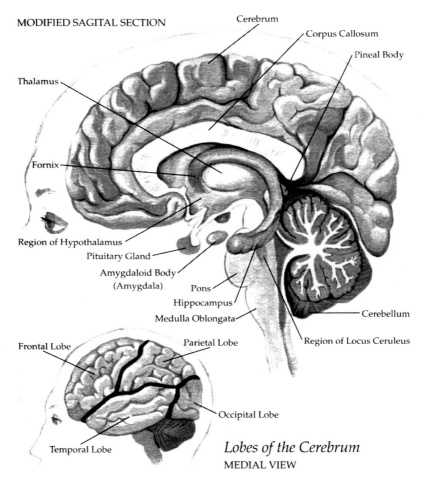

MODIFIED SAGITAL SECTION

Cerebrum

Corpus Callosum

Pineal Body

Thalamus

Fornix

Region of Hypothalamus

Pituitary Gland

Amygdaloid Body
(Amygdala)

Pons

Hippocampus

Medulla Oblongata

Cerebellum

Region of Locus Ceruleus

Frontal Lobe

Parietal Lobe

Occipital Lobe

Temporal Lobe

Lobes of the Cerebrum
MEDIAL VIEW

FIGURE 2.1   Selected structures of the brain. (Reprinted from
*A Primer on the Complexities of Traumatic Memory of Childhood
Sexual Abuse: A Psychobiological Approach*, 1996, by Fay Honey
Knopp and Anna Rose Benson, by permission of the Safer Society
Foundation, Inc. Illustration by Barbara Poeter.)

meaning. It is here that the sights, sounds, smells, tastes, proprioceptive, and touch sensations of an experience are brought together and remembered (Reiser, 1994). The hippocampus has been referred to as the "gateway" to the limbic system (Winson, 1985, 1993). It is here that information from the neocortex is processed and transmitted to the limbic system, where memory and emotion are integrated (Reiser, 1994). This is accomplished through extensive two-way connections with various cortical association areas and through the direct and indirect connections with other limbic structures such as the septal nuclei and the hypothalamus (P. Brodal, 1992). This complex structure is known to play a central role in memory, particularly the retrieval of memories for approximately three years following the registration of the experience (P. Brodal, 1992; Reiser, 1994).

The hippocampus is particularly important for the memory of events, objects, words, and other types of information. Observations of patients in whom the hippocampus has been destroyed by disease or trauma indicate that they suffer from global amnesia. They cannot remember anything that happened during the three years preceding the onset of the disorder (retrograde amnesia), although they can remember things that happened prior to it. Moreover, they cannot lay down any new memories at all (anterograde amnesia). Anything that happens to them now cannot, without rehearsal, be remembered for more than a few minutes (Bloom & Lazerson, 1988; P. Brodal, 1992; Reiser, 1994; Walsh, 1987). While the amygdala retains the emotional flavor of memory, the hippocampus retains the dry facts. It appears to process memory in terms of perceptual patterns and contexts (LeDoux, 1992; van der Kolk, 1994). It is the hippocampus that recognizes the different significance of a bear in the zoo versus one in your backyard (Goleman, 1995). It also differentiates the significance of events that happened long ago from those that are recent.

The brain's damper switch for the amygdala appears to lie at the other end of a major circuit to the neocortex, in the left prefrontal lobe, just behind the forehead. Some of this circuitry is also found in the temporal lobe. This dorsolateral prefrontal part of the brain brings a more analytic and appropriate response to our emotional impulses, modulating the amygdala and other limbic areas (Goleman, 1995; LeDoux, 1986).

The prefrontal cortex is the brain region responsible for working memory. Besides the structural bridge between these areas, there is also a biochemical one. Both contain areas that have a high concentration of serotonin receptor sites. The presence of circuits connecting the limbic brain to the prefrontal lobes implies that the signals of emotion—anxiety, anger, and terror—generated in the amygdala can create neural static, sabotaging the ability of the prefrontal lobe to maintain working memory and homeostasis (Selemon, Goldmanrakic, & Tamminga, 1995). Similar observations have been made by van der Kolk (1994). He notes that external and internal stimuli, including stress-induced corticotropin-releasing factor (CRF) production, decrease hippocampal activity. When stress interferes with "hippocampally mediated memory storage and categorization, some mental representation of the experience is probably laid down by means of a system that records affective experience but has no capacity for symbolic processing or placement in space and time" (p. 261).

Recent studies of the amygdala have discovered a role that is pivotal in the understanding of trauma, as well as shedding new light on maturation and development (LeDoux, 1986, 1992, 1994). In the brain's architecture, the amygdala is poised like an alarm. Incomplete or confusing signals from the senses let the amygdala scan experiences for danger. Sensory signals from the eyes, mouth, skin, and ears travel first in the brain to the thalamus, and then across a single synapse to the amygdala. Sensory signals from the nose are routed directly to the amygdala, bypassing even the thalamus. A second signal from the thalamus is routed to the neocortex—the thinking brain. This branching allows the amygdala to respond before the neocortex, which mulls over information through several layers of brain circuits before it fully perceives and initiates a response (LeDoux, 1986). Prior to LeDoux's observations, it was thought that the limbic system had to wait for the neocortex to give permission for the amygdala to react. LeDoux's studies have shown that anatomically the "emotional" amygdala can act independently of the neocortex. He posits that some emotional reactions and memories can be formed with no cognitive conscious participation.

The amygdala can mediate memories and initiate response repertoires that we enact without consciousness, because the shortcut from the thalamus to the amygdala bypasses the neocortex. As the amygdala becomes aroused, either from external stress or internal anxiety, a nerve running from the brain to the adrenal gland triggers a secretion of epinephrine and norepinephrine, which then surge through the body, eliciting alertness. These neurotransmitters activate the receptors on the vagus nerve. While the vagus nerve carries messages from the brain to regulate the heart, it also carries signals back into the brain, triggered by epinephrine and norepinephrine. The amygdala is the main site in the brain where these signals are carried. They activate neurons within the amygdala to signal other brain regions to strengthen the memory of what just happened. This amygdaloid arousal seems to imprint in memory most moments of emotional arousal with an added degree of strength (Goleman, 1995). The more intense the amygdaloid arousal, the stronger the imprint (LeDoux, 1986).

Similarly, van der Kolk (1994) notes that when people are under severe stress, they secrete endogenous stress hormones that affect the strength of memory consolidation. He posits that "massive secretion of neurohormones at the time of the trauma plays a role in the long-term potentiation (and thus the overconsolidation) of traumatic memories" (p. 259). He cites LeDoux's work in noting that this phenomenon is largely mediated by the input of norepinephrine to the amygdala. This excessive stimulation of the amygdala interferes with hippocampal functioning, inhibiting cognitive evaluation of experience and semantic representation. Memories are then stored in sensorimotor modalities, somatic sensations, and visual images (van der Kolk & van der Hart, 1991).

Pathophysiology

Therefore, as a traumatic event ensues, the amygdala sounds the alarm and sends urgent messages to every major part of the brain. It triggers the secretion of the body's fight or flight hormones, and the hypothalamus is signaled to order the pituitary gland to produce CRF. It mobilizes the cerebellum for movement and signals the medulla to activate the cardiovascular system, the muscles, and other systems. Other circuits signal the locus coeruleus for the secretion of norepinephrine to heighten the reactivity of the brain centers, suffusing the brainstem, limbic system, and neocortex. The hippocampus is signaled for the release of dopamine to allow for the riveting of attention (Goleman, 1995; van der Kolk, 1994). In most cases, the traumatic event wanes and the systems return to baseline.

If the trauma continues unabated, a feeling of loss of control and helplessness begins. The brain permanently maintains the action systems of fight or flight and enters the state that we know as posttraumatic stress disorder (Goleman, 1995; Kolb, 1987). The locus coeruleus becomes hyperactive, secreting extra-large doses of norepinephrine in situations that hold no danger but are somehow reminiscent of the trauma. The hypothalamus becomes hyperactive, continuing to signal the pituitary gland to secrete CRF, alerting the body to an emergency that isn't there. The aroused amygdala signals opioid centers in the cortex to release endorphins. This triggers numbing and anhedonia (van der Kolk, 1994). In effect, the neocortex is taken out of the loop. The left prefrontal cortex is unable to shut the emergency systems down.

Since norepinephrine levels are extremely high, the functioning of the systems that mediate rapid-eye movement dream sleep decreases or fails. REM sleep is disturbed or fully inhibited. The information that should be processed for a more adaptive tomorrow is misprocessed. As this continues for days, REM deprivation ensues. The emotional and cognitive interpretations of the event are distorted. The response and alarm are locked in the amygdala, and the neocortex is unavailable to mediate.

From an evolutionary perspective, this is adaptive and allows animals to react quickly and protect themselves. Overreacting is obviously more adaptive for survival than underreacting (LeDoux, 1994). For humans, this method of allowing highly charged, emotionally imprinted memories to control our present-day functioning and relations is maladaptive.

Research

Llinas (1998, 2001), Llinas and Ribari (1993), and Llinas, Ribari, Contreras, and Pedroarena (1998) describe thalamic oscillations and thalamo-cortical-temporal binding. They theorize from their research that the thalamus mediates the synchronous neuronal oscillation of all functional areas of the brain, thereby constituting the platform on which felt perceptual, somatosensory, cognitive, and memorial integration take place.

With regard to the neuroimaging of PTSD, the most replicated findings include decreased activation (with respect to nontraumatized controls) of the anterior cingulate cortex (Brodmann's Areas 24 and 32) and the dorsolateral prefrontal cortex (BA 9 and 10; Bremner, Staib, & Kaloupek, 1999; Lanius, Williamson, & Densmore, 2001; Lanius, Williamson, & Hopper, 2003; Shin, McNally, & Kosslyn, 1999; Shin, Whalen, & Pitman, 2001). As was noted above, these structures are known to serve several key emotion-processing functions. The anterior cingulate is involved in the executive (effortful, intentional) control of attention in terms of regulating emotional, cognitive, and autonomic responses (Botvinick, Braver, & Barch, 2001; Frewen & Lanius, 2006; Phan, Fitzgerald, & Pradeep, 2005). In patients who suffer from PTSD, the relative inactivity of the anterior cingulate cortex is therefore in accord with clinical observations that these patients are unable to modulate their autonomic and affective response (Frewen & Lanius, 2006). Concomitantly, these responses must be partly mediated by an overactive amygdala, which has been noted in neuroimaging studies (Liberzon, Taylor, & Amdur, 1999; Rauch et al., 1996; Shin et al., 1999; Shin, Wright, & Cannistraro, 2005). Lowered activation of the left dorsolateral prefrontal cortex, in cases of PTSD, is consistent with the hyperarousal response that is noted. Studies have found a reverse correlation between the dorsolateral prefrontal cortex and amygdala activation (Frewen & Lanius, 2006; Gilboa, Shalev, & Laor, 2004; Shin et al., 2005).

Regarding neuroendocrine studies, Yehuda (2006) notes that the initial observation of low cortisol in a disorder precipitated by extreme stress directly contradicted the popular speculation that PTSD, like other disorders of stress, was thought to be driven by hypercortisolism. She observes further that the majority of reports published since the initial observation (reviewed in Yehuda, 2002) of low urinary cortisol excretion in people with PTSD support the idea that cortisol alterations in PTSD are different from those observed in acute and many types of chronic stress, as well as those associated with major depressive disorder. This essentially gives PTSD a neuroendocrine marker that differentiates it to date from all other stress disorders. The implications of such a neuroendocrine profile have yet to be fully understood.

Imaging studies with respect to hippocampal volume in PTSD have been inconclusive (Teicher, Tomoda, & Andersen, 2006). Most studies indicated reduced volume (Bremner, Vythilingam, & Vermetten, 2003; Gilbertson, Shenton, & Cizewski, 2002; Gurvits, Shenton, & Hokama, 1996). On the other hand, De Bellis et al. (1999) conducted detailed volumetric analysis of the hippocampus in forty-four maltreated children with PTSD and sixty-one healthy controls. They failed to observe a significant difference in hippocampal volume. Carrion et al. (2001) also failed to find a significant reduction in volume. So this issue remains muddled.

With respect to hemispheric laterality, Schiffer, Teicher, and Papanicolaou (1995), utilizing electroencephalography (EEG) with a focus on auditory evoked potentials, studied patterns of hemispheric lateralization in control versus traumatized (abused) groups. The finding in the traumatized group showed right hemispheric evoked-potential suppression, causing a marked laterality in favor of the right hemisphere and a concomitant diminished left hemispheric functioning during recall of distressing memories. Interestingly, during the neutral memory task, evoked potentials were strongly suppressed over the left cortex, indicative of enhanced left cortical activity. The controls showed no significant laterality during the recall of distressing memories. The authors suggest that the two hemispheres function more autonomously (less synchronized) in patients with childhood abuse.

Teicher et al. (1997) used EEG coherence to study lateralization in fifteen hospitalized children with histories of intense physical or sexual abuse. These were compared to fifteen nonabused volunteers of equal age. EEG coherence was used to ascertain the degree of connectivity between different brain regions. Abused children differed significantly from the controls. They evidenced higher levels of left hemisphere coherence and a reversed asymmetry, with left hemisphere coherence significantly exceeding right hemisphere coherence. Detailed analyses suggested that the increased left coherence stemmed from a deficit in left cortical functioning.

In addition to replicating findings with respect to the anterior cingulate and the dorsolateral prefrontal cortices, Lanius et al. (2001, 2003) identified reduced thalamic activation in patients who suffer from PTSD, replicating similar findings by Bremner et al. (1999) and Liberzon et al. (1999). The consequences of this thalamic impairment are failures of the following:

1. Somatosensory integration, manifested by fragmentation with respect to olfactory memories, auditory memories, oral (taste) memories, visual flashbacks, and disturbing kinesthetic (bodily) sensations
2. Cognitive integration, manifested by distorted self-blame and shame
3. Memory fragmentation, manifested by overconsolidated episodic memory coupled with impaired semantic memory

Discussion

Therefore, rather than processing traumatic memories in a nonaroused and integrated manner, primary dissociative responses in PTSD involve the emotional and phenomenological reliving of traumatic memories as if they are occurring at the moment of recall. The primary structural dissociation of PTSD produces a dissociated self-state or EP that is, essentially, mediated by the inborn and evolutionarily derived defensive action systems of Fear or Rage. As complex action systems, they encompass various subsystems, such as flight, freeze, and fight. The adult self or ANP appears to be more engaged in everyday life. Its function in the structural dissociation of PTSD is detachment from trauma, and it utilizes the action systems of Seeking and Panic, which control functions in daily life (such as exploration of the environment and energy control), and the ones that are dedicated to survival of the species (reproduction, attachment to and care for offspring); (Nijenhuis et al., 2004; van der Hart et al., 2006). The adult self or ANP was considered by Myers (1940) and van der Hart et al. as "apparently normal" due to the fact that in order to detach from the trauma and continue functioning, it utilizes degrees of amnesia for the trauma, as well as intermittent anesthesia of various sensory modalities (Nijenhuis et al., 2004). Therefore, the primary structural dissociation of PTSD produces a dissociated traumatized self or EP characterized by animal defense-like reactions, wherein EPs are fixated on threat cues. Simultaneously, the adult self or ANP is characterized by avoidance of these threat cues. According to van der

Hart, Nijenhuis, and Steele in their various writings, PTSD is viewed as a manifestation of dissociation because EPs and ANPs have different psychobiological stress responses (which do not integrate) to unconditional and conditional threat-related stimuli, even if these stimuli are experienced precognitively.

THE NEUROBIOLOGY OF SECONDARY DISSOCIATION

In contrast to primary dissociation, which emphasizes sensations of reliving traumatic memories, van der Kolk et al. (1996) define secondary dissociation as the mental "leaving" of the body and observing the trauma from a distance. They stress that this manner of psychological distancing of one's conscious awareness limits pain and suffering and "puts people out of touch with the feelings and emotions related to the trauma.... It anesthetizes them" (p. 308). Frewen and Lanius (2006) note that these symptoms are not diagnostic indicators of PTSD, but rather of depersonalization disorders.

As was noted in the previous section on primary dissociation, an essential principle of the developmental psychopathology perspective is that atypical development can only be understood in the context of typical development, and so the following focus is on underlying mechanisms common to both.

Developmental Physiological Mechanisms

Schore (1994, 2001a, 2001b, 2003) posits that the inceptive stages of development represent a maturational period of specifically the early-maturing right brain, which is dominant in the first three years of human life. The right brain is centrally involved in not only processing social-emotional information, promoting attachment functions, and regulating bodily and affective states, but also in the organization of vital functions supporting survival and enabling the organism to cope dynamically with stress (Wittling & Schweiger, 1993). The maturation of these adaptive right-brain regulatory capacities is experience dependent and is embedded in the attachment connection between the infant and primary caregiver. Attachment theory is in essence a regulatory theory (Schore, 2001a, 2001b). More specifically, in attachment transactions the secure mother, at an intuitive, unconscious level, is continuously regulating the baby's labile arousal levels and therefore emotional states. It is these interactive regulatory transactions that cocreate a secure attachment bond that also impacts the development and expansion of the infant's regulatory systems involved in appraising and coping with stress (Schore, 1994, 2001b).

In describing stress, a concept that lies at the interface of the biological and psychological realms, Weinstock (1997) states,

> The survival of living organisms depends upon the maintenance of a harmonious equilibrium or homeostasis in the face of constant challenge by intrinsic or extrinsic forces or stressors. Stress is a term that is widely used to describe both the subjective experience induced by a novel, potentially threatening or distressing situation, and the behavioral or neurochemical reactions to it. These are designed to promote adaptive response to the physical and psychological stimuli and preserve homeostasis.... Successful equilibrium is reflected by a rapid neurochemical response to these stimuli, which is terminated at the appropriate time, or gives way to counter-regulatory measures to prevent an excessive reaction. (p. 1)

There is now concurrence that these crucial functions are mediated by the sympathetic-adreno-medullary (SAM) axis and the hypothalamo-pituitary-adrenocortical (HPA) axis. Furthermore, an emergent body of studies indicates that the threshold for stimulation of the SAM axis is lower than that for stimulation of the HPA axis (Malarkey, Lipkus, & Cacioppo, 1995), and that the neurochemistry of the former is regulated by the major stress hormone, CRF, which regulates catecholamine release in the sympathetic nervous system (Brown et al., 1982), and the neurochemistry of the latter by the glucocorticoid cortisol, the major antistress hormone (Yehuda, 1999). Yehuda points out that the greater the gravity of the stressor, the higher the levels of these neurochemicals, and also that the actions of these two systems are synergistic: "Whereas catecholamines facilitate the availability of energy to the body's vital organs, cortisol's role in stress is to help contain, or shut down, sympathetic activation" (p. 257).

In other words, alternations of the energy-expending sympathetic and energy-conserving parasympathetic components of the autonomic nervous system (ANS) regulate the autonomic, somatic aspects of not only stress responses but emotional states.

Functional Anatomy

The organizing system that integrates the psychological and biological realms of mind and body is the orbitofrontal cortex, in the right hemisphere. This structure exerts executive management over the functioning of the entire right hemisphere. It sits at the apex of the rostral limbic system and mediates the functions of the anterior cingulate gyrus, thalamus, hypothalamus, insula, hippocampus, amygdala, mesencephalon, pons, and medulla oblongata. The orbitofrontal cortex is known to play a crucial role in the processing of interpersonal signals required for the initiation of social interactions between individuals (Schore, 1994). Orbitofrontal neurons, in particular, process visual and auditory information associated with emotionally expressive faces and voices (Romanski et al., 1999; Scalaidhe, Wilson, & Goldman-Rakic, 1997). But this frontolimbic system is also involved in the representation of highly integrated information on the organismic state (Tucker, 1992). The systems that biochemically regulate all brain and bodily state phenomena are located in discrete groups of arousal-regulating bioaminergic neurons of the subcortical reticular formation that innervate wide areas of the brain through diffuse projections (Lydic, 1987). It is now thought that the most basic level of regulatory process is the regulation of arousal (Tucker, Luu, & Pribram, 1995). The orbitofrontal cortex, in the right hemisphere, "is involved in both generation and afferent feedback representation of arousal" (Critchley, Corfield, & Chandler, 2000, p. 267).

The ventral sympathetic frontal area of the orbitofrontal cortex mediates dopaminergic arousal (Iversen, 1977) via its direct reciprocal connections with dopamine neurons in the ventral tegmental area of the anterior reticular formation. It also projects to the ventral striatum and the core of the nucleus accumbens, a basal ganglia structure innervated by dopamine neurons and centrally involved in motivated behavior (Haber, Kuneshio, Mizobuchi, & Lynd-Balta, 1995; Mogenson, Jones, & Yim, 1980), in the nonverbal decoding of positive facial expressions (Morris, Robinson, Raphael, & Hopwood, 1996), and in mechanisms of pleasurable reward and motivation (Robbins & Everitt, 1996). Accordingly, this excitatory limbic circuit, the ventral tegmental limbic fore brain-midbrain circuit (Schore, 1994, 2001a), is involved with the generation of positively valenced states associated with approach behavior, motivational reward, and active coping strategies.

The lateral regions of the orbitofrontal cortex have reciprocal connections with arousal-regulating noradrenergic neurons in the medulla oblongata, solitary nucleus, the vagal complex in the brain stem, caudal reticular formation, and subcortical targets in parasympathetic autonomic areas of the lateral hypothalamus. This comprises the later-maturing limbic circuit, the lateral tegmental limbic forebrain-midbrain circuit that activates the onset of a parasympathetic inhibitory state, regulates negative affect, and is associated with avoidance and passive coping (Schore, 1994, 2001a). Stimulation of orbitofrontal noradrenergic inhibitory circuits results in "behavioral calming" (Arnsten, Steere, & Hunt, 1996).

The functioning of these two limbic circuits in the orbitofrontal cortex "underlies the observation that emotions organize behavior along a basic appetitive-aversive dimension associated with either a behavioral set involving approach and attachment, or a set disposing avoidance, escape, and defense" (Schore, 2001a, p. 37). In concert with this observation, van der Kolk (2006) writes about recent findings with respect to fixed action patterns, noting that "both neurochemistry and emotions are activated in order to bring about action; either to engage in physical movement to protect, engage, or defend or displaying bodily postures denoting fear, anger, or depression that invite others to change their behavior" (p. 281). Therefore, these circuits mediate and organize the action systems noted above.

Pathophysiology

In severe attachment pathologies the developing infant or toddler is repeatedly exposed to the ambient cumulative trauma that emanates from an interactive dysregulating context with a misattuned caregiver. Since this growth-inhibiting environment generates prolonged levels of negative affect in the infant, for self-protective purposes it severely restricts its overt expressions of an attachment need for dyadic regulation. The child thus significantly reduces the output of its emotion-processing, limbic-centered attachment system. And so for defensive functions it shifts from interactive regulatory modes into long-enduring, less complex autoregulatory modes. These subcortical-limbic organizational patterns are primitive strategies for survival, and therefore they become self-organizing attractor states. This sets the stage for primitive autoregulation and for the habitual use of dissociation. Indeed, individuals manifesting Type D attachment (disorganized/disoriented) utilize dissociative behaviors in later life (Schore, 1994, 2001a, 2001b).

As mentioned above, the right orbitofrontal cortex sits at the apex of the rostral limbic system and functions, optimally, as its executor. Therefore, when functioning adequately this structure exerts inhibitory control over intense emotional arousal by "taking over amygdala functions" (Schore, 2001b, p. 227).

A large body of evidence supports the principle that cortical and subcortical networks are generated by a genetically programmed initial overabundant production of synaptic connections, which is then followed by an environmentally driven process of mechanisms to select those connections that are most effectively entrained to environmental information. This parcellation, the activity-dependent fine-tuning of connections and pruning of surplus circuitry, is a central mechanism of the self-organization of the developing brain (Chechik, Meilijson, & Ruppin,

1999; Schore, 1994). This process is energy dependent and can be altered, especially during its critical period of growth. Schore (1994, 2001b, 2003) proposes that excessive pruning of cortical-subcortical limbic-autonomic circuits occurs in early histories of trauma and neglect, and that this severe growth impairment represents the mechanism of the genesis of a developmental structural defect. Therefore, this severe, experientially driven pruning of these internal limbic connections would allow for amygdala-driven states, such as fear-flight states, which would be expressed without cortical inhibition.

In optimal contexts, both the amygdala and the orbitofrontal cortex have direct connections with the lateral hypothalamus, an area known to activate parasympathetic responses through interconnections with the vagus nerve, in the medulla. Porges (1997, 2001) notes that embedded in the mammalian nervous system are neuroanatomical structures related to the expression and experience of social and emotional behavior. Several of these structures are shared with other vertebrates and represent the product of phylogenetic development. Via evolutionary processes, the mammalian nervous system has emerged with specific features that react to challenge in order to maintain visceral homeostasis. These reactions alter physiological state and, in mammals, restrict sensory awareness, motor behaviors, and cognitive potentials. The evolution of the autonomic nervous system provides substrates for the emergence of three adaptive stress and coping subsystems, each coupled to structures that evolved during identifiable phylogenetic stages. Porges calls these systems "polyvagal" to highlight and detail the neurophysiological and neuroanatomical distinction between two branches of the tenth cranial nerve (the vagus) and to propose that each vagal branch is associated with a different adaptive behavioral strategy. The vagus nerve, a primary component of the autonomic nervous system, is located in the brainstem and has branches that regulate the striated muscles of the head and face (facial muscles, eyelids, middle-ear muscles, larynx, pharynx, muscles of mastication) and in several visceral organs, such as the heart and gut. The three branches of the polyvagal system are as follows:

1. The *dorsal vagal complex* (DVC), situated in the dorsal motor nucleus of the medulla, a parasympathetic system that is a vestigial immobilization mechanism. In humans, it mediates the shutdown of metabolic activity and the freeze response.
2. The *ventral vagal complex* (VVC), situated in the nucleus ambiguous of the medulla, a parasympathetic system that enables rapid engagement and disengagement in the environment by applying a more subtle and flexible gentle braking when needed.

3. Both systems respond to the *sympathetic reticular activation system* (RAS), in the brainstem (medulla, pons, and mesencephalon).

Porges's polyvagal theory proposes that during danger or threat the older, less social systems (DVC and RAS) are recruited. The older systems, although functional in the short term, may result in damage to the mammalian nervous system when expressed for prolonged periods. Therefore, the stress and coping neurophysiological strategies that are adaptive for reptiles, such as apnea, bradycardia, and immobilization, may be lethal for mammals.

Relational trauma in this critical period (the first three years of life) promotes excessive sympathetic arousal, which is reflected in excessive levels of the major stress hormone CRF, which in turn regulates catecholamine activity in the sympathetic nervous system (Schore, 1994). In reaction, norepinephrine and epinephrine levels are rapidly elevated, triggering a hypermetabolic state within the brain. In such a kindled state, excessive pruning of neurons is provoked (Schore, 2001b). The RAS is now in full flame. Unable to sustain this hypermetabolic sympathetic state, the child's underdeveloped orbitofrontal cortex reacts by engaging the DVC. This hypometabolic, parasympathetic state of conservation/withdrawal initiates the process of pathological dissociation (Schore, 2003). In this passive state, pain-numbing and blunting endogenous opiates are elevated, instantly triggering pain-reducing analgesia and immobility. Schore (2003) notes,

> In the developing brain, states organize neural systems, resulting in enduring traits. That is, traumatic states, in infancy, trigger psycho-biological alterations that effect state-dependent affect, cognition and behavior. But since they are occurring in the critical period of growth of the emotion-regulating limbic system, they negatively impact the experience-dependent maturation of the structural systems that regulate affect, thereby inducing characterological styles of coping that act as traits for regulating stress. (p. 189)

Recall Hebb's (1949) axiom that "any two cells or systems of cells that are repeatedly active at the same time will tend to become 'associated,' so that activity in one facilitates activity in the other" (p. 70). This has been loosely translated as "neurons that fire together, wire together." The result is a developmentally impaired, inadequate orbitofrontal regulatory system that cannot connect to and engage the VVC, thereby allowing for amygdala-driven states, such as fear/flight/freeze, to be later expressed without cortical inhibition. This intense sympathetic state would then quickly shift into more parasympathetic activation, as the dorsal vagus attempts to shut things down. Schore (2001b) notes that "this is like riding the gas and the brake at the same time" and that this simultaneous activation of the excitation and higher inhibition results in the "freeze response" (p. 231). As these mechanisms become entrenched and stable, dissociation in all its permutations becomes the organizing mechanism of the person's psychic functioning. Action systems, rather than being engaged with subtlety and flexibility, are engaged in the extreme. This is in stark contrast to growth-facilitating environments, where the orbitofrontal system enhances its inputs into the nucleus ambiguus of the medulla, allowing it to engage the VVC and expand its affect-regulatory capacities (Schore, 1994, 2001b, 2003).

Research

Lanius, Williamson, and Boksman (2002), utilizing fMRI, compared brain activation between seven subjects exhibiting secondary dissociative responses and ten nonpsychiatric controls. In contrast to the decreased activation of the anterior cingulate and dorsolateral prefrontal cortex, found in primary dissociation, subjects exhibiting secondary dissociative responses showed increased right anterior cingulate cortex and left dorsolateral prefrontal activation. Frewen and Lanius (2006) propose that this profile may suggest a possible enhanced suppression of limbic emotion circuits in secondary dissociation. In addition, they found that individuals with secondary dissociative symptoms showed increased activation of the superior and middle temporal gyri (BA 38, 39), the right parietal lobes (BA 7), and the left occipital lobe (BA 19). These findings of increased temporal lobe activation in secondary dissociation are consistent with hypothesized parallels between trauma-induced depersonalization and the symptoms provoked by temporal lobe epilepsy (Frewen & Lanius, 2006; Teicher et al., 1997). Lanius, Williamson, and Bluhm (2005) found that although the sensory thalamus remains online during secondary dissociation, in contrast to primary dissociation, its transmissions with the cortex appear to be disturbed.

Discussion

Frewen and Lanius (2006) posit that these results, at a neurobiological level of analysis, support the validity of the categorical distinction between primary and secondary dissociation. They note further that these differences support state/phase models of animal defensive reactions to external threat, such as fight, flight, and freeze. With respect to secondary dissociation, they concur with van der Hart and Nijenhuis (1998), viewing freeze as a hypervigilant and hyperaroused state of readiness. When an attack becomes imminent, freeze is often combined with analgesia. This defensive reaction is believed to potentially reduce the likelihood of continued attack. If the continued attack is not reduced, the analgesia or anesthesia minimize the subjective impact. Therefore, during secondary dissociation, it seems as though, at least temporarily, the mind has given up on the body and the capacity to alter the situation. Secondary dissociation becomes, by default, the solution to helplessness.

THE NEUROBIOLOGY OF TERTIARY DISSOCIATION

Van der Kolk et al. (1996) define tertiary dissociation as the development of "ego states that contain the traumatic experience, consisting of complex identities with distinctive cognitive, affective, and behavioral patterns" (p. 308). They also propose that ego states or identities may represent different emotions (pain, fear, or anger) or different components of one or more traumatic experiences and are therefore central to the diagnostic profile of dissociative identity disorder. Although significant progress has been made in understanding tertiary dissociation psychologically and phenomenologically, little is known about its unique neurobiology.

Pathophysiology

Schore's (1994, 2001b, 2003) work, in the absence of specific data regarding tertiary dissociation, views the underlying neurobiology as driven by increased amounts of trauma and parental dysregulating, thereby driving the mechanisms, noted in secondary dissociation, to further extremes. Therefore, the markedly increased neurochemical and neuroendocrine dysregulating produces profoundly greater disruption of the orbitofrontal regulatory system. At this level of profound underdevelopment and impairment, the orbitofrontal's input connections to the dorsal motor nucleus of the medulla are all that is available to it. The DVC is engaged, bringing forth increased states of freeze, analgesia, or anesthesia. The lack or underdevelopment of connections to the nucleus ambiguus of the medulla precludes the availability of the VVC, thereby allowing for amygdala-driven states, such as fear/flight/freeze, to be continually expressed without cortical inhibition.

This profound sympathetic arousal quickly shifts into a marked parasympathetic activation, as the dorsal vagus attempts to shut things down. It is in this profoundly dysregulated environment that increased fragmentation of self-states proliferates, creating separate alters consisting of complex identities with distinct cognitive, affective, and behavioral patterns. Phenomenologically, this produces severely chaotic and profoundly dissociated and dysregulated alter identities containing the traumatic experience, often with little or no co-consciousness of each other. The specific mechanisms that underlie the formation of ego states or alters are as yet unknown.

Research

In a landmark inaugural study by Reinders, Nijenhuis, and Paans (2003), eleven women diagnosed with DID underwent positron emission tomography (PET) imaging while switching identity states in a controlled and practiced manner. The authors reported that as a result of treatment, the subjects in their sample had developed the capacity to perform self-initiated and self-controlled switches between one of their neutral and one of their traumatic personality states at the time of the scanning. Neural activity was recorded under the following four conditions:

1. Listening to a neutral memory in a neutral personality state (NPS)
2. Listening to a neutral memory in a trauma personality state (TPS)
3. Listening to a trauma memory in the NPS
4. Listening to a trauma memory in the TPS

Brain activation in response to the neutral scripts did not differ between NPS and TPS. In contrast, activation in the left parietal operculum and left insula during the traumatic script was greater in the TPS than the NPS. In comparison, the NPS was associated with greater activation than the TPS in the right medial prefrontal cortex, the rightmost area of the dorsolateral prefrontal cortex (BA 10), the lateral middle frontal gyrus (BA 6), and the bilateral parietal-occipital sulcus (BA 18). Reinders et al. (2003) relate their outcomes to studies of differences between autobiographical and nonautobiographical episodic memory retrieval, which typically show increased dorsolateral prefrontal involvement in the former. Additionally, the authors interpret increased parietal occipital blood flow during the NPS processing of traumatic memories as indicative of a low level of somatosensory awareness and integration in DID in their neutral personality states (Frewen & Lanius, 2006; Reinders et al., 2003). Obviously more studies are needed in order for patterns to become evident. Frewen and Lanius predict that calculating where to look in order to locate diverse dissociative identities will be a daunting undertaking. They posit further that "to the extent that differing identity states are complex, it is unlikely that encoded neural representations of the different states will be found simply in discrete areas of the brain (for example, adjacent columns in a structure). Rather, it is far more likely that identity states will be encoded within distributed representations across shared neuron groups" (p. 124).

DISSOCIATION AND MEDICAL ILLNESSES
OF UNKNOWN ORIGIN

Schore (1994) notes that three streams of research are converging on the centrality of mutual connections between the nervous and immune systems: biological studies of cellular components of systems, developmental studies of the effects of early experience on later immuno-competent capacities, and clinical studies of the effects of psychological factors on the outcome of particular diseases. He states further that "the hypothalamus, which releases its neuropeptides into circulation, and the organs of the immune system that deliver its cellular agents into circulation, share an identical set of signal molecules. Connections between hypothalamic limbic areas and cortical frontal limbic areas of the right hemisphere allow for an integrated circuitry that can modulate and be modulated by peripheral immune activity" (p. 442). Schore concludes that the developmental failure of these systems is responsible for future vulnerabilities to disease.

In the past few years, Scaer (1999, 2001, 2005) has also examined the relationship between chronic dissociative disorders and medical illnesses of unknown origin. Using examples of animal models (action systems) and clinical features of the whiplash syndrome, he has articulated a model of dissociation linked to the phenomenon of the freeze/immobility response. In addition, employing the above-mentioned concepts of psychobiology, he proposes a model of PTSD and dissociation linked to cyclical autonomic dysfunction, triggered and maintained by sympathetically driven neural kindling, alternating with profound parasympathetic dorsal vagal tone and endorphinergic systems. He posits that the autonomic lability and dysregulation inherent in chronic dissociative states may very well be the substrate of autonomic inflammation and autoimmune compromises inherent in a diverse group of chronic diseases of unknown origin, including reflex sympathetic dystrophy (RSD), chronic pain, fibromyalgia, chronic fatigue syndrome, and rheumatoid arthritis. It is beyond the scope of this chapter to detail the pathophysiology inherent in these illnesses. The reader is referred to works of Scaer and Schore for elaboration.

CONCLUSION

A great deal of confusion exists in both our society and our profession regarding trauma, the extent and pervasiveness of familial neglect, and the nature of dissociative processes. For centuries society has recoiled from the notion that trauma and neglect are pervasive. Rather than understanding that our history as a human race is pervasively traumatic, we choose to believe that we have survived and adapted. We apply the same lack of vision to our children, believing that come what may, they are resilient. Within our various professions, academicians at the most prestigious universities tell us that traumatic and dissociative disorders are the creations of therapists and false memory syndromes. We in the traumatology community try to shed light on this darkness, but psychological and phenomenological explanations are insufficient. Many of the finest, cutting-edge, inpatient psychiatric units that specialized in dissociative disorders have been closed. It is only through a neurobiological understanding that our ideas will be given the utmost credibility. We must be able to show clearly that the unusual and often bizarre symptoms that we label dissociative disorders are the outcomes of dysregulated, evolutionarily based, physiological systems that are completely predicated by the nature of the attachment between infants and their caretakers.

REFERENCES

Arnsten, A. F. T., Steere, J. C., & Hunt, R. D. (1996). The contribution of a-noradrenergic mechanisms to prefrontal cortical cognitive function: Potential significance for attention-deficit hyperactivity disorder. *Archives of General Psychiatry, 53,* 448–455.

Bloom, F., & Lazerson, A. (1988). *Brain, mind, and behavior.* New York: Freeman.

Botvinick, M. M., Braver, T. S., & Barch, D. M. (2001). Conflict monitoring and cognitive control. *Psychological Review, 108,* 624–652.

Bremner, J. D., Staib, L., & Kaloupek, D. (1999). Neural correlates of exposure to traumatic pictures and sound in Vietnam combat veterans with and without posttraumatic stress disorder: A positron emission tomography study. *Biological Psychiatry, 45,* 806–816.

Bremner, J. D., Vythilingam, M., & Vermetten, E. (2003). MRI and PET study of deficits in hippocampal structure and function in women with childhood sexual abuse and posttraumatic stress disorder. *American Journal of Psychiatry, 160,* 924–932.

Brodal, A. (1980). *Neurological anatomy in relation to clinical medicine.* New York: Oxford University Press.

Brodal, P. (1992). *The central nervous system: Structure and function.* New York: Oxford University Press.

Brown, M. R., Fisher, L. A., Spiess, J., Rivier, C., Rivier, J., & Vale, W. (1982). Corticotropin-releasing factor: Actions on the sympathetic nervous system and metabolism. *Endocrinology, 111,* 928–931.

Carrion, V. G., Weems, C. F., Eliez, S., Patwardhan, A., Brown, W., Ray, R. D., et al. (2001). Attenuation of frontal asymmetry in pediatric posttraumatic stress disorder. *Biological Psychiatry, 50,* 943–951.

Chechik, G., Meilijson, I., & Ruppin, E. (1999). Neuronal regulation: A mechanism for synaptic pruning during brain maturation. *Neural Computation, 11,* 2061–2080.

Classen, C., Pain, C., Field, N. P., & Woods, P. (2006). Posttraumatic personality disorder: A reformulation of complex posttraumatic stress disorder and borderline personality disorder. In R. A. Chefetz (Ed.), Dissociative disorders: An expanding window into the psychobiology of the mind. *Psychiatric Clinics of North America, 29*(1), 87–112.

Critchley, H. D., Corfield, D. R., & Chandler, M. D. (2000). Cerebral correlates of autonomic cardiovascular arousal: A functional neuroimaging investigation in humans. *Journal of Physiology, 523,* 259–270.

DeBellis, M. D., Baum, A. S., Birmaher, B., Keshavan, M. S., Eccard, C. H., Boring, A. M., et al. (1999). Developmental traumatology, part I: Biological stress systems. *Biological Psychiatry, 45,* 1259–1270.

Devinsky, O., Morrell, M., & Vogt, B. (1995). Contributions of anterior cingulate cortex to behavior. *Brain, 118,* 279–306.

Fanselow, M. S., & Lester, L. S. (1988). A functional behavioristic approach to aversively motivated behavior: Predatory imminence as a determinant of the topography of defensive behavior. In R. C. Bolles & M. D. Beecher (Eds.), *Evolution and learning* (pp. 185–212). Hillsdale, NJ: Erlbaum.

Frewen, P. A., & Lanius, R. A. (2006). Neurobiology of dissociation: Unity and disunity in mind-body-brain. In R. A. Chefetz (Ed.), *Dissociative disorders: An expanding window into the psychobiology of the mind. Psychiatric Clinics of North America, 29*(1), 113–128.

Gilbertson, M. W., Shenton, M. E., & Cizewski, A. (2002). Smaller hippocampal volume predicts pathologic vulnerability to psychological trauma. *Natural Sciences, 5,* 1242–1247.

Gilboa, A., Shalev, A. Y., & Laor, L. (2004). Functional connectivity of the prefrontal cortex and the amygdala in posttraumatic stress disorder. *Biological Psychiatry, 55*(3), 263–272.

Goleman, D. (1995). *Emotional intelligence.* New York: Bantam Books.

Gurvits, T. V., Shenton, M. E., & Hokama, V. (1996). Magnetic resonance imaging study of hippocampal volume in chronic, combat-related posttraumatic stress disorder. *Biological Psychiatry, 40,* 1091–1099.

Haber, S. N., Kuneshio, K., Mizobuchi, M., & Lynd-Balta, E. (1995). The orbital and medial prefrontal circuit through the primate basal ganglia. *Journal of Neuroscience, 15,* 4851–4867.

Hebb, D. O. (1949). *The organization of behavior.* New York: Wiley.

Herman, J. L. (1992). *Trauma and recovery: The aftermath of violence—From domestic abuse to political terror.* New York: Basic Books.

Iverson, S. D. (1977). Brain dopamine systems and behavior. In S. D. Iversen & S. H. Snyder (Eds.), *Drugs, neurotransmitters and behavior: Handbook of psychopharmacology.* New York: Plenum.

Kolb, L. C. (1987). Neurophysiological hypothesis explaining posttraumatic stress disorder. *American Journal of Psychiatry, 144,* 989–995.

Lanius, R. A., Williamson, P. C., & Bluhm, R. L. (2005). Functional connectivity of dissociative responses in posttraumatic stress disorder: A functional magnetic resonance imaging investigation. *Biological Psychiatry, 57,* 873–874.

Lanius, R. A., Williamson, P. C., & Boksman, K. (2002). Brain activation during script-driven imagery-induced dissociative responses in PTSD: A functional MRI investigation. *Biological Psychiatry, 52,* 305–311.

Lanius, R. A., Williamson, P. C., & Densmore, M. (2001). Neural correlates of traumatic memories in posttraumatic stress disorder: A functional MRI investigation. *American Journal of Psychiatry, 158,* 1920–1922.

Lanius, R. A., Williamson, P. C., & Hopper, J. (2003). Recall of emotional states in posttraumatic stress disorder: An fMRI investigation. *Biological Psychiatry, 53,* 204–210.

LeDoux, J. (1986). Sensory systems and emotions. *Integrative Psychiatry, 4,* 237–248.

LeDoux, J. (1992). Emotions and the limbic system concept. *Concepts in Neuroscience, 2,* 169–199.

LeDoux, J. (1994). Emotion, memory and the brain. *Scientific American, 270,* 50–57.

Liberzon, I., Taylor, S. F., & Amdur, R. (1999). Brain activation in PTSD in response to trauma-related stimuli. *Biological Psychiatry, 45,* 817–826.

Llinas, R. R. (1988). The intrinsic electrophysiological properties of mammalian neurons: Insights into central nervous system function. *Science, 242,* 1654–1664.

Llinas, R. R. (2001). *I of the vortex: From neurons to self.* Cambridge, MA: MIT Press.

Llinas, R. R., & Ribari, U. (1993). Coherent 40 Hz oscillation characterizes dream state in humans. *Proceedings of the National Academy of Sciences, USA, 98,* 2078–2081.

Llinas, R. R., Ribari, U., Contreras, D., & Pedroarena, C. (1998). The role basis for consciousness. *Philosophical Transactions of the Royal Society, 353,* 1841–1849.

Lydick, R. (1987). State-dependent aspects of regulatory physiology. *The Federation of American Societies for Experimental Biology Journal, 1,* 6–15.

Malarkey, W. B., Lipkus, I. M., & Cacioppo, J. T. (1995). The dissociation of catecholamine and hypothalamic-pituitary adrenal responses to daily stressors using dexamethasone. *Journal of Clinical Endocrinology and Metabolism, 80,* 2458–2463.

Mogenson, G. J., Jones, D. L., & Yim, C. Y. (1980). From motivation to action: Functional interface between the limbic system and the motor system. *Progress in Neurobiology, 14,* 69–97.

Morris, J. S., Robinson, R. G., Raphael, B., & Hopwood, M. J. (1996). Lesion location and poststroke depression. *Journal of Neuropsychiatry and Clinical Neurosciences, 8,* 399–403.

Myers, C. S. (1940). *Shell shock in France, 1914–1918.* Cambridge, England: Cambridge University Press.

Nijenhuis, E. R. S., van der Hart, O., & Steele, K. (2004). *Trauma-related structural dissociation of the personality: Traumatic origins, phobic maintenance.* Retrieved May 19, 2007, from http://www.trauma-pages.com/a/nijenhuis-2004.php

Orr, S. P., McNally, R. J., & Rosen, G. M. (2004). Psychophysiological reactivity: Implications for conceptualizing PTSD. In G. M. Rosen (Ed.), *Posttraumatic stress disorder: Issues and controversies* (pp. 101–126). New York: Wiley.

Panksepp, J. (1998). *Affective neuroscience: The foundations of human animal emotions.* New York: Oxford University Press.

Phan, K. L., Fitzgerald, D. A., & Pradeep, J. N. (2005). Neural substrates for voluntary suppression of negative affect, a functional magnetic resonance imaging study. *Biological Psychiatry, 57,* 210–219.

Porges, S. W. (1997). Emotion: An evolutionary byproduct of the neural regulation of the autonomic nervous system. *Annals of the New York Academy of Sciences, 807,* 62–77.

Porges, S. W. (2001). The polyvagal theory: Phylogenetic substrates of a social nervous system. *International Journal of Psychophysiology, 42,* 29–52.

Rauch, S., van der Kolk, B., Fisler, R., Alpert, N., Orr, S., Savage, C., et al. (1996). A symptom provocation study of posttraumatic stress disorder using positron emission tomography and script-driven imagery. *Archives of General Psychiatry, 53,* 380–387.

Reinders, A. A., Nijenhuis, E. R. S., & Paans, A. M. (2003). One brain, two selves. *Neuroimage, 20,* 2219–2225.

Reiser, M. (1994). *Memory in mind and brain: What dream imagery reveals.* New Haven, CT: Yale University Press.

Robbins, T. W., & Everitt, B. J. (1996). Neurobehavioral mechanisms of reward and motivation. *Current Opinion in Neurobiology, 6,* 228–236.

Romanski, L. M., Tian, B., Fritz, J., Mishkin, M., Goldman-Rakic, P. S., & Rauschecker, J. P. (1999). Dual streams of auditory afferents target multiple domains in the primate prefrontal cortex. *Nature Neuroscience, 2,* 1131–1136.

Scaer, R. (2001a). The Neurophysiology of dissociation & chronic disease. *Applied Psychophysiology and Biofeedback, 26* (1), 73–91.

Scaer, R. (2001b). *The body bears the burden: Trauma, dissociation and disease.* Binghamton, NY: Haworth Press.

Scaer, R. (2005). *The trauma spectrum: Hidden wounds and human resiliency.* New York: Norton.

Scalaidhe, S. P., Wilson, F. A. W., & Goldman-Rakic, P. S. (1997). Areal segregation of face-processing neurons in prefrontal cortex. *Science, 278,* 1135–1138.

Schiffer, F., Teicher, M., & Papanicolaou, A. (1995). Evoked potential evidence for right brain activity during recall of traumatic memories. *Journal of Neuropsychiatry and Clinical Neurosciences, 7,* 169–175.

Schore, A. N. (1994). *Affect regulation and the origin of the self: The neurobiology of emotional development.* Hillsdale, NJ: Erlbaum.

Schore, A. N. (2001a). The effects of a secure attachment relationship on right brain development, affect regulation and infant mental health. *Infant Mental Health Journal, 22*(1–2), 7–66.

Schore, A. N. (2001b). The effects of early relational trauma on right brain development and infant mental health. *Infant Mental Health Journal, 22*(1–2), 201–269.

Schore, A. N. (2003). *Affect dysregulation and disorders of the self.* New York: Norton.

Selemon, L., Goldmanrakic, P. S., & Tamminga, C. (1995). Prefrontal cortex and working memory. *American Journal of Psychiatry, 152,* 155.

Shin, L. M., McNally, R. J., & Kosslyn, S. M. (1999). Regional cerebral blood flow of script-driven imagery in childhood sexual abuse-related PTSD: A PET investigation. *American Journal of Psychiatry, 156*(4), 575–584.

Shin, L. M., Whalen, P. J., & Pitman, R. K. (2001). An fMRI study on anterior cingulate function in posttraumatic stress disorder. *Biological Psychiatry, 50,* 932–942.

Shin, L. M., Wright, C. I, & Cannistraro, D. A. (2005). A functional magnetic resonance imaging study of amygdala and medial prefrontal cortex responses to overtly presented fearful faces in posttraumatic stress disorder. *Archives of General Psychiatry, 62,* 273–281.

Steele, K., van der Hart, O., & Nijenhuis, E. R. S. (2001). Dependency in the treatment of complex posttraumatic stress disorder and dissociative disorders. *Journal of Trauma and Dissociation, 2*(4), 79–116.

Teicher, M. H., Ito, Y., Glod, C., Anderson, S., Dumont, N., & Ackerman, E. (1997). Preliminary evidence for abnormal cortical development in physically and sexually abused children, using EEG coherence and MRI. *Annals of the New York Academy of Sciences, 821,* 160–175.

Teicher, M. H., Tomoda, A., & Andersen, L. (2006). Neurobiological consequences of early stress and childhood maltreatment: Are results from human and animal studies comparable? *Annals of the New York Academy of Sciences, 1071,* 313–323.

Tucker, D. M. (1992). Developing emotions and cortical networks. In M. R. Gunnar & C. A. Nelson (Eds.), *Minnesota Symposium on Child Psychology: Vol. 24. Developmental behavioral neuroscience* (pp. 75–128). Hillsdale, NJ: Erlbaum.

Tucker, D. M., Luu, P., & Pribram, K. H. (1995). Social and emotional self-regulation. *Annals of the New York Academy of Sciences, 769,* 213–239.

van der Hart, O. (2000). *Psychic trauma: The disintegrating effects of overwhelming experience on mind and body.* Melbourne, Australia: University of Melbourne, Faculty of Medicine, Dentistry, and Health Sciences.

van der Hart, O., & Nijenhuis, E. R. S. (1998). Recovered memories of abuse and dissociative identity disorder. *British Journal of Psychiatry, 173,* 537–538.

van der Hart, O., Nijenhuis, E. R. S., & Steele, J. (2005). Dissociation: An insufficiently recognized major feature of complex posttraumatic stress disorder. *Journal of Traumatic Stress, 18*, 413–424.

van der Hart, O., Nijenhuis, E. R. S., & Steele, K. (2006). *The haunted self: Structural dissociation in the treatment of chronic traumatization.* New York: Norton.

van der Hart, O., Nijenhuis, E. R. S., Steele, K., & Brown, D. (2004). Trauma-related dissociation: Conceptual clarity lost and found. *Australian and New Zealand Journal of Psychiatry, 38*, 906–914.

van der Hart, O., van der Kolk, B. A., & Boon, S. (1998). The treatment of dissociative disorders. In J. D. Bremner & C. R. Marmar (Eds.), *Trauma, memory, and dissociation.* (pp. 253–283) Washington, DC: American Psychiatric Press.

van der Kolk, B. A. (1994). The body keeps the score: Memory and the evolving psychobiology of posttraumatic stress. *Harvard Review of Psychiatry, 1*, 253–265.

van der Kolk, B. A. (2001). The assessment and treatment of complex PTSD. In R. Yehuda (Ed.), *Traumatic stress.* New York: American Psychiatric Press.

van der Kolk, B. A. (2006). Clinical implications of neuroscience research in PTSD. *Annals of the New York Academy of Sciences, 1071*, 277–293.

van der Kolk, B. A., & McFarlane, A. C. (1996). The black hole of trauma. In B. A. van der Kolk, A. C. McFarlane, & L. Weisaeth (Eds.), *Traumatic stress: The effects of overwhelming experience on mind, body, and society* (pp. 3–23). New York: Guilford Press.

van der Kolk, B. A., Perry, C., & Herman, J. L. (1991). Childhood origins of self-destructive behavior. *American Journal of Psychiatry, 148*, 1665–1671.

van der Kolk, B. A., & van der Hart, O. (1991). The intrusive past: The flexibility of memory and the engraving of trauma. *American Imago, 48*, 425–454.

van der Kolk, B. A., van der Hart, O., & Marmar, C. (1996). Dissociation and information processing in posttraumatic stress disorder. In B. A. van der Kolk, A. C. McFarlane, & L. Weisaeth (Eds.), *Traumatic stress: The effects of overwhelming experience on mind, body, and society* (303–327). New York: Guilford Press.

Walsh, K. (1987). *Neuropsychology: A clinical approach* (2nd ed.). New York: Churchill Livingstone.

Weinstock, M. (1997). Does prenatal stress impair coping and regulation of hypothalamic-pituitary-adrenal axis? *Neuroscience and Biobehavioral Reviews, 21*, 1–10.

Winson, J. (1985). *Brain and psyche: The biology of the unconscious.* New York: Doubleday/Anchor Press.

Winson, J. (1993). The biology and function of rapid eye movement sleep. *Current Opinion in Neurobiology, 3*, 243–248.

Wittling, W., & Schweiger, E. (1993). Neuroendocrine brain asymmetry and physical complaints. *Neuropsychologia, 31*, 591–608.

Yehuda, R. (1999). Linking the neuroendocrinology of posttraumatic stress disorder with recent neuroanatomic findings. *Seminars in Clinical Neuropsychiatry, 4*, 256–265.

Yehuda, R. (2002). Current status of cortisol findings in posttraumatic stress disorder. *Psychiatric Clinics of North America, 25*, 341–368.

Yehuda, R. (2006). Advances in understanding neuroendocrine alterations in PTSD and their therapeutic implications. *Annals of the New York Academy of Sciences, 1071*, 137–166.

CHAPTER 3

Combining Hypnosis with EMDR and Ego State Therapy for Ego Strengthening

Maggie Phillips

From the beginning of modern psychotherapy, practitioners and theo-reticians alike have stressed the importance of ego strengthening. Freud (1923/1961) stated that his central goal of treatment was "to strengthen the ego...to widen its field of perception and enlarge its organization" (p. 80). Experts who have followed, though not necessarily Freudian in orientation, have emphasized in varied ways that strengthening and ex-panding the organizing capacity of an individual is a central focus of therapy.

This is particularly important for clients who have withstood signifi-cant traumatic experiences in that trauma and dissociation have such a serious impact on the development of the core self. For traumatized in-dividuals, certain ways of defending against the trauma tend to become exaggerated and overused, while other coping skills either fail to develop or stagnate from lack of use. Experts in the field agree that trauma-related deficits include intellectual and learning difficulties; negative and constrict-ing beliefs; impaired ability to achieve safety, trust, and intimacy; problems recognizing, regulating, and expressing emotion; and limited capacity to connect with positive somatic experience (Frederick & McNeal, 1998).

Nurturing expanded ego strength is paramount in helping to correct these types of trauma-related deficiencies. This goal can be accomplished by helping the trauma client discover and develop valuable functional resources through the curative relationship with the therapist as well as through numerous techniques that help to stimulate more effective responses to internal and external challenges.

This chapter will explore several uses of hypnosis and EMDR that can help to accomplish these objectives. Expert consensus is that trauma clients must move through an ordered process designed to strengthen and stabilize them before progressing to the uncovering, exploration, reworking, and integration of painful past experiences. The SARI model (Phillips & Frederick, 1995) is presented here as a framework for the recommended sequence of treatment. "SARI" is an acronym for the following stages and tasks of therapy:

_S_afety and _S_tabilization
_A_ctivation of inner resources and the origins of current symptoms
_R_esolution of presenting problems and their related inner conflicts
    and the _R_enegotiation of past dissociated trauma experiences
_I_ntegration of therapy experiences and personality functioning and
    development of new _I_dentity

This sequence parallels the basic sequence of recovery from trauma identified by numerous experts in the trauma and dissociation field. Hypnosis is featured in the SARI model throughout all four stages to facilitate the mastery of specific therapy goals.

Although hypnosis is widely recognized as an effective method for treating trauma as well as for helping patients extend and expand their ego strength, many questions surround its use. For example, there are a variety of theories regarding the nature of hypnosis. Generally, these involve either the assumption that hypnosis is an altered state of consciousness with many unique characteristics, or the belief that hypnotic effects result from a specific type of social interaction and the related expectations and roles that arise therein (Lynn & Rhue, 1991). There is agreement, however, that hypnosis refers to an experience of highly focused attention that may result from multiple factors, including the interpersonal relationship between hypnotist and subject, the roles and expectations of this dyad, and the psychological makeup of the person being hypnotized (Banyai, 1991).

Hypnotic phenomena are not easily measured or quantified. To some extent, hypnotic responses can be evaluated by any of the existing instruments that gauge suggestibility, hypnotic susceptibility, or the capacity for imagery. The complexity in using hypnosis, however, lies in the fact that its manifestations tend to be as much subjective as they are objective. In clinical situations, clients who experience hypnosis vary widely in their reactions, with some of them astonished to have discovered such a significantly different state of mind from their usual waking state, while others maintain that nothing out of the ordinary took place.

There is general acceptance that people are led into hypnosis through a process called *hypnotic induction* that involves listening to the therapist's voice giving them suggestions that help them to become more relaxed and comfortable and to focus their attention on more inward experience. Hypnotic phenomena vary greatly from person to person and are greatly dependent on the types of suggestions given. Responses to hypnotic suggestion can include slower heartbeat and respiration; catalepsy, or a sense of inertia; heaviness, or inability to move; an experience of involuntary movement such as levitation or ideomotor finger movement; time distortion, including constricted or expanded time sense; and dissociation of one or more aspects of the sensory experience (Hammond, 1990).

There is also agreement in the literature that indirect, permissive language may be more effective and less problematic than authoritarian suggestion. For example, a client might respond more to the suggestion "You *might* experience a light, comfortable sensation" than to the directive "You *will* experience a light, comfortable sensation."

Because of the complexity of the hypnotic experience and the lack of agreement concerning its mechanisms, it is extremely important that the professional who uses hypnosis be well trained and have received adequate consultation in understanding its effects. Generally, this type of training can be obtained through any of the three national professional hypnosis organizations (the American Society of Clinical Hypnosis, the Milton H. Erickson Foundation, and the Society for Clinical and Experimental Hypnosis) as well as through local professional societies. It is important for the reader to note that adding hypnosis to the practice of EMDR may not only increase its effectiveness but may also add complexity for some clients, such as amplification of transference reactions. For those reasons, the synthesis of hypnosis and EMDR is not recommended for any practitioner who is not well trained in both modalities.

Although some authors have raised questions about the similarity of experience during EMDR and hypnosis, such as the activation of relaxation, others (Hollander & Bender, 2001; Nicosia, 1995; Shapiro, 1995) have pointed out that EMDR is a treatment modality carried out in a state of conscious awareness and is dissimilar to hypnosis. Shapiro and Silk Forrest (1997) have concluded that there are significant differences between the two methods in EEG recordings, suggestibility, and memory processing.

Previous studies have suggested that hypnosis can be used effectively in the EMDR protocol to accomplish a variety of objectives:

- To address defenses and other obstacles that may be blocking the effective use of EMDR (Beere, Simon, & Welch, 2001)
- To explore therapy issues in more depth and to promote mind/body processing (Bjick, 2001)
- To help the client cope with distressing affect (Beere et al., 2001)

- To facilitate negotiation of ego state conflicts and promote co-consciousness between them in order to foster new behaviors (Wade & Wade, 2001)
- To assist in resolving phobias (McNeal, 2001)
- To promote more rapid stabilization, reprocessing of specific fragments of traumatic experience, and more secure structure for abreactions with clients with dissociative disorders (Fine & Berkowitz, 2001)
- To promote ego strengthening for a wide variety of clinical clients (Phillips, 2001b)

One model for the synthesis of hypnosis and EMDR is ECEM (Eye Closure Eye Movements). Although eye movements often occur spontaneously in hypnosis, they are usually ignored. The ECEM method involves the intentional and self-paced creation of eye movements after the patient has been hypnotically induced into a trance state. Hypnotic suggestions are used to emphasize inner safety and stability, the deepening of rest and relaxation, the reintegration of dissociated sensory experience, and the enhancement of revivification (heightening the vividness of recall), positive reframing, and future orientation (Hollander & Bender, 2001). The case example that follows illustrates the use of ECEM to promote ego strengthening and the reduction of anxiety following the trauma of a car accident.

JOYCE: RESOLVING ANXIETY THROUGH HYPNOSIS AND ECEM

Joyce, a fifty-five-year-old librarian for a graduate school program in the San Francisco Bay Area, was referred to me for treatment of anxiety symptoms triggered by a recent car accident. Although she had returned for support to the psychotherapist who had treated her for depression and relationship problems in the past, she continued to struggle with reactions that compromised her work life as well as leisure pursuits. These included panic attacks while driving and during meetings at work, difficulty sleeping, and feelings of hopelessness and despair when alone as well as with close friends.

Joyce contacted me for help in resolving these specific difficulties at the suggestion of a therapist friend who believed I could offer therapy methods such as hypnosis and EMDR that might promote more rapid relief. After a consultation session in which I assessed Joyce's history and current situation, I agreed to provide symptom-focused treatment concurrent with her conventional therapy (see chapter 10).

During our first two meetings, Joyce and I discussed several possible treatment methods that might help her, including hypnosis, EMDR, and a combined hypnotic and EMDR approach. Joyce had experienced both hypnosis and EMDR for a few brief sessions with two different practitioners several years before during the breakup of her ten-year relationship. Although she had found both approaches somewhat helpful, she remained disappointed by her responses to them. That is, she had experienced only a very slow, partial relief of her symptoms without confidence that either approach had contributed significantly to her progress.

Because of her previous disappointment, I believed it was particularly important for Joyce to experience immediate success with whatever treatment methods we used in order to enhance her current negative feelings of esteem and efficacy. I suggested that we might want to combine the two approaches, explaining that these modalities have a synergistic effect when used together (Phillips, 2000).

During the next few sessions, I used hypnotic suggestion to help Joyce identify several positive past experiences of mastery related to her current symptoms that allowed her to feel comfortable in her body and relaxed and calm in her mental focus. As she learned to enter these conflict-free resource states more rapidly and with less and less assistance from me, I suggested that she explore the use of lateral eye movements to help integrate further the benefits she was experiencing.

When she agreed, I first helped Joyce to connect with a past experience of comfortable, enjoyable driving using a simple hypnotic induction (Phillips, 2000). When she appeared to be in a relaxed state without anxiety symptoms or signs of any inner conflict, I directed her to move her closed eyes from right to left and from left to right. She made these relatively short ECEM sets (5–10 eye movements) while focusing simultaneously on the positive sensations in her body, her emotional sense of wholeness and well-being, and related thoughts and beliefs about herself ("I am content and relaxed; I can feel just the way I want to feel"). In only a few minutes, she reported a deeper, more confident sense of these states and a richer elaboration of their qualities.

After Joyce had practiced the ECEM approach and used it in between sessions when she felt distressed or anxious, her symptoms reduced dramatically. After a total of ten sessions, she was sleeping well, no longer reporting panic reactions, and feeling more hopeful and optimistic about work as well as her personal life.

ECEM is one of only several ways of synthesizing hypnotic suggestion and principles that can be used with clients like Joyce who have had incomplete or less than satisfactory therapy experiences as they strive to resolve the aftermath of traumatic events. The approach described above is used during the preparation phase of EMDR to facilitate greater ego strength and to promote a foundational sense of increased integration. This work is conducted prior to exploring the ego state system, its inner conflicts, and its links to posttraumatic and other types of clinical symptoms, and well before reprocessing past traumatic material.

During more than twenty-five years of clinical experience with posttraumatic clients, I have found that initial attention to ego strengthening before focusing on specific trauma events, and on the inner conflicts that have resulted from attempts to cope with and contain them, is time well spent (Phillips, 2000; Phillips & Frederick, 1995). Frequently, this type of preparation shortens the time needed for direct focus on past traumatic experiences with EMDR. In some cases, as with Joyce, I have found that symptoms may be completely resolved in this initial stage of treatment, so that reprocessing is no longer necessary in order to achieve therapy goals (Phillips, 2001b). Although some associations to painful events in her past surfaced during Joyce's ECEM sessions, direct reprocessing of these experiences was not needed to achieve effective relief from her symptoms following her car accident.

Only one session was devoted to work with an ego state that appeared to be linked to inner resources of strength and creativity. This state was highly cooperative and immediately willing to help Joyce recover from the shock and helplessness of the collision that had disrupted her life. Choosing to activate and work with an ego state that is helpful in resolving symptoms, rather than a state that may be involved in maintaining them, is one of the hallmarks of an ego-strengthening approach to the treatment of inner conflicts.

Unlike Joyce, however, other clients may struggle with significantly more complexity in their ego state systems. These clients require different kinds of interventions and frequently longer courses of therapy. Since more severely fragmented clients pose greater challenges to therapists, further attention will be given to this type of clinical situation in the remainder of this chapter.

BENEFITS OF ADDING HYPNOSIS TO EMDR AND EGO STATE THERAPY

Therapy clients who seek help for symptoms related to childhood as well as adult-onset trauma frequently have incomplete or inconsistent responses to therapy because of competing inner conflicts, which can trigger further fragmentation, dissociation, and destabilization. The issue of self-division, which is believed to cause these inner conflicts (Phillips, 2001a; Phillips & Frederick, 1995; Watkins & Watkins, 1997), has been addressed from many different perspectives throughout the psychotherapy tradition.

Pierre Janet (1907) was one of the first to experiment with hypnosis to contact and work with subpersonalities, which he believed contributed to the disturbance of identity found in posttraumatic conditions, then called "hysteria" (Janet, 1887). Others who have contributed to the uses of hypnosis to treat problems that arise when multiple ego states compete to gain more complete autonomy in functioning have included William James (1890/1983), Morton Prince (1906/1969), and Alfred Binet (1890/1977).

Freud, of course, proposed a threefold model of the ego, id, and superego, which vied for conscious control of the personality. For some time, Freud used hypnosis to explore these inner dynamics before renouncing this method due to the complex reactions that were provoked in the therapy relationship. Carl Jung proposed a more complex inner system where subconscious personality clusters, called "complexes," interacted with other aspects of the interior world, including universal archetypes, and with more exterior aspects of personality known as "persona" and "shadow."

More recently, Milton Erickson (Erickson & Kubie, 1939) and Ernest Hilgard (1977), among others, conducted careful experiments involving hypnotic dissociation and personality division that led to further experimental evidence for the divided self and its treatment. John Watkins and Helen Watkins (1979, 1997) built on these efforts, evolving a model of ego state therapy that incorporates hypnosis and hypnoanalysis to activate and treat ego states within the core personality.

These hypnotic approaches to treating posttraumatic fragmentation have been enriched by the advent of EMDR. Several investigators have explored the integration of hypnosis with EMDR (Fine & Berkowitz, 2001; Hollander & Bender, 2001; Phillips, 2000, 2001b). In 2001, an entire issue of the *American Journal of Clinical Hypnosis* was devoted to this topic, and two of the seven published manuscripts focused on combining hypnosis with EMDR to work with ego states related to PTSD and dissociative conditions.

Hollander (Hollander & Bender, 2001) has pointed out that ECEM, her model for synthesizing hypnosis and EMDR, combines the stabilizing qualities of hypnosis with the rapid desensitization and reprocessing capacities of EMDR. ECEM, along with other uses of hypnosis, offers several benefits in its treatment of trauma-related sequelae. First, this approach can elicit psychophysiological calming and promote safe exploration of inner experience. Second, during reprocessing, ECEM can enhance hypnotic methods for revisiting traumatic experience and for promoting corrective, reparative, and restorative experiences. Third, ECEM appears to promote more continuity of self and greater access to resources of the present and future, and may facilitate positive future pacing and orientation (Hollander, 2003).

Previously, I have proposed that hypnosis can potentiate EMDR by permitting a more expanded focus on ego strengthening (Phillips, 2001b). Specifically, hypnosis can be used to accomplish the following:

- Extend the concept of safety
- Incorporate conflict-free target imagery for greater stabilization during the EMDR preparation phase
- Link positive cognitions and beliefs that appear spontaneously while constructing and installing conflict-free imagery with EMDR interweaves
- Utilize various types of hypnotic suggestion and imagery for developmental repair during EMDR resource development and installation (RDI)
- Expand the client's ability to engage in positive future-oriented activity through age progression and other hypnotic techniques

THE IMPORTANCE OF EGO STRENGTHENING

The clinical work with Joyce discussed above further extends these ideas by demonstrating how hypnosis can potentiate EMDR and ego state therapy. From this perspective, the whole personality can be helped through improved self-esteem and ego strength, as well as through resolution of distressing symptoms. In addition, specific ego states within the personality that often contribute to persistent symptoms and block therapeutic progress can benefit from this approach in strategic ways that can then help unlock healing potentials previously blocked by rigid, often unconscious ego state conflicts.

From the time of Freud ego strengthening has been considered important to the process of therapy. From a psychodynamic standpoint, resolution of unconscious early life conflicts expands the ability of the ego to direct an individual beyond survival to mastery.

Cognitive-behaviorists have operationalized ego strength constructs such as self-efficacy, which refers to the belief that one has the ability to complete a task. In studying the impact of self-efficacy on goal attainment, researchers have found that higher efficacy results in higher and more consistent goal attainment (Bandura, 1977).

Principles of systems theory, as applied to families and organizations, and more recently to internal ego state families, have incorporated strengthening approaches to increase access to positive, healthful aspects of the system and extend their influence over immature or less constructive aspects. This is also true of hypnotic ego state therapy, which works with the internal system of self to increase the interaction between more mature, functional aspects of personality and extend their influence over more childlike and dysfunctional states (McNeal & Frederick, 1993; Phillips & Frederick, 1995).

Presenting the Concept of Ego Strengthening to Clients

Most clients who seek psychotherapy are interested in becoming stronger in a number of ways. Those who have experienced significant trauma in childhood or as adults, however, may not fully understand the importance of devoting time in therapy specifically for the purpose of ego strengthening. They are usually quite anxious to "get down to business," which to some of them means getting the painful examination of past trauma over with as quickly as possible. Launching into trauma work without adequate preparation, however, can be quite destabilizing and therefore damaging to the client and to any foundation laid thus far for therapy.

As part of my orientation to treatment during initial sessions, I often talk with clients about my belief in a phase-oriented approach to therapy, the SARI model (Phillips, 2001a, 2001b; Phillips & Frederick, 1995).

The first stage (S) begins with stabilizing, safety, and strengthening as the cornerstones for all subsequent work. This stage may take longer for the complex client, but once mastered, leads naturally into the second stage (A), which emphasizes the activation of traumatic experience and of related inner conflicts, and access to healing inner resources. The third stage (R) is focused on the resolution of symptoms and ego state conflicts, and the renegotiation of past trauma experience. These two stages (A and R) may occur somewhat simultaneously; usually, there is at least some interplay between them. In the fourth and last stage (I), therapy experiences are further integrated so that a new identity is developed.

Sometimes I use the metaphor of preparing for a rigorous journey. I explain to clients that it is as if we are going on an expedition to the Himalayan Mountains. Because there can be dire consequences if we are not fully prepared and equipped for this type of joint venture, it is important to detail the resources we will need to have available, how we will collect and organize these efficiently, and how we will divide the responsibilities that are involved in our undertaking.

During this S or beginning stage of therapy, we will not be exploring the origins of symptoms. Instead, we will discuss how we can utilize these symptoms to lead to a sense of mastery and positive control. For example, I have often worked with women clients who struggle with flashbacks connected with childhood sexual abuse that interfere with current sexual response. I might suggest that a client begin to notice how the onset of flashbacks might allow her to slow down the pace of sexual activity to allow for a more gradual sense of safety, provide an opportunity for deepening communication with her partner, and help her to focus on her own inner needs rather than the needs and wishes of her partner (Phillips, 2001a). Utilization of flashbacks in this way can help clients achieve a sense of mastery and provide for important self-learning.

As discussed above, ego strengthening is provided in some way through almost every type of therapy. Yet, it appears that many "talk" therapies rely on the alliance with the therapist to provide strengthening in a fairly general way (Frederick & McNeal, 1998). Even EMDR had a minimal focus on techniques designed to promote initial strengthening until the fairly recent addition of resource development and installation during the preparation phase (Phillips, 2001b).

Hypnotic Ego Strengthening

Especially in the areas of self-calming and self-management, which are typically intensive needs of the posttraumatic patient at the beginning of therapy, hypnosis may provide many effective options. The use of direct and indirect hypnotic suggestion is part of a rich tradition that has focused on helping clients achieve specific goals such as deeper internal safety, improved ego strength, and more lasting stability through experiences of mastery and ego strengthening.

Hypnosis has long been used to facilitate the therapeutic task of ego strengthening in a variety of ways. John Hartland (1965, 1971) first popularized hypnotic ego strengthening through general, supportive, direct suggestions to increase self-confidence, enhance coping, and reinforce a positive self-image (Hammond, 1990). Spiegel and Linn (1969) have demonstrated that mastery of symptoms accomplished through hypnotic suggestion can create a positive "ripple effect" of widespread clinical improvement and growth. Stanton (1989) added imagery to hypnotic suggestion designed to further enhance ego functioning. Gardner (1976) and Dimond (1981) have also used imagery and hypnosis to strengthen mastery and a sense of internal control.

Indirect hypnotic suggestions were popularized by the work of Milton Erickson (Rossi, 1980). His contributions included metaphor and storytelling, paradox, and naturalistic and conversational suggestions to help individuals access and utilize internal resources. According to his principle of utilization, even attributes and experiences normally deemed dysfunctional or aversive can be viewed as assets to the therapy process. With more challenging clients who present diverse barriers to change, the more Ericksonian, permissive approaches that allow clients to proceed at their own pace can be especially useful. This approach sends the important message that clients' existing competencies are adequate for transformative experiences.

Hypnoanalysts (Brown & Fromm, 1986) have used hypnoprojective techniques such as dreams, the inner screen, and the ideal self to facilitate the discovery and enhancement of inner coping strategies. Other recent advances with hypnosis include the use of hypnotic age progressions to promote positive views of the future (Frederick & Phillips, 1992; Phillips & Frederick, 1992); age regression to past experiences of mastery and renurturing (Murray-Jobsis, 1990; Phillips & Frederick, 1995); the activation of positive internal energies such as "inner strength" and "inner love" (Frederick & McNeal, 1998; McNeal & Frederick, 1993); the use of hypnotic suggestion to increase ego functioning by strengthening specific ego states (Phillips, 1996); and projective and evocative techniques that encourage self-development in terms of internal boundary formation, self-soothing, affect regulation, and strengthening of the core self (Frederick & McNeal, 1998).

INTRODUCING HYPNOSIS TO EMDR CLIENTS

When I meet clients for the first time, we explore the nature and history of their problems and the type of help they are seeking. Many clients who call me have been referred specifically for EMDR or hypnosis; others are seeking general treatment of difficulties related to current or past traumatic events that have not responded to previous therapies. A typical referral to my practice usually involves several failed attempts at prior therapy. These might result from an improper fit between client and therapeutic style or approach, from misdiagnosis or from failure to diagnose PTSD or dissociative problems, or from problems in the therapy relationship that stem from transference and countertransference reactions that have not been worked through sufficiently.

Because there are many myths related to the uses and misuses of hypnosis, whenever I discuss hypnosis as a treatment possibility, I spend time demystifying its nature and clinical applications. I ask questions informally to assess the appropriateness of hypnosis for a particular client and then begin to build rapport and a positive working alliance (Phillips & Frederick, 1995). Generally speaking, individuals who score high on scales of hypnotizability and are highly suggestible respond best to formal hypnosis, while those who are less hypnotizable may work better with indirect, more conversational uses of hypnosis. For this reason, further screening may be conducted using standardized tests such as the Hypnotic Induction Profile (Spiegel, 1972).

With clients who demonstrate dependency issues, performance concerns, and other fears such as loss of control, I am more careful to take adequate time with this initial step. We may decide to defer formal hypnosis if the client's concerns are significant, and reevaluate at a later time when the client feels safer about considering hypnosis. Another option is to use a slower-paced approach. We might experiment first with specific tasks related to formal hypnosis, such as comfortable eye closure, the ability to start, stop, and sustain an internal focus of attention, and the capacity to permit and experience sensations of relaxation in the body in response to verbal suggestions (Phillips, 2001a).

Once a client has achieved positive competency for these and other hypnotic skills, we next determine whether we will use formal hypnosis by itself as a treatment modality, or whether we might combine hypnosis with EMDR or even with a third modality such as a meridian therapy technique drawn from energy psychology (Phillips, 2000). Although these choices depend on the nature of each clinical situation, as a general rule, with more complex clients, I prefer to use one modality at a time so that we can more easily monitor the variables involved in their therapy experience. When there is less complexity in terms of diagnosis, diminished chronicity of symptoms, and less negative previous therapy experience, I feel freer to suggest a more experimental approach.

If the client and I decide on a more experimental route, I explain how the practice of combining approaches can sometimes result in a more powerful therapy outcome. I refer to the mechanism of the AIDS cocktail treatment, which attributes its pharmacological efficacy to the potency of multiple medications, which work exponentially better in combination than as separate compounds. Ultimately, of course, the most effective therapy modality for any client is one that evolves from a trusting therapeutic alliance and through careful evaluation of the client's responses to every step taken in treatment. And no matter what course is chosen, obtaining each client's informed consent is an essential aspect of the initial phase of treatment.

SEQUENTIAL USES OF HYPNOSIS IN THE STANDARD EMDR PROTOCOL: AN EXTENDED CASE STUDY

Jeremy was a thirty-two-year-old rising star engineer in a large computer software company when he was referred to me by the therapist who had been working with him for about five years. Although their therapy relationship was a good one, Jeremy had made little progress with night terrors, insomnia, panic attacks, and organizational problems that had plagued him since childhood. For the first few months, I saw Jeremy concurrently with his regular therapist (see chapter 10) in adjunctive bimonthly sessions. During this time, consisting of approximately six hourly sessions, I conducted an assessment of his therapy needs, formulated a working diagnosis, took a thorough history, and discussed various possibilities for treatment of his symptoms.

Step 1: History Taking, Initial Assessment, and Treatment Planning

Jeremy shared a voluminous amount of information about his family background, the evolution of his symptoms, and the therapy he had undertaken thus far to treat them. During these first six sessions, a detailed picture emerged of his experiences growing up in an alcoholic family where there had been both abuse and neglect.

Jeremy believed that his birth and first two years of life had been fairly normal and uneventful, commenting that his parents had really wanted this first pregnancy and that his father's drinking problem was in its very early stages during that time. He recalls being told that he was a healthy, lively child and that his parents were very happy about beginning their family, though he reported little actual memory of experiences under the age of ten.

By the time their second child, Jeremy's sister, was born three years later, however, this family portrait had changed dramatically. Jeremy's father had changed jobs, shifting from a well-paid administrative position at a corporation to a teaching position in their local community college and subsequently to jobs teaching in high schools, followed by a failed attempt at starting his own business. Although at the time these changes were explained as being due to "political differences" with his supervisors, Jeremy believed that this period marked the beginning of his father's alcoholism, auguring the subsequent shifts from school to school and town to town as his father began having more and more interpersonal conflicts and difficulties managing his responsibilities.

Jeremy recalled dramatic tensions between his parents with several separations and reunions. During these times, his mother would leave and move with the three children (as by then Jeremy's brother had been born) to her parents' house, which was a day's drive away. These moves were disruptive to Jeremy's continuity in school experience as well as in his family relationships. When the family was away from his father, Jeremy shifted into a parental child role, serving as his mother's confidant and closest ally. At times he even slept in the same bed as his mother, and he remembered several experiences of sexualized touching.

Each time his mother reconciled with his father, Jeremy's life was thrown into a painful turmoil. He lost his position as his mother's primary companion; in fact, his mother was impatient with his needs for attention from her. Both his parents demeaned his behavior as "clingy," with his father taunting him for being a "little girl."

As his father's drinking accelerated further during Jeremy's late grade school and junior high years, Jeremy was singled out as a frequent scapegoat. His father berated him verbally and beat him physically with a belt. Jeremy learned not to bring friends home from school because their presence triggered episodes of painful humiliation whenever his father appeared. When he received phone calls or mail, his father often intercepted them and subjected Jeremy to further taunting and abuse. During this time, his mother was emotionally and physically absent, since she was forced to take on two jobs to support her family during the increasingly frequent times when his father was between jobs.

Jeremy told me that he coped with these circumstances by learning to compartmentalize, shifting into a different persona while at school and visiting with his friends away from home. He began to construct a different reality outside his family that everything was "just fine." With no one to protect him or his younger siblings from his father's abuse and his mother's neglect, Jeremy fell into the role of protector for his brother and sister, deriving some satisfaction from keeping them out of harm's way.

As he moved into high school, Jeremy continued to make high grades in school, though he received little encouragement or recognition at home. He also received no guidance about attending college and absorbed his mother's fears that he would somehow become a failure like his father. He believed that "something was wrong with him" because his life was so different from that of his peers, though he also harbored compensatory fantasies that someday he would show everyone his superiority, achieving great fame and success in his work life and an enviable marriage in his personal life. As Jeremy put it, "It's as if one part of me created this elaborate fantasy world to help me get through all the painful times. 'Don't worry,' it would say, 'someday you'll show everybody when you have your beach house, Mercedes, and a beautiful, devoted wife and beautiful children. This problem will pass. You're too good for these people anyway. They just don't appreciate you.'"

Jeremy struggled to complete his degree at a small local college, putting himself through school by working several jobs. After graduation, he moved from job to job trying to "find himself" and living in a dilapidated trailer from paycheck to paycheck. He was fortunate to attract several older adult mentors who helped him to believe in himself, and he returned to night school, specializing in computer science.

Jeremy's personal life during these years was also difficult. He never dated in high school for fear of family reprisals, and he avoided intimacy during college, believing this would only complicate his already troubled existence. Several of his adult mentors were women, however, and they encouraged him to engage with them sexually as well as emotionally.

By the time Jeremy won his first good job in a highly respected computer company at the age of twenty-seven, he realized that he needed help and sought out his current therapist for individual treatment. In working with her, he discovered that he was addicted to alcohol and began the process of recovery through Alcoholics Anonymous and group therapy for adult children of alcoholics. Though he found his therapist helpful and supportive, he was disappointed that somehow he could not achieve a sense of normalcy in his personal relationships.

Like many survivors of childhood trauma, Jeremy also suffered from multiple anxiety symptoms. These included difficulty falling asleep, as Jeremy suffered from intense nightmares that occurred almost nightly and so avoided going to bed. He had panic attacks during meetings at work, and often had to hide in the bathroom to calm his hyperventilation, racing heart, and sweaty palms. Medication helped marginally with these symptoms, but did nothing to help him with his problems concentrating, completing daily tasks such as paying bills, and organizing his work schedule and leisure time activities. He realized that these problems were compromising his ability to advance at work and might also be undermining his confidence about moving forward in his personal life.

Assessment of Ego State Problems and Treatment Planning. As we explored his history and current difficulties, I also began to evaluate Jeremy for the likelihood of divided-self or ego state problems. I do so routinely whenever I am consulting with an individual whose therapy outcome is incomplete despite a strong therapeutic alliance. I also look for the following indicators: amnesia for significant portions of childhood; incidence of childhood trauma and abuse; the presence of symptoms that are ego dystonic; use of the language of parts when describing symptoms or difficulties; references to dissociative defenses such as loss of time and excessive fantasy and compartmentalization; and evidence of intrusive phenomena such as nightmares, flashbacks, and panic attacks (Phillips, 2001b; Phillips & Frederick, 1995).

In Jeremy's case, I noted that he displayed all of these criteria, and I talked with him about the diagnostic possibility that dissociation had fragmented his sense of self and that inner conflicts between different parts of him might be driving and maintaining his symptoms. This hypothesis made sense to Jeremy. I explained further to him that if this assumption were true, his symptoms would not improve significantly unless we treated the underlying condition of ego state conflicts.

We talked together about various treatment options to address internal conflicts. I emphasized that regardless of which methodology we might use, we would begin with a focus on strengthening, stabilizing his symptoms, and helping him to achieve a greater sense of inner safety. In evaluating different possibilities, Jeremy told me that his therapist had already talked with him about hypnosis and he was intrigued with the idea of finding ways to help himself beyond the scope of his conscious mind.

Although there are many approaches that can activate the unconscious, including hypnosis and EMDR, we decided to begin with hypnotic work first. The idea was to introduce hypnosis to Jeremy within an ego-strengthening context, especially since we might want to use this method later on to work with divided-self issues in conjunction with EMDR. This sequence also made sense in terms of my clinical experience, which has demonstrated that complex posttraumatic clients generally have more issues in responding to hypnosis than EMDR, largely because of the issue of control.[1] Therefore, introducing hypnosis early on in treatment as a tool that would help him gain gradual control over his anxieties seemed an important intervention.

Preparation for Hypnosis During the S Stage. In addition to the procedures described above for introducing hypnosis to clients through simple hypnotic tasks, I also evaluate the client's responses to direct and indirect uses of hypnosis that can help achieve the S-stage goals of safety, stability, and stabilization.

During my first hypnotic session with Jeremy, I began with applications of Milton Erickson's indirect utilization approach (Erickson, 1959), which is the acceptance of all symptoms as potential resources in the therapy process without the expectation of changing the symptoms. In this case, I suggested to Jeremy that he gauge the intensity of his anxiety symptoms on any given day as an indicator of his need for self-care. We discussed the concept of self-care as a way that he could learn to give to himself to address some of the ways his needs had been neglected in childhood.

One example of how the utilization approach worked with Jeremy involved a focus on his avoidance of bedtime. When we explored the circumstances surrounding bedtime in childhood, Jeremy revealed that bedtime had been chaotic and inconsistent, a time when tensions between his parents tended to escalate and often resulted in violence. We agreed that he would approach bedtime as he wished his parents had back then, with a gradual slowdown in activity, a focus on calming and quieting through reading and listening to classical music, and journaling to provide positive closure for the day. We applied a similar approach to his other symptoms, and within two weeks Jeremy reported marked improvement. His nightmares and insomnia had lessened and he experienced considerably less panic at work.

During this time, we also instituted the achievement of an inner safe place or sanctuary, a procedure common to both hypnosis and EMDR, and essential to the S stage of treatment. Before Jeremy could begin any focus on past trauma, it was necessary for him to develop islands of internal safety to which he could retreat at any time he felt overwhelmed or flooded by reactions connected with traumatic events.

For clients like Jeremy, the involuntary mechanism of dissociation or withdrawal can be a significant issue (whether or not a formal diagnosis of dissociative disorder has been made). It is therefore particularly important to teach the idea of planned or chosen retreat to instill a further sense of mastery and to help the client practice retrieving this place with and without the use of bilateral stimulation (BLS), hypnotic induction, or other formal technique. Jeremy identified the image of a beautiful house on the beach, with many large windows and skylights, in a serene ocean setting. This image was connected with feelings of relaxation and comfort and a sense of safety and well-being. Later on during ego state work, we would expand his safe place so that each ego state could participate.

Because Jeremy's problems with concentration and organization seemed so far unresponsive to indirect hypnosis methods, I introduced him to more direct uses of hypnosis during our third hypnosis session (fifth introductory session). I taught him how to use ideomotor signals (Cheek & LeCron, 1968), a technique that helps to develop a sense of safe inner control and trust in internal boundaries (Phillips & Frederick, 1995). With this method, finger signals are identified through hypnotic suggestion to convey "yes," "no," and "I'm not ready to tell you."[2] Jeremy learned that when his fingers signaled "yes," it was safe to proceed and that his internal search would produce positive results. When his fingers signaled "no," he learned the importance of honoring this limit and shifting directions to more solid ground inside.

Using the ideomotor signaling process, I instituted positive age regression, asking Jeremy to go back to a time in his experience when he had felt organized, focused, and competent in managing his time. He easily retrieved several appropriate experiences of competent times to serve as resources and explored these while in a comfortable state of relaxation.

Introducing the Synthesis of Hypnosis and EMDR for Further Stabilization. I then introduced Jeremy to EMDR as a way of stimulating both sides of his brain to provide strengthening, desensitization, and reprocessing experiences related to past trauma. We deepened and extended his past experiences of competency using several short sets of ECEM while he was connected to the resource states through hypnotic ideomotor signaling. Finally, I invited Jeremy to practice evoking these experiences at times in between sessions when he felt distressed about being disorganized and unfocused, and to anchor them more securely using ECEM.[3]

Although Jeremy felt good about being able to develop this skill and felt less general anxiety, he made little progress in improving his concentration or his organizational skills. In order to go further, it seemed important to initiate ego state work using hypnosis and EMDR.

Step 2: Preparation for EMDR and Ego State Therapy

Before we could begin exploration of Jeremy's ego state system and the relationship of specific states to his anxiety symptoms, there were several aspects of preparation that needed to be completed. First, we discussed the basic principles and practices of ego state therapy and how they fit within the four-stage SARI model of phase-oriented treatment (Phillips & Frederick, 1995; Watkins & Watkins, 1997).

Reviewing Standard Protocols for Ego State Therapy and EMDR. We also reviewed Jeremy's beliefs and feelings about having inner parts and connected these to his family of origin and the history he had shared in the first phase of our work. Even though Jeremy was comfortable with the idea of having inner parts and with revealing past awareness of their presence, he was worried that working with them directly might cause more problems instead of helping him to come together.

This is a common concern for many clients,[4] and it is important to take sufficient time to identify and address any and all reservations the client may have about beginning this kind of work. I explained to Jeremy that most clients experience greater feelings of wholeness during ego state therapy. I told him that on rare occasions when this did not occur, however, it would be crucial to process together any negative effects or reactions he was experiencing so that we could learn what additions or adjustments we might make in order to keep the experience fully positive for him.

In addition, we discussed the standard protocol for EMDR. I explained to Jeremy that EMDR—similar to hypnosis although working through a different mechanism—was useful in stimulating multilevel change. This would occur by first targeting a distressing event that encompassed a problem or past trauma that he wanted to resolve. Jeremy would be asked to visualize the target and to describe his initial feelings, beliefs, and reactions related to the target. We would also identify the negative cognition, or negative self-belief related to the trauma, and a positive cognition, or what he wanted to be able to believe about himself in relation to the trauma. He would then use the Validity of Cognition (VOC) Scale to rate the positive cognition as to how true it seemed before EMDR and the Subjective Units of Disturbance (SUD) Scale to rate his emotions while viewing the target scene. Finally, I would ask him to notice and describe any body sensations that occurred while completing the previous steps. We also discussed how BLS, ECEM, or some other combination of hypnosis and dual stimulation would be used to help him reprocess the target event and the negative beliefs, feelings, and body sensations associated with it to move the SUD to 0 and to increase his confidence in the positive cognition he wanted to achieve.

Uses of Conflict-Free Imagery. Another important preparation task is to further strengthen the client's entire personality before working with its individual parts. Such an undertaking builds on a foundation of wholeness and may reduce the need for protective dissociation (Phillips, 2000).

One way of accomplishing this is to introduce the conflict-free (CF) image. This type of image represents an area of functioning where the client is free of all symptoms, anxieties, and inner conflicts. Unlike the safe-place image, the conflict-free image tends to be action oriented. It focuses on daily experience that crystallizes ways in which the individual has already achieved integrative functioning and on evidence of a positive self-image that has already been actualized (Phillips, 2001b). It is important that the image be connected with everyday life experience, as this tends to be more strengthening and accessible than a more rare "peak" experience that might occur unexpectedly. It is also more self-reinforcing because there will be more frequent reminders.

I directed Jeremy, "Think of a time in your everyday life when you are just the way you want to be more of the time. You aren't experiencing any of the difficulties you came here to deal with. This is a time when all of you is engaged in a positive manner and you experience only positive feelings about yourself." Jeremy immediately thought of reading historical novels in his favorite chair while his cat lay curled up in his lap. To him, this image captured a time of freedom to focus on his own relaxation and comfort. He felt good about stretching his mind at the same time he was relaxing his body and feeling connected to the reassuring presence of his cat. This image represented a time of balance and inner harmony, when all was well in his outer and inner worlds.

We tested this image (Phillips, 2000) first to make sure that it evoked wholly positive reactions (which it did), and then to determine whether its strength was greater than at times when Jeremy was symptomatic or anxious. I asked him first to evoke the image, exploring positive thoughts, feelings, and sensations connected with it as a resource state. Next, I asked him to think of a time when he felt far away from that experience. He reported a recent incident at work when he felt panicked about his performance. We then explored the distressing thoughts, feelings, and sensations connected with the second problem image.

When I asked him to refocus on the conflict-free image and then to recall the problem issue, Jeremy was surprised to report that the second image seemed further away in his mind. "It just doesn't matter as much," he said. "I can remember what is most important to me instead of dwelling on the negative." A few sets of eye movements helped to further strengthen this response. I suggested that he practice evoking his conflict-free image when he was feeling anxious at work. At the next session, Jeremy reported that he had successfully used his CF image to defuse the onset of a panic attack during a meeting and felt more optimistic about being able to change some of his more intractable difficulties of concentration and focus.

In addition to adding further ego-strengthening possibilities during the preparation phase, conflict-free imagery can also be used for strengthening when first initiating EMDR and ego state therapy, at the beginning of trauma reprocessing, and throughout treatment for stabilization.

Step 3: Initiating Ego State Therapy Using EMDR and Hypnosis

Our next step was to begin to use EMDR and ego state therapy to address Jeremy's symptoms related to concentration and organization. He felt particularly urgent about making progress in this area because his bank accounts were overdrawn and he was behind in paying many of his bills. Unfortunately, this problem had plagued him throughout his adult life. He had also had trouble with organization during college years, and had been tested for attention deficit disorder, though that diagnosis had been ruled out. Although there were other difficulties Jeremy needed to address, including his difficulties with intimacy, we targeted this area as a starting point.

As we began to explore Jeremy's ego state system, and the possibility that the organizational and focusing issues might be related to a conflict there, I asked Jeremy what he already knew about inner parts of himself that might be blocking his ability to concentrate. He replied that he had become aware, due to our recent conversations about ego states, that when he sat down to arrange his calendar at work, he could hear a negative voice inside that said, "You're not going to remember everything you need to write down. This is going to be a mess!"

Jeremy speculated that the voice had probably come out of numerous experiences when he had forgotten to put meetings on his calendar. Because of his personable manner, he had been able to compensate so that no significant damage had occurred, but he was always left feeling vulnerable and upset after these episodes. He also told me that he had felt on many occasions that there was a force inside that kept him from sitting down at home to look at his finances. "It's as if some part of me is saying, 'I don't want to look. Please don't make me.' It sounds silly, I know, but that part of me seems really frightened."

Since Jeremy had clear access to these two parts, we decided to use EMDR to target these two states and the situations Jeremy was already aware of that were connected with his symptoms. Before beginning to work with these two states, however, I suggested that we begin by finding a part inside that had mastered concentration and organization.[5]

Beginning with a Positive Ego State. To find this ego state, I asked Jeremy to recall a time that best represented successful concentration and organization. We constructed a conflict-free image based on this experience that involved completion of a work project, and made sure that the feelings, thoughts, and body sensations evoked were both wholly positive and stronger in intensity than his reactions to times when he had difficulty with these tasks. Because this experience came to mind easily for Jeremy, a hypnotic induction was not necessary, but could have been useful if that had not been the case.

Next, we used a few brief sets of eye movements to deepen and strengthen the CF image. When Jeremy seemed fully connected to this experience with all of his senses, I suggested, "During the following set of eye movements, I'd like to ask the part of you inside who helped you to complete the project at work and who is very good at concentration and at organizing details to come forward so that we can get to know him in some way."

Following the eye movements, Jeremy reported that he saw an image of a young boy with horn-rimmed glasses who looked a bit like Harry Potter. "He told me he liked to put things together and that he was good at it," Jeremy added. "Now that I think of it, I always liked to work puzzles when I was a kid. I'll bet this part of me was around then."

During several more sets of eye movements, further information emerged about this part of him who wanted to be called the "Scheduler." We learned that this ego state often felt frustrated by another part inside who was scared to look at things. "He told me that this scared part comes in and breaks his concentration so that he can't get it back again," Jeremy explained.

Working with Ego States Connected to the Symptom. Since we encountered information about an ego state who seemed to be connected to the targeted problem we were working on, we discussed how to begin to work with both of these parts, who were obviously in conflict. I reminded Jeremy about the *A* stage of the SARI model, and how we would work with both resource and problem states to shift the inner conflict, which would, in turn, shift the symptom. We decided to work with one state at a time during subsequent sets of eye movements, and then find a way to bring them together.

During several sets, we made contact with a young part who appeared to be about eleven years old. Jeremy described him as being rather scruffy in appearance and sensed that his role was to watch other people to make sure he did things right. As we communicated further with the "young part," the ego state told Jeremy, "I don't want to look at things. I just want to get through them as fast as I can. If I look, it slows me down and then someone might see that I've done something wrong. Then they'll try to help me and it won't be mine anymore. They will take my ideas away." When asked how things had come to be this way for him, the young part seemed to close down and gave no more new information in subsequent sets. In fact, Jeremy reported that he disappeared altogether.

Using Hypnosis to Provide Corrective Experiences. At this point, it appeared that we had encountered a less mature part who needed intensive attention so that we could begin to shift some of his beliefs and open him to new learning. In order to do so, we needed to begin by helping this ego state to experience greater safety in the therapy situation.

Although there are many ways of accomplishing these tasks, because Jeremy had found that our earlier hypnotic work seemed to help him feel relaxed and safe, I suggested that we use hypnosis to find a safe place for this young part and then continue to work with him through ECEM.

We instituted ideomotor finger signals following a brief induction for relaxation and deepening of awareness, and this time the young part responded to the request that he come forward inside. He verified that he had retreated because he believed we were critical of him and wanted to change him in some way. Since he no longer felt safe with us, he was willing to find a safe place inside that belonged only to him.

When invited to find this safe place, he indicated he had found a room that was the kind of room he had always wanted to have. There was a strong lock on the door and skylights that let in a lot of sunlight. The room was hidden on the back of the beach house that Jeremy had selected in an earlier session. The young part became calmer and more relaxed as he explored the room. I invited him to test its security by finding out whether we or anyone else could enter his room. He appeared satisfied: "No, you can't follow me here. I have to let you in or give you the combination to the lock and I'm not going to do that!" After supporting his discoveries, we used several sets of ECEM to deepen and strengthen his connection with his safe place. He then agreed to talk with us further during the next session.

We discovered in our next hypnotic encounter that the young part had learned to fear sitting still to "look at things" because, beginning in about fifth grade, whenever he started to do homework, his mother was working nights and his father was drunk and "on the prowl." Often, his father would burst into his room, snatch his homework away and ridicule him for "not doing it right," and then begin to rage at him for other shortcomings, ultimately hitting him or threatening violence. This young part also told us that he did not trust the other parts inside any more than he trusted his father because they criticized him and tried to force him to do things their way. "I don't always know what to do," he said poignantly. "So all I can do is hunker down and just get through it as fast as I can."

Jeremy and I agreed that we needed to provide help for this ego state, and that it needed to be offered in a way that he could accept. We again "called him out" using ideomotor signals, and I explained the process of EMDR and ego state therapy to him.[6] Though he had doubts as to whether this approach could help him, he agreed to cooperate.

Step 4: Reprocessing Past Trauma with Individual Ego States

When using ego state therapy, one of the therapeutic issues is deciding when to work with the whole personality, when to work with strategic groups of ego states, and when to focus work on one particular ego state. In this instance, it appeared that the "young part" held the key to shifting Jeremy's disorganization and inconsistent concentration. Because he was distrustful of all of the other inner parts, it seemed important to work with him alone.

We began this phase of our work by targeting the young part's experiences of Dad's intrusion and violence when he was attempting to do his homework. At this point, the ego state was accessible without the use of hypnosis. Jeremy could both visualize this part and have access to his inner thoughts. Because this ego state was fearful about working with this memory, I suggested we do some strengthening first.

I asked the young part to go to his safe room at the beach house, and we strengthened his connection with several sets of BLS. I asked him if there was anything further he needed in order to feel strong enough and safe enough to do the work involving his father. The young part hesitated and said, "I do need something because I feel scared but I don't know what it is." I suggested that the young part hold the thought "I need something more to feel safe and strong" during several sets of BLS. What emerged was that he wanted someone to be with him so he wouldn't be alone, and that his maternal grandfather, to whom he had always felt close, could be there.

While Jeremy held a focus on the young part and grandfather, we reviewed the target memory of his father grabbing his homework, yelling at him, and hitting him because he was not doing it right. The negative cognitions were "I'm stupid" and "I'm unable to look at this because I'll be wrong and in danger." The young part's belief in the positive cognitions "I'm competent" and "I'm able to look at anything and be OK" were a 4 out of 7 and a 2 out of 7 respectively on the VOC Scale. His overall distress was an 8 out of 10 on the SUD Scale. He reported that his body felt tense all over and very tight in his chest. I reminded the young part that at any time he felt overwhelmed as we focused on the past memory, he could go to his safe room with or without his grandfather. To reassure him further, we practiced first; he shifted from the scene with his father back to the safe room easily and successfully.

I also discussed the modalities for BLS with the young part as I had done earlier with Jeremy during step 3. Though Jeremy had chosen to track my fingers with his eyes, the young part wanted to listen to ocean sounds with the headphones and to hold the tactile device in each hand. We began with a focus on the scene with his father, the "I'm stupid" and "I can't look at this because I'll be wrong and in danger" cognitions, the image of his grandfather holding his hand, and the tension in his body. Very soon in the unfolding sets, the young part reported, "My grandfather is telling me that he knows I'm very smart. I know I can do my homework. It's just that I'm anxious when my dad interrupts me and then I can't focus."

With support and feedback from his grandfather, the young part was able to confront Dad and tell him to leave the room so he could do his work properly. When Dad angrily threatened to hit him for talking back, the young part replied, "You've been drinking, Dad. Please don't talk to me that way." Jeremy reported that Dad looked chastened and left the room. When we checked on progress, the distress had dropped to 2 on the SUD Scale, and Jeremy reported a little worry about future times that Dad might interrupt him. We targeted that worry for several more sets, but no more new information appeared.

I then introduced an interweave, asking the young part, "What would Grandfather want you to do if this were to happen again?" His immediate response was, "I'm going to sit down with Mom and Grandfather and tell them I don't want to be left alone in the house with Dad at night. I can go to my best friend's house or to my neighbor's. There are other places I can be if I can't be safe at home." We continued with several sets of BLS, after which the distress level fell to 0. Jeremy reported a 7 on the VOC Scale for both the "I am competent," and the "I can look at this and be OK" cognitions. I asked him to help the young part hold the target image in mind along with the positive cognitions for a few sets to strengthen this link. A subsequent body scan indicated that the tension was gone, and Jeremy reported a deep feeling of relaxation and calm spreading throughout his body.

As a final step, I decided to institute a positive future template that involved the Scheduler. I asked the young part if he knew this part inside and if he felt he was anything like his father. "He's just like my father, always wanting me to do something his way." I commented that I thought it was important for the young part to hear what the Scheduler thought about the scene we had just worked with. Reluctantly, the young part was willing to meet with him during the next set of eye movements.

During that set, the young part was surprised to discover that the Scheduler was glad that he had stood up to Dad and that he wanted to help the young part do his best work by helping him sit down and focus without any anxiety from the past. During several more sets, we strengthened the young part's trust in the Scheduler ego state by asking him to imagine what it would be like in the future if he was asked to sit at his desk and organize his calendar. During several short sets of BLS, the young part reported that he felt relaxed and safe because he now believed that the Scheduler really wanted to help him and that together they could do whatever was needed. Jeremy's final future image was one of sitting at his desk at work, looking at his neatly annotated calendar, and feeling confident and proud of his progress.

Step 5: Integration and Closure

During the next session, Jeremy reported that he had felt much more confident at work, that his focus seemed sharper, and that he had been able to retain more specific details related to work tasks and scheduling. He also noticed that although he experienced a slight hesitation when he scheduled meetings or appointments on his calendar, he was able to move through this easily into a place of feeling centered and at ease. He was excited about the possibilities that our work presented and eager to work on straightening out his finances.

Jeremy told me he felt very good about the changes he had made and wanted to continue working with me. We had met for a total of twenty sessions spread over seven months; the last fourteen sessions after the initial assessment phase had been extended to seventy-five minutes each. Jeremy had made significant improvements in his sleep cycle, and many of his anxiety and panic symptoms had dissipated. He also believed he had been able to make a shift in his problems with organization, reporting that the reprocessing work with the young ego state had resulted in his spending more time focusing effectively at work, specifically in the management of his schedule.

As we evaluated our work and discussed his remaining needs, Jeremy told me that he wanted to work with me as his primary therapist. He had already discussed this with his other therapist, and we agreed that all of us would discuss this possibility further. Jeremy's therapist told me she was quite supportive of this plan and felt that they had reached the end of what they could accomplish together. After a month spent in a positive termination process with her, Jeremy and I instituted weekly sessions of EMDR and ego state therapy. Several years later, we have worked with about ten key ego states in a similar manner to that described above. Jeremy's management of his finances is much improved, though he still has difficulty when his stress level is high. He has corrected many of his organizational habits at work, and the rapid rise of his career path has presented frequent challenges that have triggered setbacks as well as further opportunities for reprocessing past traumatic events.

CONCLUSION

Although this case review involves only one segment of EMDR and ego state therapy rather than a complete course of treatment, several conclusions can be drawn from the results, particularly in regard to clients with complex posttraumatic stress disorder.

First and foremost, the importance of ego strengthening in every stage of work cannot be overstated. In the work with Joyce presented at the beginning of this chapter, the initial focus on identifying and deepening past experiences of mastery strengthened her sense of confidence in being able to master the aftermath of a recent car accident. Hypnotic suggestion was used to help her access these resources, and ECEM, a combination of EMDR and hypnosis, helped her to deepen the positive intensity of her resources. It is also evident that strong emphasis on strengthening experiences at the beginning of treatment may have allowed Joyce to resolve her symptoms without a need for reprocessing past trauma.

In Jeremy's case, a more indirect strengthening approach was used first that involved the utilization of his symptoms. This allowed him to experience a positive shift in becoming more consciously aware of his difficulties, and using them as self-learning devices, without requiring him to make a definite change. This method was followed by more direct strengthening techniques of creating an inner safe place and constructing conflict-free images.

Conflict-free images are a particularly useful tool in EMDR and ego state work because they serve as containers for integrative moments that already exist for the client. Because they may be used with the whole personality or with individual ego states, as they were with Jeremy, they can evoke responses that help to contribute to a sense of self-cohesion and a more integrated self. For Jeremy, these experiences were further enhanced through the use of BLS as a positive introduction to EMDR. The S stage of the SARI model is presented within these two case examples as a model for introducing and implementing direct and indirect ego-strengthening experiences within a flexible protocol.

Second, when working with a posttraumatic client who is not fully responding to therapy, it is important to evaluate for the likelihood of self-division or ego state problems. This can be done through conversational approaches, as illustrated with Jeremy, or through more formal assessment instruments. If there is some evidence that inner conflict can be contributing to the client's more refractory symptoms, it is also important to assess the degree of dissociation that may be involved. This type of assessment can be used to determine the methods that will be most useful for conducting ego state work.

In working with Joyce, where there was little evidence of self-division, finding a helper ego state appeared to further strengthen her and may have sped up the process of resolving her symptoms. Joyce was therefore able to work her way through the four stages of the SARI model to resolve the traumatic stress symptoms related to a recent traumatic event in only ten sessions. And when working with more complex issues of self-division, which Jeremy displayed, the practice of beginning ego state therapy with an ego state that can contribute assistance and insight into the client's problems is a highly efficient and effective approach.

The two cases presented also illustrate the positive contribution of hypnotic suggestion to EMDR therapy. Such a combined approach appears to have facilitated a sense of containment, deepening and strengthening both clients' experiential connections with positive imagery. The use of ideomotor signals also helped Jeremy to learn about and trust the boundaries of his less conscious experience. They also helped us to move through an apparent impasse with a pivotal ego state and to facilitate improved communication and feelings of safety for him. Finally, hypnosis helped to provide important renurturing experiences, connecting the young part with the ego strength of his supportive grandfather.

Although hypnotic suggestion can help to create numerous possibilities in EMDR and ego state therapy, there are some caveats. Therapists who want to use this approach must be fully trained in EMDR, as well as in hypnosis and in ego state therapy. Introducing hypnosis may also require careful attention to the exploration of a client's mythology and fears related to this approach, due to the misconceptions about hypnosis that continue to linger in the popular press.

Finally, it is important to acknowledge the legacy of Milton Erickson and his indirect approaches to hypnotic suggestion. Erickson's emphasis on mutual cooperation is a helpful paradigm for clarifying the roles of client and therapist as well as the boundaries between ego states as subpersonalities. When the principles of cooperation, utilization, and future orientation are applied effectively within the EMDR protocol as a way of working with an inner family that has been shattered by past trauma, the possibilities of achieving wholeness and integration can be greatly multiplied.

In this age of increasing violence, abuses of power, and boundary confusion, imagine for a moment what our world might be like if we could use the powerful methods described in this book to treat the pervasive condition of "negative otherness" or alienation (Gilligan, 2002). Welcome to a world of hope made possible by applying the lessons of EMDR and ego state therapy. Hypnosis may simply help us open this promising portal a little bit wider.

NOTES

1. The common myth persists that hypnosis induces a state in which the client is defenseless and surrenders conscious control. This perception may stem from media portrayals of the hypnotist as a Svengalian operator who will force clients to do and say things against their will. Clients also fear that they cannot be hypnotized, a related notion that arises from the belief that they must surrender their control and will to the hypnotist. Since posttraumatic clients are very fearful of being overwhelmed against their will, as they were historically during experiences of trauma and abuse, this notion of hypnotic surrender is understandably terrifying for them.
2. Details of this method can be found in Phillips and Frederick, 1995 (pp. 50–51), and in Phillips, 2000.
3. Similar results can be obtained using BLS with past resources identified during RDI without using hypnosis.
4. Others include fears of becoming schizophrenic, a multiple personality (dissociative identity disorder), or otherwise "going crazy"; decompensating or losing further control over their functioning; and various nameless fears that may be related to what Freud termed "death anxiety" or "free-floating anxieties."
5. This is similar to the work I did with Joyce, described at the beginning of this chapter. Here, I start our ego state work with a positive state that will be further strengthening and stabilizing for Jeremy.
6. With dissociated ego states, whether or not there is a formal diagnosis of dissociative disorder, it is often necessary to explain treatment approaches you may have already reviewed for the core personality. In this case, I asked the ego state if he had been present when Jeremy and I discussed treatment options, and he told us he had not. Therefore, I reexplained the principles and practices of both EMDR and ego state therapy to obtain the ego state's informed consent. This is a necessary practice in order to strengthen alliances and facilitate greater cooperation and trust throughout the entire ego state system.

REFERENCES

Bandura, A. (1977). Self-efficacy: Toward a unifying theory of behavior change. *Psychological Review, 84*, 191–215.

Banyai, E. (1991). Toward a social psychobiological model of hypnosis. In S. J. Lynn & J. W. Rhue (Eds.), *Theories of hypnosis: Current modes and perspectives* (pp. 564–598). New York: Guilford Press.

Beere, D., Simon, M., & Welch, K. (2001). Recommendations and illustrations for combining hypnosis and EMDR in the treatment of psychological trauma. *American Journal of Clinical Hypnosis, 43*(3–4), 217–232.

Binet, A. (1977). *On double consciousness*. Washington: University Publications of America. (Original work published 1890)

Bjick, S. (2001). Accessing the power in the patient with hypnosis and EMDR. *American Journal of Clinical Hypnosis, 43*(3–4), 203–216.

Brown, D., & Fromm, E. (1986). *Hypnosis and hypnoanalysis*. Hillsdale, NJ: Erlbaum.

Cheek, D., & LeCron, L. (1968). *Clinical hypnotherapy*. New York: Grune & Stratton.

Dimond, R. (1981). Hypnotic treatment of a kidney dialysis patient. *American Journal of Clinical Hypnosis, 23*, 284–288.

Erickson, M. (1959). Further techniques of hypnosis: Utilization techniques. *American Journal of Clinical Hypnosis, 2*, 3–21.

Erickson, M., & Kubie, L. (1939). The permanent relief of an obsessional phobia by means of communications with an unsuspected dual personality. *Psychoanalytic Quarterly, 8*, 471–509.

Fine, C. G., & Berkowitz, A. S. (2001). The wreathing protocol: The imbrication of hypnosis and EMDR in the treatment of dissociative identity disorder and other dissociative responses. *American Journal of Clinical Hypnosis, 43*(3/4), 275–290.

Frederick, C., & McNeal, S. (1998). *Inner strengths: Contemporary psychotherapy and hypnosis for ego-strengthening*. Hillsdale, NJ: Lawrence Erlbaum.

Frederick, C., & Phillips, M. (1992). The use of hypnotic age progressions in interventions with acute psychosomatic conditions. *American Journal of Clinical Hypnosis, 35*, 89–98.

Freud, S. (1961). The ego and the id. In J. Strachey (Ed. & Trans.), *The standard edition of the complete psychological works of Sigmund Freud* (Vol. 19, pp. 3–66). London: Hogarth Press. (Original work published 1923)

Gardner, G. (1976). Hypnosis and mastery: Clinical contributions and directions for research. *International Journal of Clinical and Experimental Hypnosis, 24*, 202–214.

Gilligan, S. (2002). The experience of "negative otherness": How shall we treat our enemies? In J. Zeig (Ed.), *Brief therapy: Lasting impressions*. New York: Harper & Row.

Hammond, C. (1990). *Handbook of hypnotic suggestions and metaphors*. New York: Norton.

Hartland, J. (1965). The value of "ego strengthening" procedures prior to direct symptom removal under hypnosis. *American Journal of Clinical Hypnosis, 8*, 89–93.

Hartland, J. (1971). Further observation on the use of ego strengthening techniques. *American Journal of Clinical Hypnosis, 14*, 1–8.

Hilgard, E. R. (1977). *Divided consciousness: Multiple controls in human thought and action*. New York: Wiley.

Hollander, H. (2003, April). *Integrating EMDR with hypnosis*. Advanced workshop presented at the 45th Annual Scientific Meeting and Workshops on Clinical Hypnosis, Alexandria, VA.

Hollander, H., & Bender, S. (2001). ECEM (Eye closure, eye movements): Integrating aspects of EMDR with hypnosis for treatment of trauma. *American Journal of Clinical Hypnosis, 43*(3/4), 187–202.

James, W. (1983). *The principles of psychology*. Cambridge, MA: Harvard University Press. (Original work published 1890)

Janet, P. (1887). L'anesthésie systématisée et la dissociation des phenomènes psychologiques. [The systematic anesthetization and dissociation of psychologic phenomena.] *Revue Philosophique, 23*, 449–472.

Janet, P. (1907). *The major symptoms of hysteria*. New York: Macmillan.

Lynn, S. J., & Rhue, J. W. (1991). *Theories of hypnosis: Current models and perspectives*. New York: Guilford Press.

McNeal, S. (2001). EMDR and hypnosis in the treatment of phobias. *American Journal of Clinical Hypnosis, 43*(3–4), 263–274.

McNeal, S., & Frederick, C. (1993). Inner strength and other techniques for ego strengthening. *American Journal of Clinical Hypnosis, 35*, 170–178.

Murray-Jobsis, J. (1990). Renurturing: Forming positive sense of identity and bonding. In D. C. Hammond (Ed.), *Handbook of hypnotic suggestions and metaphors* (pp. 326–328). New York: Norton.

Nicosia, G. (1995). Brief note: Eye movement desensitization and reprocessing are not hypnosis [Letter to the editor]. *Dissociation, 8*, p. 65.

Phillips, M. (1996, March). *Strengthening observing and experiencing ego functioning in ego state therapy.* Paper presented at the 37th Annual Scientific Meeting of the American Society of Clinical Hypnosis, San Diego, CA.

Phillips, M. (2000). *Finding the energy to heal: How EMDR, hypnosis, imagery, TFT and body-focused therapy can help restore mind-body health.* New York: Norton.

Phillips, M. (2001a). Ericksonian approaches to dissociative disorders. In B. Geary & J. Zeig (Eds.), *The handbook of Ericksonian psychotherapy* (pp. 313–332). Phoenix, AZ: Milton H. Erickson Foundation Press.

Phillips, M. (2001b). Potential contributions of hypnosis to ego strengthening procedures in EMDR. *American Journal of Clinical Hypnosis, 43*(3/4), 247–262.

Phillips, M., & Frederick, C. (1992). The use of hypnotic age progressions as prognostic, ego strengthening and integrative techniques. *American Journal of Clinical Hypnosis, 35*, 90–108.

Phillips, M., & Frederick, C. (1995). *Healing the divided self: Clinical and Ericksonian hypnotherapy for posttraumatic and dissociative conditions.* New York: Norton.

Prince, M. (1969). *The dissociation of a personality.* Westport, CT: Greenwood. (Original work published 1906)

Rossi, E. (Ed.). (1980). *The collected papers of Milton H. Erickson on hypnosis* (Vols. 1–4). New York: Irvington.

Shapiro, F. (1995). *Eye movement desensitization and reprocessing: Basic principles, protocols, and procedures.* New York: Guilford Press.

Shapiro, F., & Forrest, M. S. (1997). *EMDR: The breakthrough therapy for overcoming anxiety, stress, and trauma.* New York: Basic Books.

Spiegel, H. (1972). An eye-roll test for hypnotizability. *American Journal of Clinical Hypnosis, 15*, 25–28.

Spiegel, H., & Linn, L. (1969). The "ripple effect" following adjunct hypnosis in analytic psychotherapy. *American Journal of Psychiatry, 126*(1), 53–58.

Stanton, H. (1989). Ego enhancement: A five-step approach. *American Journal of Clinical Hypnosis, 31*, 192–198.

Wade, T., & Wade, D. (2001). Integrative psychotherapy: Combining ego-state therapy, clinical hypnosis and EMDR in a psychosocial developmental context. *American Journal of Clinical Hypnosis, 43*(3–4), 233–246.

Watkins, J. G., & Watkins, H. H. (1979). The theory and practice of ego state therapy. In H. Grayson (Ed.), *Short-term approaches to psychotherapy* (pp. 176–220). New York: Human Sciences Press.

Watkins, J. G., & Watkins, H. H. (1997). *Ego states: Theory and practice.* New York: Norton.

CHAPTER 4

Changing Cognitive Schemas through EMDR and Ego State Therapy

Michael C. Paterson

Often clients require extensive preparatory work to ensure that they have the ego strength to allow them to experience EMDR. Failure to do this may result in harm to the client and litigation against the therapist. Ego strengthening is required where the client's personality is less than totally integrated, usually indicated by the presence of enduring irrational beliefs and behavior. Such beliefs exist despite extensive evidence to the contrary; for example, a man may believe he is worthless and a failure despite being in a stable marriage and also holding a college degree. Similarly, irrational beliefs often prevent clients from progressing in therapy due to the blocking action they exert on cognitive processing.

Extreme fragmentation of personality, such as with borderline personality disorder, is often treated by cognitive therapists using Schema-Focused Cognitive Therapy (Young, 1994; Young, Klosko, & Weishaar, 2003). This approach holds that all people develop maladaptive cognitive schemas, enduring patterns of self-belief that are usually laid down in childhood (for example, "I'm a failure") and become ingrained in the individual's personality. These beliefs are resistant to change and are manifested in characteristic patterns of nonadaptive behavior. For example, the client with the failure schema may display perfectionism in routine tasks in an attempt to break away from the negative self-belief. The usual effect is one of setting oneself up to fail. Treatment involves confronting and challenging the maladaptive schemas using emotive, interpersonal, cognitive, and behavioral techniques, thus weakening the schemas and allowing the healthy part of the individual's personality to come to the fore.

Maladaptive cognitive schemas are accessed through the negative cognition in EMDR. For EMDR to be effective, the schema must be triggered in order to generate the associated emotion and somatic sensation. The wording of the negative cognition is therefore important, as some statements will only approximate the schema but others will trigger it. For example, the negative cognition "I'm no good" may be better replaced with "I'm worthless."

Ego state therapy, seen traditionally as being psychodynamic in origin (Watkins & Watkins, 1997), achieves similar results to the schema-focused approach. The theory holds that everybody has a number of ego states (personality patterns), each representing certain beliefs and behavior. Each ego state is separated from other states by boundaries that are more or less permeable. This means that most people can move easily between ego states to deal with situations as they arise. Where boundaries between ego states are less permeable, then individuals can remain stuck in a particular state and only escape when they switch suddenly to an alternative state, such as with borderline personality disorder.

As with the schema-focused approach, ego state theory holds that people develop maladaptive states, often in childhood, but these are at a different level from schemas. For example, clients may be aware of a critical inner voice that abuses them verbally when they get it wrong. They may have a failure schema, but the Critic is a part representation of that. Thus the aim of ego state therapy is changing the roles of maladaptive ego states to more functional ones.

Schema-Focused Cognitive Therapy views schemas as stable and enduring patterns of beliefs and feelings about oneself that are resistant to change. More recently, Young et al. (2003) explained their concept of schema modes as "the moment-to-moment emotional states and coping responses—adaptive and maladaptive—that we all experience" (p. 37). These authors identify ten schema modes, which they group into four categories: Dysfunctional Coping modes, Child modes, Dysfunctional Parent modes, and a Healthy Adult mode. Upon examination, these modes are akin to ego states.

Young (1994) points out that schemas are not always in conscious awareness but, when triggered, dominate one's thoughts and feelings and determine subsequent behavior. The same principle applies to ego state theory. Watkins and Watkins (1997) have drawn on the work of early psychodynamic theorists to propose that ego states exist subconsciously until they are invested with self-energy (ego cathexes) and take the "executive" position; in other words, that part of the person is in charge.

Other ego states remain dormant and usually aware of what is happening outside their host; they have been invested with object energy (object ca-thexes). In dissociative identity disorder, however, ego states are usually unaware of the presence of other states and are amnesiac when switching between states occurs. For example, when in a particular state the client does not recognize clothes in the wardrobe bought while in a different state. A similar phenomenon occurs with state-dependent memory.

The ego state and schema-focused approaches agree that what they are targeting is the result of one's personality development. Both approaches accept that adaptive and maladaptive states can and do develop. Where these theories appear to differ is in what they include.

Watkins and Watkins (1997) incorporate the development of adap-tive ego states through normal differentiation, and they accept dissoci-ation as a phenomenon in which different states are manifested. This means that patterns of thinking, emotions, and behaviors that serve the client well in the present have developed through stable life experiences. Through dissociation, other less adaptive states can develop under the umbrellas of depersonalization and derealization.

Young (1994) differs in his approach by concentrating on the de-velopment of early maladaptive schemas and their maintenance; he sees dissociation as one way of maintaining these. When in a dissociated state, clients experience depersonalization or derealization and are not in full contact with what is happening in the world around them. Because of this it is difficult to trigger schemas using Young's schema-focused ap-proach. However, the introduction of schema modes to the approach (Young et al., 2003) makes this less of a problem. Effectively, Young (1994) holds that dissociation is a barrier to progressing through therapy, while the Watkins duo sees dissociated ego states as being able to enhance therapy.

From appreciating the subtleties of both the schema-focused and ego state approaches much can be learned about the maintenance and change of enduring irrational beliefs and behavior. Cognitive analytic therapy (CAT; Ryle, 1998) has gone some way to provide this. Ryle's model al-lows a place for adaptive ego states, transition between states, dissocia-tion, and schema maintenance.

CAT maintains that in early life people learn reciprocal roles that, through their experience of these and the meaning they attach to them, determine how their personality develops. For example, emotional de-privation by Mother in childhood is acted out in play and later adopted as a pattern of thinking and behaving whereby the mature adult believes that emotional needs cannot be met by others. These reciprocal roles form basic role patterns (self-states), have stable and recognizable char-acteristics, and are resistant to change. Ryle proposes that therapists help clients identify the different self-states and reciprocal role patterns and display them as a therapeutic tool in the form of a Self States Sequential Diagram. This permits clients to see in a flowchart what triggers their ego states, how these are maintained, and what occurs as a result.

MAINTENANCE OF IRRATIONAL BELIEFS AND BEHAVIORS

Schemas and ego states are maintained in their existing forms through a lack of evidence to influence change. This means that evidence that may dispose people to think differently about themselves is avoided or distorted to fit with existing beliefs. For example, a student with a core belief of "I'm a failure" who scores an A+ on an assignment may minimize that success with a statement indicating that anybody could achieve it with a little effort.

I believe that schemas, as enduring beliefs and feelings, are at a more complex level than separate ego states. As part-selves, a number of ego states can influence the overall belief and its associated feelings. By way of example, an adult in the work environment receives constructive feedback from his boss, but instead of accepting this as a learning experience and a way to improve his performance, he finds that he experiences a sense of failure, which triggers feelings of despair. From the schema perspective, the adult worker's failure schema was triggered and was maintained by discounting previous successes and ignoring assurances that not all of the performance was weak. In terms of ego states, this would have triggered a child state that developed as a result of frequent parental criticism. It would be maintained by another ego state, the Critic, that formed as a parental introject. This part-self would block any adaptive information that could modify the reasoning of other parts.

Depending on the theoretical approach, authors propose a range of ways, often overlapping, in which the maladaptive states and schemas are maintained. Young (1994) believes that maladaptive schemas formed at an early age are most resistant to change. He cites three processes by which change is prevented: *schema maintenance*, *schema avoidance*, and *schema compensation*. In schema maintenance, information contrary to the schema is discounted (for example, a failure schema rejects or distorts evidence of success), and self-defeating behavior can occur (for example, being involved halfheartedly when faced with a new project). In schema avoidance, behavioral triggers for the schema are avoided (for example, vulnerability is prevented by avoiding crowds), while cognitively and emotionally there are voluntary and involuntary efforts to avoid thinking of events or experiencing painful emotions. With schema compensation one behaves opposite to what the schema suggests. For example, instead of avoiding relationships, a man with an abandonment schema who tries to compensate for this may seek out relationships and smother women with attention. The women may likely feel trapped and leave the relationship, thus abandoning the man and reinforcing his negative self-belief.

In the cognitive analytic view dysfunctional patterns of thinking and acting are maintained by *traps*, *dilemmas*, and *snags*. Traps are when one is unable to escape from circular thoughts and behavior. For example, a low-in-mood, "worthless" adolescent believes she will not do well on a class test; poor performance results and the belief is confirmed. Dilemmas occur when people act in a certain way because the alternatives seem bad or worse. For example, a man does not express how he feels as he risks being rejected. Snags appear when one wants to change one's behavior, but the alternative will be prevented by the creation of internal conflict by either running contrary to what significant others want for the individual or through feelings of not deserving the alternative. For example, a trainee computer systems engineer who felt guilty about success failed the level 4 professional exam on three occasions but was able to pass exam 5, for which he had to know the material for the earlier exams.

In terms of ego state theory, Watkins and Watkins (1997) reiterate what is demonstrated above. They indicate, first, that states are maintained by a present-day anticipation, often unconscious, of the reoccurrence of certain childhood experiences. Although the person has developed chronologically, the early maladaptive learning is reinforced through not moving beyond the early maladaptive states (schema maintenance). Second, Watkins and Watkins suggest that there can be a present-day desire to change the past (schema compensation). They give an example of a woman who seeks out an abusive relationship because as a child she was abused by a trusted adult. Instead of breaking away from the abused child state the victim recreates it, thus maintaining the maladaptive state.

I suggest that through understanding other theoretical perspectives in addition to the ego state field, clinical practice can be enhanced. A useful starting point with clients is to identify, through clinical interview, which schemas are maladaptive. Clinical intuition could be supported with Young's Schema Questionnaire (Young, 1994; Young et al., 2003), which examines up to eighteen different schemas. Next, clinicians may wish to use Ryle's (1998) technique and provide a Self States Sequential Diagram to unravel for their clients the complex interplay of state switches, emotions, and subsequent behaviors. Using these two tools therapists will be able to structure their approach for maximum effectiveness. They can identify the preparatory work necessary to stabilize the client and the potential targets for EMDR, and then agree on these with the client.

TERRORISM AND TRAUMA IN NORTHERN
IRELAND: POLICE AS VICTIMS

The case study below is that of Margaret, a former police officer in Northern Ireland who had been retired on medical grounds with a diagnosis of depression. She had served in the Royal Ulster Constabulary (RUC) during the terrorist campaign in the latter third of the 20th century. The RUC was the police service in Northern Ireland from 1922, when the island of Ireland was partitioned into two states: Northern Ireland (British) and the Republic of Ireland (Irish). In 2002, following terrorist cease-fires and a major review of policing in Northern Ireland, the RUC was restructured and named the Police Service of Northern Ireland (PSNI). She served in the RUC from 1979 to 1983 and sustained amputation of both arms in a terrorist rocket attack on her police vehicle in 1981.

The nature of policing in Northern Ireland during the terrorist campaign was such that officers had to carry out normal policing duties under risk of attack. When they signed off from duty the risks remained: many officers were attacked, and some murdered, when at home or engaged in an activity outside the home. During "the Troubles" that started with civil disturbances in 1968, 302 RUC officers have been killed and hundreds more injured, many maimed for life. Over 3,000 people died as a result of the Troubles, representing around 0.2 % of the population. In terms of the United States, this would be equivalent to some 453,000 people.

Policing in Northern Ireland was not easy in psychological terms as officers were required to attend murder scenes where mutilated bodies were often to be found. Training was on the job and nothing was done in the early years to prepare officers for what they had to face. In my first week of operational duty in 1979, I was sent with colleagues to recover body parts following a bomb blast with multiple fatalities at Narrow Water, a scenic area near Newry in County Down. During the early 1970s, some officers in Belfast, the largest city, attended several bomb scenes during one shift.

Studies of former RUC officers (McConnell, Paterson, & Poole, in preparation; Paterson, Poole, Trew, & Harkin, 2001) have found that policing in Northern Ireland has left its mark. Depending on the tenure of employment in the RUC (the career grade of regular officer or the auxiliary reserve officer), levels of psychological symptoms differed. Some 35% of retired regular officers met criteria for "psychiatric caseness" (as it is referred to in Ireland) on the General Health Questionnaire and 11% for posttraumatic stress disorder; retired reserve officers were 44% and 17%, respectively.

As a clinical psychologist in Belfast, I head an organization with a psychiatric colleague that specializes in the assessment and treatment of posttraumatic stress. I work extensively with serving and retired officers such as Margaret who have developed psychological difficulties as a result of their police service. I use EMDR as a treatment of choice for traumatic stress and weave in ego state therapy when reprocessing appears to meet resistance. Ego state therapy, in its own right, has proved effective for preparation with clients whose negative self-beliefs appear to be causing internal conflict that needs resolution before using EMDR.

MARGARET: A CASE STUDY OF TRAUMA IN NORTHERN IRELAND

Margaret's Story

Margaret's medical retirement from the RUC followed a diagnosis of depression. Her ability to function within the policing environment was severely affected in that she was unable to concentrate on her job, her sleep was poor and its pattern erratic, and she had lost interest in most things in her life. She had been experiencing frightening dreams and intrusive thoughts at the time of her medical retirement, but these were not cited as part of her official diagnosis. When she came to see me her Social Security benefits had been terminated; this led to her feeling more distressed and later, following a former colleague's advice, to attend the Police Rehabilitation and Retraining Trust where I worked. Apart from seeing a psychiatrist for her diagnosis of depression and prescription of antidepressants, which she declined to take, Margaret had never been treated for her difficulties.

Now age forty-seven, Margaret lives as a single parent with her ten-year-old son, never having lived with her son's father; he was married and living with his wife. When I met her, Margaret presented with posttraumatic stress disorder with comorbid depression relating to incidents during her police service when colleagues and civilians had lost their lives in terrorist attacks. She reported feelings of guilt relating to her perceived role in one incident, and often a feeling of being numb, distant to what was going on around her. It transpired that when emotional demands became so intense she dissociated, which she described as feeling like a "fluffy cloud." This was like looking at the current scene from a different viewpoint and feeling numb. The same phenomenon occurred when Margaret experienced high levels of pain: she did not require any pain relief when giving birth to her son. During the early stages of my contact with her, Margaret was resistant to allowing her emotions to be exposed. She always found this uncomfortable, at least until she went onto the "fluffy cloud."

Margaret was born into a working-class family in the Roman Catholic faith during the 1950s in a rural part of Northern Ireland. She was the youngest of seven children at a time when traditionally large families were the norm; parish priests, whose instruction was generally obeyed, forbade the use of contraception as it was contrary to the philosophy of their church.

During her formative years Margaret felt separate from the middle five children ("the middle group"), but close to her oldest brother, who was also an "outcast." Margaret had a reasonable relationship with her mother, who died when Margaret was age twenty-two. During Margaret's childhood, her mother had to spread her affections across all her children, but Margaret, as the youngest, received her share. After her mother's death, Margaret cared for her elderly father, with whom she never had had a good relationship. Throughout Margaret's life he was emotionally distant and gave little attention to her. As a widower he became demanding of her time when she was working long hours in the RUC. Margaret resented this and moved out from the family home.

Margaret performed well at school but was angered when her family moved to England when she was age fourteen, apparently on the insistence of an older brother who was in the "middle group." Margaret left school at age fifteen and went to work in a factory. She had never felt part of her family, and in her desire to escape from the family environment, she joined the British army. Margaret had a need to be accepted by her new army colleagues and, in an attempt to be accepted into the culture, allowed a lesbian colleague to kiss her passionately. After another colleague reported the couple there was an investigation by the Military Police but no charges were proffered. This was an isolated incident as Margaret did not have lesbian tendencies. She regretted the experience bitterly and subsequently carried feelings of guilt; she left military service after three months. When she was nineteen years old, Margaret's family decided to resettle in Northern Ireland, apparently following a decision by one of Margaret's siblings. Nobody asked Margaret for her view.

Upon her return to Northern Ireland Margaret decided to join the RUC, perhaps as a punishment to her family. Her relatives were dismayed: they saw Margaret as letting them down by joining what they viewed as a Protestant police force. The family was Irish Nationalist in their political views and saw the RUC as oppressive to the Catholic minority.

Throughout her police service, Margaret was exposed to death, not only caused by terrorists but also due to car wrecks and other sudden deaths. Deaths of children had a particular effect, with Margaret recalling vividly the sight of dismembered corpses in two particular incidents where children were not the intended victims: a bomb explosion in Belfast during the 1970s and another in County Down in the 1990s. She also felt responsible for the shooting deaths of three colleagues, one of whom she had challenged for not being on the ground as much as other officers.

The risk of clearly identifying Margaret, a pseudonym, prevents more detail about these incidents being given.

From her life experience with family and others, Margaret had always felt she was on her own and was apprehensive about trusting people; her view was that people would take advantage in some way. The guilt she had carried from her same-sex contact was so intense it drove her to invite divine retribution upon herself. She often drank heavily and drove her car fast but never came to harm. When terrorist incidents occurred, she escaped unscathed, often having left the scene a short time previously. This resulted in a distorted belief that God wanted to torture her even more. In her early forties she was diagnosed with ovarian cancer and was treated successfully with a total hysterectomy.

Understanding Margaret's Problem

When I carried out my assessment in early 2000, I found that Margaret had developed certain core beliefs about herself that were not currently self-serving, what Young (1994) termed "early maladaptive schemas." Margaret's family life was responsible for these on the whole. The first schema, Emotional Deprivation, is an expectation that one's primary emotional needs will not be met by others. Margaret's mother's affections were shared across seven children and a husband. She saw the five siblings in the "middle band" as caring little about her, and Father just did not bother. The second schema, Social Isolation/Alienation, produces a belief of not belonging to any particular group, separate from the rest. Margaret's sense of isolation in the family caused this to develop, and it was reinforced throughout life. Third, Mistrust/Abuse results in a belief that others will purposely take advantage in some way. The trust Margaret placed in her older siblings and parents was not fulfilled; her siblings rejected her, and her parents were not physically or emotionally available to her. Fourth, Defectiveness/Shame results in a belief that there is an internal flaw, and if others get close they will recognize this and withdraw from the relationship. It appeared that the same-sex contact had the effect of exacerbating this belief. Margaret had avoided relationships until her son's father persuaded her to go out with him.

I noted a complex interplay of these schemas that were each triggered by certain events. Faced with these and with Margaret's PTSD with comorbid depression, I decided that extensive preparatory work needed to be done before I used EMDR on the traumatic memories. I was aware that Margaret's perspective and mood could shift rapidly, and I needed to establish a significant level of stabilization. A few months previously I had become familiar with ego state therapy and knew that it was capable of working with different "parts" of Margaret to create internal harmony.

Young et al.'s (2003) schema modes were unpublished when I was working with Margaret.

My expectation was that internal harmony would create the safe circumstances whereby I would be able to use EMDR on Margaret's disturbing memories, particularly the deaths of children and the murders of her three colleagues. She also had discomfort on feeling closed in with people surrounding her, which, I suspected, may have related to an early life experience.

At this point, it was difficult to know where to start with ego state therapy so I drew on Ryle's (1998) CAT approach and sketched a Self State Sequential Diagram (see Figure 4.1), the explanatory flowchart that showed Margaret and me when, and in what circumstances, emotions and thoughts about herself seemed to switch without warning.

In Figure 4.1, it can be seen that Margaret's state of feeling vulnerable and lonely was influenced by a number of her life experiences. She regularly switched to an Untouchable state named Joker in which she had a devil-may-care attitude and felt as if nothing could harm her. In the past, this state experienced harm happening to others while Margaret remained unscathed; the ensuing guilt, which appeared in the form of the state called Robed One, she felt was exacerbated by her Roman Catholic upbringing and the memory of her same-sex contact. In an effort to punish herself, Margaret wanted God to strike her down and even took risks in an attempt to come to harm. Another state that Margaret experienced, named Bossy, related to a need to protect herself or others, but this was often in conflict with the Vulnerable and Lonely state. A further state, called Watchful, tended to act as a peacekeeper. Margaret's dissociated depersonalized state, which she described as the Fluffy Cloud state named Elizabeth, was an escape when things got to be too much.

Margaret's Rebirth

Initially, I intended to use hypnosis to attempt ego state therapy with Margaret, but she was particularly defensive and only achieved a comfortable, relaxed state. I had suggested an image of a derelict villa in the mountains in which to gather together Margaret's ego states, but despite my best efforts I was unsuccessful until I used a little subterfuge. To help Margaret access her ego state system, I described a group of urns in a corner and asked her to be aware of a sound coming from one of them. In her relaxed state, she accessed an image of a shadowy figure that remained for a brief period before it disappeared again. I felt disillusioned with hypnosis as a vehicle to access ego states and considered briefly that my failure might have been due to lack of skill. To overcome this I decided to try the same bilateral stimulation that I used with EMDR.

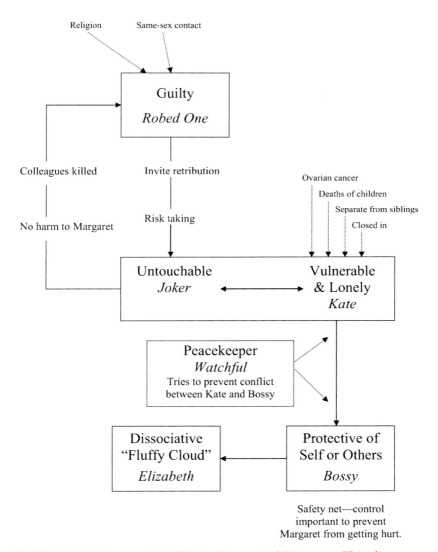

FIGURE 4.1   Margaret's Self State Sequential Diagram. This diagram by the therapist shows six ego states, their interrelationships and roles, and the major life events that have impacted them.

Alternating bilateral auditory tones (BATs) had worked well for a different client with a simpler presentation, so I thought I would try these with Margaret. These were used thereafter.

Fortunately for me, Margaret dropped her defenses in the next session. The father of her child, with whom she was in dispute for child support payments, was in the same building for a training course. Having served in the police I knew this man and was able to arrange for Margaret to be directed immediately to my consulting room, in case the two would meet. Through this, Margaret felt she could trust me, a shift in her core schema of Mistrust/Abuse.

From my knowledge of Margaret's sequencing of her ego states, I felt it appropriate to target first her schemas of Isolation and Vulnerability. With the BATs playing constantly through headphones, I asked Margaret to visualize walking down a forest path to reach a small clearing in the woods. I described the path and clearing in a manner whereby Margaret was able to create a personalized image. The clearing had a circle of logs in the center that could act as seats for ego states that might come in. I asked Margaret to invite in any parts of her that knew something, or wished to say something about the feelings of isolation and vulnerability she had. I also added that if nothing was coming in that was okay.

Thankfully, an image of a figure entered Margaret's awareness. Having described this first ego state to me she named him Bossy, a state that existed to protect Margaret. He jealously guarded his control due to a childlike belief that this would prevent Margaret from getting hurt (a trap). I was able to hold a conversation with each ego state by asking Margaret if I could speak directly to that part; as I directed my question to the ego state Margaret moved easily into that role. Another ego state, a sad part that Margaret named Kate, felt that Margaret had to move on and stop living in the past, but to do this the states had to agree. Bossy was resistant to changing (a dilemma), but the assurances of another ego state, Competent Adult (Margaret's executive ego state), that she would take responsibility to plan their direction and set goals was sufficient to allow Bossy to agree to give this redefinition of roles a try for the common good. In order to consolidate the newfound agreement between these ego states, I asked Margaret to visualize herself in the midst of them and drawing them closer, thus allowing Bossy, Kate, and Competent Adult to blend with her and become part of her at the end of the session.

At the start of session 3, Margaret reported that she realized she had been obstructive with me and had resolved to change. At home as she was again using a relaxing room she had avoided for years and was listening to music she had put away several years previously. We spent some time talking and helping Margaret adjust to her new mind-set.

Margaret still felt isolated, however, and said she "didn't belong." In session 4 this isolation took the form of Kate appearing in the forest clearing. The ego states Bossy, Watchful, and Joker were present, too. Bossy said that his new role of having less control was "not so bad" and agreed to continue with it. Kate recognized that she did not have much in common with the other ego states but that she would have to be more open to new information to allow the others to be able to work with her. Watchful, who previously prevented clashes between Bossy and Kate, felt that she now had less to do but was prepared to use negotiation rather than being confrontational.

At the end of the session the ego states were in agreement to work together. I asked Margaret to invite the ego states to join her in the center of the forest clearing and draw them in close to her. I then asked her to notice their bodies against hers and to draw them in closer still, being aware of their bodies blending with her and becoming part of her. As this was happening I checked with Margaret that this was a positive experience for her. After the ego states blended I requested that Margaret leave the forest clearing and return to the room with me. At this stage Margaret was able to report a sense of wholeness.

At her next session (5), one week later, Margaret reported that she was now able to concentrate to read novels and had started genealogical research on her family history. An old memory had been disturbing her though: fainting in church at age seven when closed in by adults. Margaret recalled the scene and described the interior of the chapel as being small with whitewashed stone walls, being crammed with people, and having a smoky atmosphere due to the burning incense. She also recalled three elderly ladies behind her, all of them dressed in black. She named these people "the nuns," though her description would have fit witches better. I decided to use EMDR on the affected child ego state with the adult Margaret present throughout. The memory held a SUD rating of 6 and a belief of not having any control. Desensitization took around fifteen minutes, with a number of somatic sensations evident. The child ego state reported feeling nauseous and faint. After a few sets of BATs this eased and then the smoky atmosphere cleared. With more sets of BATs an adult perspective emerged and Margaret reported seeing the "nuns" for who they really were: three elderly country women dressed in black clothes, common for women of their generation.

Sessions 6 and 7 focused on the Vulnerable and Lonely ego state Kate. Margaret had presented with a feeling of not belonging. She reported that she had always wanted to be included in activities but had behaved in a way that made it impossible (schema compensation). By this she meant that she teased others in order to get attention. It transpired that Joker was the ego state that initiated the schema compensation.

Kate's worst fear was being rejected, but she was suspicious of the motives of the other ego states. She realized she needed to accept things as they are and stop analyzing. The other ego states present—Bossy, Watchful, and Joker—agreed to accept Kate.

After Kate's acceptance by the other ego states, I felt it would be appropriate if Kate could feel accepted by the "middle band" of siblings. In the next session (8), based on Kate's earliest memory of not belonging, I created imagery of Margaret's siblings playing without her. Kate approached them gingerly, joined in the game, and reported feeling that she had fitted in with them. I then checked which memory of not fitting in was the worst for Kate. She recalled Margaret's mother's death. Kate reported a chasm between her and the family and a sensation in her upper body. Focusing on the sensation, Kate began crying and saw herself hugging two of Margaret's brothers. When the session ended and Margaret was debriefed, she was still quite emotional.

The next two sessions (9 and 10) involved EMDR with Kate, helping desensitize her to the breakup with Margaret's son's father (when Margaret felt vulnerable) and the military police investigation of the same-sex contact (about which she reported feeling vulnerable and guilty). At the end of reprocessing, Kate reported feeling strong and no distress over the breakup with Margaret's child's father. With regard to the military police investigation, Kate saw two empty chairs in the interrogation room and reported a feeling of being secure and not to blame for the incident where she and the lesbian colleague kissed. It became evident that Margaret's colleague had caught her unawares and had taken advantage of her loneliness.

In session 11, I judged that I could use EMDR with the whole Margaret. During this session her ego states were present but quiet. Margaret had returned from a camping holiday feeling very vulnerable: "There was only a thin piece of canvas between me and the outside world." I asked Margaret to identify the negative cognition that went with this and the associated emotion and somatic sensation. I then asked her to hold the cognition, emotion, and body sensation together and float back in her memory to identify what old memory this fear linked to. Margaret had been forced to move home seventeen years previously after receiving an intelligence report of a terrorist threat against her. She had not settled comfortably in a residence since and was prone to compulsive checking of doors, windows, and locks. Being in a tent led to her feeling extremely vulnerable. I used EMDR to desensitize the memory of the enforced house move and also the experience of being under canvas. Both memories saw the SUD reduce to 0 and had positive cognitions installed.

On her next visit (session 12), Margaret reported feeling safer in her home and was checking locks in "the normal fashion." She then asked me to help her overcome her feelings associated with her total hysterectomy following ovarian cancer. This was achieved with EMDR working with the whole person.

When Margaret returned for session 13, an opportunity arose to use ego state therapy again. Margaret was targeting with EMDR her memory of the murder of three colleagues in a terrorist gun attack. On a sunny summer afternoon, these officers had parked their police vehicle in a busy thoroughfare in a market town. People streamed by, going about their business as the officers relaxed watching the activity. Out of the crowd three gunmen approached and opened fire on the police officers. They all died in a hail of bullets. Luckily, Margaret was not present at this incident, but she had blamed herself irrationally for these deaths as she had challenged one of the deceased officers for not being out on the ground as much as he should be.

Using EMDR, I found that processing was blocked by a somatic sensation in Margaret's forehead. This cleared through using a technique introduced to me by David Grand. I asked Margaret to picture what color the uncomfortable feeling was, identify where she was comfortable and notice that color, then notice both colors and be aware of what happened. Further into the session, Margaret reported a tug-of-war between two ego states, Robed One and Watchful. Robed One felt that Margaret was to blame for the deaths because she was "too laid back" (that is, slow to respond). During the discourse that followed, Robed One conceded some ground but still maintained that Margaret had an element of responsibility. This assertion diminished for this session as an associated negative somatic sensation was overcome by a positive sensation using the David Grand technique described above.

In session 14, Margaret was unable to access the memory of the murders of her three colleagues. I used ego state therapy to try to identify what may have been blocking this from coming up and found that Joker was the executive ego state. Margaret had booked a vacation at short notice and Joker was in a party mood. Margaret's other ego states appeared to her dressed in bright clothes and carrying suitcases. However, one ego state, Robed One, was excluded by the group. When I asked them the reason for excluding Robed One, the other ego states agreed in unison that he was a "misery guts" (that is, not fun to be with). Robed One rejected this comment, seeing himself more as reality focused because of Margaret's self-blame attached to her colleagues' deaths. Through Socratic questioning (that is, structured questioning leading to a logical conclusion), Robed One became more accepting that the terrorists were to blame. The other ego states became more accepting of Robed One, who now had acquired a light-colored robe and a suitcase for his vacation.

Upon returning from her vacation, Margaret was ready to reprocess her memory of an incident where a young child had been caught in a

bomb blast and killed (session 15). The child and her family were returning from vacation when their car was caught in the blast of a land mine
explosion that was detonated to kill a man in the car in front of them.
Margaret went to the mortuary to gather together body parts for identification. She recalled with tears in her eyes seeing the family's holiday pho-
tographs with the child alive and smiling happily. The meaning this had
for Margaret, in terms of her negative cognition, was "I'm helpless."

To address the traumatic memory I started Margaret on EMDR and
found that she was processing somatic sensations and colors. When she
reached a plateau in her reprocessing, I brought her back to target and
she dissociated. This was manifested by glazed eyes with a distant look,
complete stillness, and lack of affect. Previously when Margaret had dissociated, I had grounded her and returned to the matter in hand: I had
asked her to notice the floor under her feet, notice the wooden arms of
the chair as she squeezed them, and then draw herself back into her body
through the sensations in her hands and feet. This time I inquired further
and found that the dissociated state was a child named Elizabeth. This
female ego state took over the executive position at her own discretion,
often to the anger of the other ego states. Elizabeth was unaware that
they got cross at this and willingly agreed to relinquish her control to
Margaret herself. Due to lack of time the memory of the child who died
was not resolved until two sessions later.

In the period before session 16, Margaret had required medical treatment for an eye injury. She reported having been dissociated during and
after her hospital treatment. In ego state therapy, the ego states thanked
Elizabeth for taking over and saving them from the pain; however, they
insisted that Elizabeth ask first the next time she felt she needed to take
control.

In Margaret's childhood home there were many arguments with Margaret, the youngest child, looking on. When decisions were made Margaret
the child did not have a say. It transpired that the ego state Elizabeth was
created to help deal with the disturbance and the isolation that Margaret
felt. In session 16, the group of ego states accompanied Elizabeth to the
childhood home. Margaret reported somatic sensations being reprocessed
and then Elizabeth being able to take an adult perspective on the scene, realizing she did not own the family dysfunction. At the end of this session,
Elizabeth was blended comfortably into the whole Margaret.

In therapy session 17, Margaret laid to rest the traumatic memory of
the dismembered child. Desensitization took the SUD rating to 0 in less than
thirty minutes, and a positive cognition of "I am in control" was installed.

In two further sessions (18 and 19), we discussed practical issues regarding facing new situations. Margaret identified an expected difficulty in
speaking to strangers and also in organizing herself to apply to a university

program. I used EMDR in developing a future template for whenever Margaret met strangers; she had only a little anxiety at this stage and it reduced with BATs. I was not an expert in finding the route to university for others, so I arranged an appointment for Margaret with a specific career counselor at the Police Rehabilitation and Retraining Trust. From my knowledge of both women, I knew they would hit it off.

I had taken Margaret as far as I thought I could. Rather than discharge her I offered her the opportunity to return for a top-up session if she needed it. This gave her the confidence to try new things, knowing I was available by phone.

After my initial difficulty in accessing Margaret's ego states, she turned out to be a joy to work with for she responded very well to ego state therapy. I have found that people who experience dissociative episodes are excellent subjects for ego state therapy. They appear to be processing information at a deep level and as such achieve greater shifts. For Margaret, Socratic questioning of the more mature ego states led each state's thinking to logical, rational conclusions. Dealing with immature ego states, such as Elizabeth, required a more child-friendly approach. By using what was right for each ego state, Margaret moved relatively quickly to resolution of her difficulties.

At a follow-up nine months later Margaret was functioning well. She was no longer disturbed by frightening dreams, intrusive thoughts, or negative beliefs about herself. Furthermore, she had not dissociated since Elizabeth agreed to seek permission of the other ego states before taking over protective executive control under stress. Switching to the ego state Elizabeth was always an escape from reality for Margaret. Removing the triggers for Elizabeth and placing adaptive ego states in Elizabeth's former role ensured that Elizabeth remained in a safe place.

Margaret's early maladaptive schemas were altered to more adaptive functioning. Emotional Deprivation—the expectation that her primary emotional needs would not be met by others—had shifted to a core belief represented more by emotional stability. Through ego state therapy and EMDR Margaret healed the wound felt by the ego state Kate. As a result, she was able to develop close social relationships and be comfortable with them. Her sense of separateness from others, characterized by Social Isolation/Alienation, had gone; Margaret was even mixing comfortably with her siblings and their families. The work done with the ego states Kate and Joker played a major role here. This had a secondary effect on the schema of Mistrust/Abuse, with the ego state therapy involving Watchful, Bossy, and Elizabeth, helping Margaret to be able to start trusting people.

Defectives/Shame also shifted, primarily through the work done with the ego state Robed One. Although Margaret had not yet engaged in an intimate relationship with a significant other, she was able to recognize that she did not have an internal flaw and did not discount the possibility of intimacy in a relationship in the future.

When I first met Margaret, she was existing rather than living. She had no plans for the future and was functioning only to provide for her son. Having experienced ego state therapy and EMDR, Margaret had found a new life and her young son told her that he did not want "that other mummy" to come back. At the time of writing, Margaret had enrolled in a university course and was active in a local community group pressuring the municipal roads department to introduce traffic-calming measures on her access road. Margaret was going out socially and mixing with people she would previously have avoided, including family. She was full of praise for ego state therapy and EMDR and my patience with her. I learned from Margaret and am grateful for the teaching she gave me.

CONCLUSION

My experience of using ego state therapy to address dysfunctional schemas has improved my clinical practice significantly. Because of the cognitive-behavioral influence in my clinical training I was unsure initially of the validity of the psychodynamic theory in ego state therapy. However, thinking in terms of schemas and Self State Sequential Diagrams has helped me to accept concepts that initially seemed intangible.

Helping clients access their ego states allows the unconscious to deliver up its unresolved conflicts, such as would occur during dreaming in REM sleep. The benefit of therapeutic input means that the dilemmas, traps, and snags maintaining maladaptive schemas can be challenged and the blocks to improvement removed.

In Northern Ireland, people experience early life situations and traumas similar to those in other parts of the world. Sadly, poor parenting and abuse of children in all its forms knows no borders, and children go on to develop maladaptive schemas that hold them back in later life. Where maladaptive schemas form a weak foundation for the building of the remainder of one's life, the structure of that life is unsteady. Add to this the impact of exposure to psychological trauma through the Troubles and those people can develop chronic psychological problems, possibly leading to enduring personality disorders. Ego state therapy and EMDR continue to work well together in my clinical practice. Margaret is one of a series of successes, and I used her as an example here because I was able to offer evidence at nine-month follow-up. Margaret's life has been enhanced as a result of ego state therapy and EMDR, and it would be true to say that mine has too. These approaches permit me to change people's lives within a few sessions and rapidly overcome blocking beliefs and resistant somatic sensations. That is what I call fulfillment.

REFERENCES

McConnell, N., Paterson, M. C., & Poole, A. D. (Manuscript in preparation). The psychological and physical health of retired members of the Royal Ulster Constabulary Reserve.

Paterson, M. C., Poole, A. D., Trew, K. J., & Harkin, N. (2001). The physical and psychological health of police officers retired recently from the Royal Ulster Constabulary. *Irish Journal of Psychology, 22*(1), 1–27.

Ryle, A. (1998). *Cognitive analytic therapy and borderline personality disorder: The model and the method.* Chichester, England: Wiley.

Watkins, J. G., & Watkins, H. H. (1997). *Ego states: Theory and therapy.* New York: Norton.

Young, J. E. (1994). *Cognitive therapy for personality disorders: A schema-focused approach.* Sarasota, FL: Professional Resource Press.

Young, J. E., Klosko, J. S., & Weishaar, M. E. (2003). *Schema therapy: A practitioner's guide.* New York: Guilford Press.

CHAPTER 5

Treating Dissociative Identity Disorder with EMDR, Ego State Therapy, and Adjunct Approaches

Sandra Paulsen

TALKING TO PARTS

Therapists who choose to work with clients with dissociative identity disorder (DID) enter into the complex, confusing worlds of some of the most wounded clients they will ever encounter. For that very reason, they are the people who are most in need of our best personal and professional resources: our deepest compassion, our most enduring patience, our courage, and our best technical strategies—offered to not just one personality, but many parts of the psyche within a single individual. Those parts are at war with one another, and it is up to the therapist to show the way to peace.

I have been working with clients with DID in my private practice since 1992, when I stumbled across the phenomenon while beginning to use EMDR. EMDR training did not at that time caution therapists to screen clients for dissociation, as is now accepted practice. Though I used the standard EMDR protocol, within a particular two-week period I observed atypical results in three clients in treatment for PTSD or phobias. Astonishingly, all three clients exhibited amnesia for things like knowing me, having given consent to do EMDR, present time and place, their own identity, or the fact that we were *working with* a memory, rather than *being in* the memory again.

Quite naturally and spontaneously I worked with those found parts of the client's self by honoring the point of view that revealed itself, and giving a voice to that aspect of self evidencing amnesia, according respect and curiosity for its concerns.

While studying DID I learned about ego state therapy, an approach involving giving a voice to aspects of the self to resolve inner conflicts and trauma, developed by John G. Watkins and Helen Watkins many years prior. John Watkins and I have collaborated since 2004, presenting together on ego state therapy and EMDR at international conferences (Watkins & Watkins, 1997).

"Talking to parts" continues to be a natural way for me to work. About a third of my practice is with clients with DID, and I have taught and provided both individual and group consultation on the subject of using EMDR with dissociative clients for fifteen years as of this writing.

I choose to work with individuals with DID because it is highly rewarding. DID people are often highly gifted, deeply spiritual, and courageous even in their despair and terror. I feel privileged to walk the path of healing with them. I am personally transformed and uplifted by the miracles I witness through EMDR and ego state therapy with this most severely injured group of people. For me, it is a sacred trust to be a vehicle for their transformation against all odds, all betrayal, and all violation of trust. Moreover, it is the very stuff of the mystery of human existence, namely, to emerge from the abyss of suffering, to find the courage to embrace transformation, to open the heart, and for some, to achieve radiance seemingly more brilliant because of the difficulty of the journey.

THE CRUX OF THE PROBLEM AND NEW TREATMENT APPROACHES

DID almost always occurs following severe, chronic, and inescapable childhood trauma. Since the child can neither fight nor flee, freezing is the only possible response. Thus the trauma is set aside (dissociated) without resolving it. The unresolved trauma is held in separate parts of the self, out of the awareness of the "front" or "apparently normal parts" of the self.

Once thought to be extremely rare, the prevalence of DID has been found to be about 1 percent of the general population, and higher in clinical practice, especially among therapists who treat trauma. Therefore, most EMDR therapists can expect that they will indeed have clients with DID in their practice.

DID has historically been held to be very challenging to treat, and the treatment has typically been very long. Reasons for the complexity and length of the treatment include the special skills required of the therapist; the abhorrent nature of the trauma; the difficulty of supporting the client while avoiding iatrogenic problems; chronic suicidality and boundary issues; reenactment of traumas in the therapeutic relationship; and more.

In the past DID has been treated with hypnosis and a psychodynamic approach. Those methods are still important today, but three new treatment tools have arisen that significantly shorten treatment. First, early screening of all clients for dissociation can save years by providing a correct diagnosis that points to an appropriate course of treatment. Second, ego state therapy—and specifically the Dissociative Table Technique (Fraser, 1991)—provides a very practical application of psychodynamic therapy that enables rapid access to deep psychic structures that the client can see, hear, and feel, speeding up treatment. Third, the judicious addition of EMDR can accelerate the portions of the treatment that focus on detoxifying and making meaning of the trauma. As a result, in my experience treatment of DID with EMDR can be shorter than without it (though there are as yet no controlled studies of the treatment of DID with or without EMDR).

Working through traumatic memories with hypnosis alone is like rowing a boat across a lake: you can get to the other side, but it is very effortful. I think of EMDR as adding a powerful motor to the therapeutic boat, allowing detoxification of trauma to progress more rapidly— though, as with motorboats, appropriate pacing is key to keep the boat upright.

This chapter addresses the use of EMDR with clients on the severe end of the dissociative continuum. For many, but not all, highly dissociative clients, EMDR has a central place in treatment when used in combination with ego state therapy and within a careful and phased approach to treatment. In these cases, EMDR cannot be successfully conducted without working with the ego states involved, because of the fixity and relative impermeability of dissociative barriers. EMDR tends to thin or remove dissociative barriers and cause associative linkages to dissociated material. Therefore, failure to prepare or work with the structure of the self prior to doing EMDR can result in sudden and severe flooding, disorganization, and decompensation (Paulsen, 1995, 2004a).

This chapter will offer an understanding of DID and how to use EMDR and ego state therapy to treat it. I will also introduce two specific modalities to strengthen the treatment: the ACT-AS-IF approach (Paulsen, 2006) to prepare highly dissociative clients for EMDR, and ARCHITECTS (Paulsen, 2006), a stepwise protocol for conducting an EMDR session with a client with DID. My objective will be to shed light on how EMDR must be modified to deal with clients with DID safely. The practical concepts will be illustrated by several case studies.

WORKING WITH THE DYNAMICS OF
DISSOCIATIVE IDENTITY DISORDER

Diagnostic Criteria, Etiology, and Manifestation

Throughout this book, ego state therapy is used to access, explore, and resolve inner dividedness. For some individuals, that dividedness takes extreme proportions. The *DSM–IV* defines dissociative identity disorder, formerly called multiple personality disorder, as "the presence of two or more distinct identities or personality states... that recurrently take control of the individual's behavior," accompanied by "an inability to recall important personal information, the extent of which is too great to be explained by ordinary forgetfulness" (American Psychiatric Association, 1994, p. 484). This definition has been criticized for not being as robust as the clinical criteria by which specialists in dissociation conduct their differential diagnostic decision process and treatment (Dell, 2001). At the same time, the emphasis of this definition on the presence of amnesia for aspects of identity continues to be clinically useful to distinguish DID from the less severe conditions on the dissociative continuum and from the other dissociative disorders (Spiegel, 2001).

Most commonly, the severe trauma that causes DID occurs within the family of origin or foster family. In addition to the direct effects of physical, sexual, or emotional trauma, there is a simultaneous impact upon each developmental milestone that is missed because of the ruptures caused by the trauma.

In many cases, the trauma includes the betrayal and abandonment by what should have been loving caretakers, who subordinated the child's needs to their own gratification or impulses. Therefore, many individuals with DID have not successfully navigated attachment and trust milestones, let alone the subsequent developmental milestones. Traumatized children often make the best of scarce attachment possibilities in abusive families by compartmentalizing—and dissociating—traumatic material into one part of the self, so that another part of the self can preserve the illusion of a loving parent or caretaker. This results in discontinuity of the self, of time, and of memory itself.

Life is extraordinarily difficult for clients with DID. Because of these discontinuities, normal cause and effect is not present in their lives. There are alter personalities in DID that at times take complete executive control of the body, and for whose behavior other parts of the client have no memory. In some cases, those alters have distinctively different preferences and personality traits.

Clients with DID are forever being accused of things they don't remember doing and insist that they would never have done—although another part of them has outside awareness of other parts of the self. Moreover, the enormity of unresolved trauma means that there is frequent leakage of physical and emotional pain, as well as flashbacks and nightmares, from the parts of themselves that are holding the unresolved traumatic material, referred to by Braun (1988) as Behavior, Affect, Sensation, Knowledge, or BASK. Enormous amounts of energy are consumed in maintaining the dissociation, so that less energy is available for other life activities. Still, while individuals with DID are sometimes severely dysfunctional, they are often surprisingly functional, and may even hold responsible positions in society.

While it may appear that dissociation is a dichotomous variable—that is, a client either has DID or not—it is in actuality a continuous variable. The category dissociative disorder not otherwise specified (DDNOS) subsumes those clients who are very dissociative but for whom full criteria are not met. Specifically, the hallmark of DID is amnesia in present time, outside of hypnotherapeutic interventions, that isn't explainable by other factors, such as substance abuse or an organic condition. Otherwise, however, DDNOS resembles DID in its causes and treatment, but the condition may be considered milder for many DDNOS individuals. Some of the symptoms of DID are also found in DDNOS, especially derealization and depersonalization, in which individuals feel as if the world around them is somehow unreal or distorted, or as if they themselves are unreal, or as if they are standing next to or behind themselves. Individuals with DDNOS, however, by definition do not have the loss of time that is pathognomic for DID. Other chapters in this book describe treatments that are beneficial for clients who do not have full DID, and for some clients with DDNOS.

The Challenge to the Person of the Therapist

Working with clients with DID (especially those who also meet criteria for borderline personality disorder) is among the most difficult work that a therapist can do. Having a strong sense of therapeutic self, a wide range of clinical knowledge and experience, and the ability to set and hold the structure of the therapeutic frame are key to successful outcome and to avoiding clinical burnout. The cure involves the therapist listening empathically to many hours of stories of torture, abandonment, and betrayal of the worst human form, often perpetrated against the most helpless of people. It also involves the curative role of the therapeutic relationship itself, through which clients can begin to stitch together the tattered tapestry of their very self-structure and restore the humanity of shared relational experience in attachment and trust.

The treatment for DID tends to be long-term, yet DID is among the most treatable of mental illnesses. Being part of the transformation of a person from deeply divided to integrated and wholly human is one of the greatest privileges of being a mental health professional.

Even those therapists who think that they do not want to treat this difficult condition will find individuals with it in their practice, if they only look. Since the purpose of dissociation is to keep secrets from the self and the world, the therapist who does not look will not see. Therapists who ask for each and every client, "Where on the continuum of dissociation does *this* client lie?" will find DID and DDNOS throughout their client base.

Accessing the Parts of the Self

Early in the history of EMDR training, there were no caveats regarding the use of EMDR for highly dissociative individuals. When I first became aware of DID in my clients, it was evident to me that EMDR functioned as a "divining rod" (Paulsen, 1995) for dissociation, bringing dissociated material and aspects of the self into conscious awareness during EMDR processing. It was further clear that unless groundwork was appropriately laid for this processing, the EMDR could not be safely resolved at the end of the session, potentially leaving the client in a high level of arousal. As a result of this finding, the EMDR Institute modified its training procedures to caution therapists about the importance of screening for dissociative disorders using the Dissociative Experiences Scale (Bernstein & Putnam, 1989) or other appropriate screening methods prior to the use of EMDR. In 1996, this procedure was further expanded with the integration of the fractionated abreaction methodology (a deliberate working-through of a fraction of a memory to prevent flooding by the entire memory) for the most severe dissociative clients (Lazrove & Fine, 1996). More recently, the addition of the wreathing protocol (involving the interlacing of hypnosis and EMDR to lessen affective intensity; Fine & Berkowitz, 2001) has enriched the approach.

The procedure for safely combining EMDR and ego state therapy was first described by the present author; Paulsen Inobe, 2001, 2003; Paulsen & Watkins, 2003a, 2003b) as a way to resolve "looping" or stuck EMDR processing. The procedure used the Dissociative Table Technique (Fraser, 1991; Paulsen, 1995, 2006a; Paulsen & Watkins, 2005), described below, in contrast to a formal trance induction procedure, as a way to quickly and readily gain access to disowned aspects of the self. As described throughout this book, this procedure is useful for less than fully dissociative individuals as a way to create an internal workspace that enables material that might otherwise remain out of awareness to be brought into conscious awareness.

Other methods are available to access the inner personality systems of clients with DID, including formal hypnosis, guided imagery, self-hypnosis, meditation techniques, drugs such as sodium amytal, and fear or pain themselves (Fraser, 1993). Also, the Dissociative Table Technique does not always work with the extremely dissociative client whose amnesic barriers and self-structure may not permit visual accessing, especially early in treatment, or with a rare few who cannot visualize a conference room. However, the advantage of the Dissociative Table procedure is that for many people it enables rapid access to these disowned aspects of self without a formal trance induction. The EMDR therapist can then use ego state therapy when EMDR loops by asking the client to glance inside to a conference room in the mind's eye where the ego states are gathered. Whatever resistance or dissociated dynamic the EMDR processing is stuck upon is often visible in some form in the internal conference room, as a part of the self that was not engaged in the process. This occurs either because the disowned part of the self is ego dystonic to the front part of the self (also called the "host"), or was itself resistive to joining in the EMDR processing due to an internal dynamic related to its functional protective role in the self system.

Imputing identity, ego, and motives to a part of the self that is separate from the front part initially requires a leap of faith for many clinicians. However, talking about "one part of me" and "another part of me" is a basic human inclination. Speaking directly to parts energizes them, and inclines that part of the client to answer in the first person (as subject), so that the parts are "egotized," allowing them to be addressed and worked with separately (J. Watkins, personal communication, March 24, 2003). This engages the relevant dynamics more potently than referring to parts of the self as "he," "she," "they," or "it," which enables the parts to remain imbued only with object energy.

Once energy has been added to a part, it tends to be pulled forward and be either (1) fully present or copresent with another part of the self, or (2) in conscious mind and observable by the front part. If it is fully forward and present, it is said to be "ego cathected." If it is ego cathected, the client fully owns the point of view of that part, and uses the first person "I" or "we" to discuss the material it holds. If the part is not fully forward and present, but in conscious mind and visible at the conference table, it is said to be "conscious," or "co-conscious" if other parts are also at the table. If it is conscious but not present, it is said to be "object cathected," and the client uses the terms "he," "she," "it," or "they" to discuss that part. Given how easy it is to give a voice to a part of the self to move one part into ego cathexis and another into object cathexis, it is evident that the simple method of speaking to parts is a means to move energy from one part to another, and thereby rapidly access and modify internal dynamics.

TECHNICAL CHALLENGES
OF THE TREATMENT

Impermeability of Amnesic Barriers in DID

In severely dissociative individuals, the amnesic barriers between aspects of the self or personality states may be so impermeable as to render the Dissociative Table Technique less useful in the earlier phases of treatment. This occurs because the alter personalities are not capable of co-consciousness due to the psychodynamics that govern the self system. For example, if the self system of a client with DID is structured so as to accommodate two highly disparate belief systems, such as, "Daddy loves me" and "Daddy rapes me," then the parts of the self that function in each of those mutually exclusive realities cannot occupy consciousness at the same time without destabilization, inner conflict, and, for some clients, acting out. The impossible double bind was solved and continues to be solved by the structure of the self and its amnesic barriers, which precludes co-consciousness of these mutually exclusive parts.

For some clients with DID, a degree of co-consciousness may be possible using the dissociative table imagery, in which parts of the self are present at the table. EMDR undertaken too early, however, will only result in aborted processing and destabilization. This occurs when the parts of the self relevant to the material being processed "look through the eyes" of the conscious front part, bringing parts that were previously held out of awareness into consciousness and investing them with ego energy. In later processing this is desirable, but if it occurs too early the processing must necessarily get stuck or "loop" because the groundwork has not been conducted that would prepare the self system to manage the double-binding material. The two ends of the double bind cannot be tolerated in the conscious mind simultaneously due to long-held defenses and resistances that are rigidly entrenched.

In some DID cases, extensive groundwork, such as formal hypnotic induction or other accessing techniques (Fraser, 1993), is needed to bypass dissociative barriers prior to the introduction of EMDR. In others, the groundwork can be conducted using imagery or the Dissociative Table Technique without formal trance induction. At the same time, it must be remembered that highly dissociative individuals are heavily reliant on self-hypnotic methods to cope with daily life and to maintain their internal self structure. Therefore, practitioners using the Dissociative Table Technique as an imagery method and without formal trance induction should still have a working understanding of hypnotic phenomena and guidelines for the use of hypnosis. This, among other benefits, will ensure that the therapist is aware of the limitations of recall under hypnotic conditions—which means all dissociative conditions—and accordingly can adopt an appropriate therapeutic stance. Other dimensions of complexity that comprise the necessary groundwork are discussed below.

Intractable Illusions of Separateness

One of the dimensions that distinguishes severe DID from a milder form of dissociative disorder is the fixed illusion that clients with DID often have that parts of the self are actually separate people. In milder forms of dissociative conditions and even in clients without formal dissociative disorders, parts of the self may feel quite separate and may initially believe themselves to be in separate bodies. However, in with clients who do not have full DID this belief is more readily modifiable than in severe forms of DID.

In DID, the belief in separate bodies can be a serious obstacle to the therapeutic process because some parts of the self are not aware that they have an interest in the overall outcome of therapy. That is, since they believe themselves to occupy other bodies, they may say, "Who cares if s/he is suffering?" (or dies, and so on). Even in severe DID, however, this belief is modifiable in time. Progress can be made with parts of the self that are not the host personality by inviting each part to consider an experiment in which the alter "looks through the eyes" at the hand, clothes, and so on.

The therapist concretely walks the alter through the logic of "looking through the eyes that are in the head attached to the shoulders and body" and asks questions such as "Whose hand is that? Whose clothes are those?" Similar procedures have also been offered to orient the client to present time and identity (see, for example, Twombly, 2000).

Any such procedure can be quite confrontational, and the therapist is wise to back off quickly, saying, "Don't take my word for it, but just consider it this week. If I'm correct that you are in the same body, then it might have real implications for you, so I'm happy if you just consider the possibilities." The therapist then proceeds to concretely explain how the well-being and interests of one part of the self are tied to those of the others, and mediates and negotiates a solution. The therapist may offer to assist in meeting the needs or goals of the alter (within parameters of safety and appropriateness) if that alter agrees to accommodate the needs or safety of another part of the self, for an agreed upon period of time.

In short, the classic psychiatric assessment of orientation "times three" to person, place, and time must be assessed across the dissociative continuum. Where parts of self are found to be disordered to one of those elements, they should be oriented by use of methods that may be quite concrete and appropriate to the age of the part of self in question.

This step of inviting a part to "look through the eyes" adds ego energy or "I-ness" to it, so that it is fully present and executive in the client, instead of pushed away and dissociated. Because it previously may have been held only with object energy or "he/she/it-ness," it is now more fully owned by the self for having "looked through the eyes."

This procedure, which typically works well with less dissociative parts of the self, may require repetitions over time, especially with highly dissociative individuals. The host personality may persist in the illusion of separateness throughout much of the treatment. This can be framed to all parts of the self as the host doing his or her job of not knowing, and doing it well. The host's ability to not accept the reality of the trauma or the dissociation enables fractionated work (Fine, 1991, 1993) to occur behind the scenes in the mind's eye, using ego state therapy and the Dissociative Table. After the majority of a traumatic memory has been detoxified using EMDR, the host may then receive the information and process it to an adaptive resolution, with the intensity of the affect having been greatly diluted (Lazrove & Fine, 1996).

In the meantime, the therapist must often straddle the epistemological divide that is endemic to work with dissociative individuals. That is, just as the therapist must say, in regard to what happened with a specific trauma or perpetrator, "I don't know what happened, as I wasn't there, though I suspect *something* happened, as you're quite dissociative," so must the therapist also say, "If I'm right, that you are all parts of the same self and share the same body, then there are implications for what each part needs and wants." This posture enables the therapist to speak and work with all parts of the self, regardless of their particular beliefs, resolving internal conflicts and moving slowly toward integration.

The Volume of Unprocessed Traumatic Material

Another variable that adds to the complexity of DID cases is the very volume of unprocessed traumatic material. Historically, the field itself has been divided over the wisdom and necessity of processing through dissociated traumatic BASK elements. Ross (1997) considers abreaction to be a form of acting out, and no longer conducts abreactive procedures. Watkins takes the position that traumatic material must be energetically abreacted (Paulsen & Watkins, 2003b). Many maintain that sufficient ego strengthening needs to be conducted before attempting abreaction (see, for example, Phillips & Frederick, 1995), and this strategy is recommended in the ACT-AS-IF procedure, below.

The problem with the volume of unprocessed traumatic material relates to both flooding and "daisy-chaining" of traumatic memories. Flooding occurs when dissociative barriers come down prematurely, overwhelming the client with more BASK elements than there is ego strength to tolerate. Daisy-chaining of one traumatic memory to the next occurs when the barriers come down and allow flooding of associated memories, which may be related by perpetrator, type of trauma, age of trauma, or other variables. In order to reduce the probability of flooding with concomitant retraumatizing, it is often helpful to use a fractionation procedure (Fine, 1991) to moderate the intensity of affect. Premature accessing of traumatic material without an agreed upon plan with key aspects of the self system can set back therapy unnecessarily.

Attachment Issues Fracturing the Therapeutic Container

Many clients with DID exhibit profound attachment injuries, related to attachment failures in the earliest years of life (Siegel, 1999). These injuries often take the form of split object relationships, such as "bad mother/good mother" (Klein, 1975). As a result of having such primitive constructions and expectations for possible relationships and attachments, clients with severe DID often exhibit the same splitting mechanism projected into the relationship with their therapist and others in their lives. Indeed, Ross (1997) considers the terms "dissociation" and "splitting" to be synonyms. The part of the self that knows and expects the world to operate the way it did with the bad parent is often the part that is out of awareness to the part that managed to maintain an attachment, however dysfunctional, to the good parent, who was in fact the same person as the bad parent.

There may be more than one introjected parent alter personality corresponding to the good and the bad parent. Wild swings of mood or perspective and rapid switching between these frames of reference can seriously disrupt therapeutic progress. On the one hand, the client is warm and appreciative of the therapist's efforts and compassion and, on the other hand, suspects the therapist of treachery and even perpetration of the worst kind. Additionally, if there is a treatment team involved, the splitting is commonly manifested in the client's relationships with team members.

Therapists must finesse this splitting process by maintaining open communication with other members of the treatment team about the possibility of splitting. The therapist must also communicate with all parts of the client, not just the affable ones, as well as remaining aware of possible sources of distortion in clients accounts of their interactions with the therapist and with other members of the treatment team. The parts of the client's self that are vigilant to danger and perpetration can be mistrustful, hostile, even paranoid or violent. The need to address those hostile alters throughout treatment is key (Paulsen, 2004b; Putnam, 1989), and any therapist treating clients with severe DID will need appropriate boundaries regarding threats of harm from such clients (Ross, 1997).

Hostile alters can not only not be ignored (they won't go away), but they are also an important source of power to the client, whose host may manifest as weak, depleted, and overwhelmed. The therapist will need to engage hostile alters by acknowledging their importance and power, addressing and respecting any concerns they may have, reeducating hostile alters that hold cognitive distortions about separateness or the advisability of punishing or killing the self, and acknowledging their pain and the hardship of doing the difficult job of holding toxic energy, for example.

Because these alters appear to originate early, as evidenced by the developmental issues they revolve around—namely unresolved trust issues, infantile rage, and early narcissistic injuries—their logic can be primitive and their needs simple. In some cases, merely acknowledging their importance and power is enough. In others, acknowledging that they must be tired of defending and fighting all these years causes a shift in internal dynamics to a more vulnerable and cooperative affect for that alter. For some, appropriately meeting early unmet developmental needs for attachment and nurturing, via strengthening internal resources, will help. A stable therapeutic container will also help to remediate these attachment issues. However, for some clients this problem is slow to resolve and is one of the most difficult that the therapist will face in the therapy.

Irreconcilability of Double Binds

Ross (1997) has described common cognitive distortions that need to be corrected in clients with DID. In examining them, one can see that if pairs of them occurred together in the same client, they would create intolerable double binds of the kind that might be expected to produce dissociation in order to accommodate the two frames of reference. One observes that the structure of a highly dissociative client's self system often appears to have developed in order to contain two or more mutually incompatible experiences and frames of reference. Through state-dependent learning (learning that was acquired when the client was in a specific ego state and can only be recalled through that state), the client learns one repertoire of behaviors for one belief and frame of reference—or to deal with one parent or aspect of a parent—and other behaviors for another set of beliefs, frames of reference, or parts of a parent or perpetrator. Some examples of the cognitive pairs in double binds commonly found in clients with DID include Daddy loves me/Daddy hurts me; I'm a princess/I'm evil; I'm lovable/I'm loathsome;

I'm special/I don't deserve to live; I have no control or power/It's all my fault that the abuse happened.

Therapists who attempt to prematurely process a negative cognition that represents one end of a double bind in a client with DID will encounter a looping EMDR process. This is because the processing pulls in the other end of the double bind, bringing into conscious mind, perhaps without appropriate groundwork, a part of the self that is still invested in its own frame of reference. This can be useful in a less dissociative client, by inviting into simultaneous awareness the impossibility of the two ends of the dilemma. This may evoke insight and compassion through the processing that is enabled by the copresence and co-consciousness of the disparate frames of reference of the double bind.

In a highly dissociative client, however, the looping is not so easily resolved. The parts of the self involuntarily pulled in by the nature of EMDR processing may be ego invested in their own frame of reference and their separateness. Therefore, it is highly advisable that the groundwork be done ahead of time for clients with DID, with an informed consent to the processing by all parts of the self that are relevant to the issue being processed. This necessitates considerable knowledge of the structure and process of the self system on the part of the therapist prior to the first use of EMDR for trauma processing.

Self-Mutilation and Other Red Flags

There is another complicating factor in the treatment of DID that necessitates a slow and judicious use of EMDR. Many clients with DID engage in self-mutilation when they are in extreme emotional pain, which functions as a pressure-relief valve for many clients. Certainly, this function can eventually be replaced by a more appropriate way to release toxic affect and pain from unresolved trauma, such as EMDR, when the time is right and conditions are met. Premature EMDR, however, will only access the trauma but not permit the pain to be processed to an adaptive resolution, either because the mechanisms are not in place to titrate the affect through a fractionated approach, or because the parts of the self instrumental in the self-mutilation have not consented to do EMDR or do not understand it or their appropriate role in it.

Sometimes alters are aware of the EMDR and understand it, but do not agree to resolve the internal conflict lest their own power be diminished. At other times, alters may doggedly adhere to the notion that they or another part of the self deserve punishment, including death. Encountering such beliefs for the first time in a client with a history of self-mutilation or other signs of brittleness and extreme pathology is not a productive therapeutic pathway for client or therapist. It is far better to have spent the necessary time on containment and stabilization, exploring the self system and obtaining consent to proceed, negotiating the client's internal power dynamics, and strengthening the ego prior to conducting an EMDR session for processing trauma.

As put forward by the Dissociative Disorders Task Force in appendix B to Francine Shapiro's seminal book *Eye Movement Desensitization and Reprocessing* in both its editions (1995, 2001), other red flags contraindicating proceeding with EMDR without appropriate precautions and procedures in place (in addition to ongoing self-mutilation) include active suicidal or homicidal intent; uncontrolled flashbacks; rapid switching from one ego state or alter to another; extreme age or physical frailty; terminal illness; a need for concurrent adjustment of medication; ongoing abusive relationships; alter personalities that are strongly opposed to abreaction; extreme character pathology—especially a severe narcissistic, sociopathic, or borderline disorder—and serious dual diagnoses, such as schizophrenia or active substance abuse.

The task force advised that the following be in place prior to proceeding with EMDR for trauma processing when a dissociative disorder is present: good affect tolerance, a stable life environment, willingness to undergo temporary discomfort for long-term relief, good ego strength, adequate social support and other resources, and history of treatment compliance (Shapiro, 1995). The remainder of this chapter will outline a phased approach to treatment that will help ensure that those positive criteria are met.

A Phased Approach to Treatment

Since Janet, treatment of dissociative conditions has taken a phased approach (van der Kolk & van der Hart, 1989). More recently, contributors have offered other phasic approaches, including Putnam (1989), Kluft (1993a), and Phillips and Frederick (1995). These phased approaches all generally enrich and guide the therapeutic approach. Putnam's, Kluft's, and Phillips and Fredericks's approaches put special emphasis on the importance of early phases to enable containment and stabilization. Kluft has made two key observations that are especially instructive, namely, that the early stabilization emphasis will effectively "bore the client into health" (1993b, p. 96) and "the slower you go, the faster you get there" (1993a, p. 146).

In addition to these valuable phasic approaches, the EMDR clinician will also benefit from a detailed definition that enables explication of the phases of treatment from the viewpoint of the therapist. The emphasis here will be on (1) identifying the prerequisites to EMDR processing per se, and (2) clarifying points in the process of treatment where bilateral stimulation (not simply the standard EMDR trauma protocol) may be of value for some clients. The next sections describe two approaches developed by the author to meet those goals.

The ACT-AS-IF Approach

The ACT-AS-IF approach (Paulsen, 2006a) is a template for preparing clients with DID for EMDR and ego state therapy and supporting them throughout the treatment. The acronym stands for the phases of Assessment, Containment, Trauma accessing and preparation, Abreaction of trauma, Skills building, Integration, and Future templates.

The name "ACT-AS-IF" reflects the actual manifestation of DID and its treatment for three reasons: (1) the client with DID learned to act as if the abuse weren't happening, or were happening to someone else; (2) the therapist treating a client with DID necessarily acts at times as if the client were several people, but never loses sight of the fact that the client is actually one person; and (3) the therapist guides and bolsters the client's hope and expectation and acts as if healing and wholeness is possible, which it is.

Assessment

The initial phase of treatment includes assessment of a number of dimensions. First and foremost is the differential diagnosis of DID versus another dissociative disorder or no dissociative disorder using a standardized tool or appropriate clinical interview as described above. Some practitioners may use a formal assessment battery, but there are no norms for highly dissociative individuals for many instruments. Some tools have been specifically developed for assessment of dissociative disorders The most commonly used screening instrument is the Dissociative Experiences Scale (DES; Bernstein & Putnam, 1989). Others include the Dissociative Disorders Interview Schedule (DDIS; Ross et al., 1989), the Structured Clinical Interview for DSM–IV Dissociative Disorders (SCID-D; Steinberg, 1994), the Somatoform Dissociation Questionnaire (SDQ-20; Nijenhuis, Spinhoven, Van Dyck, van der Hart, & Vanderlinden, 1996), and, more recently, the Multidimensional Inventory of Dissociation (MID; Dell, 2001).

Additionally, clinical assessment of other parameters will determine the degree of stability the client exhibits and therefore the speed at which treatment can proceed. The less stable the client, the greater the precautions before and during the introduction of bilateral stimulation to the treatment. Examples of these other parameters that should be assessed include the degree of rapport between client and therapist;

the client's understanding of and ability to abide by the terms of treatment and boundaries; and the accessibility of the client's self system versus an unwillingness or inability on the client's part to permit therapist access to the self system. Other dimensions to assess include the presence of dual diagnoses, such as borderline personality disorder with concomitant red flags such as self-mutilation or splitting and active substance abuse and the need for detoxification and treatment. It is also important to determine, over the course of early treatment, the client's degree of inner dividedness and conflict, permeability of dissociative barriers, readiness and ability to engage in system mapping, and containment skills. The therapist should also assess the client's ability to respond to education and skills building regarding containment; to exhibit control over and delay switching; to stay present during the therapist's description of the approach to treatment; to collaborate with and consent to proceed with the treatment plan that the therapist describes; to commit to a healing journey; and to form an attachment to the therapist. Most clients with DID will have problems with at least some of these issues; the more severe these features are, the longer it will take to conduct the stabilization and preparation phases necessary before detoxifying traumatic memories.

In this phase of treatment, ego state therapy is relevant and useful for determining all of the above, but bilateral stimulation has little or no place in the early phase of treatment. One possible exception is to help stabilize the client in a flashback by very brief and very tentative use of a few short sets of bilateral stimulation to take the edge off of a flashback and ground the client in present time long enough to conduct a standard containment procedure. In sum, the assessment of all of these dimensions begins with the initial session and continues through the containment and stabilization phases and beyond.

Containment

The containment phase of treatment actually begins during the assessment phase, in the sense that the therapeutic relationship itself is the containment structure that will hold the client safely throughout treatment. More broadly stated, the purpose of the containment phase is to establish the client's affect-regulation skills and create and enhance stability. These skills include the ability to ground; to use mindfulness or an observing ego to "just notice" what is happening in the internal world; to name, access, and establish distance from emotions; and more.

Containment must be formally addressed early in treatment because the therapist may need to access the self system of the client in order to determine the answers to some of the questions described above (although accessing the self system of the client should be delayed in the event that it would be destabilizing). Anytime the therapist accesses the self system of the client, there must, for safety reasons, be time reserved at the end of each session to conduct a containment procedure to ensure that the client leaves in a safe and contained state and is able to drive home and function outside of the therapy office. There are many possible methods of stabilization available (Paulsen & Golston, 2005), a few of which will be mentioned here.

For some clients, the containment phase of therapy begins with addressing external safety issues. For many, early emphasis in this phase is on teaching grounding techniques, enabling the client to be in the present by tuning into one or more of the five senses. For others, the phase begins by establishing and strengthening an inner safe state using imagery and, for some clients only, limited bilateral stimulation (BLS) to anchor and vivify the experience of a safe place (Shapiro, 1995). Korn and Leeds (2002) describe a resource development procedure for stabilization purposes that employs BLS. Phillips (2000) describe the use of a conflict-free state to enhance the client's internal resources and ego strength. For some individuals, it is possible to use not only imagery but also BLS to provide the experience of positive resources.

With severe DID, attempts to supply these milestones may trip double binds and related negative cognitions, so any such efforts must be slow, careful, and tentative. For some individuals with DID, imagery without BLS may work best. For others, mediation with parts of the self that interfere with the provision of positive resources may be successful once their concerns are addressed through discussion or meeting their needs.

The containment phase of treatment may involve a range of other functions, including beginning to establish positive expectations of healing and wholeness, which will itself offer containment and reassurance; planning and visualizing a healing pathway that traverses the phases of treatment described here, which will offer structure and thereby containment; and resource building and ego strengthening by imaginal provision of a wide range of positive resources, strengths, and coping abilities, which will also provide containment and enhance stabilization.

During this phase, it may be necessary to conduct crisis management for internal or external issues. The success of these interventions will often pivot on the client's ability to allow access to the self system to intervene in internal dynamics, and follow up with closure and containment between sessions. Containment is greatly enhanced by establishing self-soothing abilities through imagery, practiced repeatedly for a conditioned response and strengthened as appropriate for a given client, with cautious use of BLS.

The most challenging of all of the above is to attempt to offer containment via attachment imagery with images and language to encourage internal nurturing. For many clients with DID, this will not be possible until much later in treatment. Others will have access to resources such as their spiritual feelings of being loved by God or a healing white light, if nothing else, from which they will receive comfort, nurturance, and, therefore, a measure of containment.

Ego state therapy is relevant during the containment phase because resourceful ego states may be strengthened or mobilized to assist depleted states. Tentatively, BLS for some clients will help strengthen and install positive imagery and expectancy with brief, short sets. For any client with DID for whom BLS is destabilizing, therapists should not pursue BLS until greater stabilization and containment are achieved.

A most critical skill to establish during this phase is the ability, on cue from the therapist, to successfully contain or "tuck in" both the aspects of the self and BASK material that have been accessed during the session (Paulsen & Golston, 2005). This conditioned response is developed through repetition of key phrases and imagery such as the following (note that there are many ways to accomplish this containment and closure; this is my own preferred language and methodology):

- "I'd like to thank all the parts of the self that helped today. Does any part need to say anything before we tuck them in?" (Reassurance is offered as needed.)
- "There's your fluffy white cloud waiting for you to climb on board, and we'll tuck you in with cloud blankets and fluff up your cloud pillows, and I'll say good-bye as the clouds pull away and take you deeper and deeper for a deep healing sleep."

This process won't work initially for some clients with DID without education and mediation among conflicted parts to concretely demonstrate that it is in their interest to allow this rhythm of therapy to develop.

Imagery for containing material may include vaults, jars, boxes, bookshelves, heavy curtains, and so on. Imagery for tucking in parts may include comfortable and nurturing resources, such as protection from Mother Mary, an angel or any other religious icon or image (as appropriate), a rocking chair, or a teddy bear (especially helpful for child parts of the self). The rationale here is that traumatic material is often contained in child parts of the self with primitive rationale, little insight, and massive attachment injuries and need for nurturance. Responding to unmet developmental needs for structure and nurturing, as a regular part of therapy that is limited and not all-consuming, can reduce terror, strengthen ego boundaries, and overall reinforce positive internal resources and render them more available.

Kluft (1993a) has described a number of hypnotic "temporizing techniques" that "interrupt processes that would or could prove overwhelming, and 'buy time' for the client and the treatment" (p. 157). These include alter substitution (relief for depleted alters), the provision of sanctuary (creation of safe places), distancing maneuvers (for example, permissive amnesia and screen techniques), bypassing time (time distortion and therapeutic sleep), bypassing affect (such as containing difficult affect in a vault), reconfiguration (bartering with dysfunctional alters for more time in treatment or in control), and attenuation of affect (fractionated abreaction), which will be described below.

An additional series of beneficial techniques for containment and stabilization is drawn from the armamentarium of somatic psychotherapy methods (Levine, 1997; Paulsen, 2006b; Paulsen & Stanley, 2005). These must be approached slowly and cautiously, as most clients with DID will be unable to attend directly to bodily sensations since somatic dissociation is a hallmark of dissociative conditions. However, with the support of the therapist and attention to providing the client with resources, carefully paced somatic procedures can be helpful. For example, tracking body sensations and internal experience in present time is an important element that establishes both grounding and mindfulness. Titrating affect by moving back and forth gently and in a paced way between discomfort and comfort begins to strengthen the client, and may even begin to transform disturbing material without the intensity of abreaction. The therapist can also invite micromovements, in which the client expresses thwarted fight or flight responses very slowly. This is hypothesized to release pent-up sympathetic arousal, and to begin initial steps toward catalyzing the body's innate tendency toward internal coherency. When introduced with caution and paced gently, these approaches can be beneficial for some but not all clients with DID.

Many clients with DID will not begin to achieve containment and stabilization until their internal dynamics have begun to shift, especially with regard to introjected perpetrators. This process may be begun in this phase and expanded in subsequent phases.

Trauma Accessing and Preparation

Using EMDR to detoxify traumatic memories can only be considered when (1) the client has exhibited both containment and stabilization and the prerequisite set of affect-regulation skills, and (2) the self system and the highlights of the trauma history—rather than the details, which could cause destabilization if recalled too soon—are reasonably well known to the therapist. In preparing for EMDR, this present phase—including the accessing of internal dynamics and traumatic memories but not the abre-active metabolizing of them—may take from months to years for clients with DID. Most importantly, a critical mass of the client's self system must be willing and able to do trauma work and reliably take the cue to begin the process of "tucking in" or containing the issues worked on during the session, as described above. If this is not achieved in advance through ego state work, and if EMDR is prematurely utilized, adverse outcomes may occur. These may include that (1) unengaged aspects of the self will resist the associative process of EMDR; (2) processing may proceed but begin to loop, outside of the client's awareness and without the therapist having sufficient information to resolve the looping; or (3) the parts of the self will resist containment and the session will end with unacceptably high levels of client arousal. Any of these outcomes is retraumatizing to both client and therapist, and destructive to treatment progress and rapport.

Another prerequisite for proceeding to detoxify trauma is to ensure that the client will reliably allow access to the internal system and work through internal conflicts to some degree, via the Dissociative Table or other accessing method. If this capacity is not in place, the EMDR will loop and the client will likely not permit the therapist the access to the system needed to resolve the looping.

Ideally, the client permits access such that relevant parts of the self system participate in the planning and preparation for trauma work. The copresence of parts of the self around the table means that greater insight is possible for the client, and there is, at least during those moments around the table "in the mind's eye," more integration than if a single alter were present. Those parts may be in a position to contribute information, cautions, perspectives, and history about the functions and dynamics of the material being planned, including cognitive distortions.

By making use of copresence without bringing the material fully into conscious awareness, the trauma work can be planned without prematurely triggering an abreaction. For some clients, this method won't work because turning the client's attention to the traumatic material may cause a full switch and bring the child alters that contain the unprocessed traumatic material into full consciousness, causing them to "look through the eyes," or become prematurely egotized. When this happens, the material can be contained using the conditioned response for containment described earlier, or, for a few clients, a very few BLS sets may take the edge off the abreaction, and then containment procedures may be employed. Assuming the use of copresence can be employed successfully using the dissociative table, the relevant parts of the self work collaboratively with the therapist to enable a planned approach to trauma processing.

Kluft (1990a) described the attenuation of affect, also called "fractionated abreaction" (Fine, 1991), which involves the deliberate or planned interruption of abreactive events after a small amount of affect has been expressed. Before proceeding to release more affect, the therapist and client must process that initial material. See the tactical integrationist approach (Fine, 1999) for another method for managing the pace of the work.

There are diverse options for managing a fractionated abreactive session, including the following:

- Double distancing: Clients sees themselves or someone just like themselves on a screen, going through the processing.
- Envisioning a library with volumes of books, each of which holds a story from the client's life and can be read once the client is ready (Kluft, 1990a).
- Examining information about a trauma while setting aside the affect temporarily in an imaginal container.
- The slow leak technique: Information emerges only at a rate that is palatable to the client (Kluft, 1990b).

The therapist and client should choose together the memory or small portion of a memory that is to be worked on, the method of fractionation that will be used, which alter will be the "star" of the abreactive work, and which alters will stand by as positive resources.

Note that fractionated abreaction should be embedded within the overall context of a collaborative approach to treatment that uses planning and skills building to enhance both the client's sense of mastery and ego strength. As a result, when it comes time to actually process the trauma through an abreactive procedure such as EMDR, the client will experience it with a sense of self-efficacy, as a process through which client cannot only survive but triumph. Indeed, this pathway to healing and wholeness, or metacognition, can itself be installed using BLS or the conference room imagery. A client equipped with coping imagery, self-soothing skills, a collaborative relationship, and an understanding of trauma work as a process that can be controlled will be in good shape to begin the most difficult work of treatment. With this phase in place, the client and therapist are ready to proceed to use EMDR.

Abreactive Synthesis

The term "abreaction" can refer to both spontaneously emerging traumatic material (such as a flashback) and deliberately working through dissociated BASK elements of a dissociated memory so that it is synthesized.

The latter use of the term is intended here (Paulsen & Watkins, 2003a, 2003b; Watkins & Paulsen, 2004).

Clinicians have used EMDR to process traumatic memories to an adaptive resolution in a planned way since 1989. For clients with DID, as previously described, the procedure is more complex, not only during the planning previously described, but during the actual EMDR processing of trauma. The more time spent on prior steps, the easier the abreactive phase will be.

In the abreactive phase of the work, the standard EMDR protocol (Shapiro, 1995) is modified for the purposes of working with a dissociative self system (Lazrove & Fine, 1996; Paulsen, 1995). For the most part, this involves conducting BLS on the fractionated piece of a previously planned traumatic memory, as described in the prior phase. The fractionated abreaction enables the therapist to divide the work into manageable pieces that both fit into the available session time and titrate the affect so the work is not overwhelming and is approachable for the client, giving the client a sense of mastery and partial relief. The abreaction procedure is described in more depth under the heading ARCHITECTS, below. First, however, I will generally describe the abreactive and subsequent phases of therapy.

It is characteristic of trauma processing in clients with DID that the therapist is always in a double bind with them just as they are always in double binds themselves. If an alliance is formed with one part of the self, another may feel alienated. The artistry is in honoring all the parts of the self, as all are there for some good reason that can be understood. In the understanding of the totality comes the resolution of the binds. In the case of trauma processing, the bind is that although the best processing is planned and fractionated, even the most extensive planning will fall short and the processing will likely take sudden and unexpected turns. Those surprises can take several forms: other alters are involved than those initially expected; the trauma being addressed is one of many or earlier ones that are triggered by the processing; the client's consent is not what was apparently agreed to in preparation for the trauma processing; or the processing loops and no alter will manifest to explain or take responsibility for the looping until there is little time left in the session. In each situation, the therapist must rely on clinical judgment, in collaboration with the client, to determine what and when to process and what and when to contain.

Typically, relevant alters will assemble in the conference room in the mind's eye, while the "star" of that piece of the work "looks through the eyes" during the processing. It may be necessary to use other devices to manage the work with appropriate containment in addition to what has been planned in advance (Paulsen, 1995). For example, overwhelmed observers can either be "tucked in" or sent off on a "fluffy white cloud," or asked to wait in an adjacent room equipped with speakers so they can hear what is going on while maintaining enough distance. Any numbers of devices can be added to secure sufficient emotional distancing to maintain the optimal level of arousal somewhere between dissociation or numbness and being overwhelmed. One alter may wish for a control panel, a Plexiglas window, or a space suit and stun gun for safety, while another may prefer a screen and a microphone, which would guarantee distance, strength, or power. An alter that falters during the processing may benefit from reconfiguring (Kluft, 1993a) the alter system by bringing one or more alters with positive resources close by to give strength to the depleted alter.

Any unforeseen switches should remind the therapist to check to see if the present alter is known to the therapist and vice versa, aware of the EMDR processing, and consenting to proceed. If permission is not present, processing should stop and a careful closure and containment procedure should be conducted. In that event, a metacognition to shape client expectancies can be installed with a few brief sets of BLS, if appropriate. One such metacognition might be of having taken one step today down a path toward healing and wholeness, with appreciation expressed among participating alters, as well as those waiting quietly for their turn.

"Containment" and "safe closure" are the watchwords here. The therapist can also make suggestions during the closure procedure that the remaining material can stay in the vault or, alternatively, be examined in a neutral way, with complete peace, safety, and relaxation (Kluft, 1990a).

Skills Building

Like the containment phase, the skills-building phase of treatment is not a discrete phase, but an iterative one. As reliance on dissociation decreases, it is important to enrich the client's armamentarium of skills. BLS can be especially valuable to accomplish this goal.

In concrete terms that the client's alter system can relate to successfully, this often involves finding the older or more cognitively oriented alters and asking them to step into slightly different roles or "job descriptions" that will be better than the ones they've been doing all these years. Alters typically express reservations, especially about losing power in the case of protector alters, or not being up to the task, in the case of child alters or parental introject-based alters, among others. The therapist's role is to provide reassurance that the therapist will assist the alter in learning the skills needed for the new role; the alter simply needs to be willing to learn (Paulsen, 2004b).

Whatever the skill is, the therapist needs to have sufficient understanding of its environmental triggers, cognitive and behavioral components, and likely consequences in order to break it down into manageable pieces. BLS can be used for some clients with DID to install and vivify components of skills and explore what it would be like to use those skills in place of dissociation. This may involve installation of alternative ways of coping so the client has a menu from which to choose, employing newfound ego strength and positive resources that can also be strengthened using BLS. The therapist helps the client or relevant alters acquire specific language and physical movements, such as those involved in speaking, assertion, conflict resolution, care taking, limit setting, and self-protection, as needed for adaptive growth. BLS can also be used to install metacognitions about how it will feel to live life with the new options and skills in place.

Integration

Again, this phase doesn't stand alone discretely, but rather continues throughout treatment, culminating, for some, in complete integration, with or without an integration ritual to take down walls that are no longer needed.

From the first use of the Dissociative Table Technique, the client takes small steps toward integration through experiencing a degree of facilitated copresence. That is, because the client sees multiple parts of the self in the conference room, there is more integration than when only a single alter is present or when a single alter is audible to another alter or the host. Their copresence is an incremental step in the direction of integration. As internal cooperation and communication emerge gradually throughout subsequent steps, greater levels of integration are achieved. For many clients, amnesic barriers eventually spontaneously disintegrate over the course of treatment. This can be understood as the natural result of an associative process.

It is critical that dissociative barriers come down when the time is right and not before. It has been recommended (Fine, 1991) the host's amnesia be maintained throughout the trauma work phase for some clients. This enables the host to continue doing its job of not knowing and being in charge of life. Behind the scenes, the alters and therapist are engaged in the arduous work of detoxifying trauma, synthesizing the results, and achieving understanding.

The addition of BLS tends to markedly contribute to the spontaneous removal of dissociative barriers. In clients with DID without red flags contraindicating early use of BLS, slow, brief sets can contribute early and throughout treatment to integrative processes such as increasing inner cooperation, mediating conflicts between alters, and increased compassion and insight.

For some clients, brief integration rituals that include BLS can be powerful additions to treatment. For example, alters may join hands, or dance together, saying, "We are one, we are I." (See Kluft, 1990c and 1990d, for other rituals that can be modified as needed for the specific client's needs, and to which BLS can be beneficially added.)

Future Templates and Follow-Up

As treatment draws to a successful close, the client who is now free of DID needs to prepare for a future life without dissociation and without regular access to the therapist, frequent appointments, or follow-up. This phase may begin with the client glancing backward, reviewing the high points and milestones of the therapeutic work from the beginning, as if the whole journey and process were a travelogue. This enables the client to fully appreciate how much has been accomplished and how many therapy miles have been traveled.

It is also beneficial to review the client's life history in totality, now that key traumas have been detoxified, so that further synthesis and meaning can occur. The standard protocol can be adapted to enhance this synthesis through associative learning.

Another step may involve glancing forward, so that the client can envision what life will mean and what it will be like now that treatment has ended and the client's life has been reclaimed, free of dissociation. One way to accomplish this is to invite imagery about what the client would like a life scrapbook to include at the end of the client's life, years from now. It would include, sadly, the pain and chaos of trauma, its resolution through treatment, and whatever other goals the client has set for the future. EMDR's performance-enhancement protocol is beneficial for this purpose. The therapist may invite a values review of work, family, creativity, physicality, spirituality, health, friends, community, service, education, happiness, avocations, and so forth. This process may include homework assignments as the client thinks through these various areas of life and returns to therapy to install vivid, realistic goals for life using BLS. Metacognitions and insights can be strengthened with BLS, as can the client's acceptance and resolution of the personal life journey.

Once the big-picture values are clarified and goals set, the steps and projects that comprise the direction the client will take independently, or with less frequent therapist contact, can be vivified and installed. This future-visioning approach has been described elsewhere (Paulsen Inobe, 2000) and is derived from the performance-enhancement approach

(Foster & Lendl, 1996) to future templates, originated for athletes and executives, and modified here for use with dissociative clients.

ARCHITECTS: A PROCESS FOR ABREACTIONS

Because working through the unresolved traumatic material is the core of the treatment, the abreactive synthesis that is the crux of EMDR trauma processing deserves a closer look. I have developed an approach called ARCHITECTS to guide therapists through an abreactive session, closely following the eight phases of Shapiro's EMDR protocol but adapting it for dissociative clients. This process is based on the fractionated abreaction approach (Lazrove & Fine, 1996) and the tactical integrationist approach (Fine, 1999). It is also consistent with the wreathing protocol offered for a similar purpose (Fine & Berkowitz, 2001), though it was developed independently from it.

The acronym "ARCHITECTS" is offered as a mnemonic tool in the therapist's armamentarium; it also serves to remind the therapist that each abreaction should be mindfully planned to move toward positive results. Architects have blueprints, not impulses. Overall, the process can be understood as titrating affect, variously accelerating or decelerating as the situation calls for. This is not required for individuals without DID, but it is necessary for the client with DID.

The ARCHITECTS approach consists of the following nine steps: Access, Refine, Consent, Hypnosis or Imagery, Titrate, EMDR/BLS, Closure, Technological Tranquility, and Stabilize, Synthesize, and Soothe.

Access: Access the client's self system using the dissociative table, if tolerated, or according to how the system presents to the therapist. As a heuristic, if a client with DID can only switch alters and cannot talk through or use the dissociative table, the use of EMDR will be more tenuous than if there is enough integration to tolerate talking through.

Refine: The target was selected in an earlier session. However, the therapist will refine this preselected target according to what presents in the dynamics of the conference room. The best plans may be set aside according to shifting system dynamics; in short, the material may select the therapist. The therapist is still better off having planned than to skip planning, even if the plans are replaced by something different.

Consent: The therapist should obtain final consent to go ahead from a sufficiency of the self system and reaffirm supportive roles for other alters. In an effort to keep the entire self safe and relatively comfortable, the therapist will remind the parts of the self that are to engage in processing that closure and containment will be necessary on their part whether the processing is finished or not. That way, when the time runs out and the SUD is not 0, the client will not be surprised to have to close down the session anyway.

_H_ypnosis or _I_magery: The therapist will use either formal hypnotic trance or imagery such as the dissociative table to supply any needed resources, ego strengthening, or affect titration. These fractionation methods typically include an intensity control knob, a vault, a Plexiglas wall, a waiting room, a rocking chair, and so on. The therapist and client are limited only by their imaginations in supplying the resources that will enable the processing to stay on track and the affect to remain within tolerable limits. Setting up the parts of the system for their roles in the processing will be determined by the history and preferences of both client and therapist. It is especially beneficial to invite the front part of the self, which manages daily life, to not be present for the processing, with the agreement that that part can return at the end of the session (Fine, 1999).

_T_itrate: The therapist accesses the traumatized neural network by asking for the relevant alter and evoking the memory of the traumatic event. That is, we make sure the salient part is egotized, or "looking through the eyes." It is necessary to keep the client in dual attention awareness, as is required by the standard EMDR protocol. It is key to keep an optimal arousal level between overarousal (indicated by flashback) and numbness. With this population, immersion in flashbacks is always a hazard. The therapist's prior months of grounding and orienting the client to the body the client lives in, and the place and time in which the client lives, will pay off here.

_E_MDR/BLS: The therapist will initiate BLS as usual. However, the therapist may wish to maintain a higher level of patter during the EMDR processing, such as uttering continuously, "That's it...I'm here...I'm right here with you....This time you're not alone....That's right...it's old stuff" to help maintain that dual attention awareness.

With a client with DID, processing is not likely to be smooth sailing, and the therapist will need to engage in problem solving as needed via titrating affect, stopping and negotiating with emerging alters, mediating internal dynamics if needed, and offering reframes appropriate to the ages of the different parts of the self. Because BLS is an associative process, and because dissociation is the paramount feature of the self system of the client with DID, unexpected material will emerge in this step, and is to be expected. Parts of the self may emerge that the therapist has never met before, that were pulled up by the process. If this occurs, the therapist should introduce himself or herself and ask if the client knows what they are doing and if it is okay to continue. If not, the session should be closed down. If so, the processing can continue. By definition, doing a fraction of a trauma means that it will not be finished completely in a single session. Clinical judgment should be used in collaboration with the client's stated preferences regarding when to stop. In the fractionated abreaction model, both therapist and client expect processing to be partial.

Closure: The therapist should be sure to stop appropriately, whether the processing gets to a resolution or not, leaving enough time in the session to close, ground, and reorient the client for travel. It is beneficial to close in two steps (Paulsen & Golston, 2005). First, the BASK material needs to be contained. A therapist might contain residual unprocessed BASK elements using imagery such as boxes, jars, or Tupperware. The container can be put in a vault and sent down an elevator behind a heavy velvet curtain, for example.

Second, the ego states must be contained. The therapist should soothe and contain participating alters, providing the resources they need via imagery and preestablished conditioned-response language to close the session. It is helpful to close the self system using classically conditioned imagery, such as tucking the alters into their safe place or having them go off on a fluffy white cloud. It is critical to return the front part of the self to the executive role for the drive home, both for safety and to ensure continued cooperation of the front.

It is important—and it will have been well established by the prior months of treatment—that the front part of the self be allowed to not know the memory until later, after it has been detoxified. The others may need to be reminded of this arrangement, in concrete terms of how it will benefit them. It is critical that both the front part of the self and the parts behind the amnesia barrier understand and accept that now is not the time to bring the front part into awareness of the traumatic material. The key to maintaining stability during the detoxification of trauma with EMDR is that the front part continue "doing life" and "being the face that meets the faces" (Paulsen, 2004a, 2004b), interacting with real people in the real world.

Technological Tranquility: The therapist should make sure that the client agrees to contain or soothe any emergent between-session residual processing via a method such as a telephone call, relaxation tape, butterfly hugs, or other well-rehearsed self-soothing procedures, as has been previously established in the client's treatment history and by office policy regarding emergencies. It is not unusual for there to be discomfort following an EMDR session, at the same time as there is relief. The front part of the self should be allowed to not know about the memories that are being processed.

Stabilize, Synthesize, and Soothe: Based on the client's state at the next visit, the therapist will emphasize synthesizing or consolidate gains via talking, imagery, or BLS. If the client feels raw, soothing and restabilizing procedures are called for rather than additional EMDR. EMDR should be continued on the next piece in the fractionated abreaction sequence only if the client is sufficiently stable. It is critical to pace the work to prevent the client from becoming overwhelmed and destabilized. It can take weeks for key memories to be synthesized. Much of the synthesis happens on a deep level, outside of conscious awareness. Associative linkages will continue to occur in waking and dream states, and many alters will have something to say about the changes and realizations. Whereas a client without DID could conduct this effort with the help of EMDR, a client with DID may not be able to tolerate more EMDR right away. The therapist should moderate the pace of the work according to cautious clinical judgment and client capacity.

CASE STUDIES

The following cases are selected to illustrate the wide variance in deciding how to use EMDR and whether it should be employed with dissociative clients, depending upon the presence or absence of key indicators described earlier. Treatment is brief for some and long and complex for others; therefore many of the details of the course of treatment are excluded for the sake of brevity. All names are fictitious and all identifying information has been altered.

Shelley: DID with No Red Flags

Shelley is a twenty-two-year-old White female referred to me by her friend following an acquaintance rape that occurred after college graduation. She was the only child of a wealthy family and lived alone in an apartment. Because of her severe PTSD symptoms, her ability to get and retain her first real job was in jeopardy. Her DES score was 32 out of a possible 100. On direct inquiry, Shelley reported depersonalization and derealization, which had been an issue intermittently throughout her life, but were highly present since the rape. Also since the rape, she had an onset of severe nightmares, flashbacks, and headaches. In an effort to self-medicate, she had increased her alcohol consumption but then decreased it once she was educated about its depressive effects. She reported commonly feeling as if she were watching herself and was losing time, up to a few hours at a time. Loss of time had not been present, by self-report, prior to the rape, although she believes it may have been present much earlier in life. Shelley reported having the impression that there may have been a history of child sexual abuse by an uncle who was responsible for baby-sitting her frequently during the day for several years.

In her second visit, Shelley readily agreed to use the dissociative table to contact several parts of herself, which she called Anger, Sadness, Shame, and Fear. Each part claimed to take executive control of her body during episodes of her amnesia, with Shame and Sadness only taking a few minutes and Anger taking the most control—a few hours by Shelley's estimates. Anger was the most invested in her separateness, but not nearly as much as in some cases of DID. Indeed, each part readily allowed contact and rapport, and responded appropriately to education. For example, the parts initially did not know they were in the same body, but upon brief reflection, they agreed to take an experimental approach to the therapist's "hypothesis" that they were one person, and moved relatively rapidly to accepting that information and its implications as true.

Additionally, each part appreciated the therapist's empathic listening and offer to assist them in meeting their needs. Inner conflict was present but was very workable and amenable to mediation using ego state therapy. For example, Anger was initially impatient with Shame and Fear, as they were viewed as too weak and "wimpy." Anger agreed to assist the therapist in helping Shame and Fear resolve their unresolved stores of traumatic memories, so that they might be more empowered as Anger wished them to be. There were no red flags contraindicating proceeding with EMDR once Shelley reduced her alcohol consumption to social levels.

The standard EMDR preparation was conducted with a fractionated abreaction variation. Each alter targeted the recent rape incident. The therapist explained to the entire self that the rape incident likely had stirred up ancient similar feelings from early life experiences, and each part readily agreed. Shelley's ego states and, with a little education, host as well agreed that it was in her collective best interests if she also addressed the parts' concerns, amnesia, and memories of childhood sexual abuse. It was understood ahead of time that if the rape material and its associations did not fit into the processing time allowed, it would be necessary to contain and soothe the residual material for processing to completion at a later time.

As planned, each part of the self was the "star" of one or more EMDR processing sessions, with the remainder being contained each time. Targets of sessions, over about twelve weeks time, were molestation incidents in childhood seen through the eyes of the ego states—Anger first, then Fear, Sadness, and Shame for separate targets of molestation itself—and then Shelley's parents' nonresponsiveness when she asked for help and to be believed.

For each session, closure was achieved using containment imagery in two phases: first, closure of residual BASK elements by containing them in Tupperware until the client heard the airtight lid snap closed, and second, closure of the self system by tucking in the parts of the self to their usual safe places, unless Anger needed to stay near the surface for vigilance and safety on the ride home. Closure also included metacognitive installation with brief BLS in which the day's work was framed as having planted seeds of progress, or taken additional steps down a healing pathway.

Processing tended not to result in disorganization or regression, and over the course of treatment Shelley reported a continual decrease in symptoms, except for one occasion when she felt raw. A deep-healing intervention using imagery was conducted to address this slight regression. The EMDR sequence resulted in immediate cessation of nightmares and flashbacks. There were no crisis calls between sessions, and on follow-up, each remaining part had understood and complied with the request to contain its piece of the material between sessions.

The host did not resist any of these tactics, with the exception that Shelley sometimes required a considerable portion of the double session to chat about current life issues surrounding family, a boyfriend, or job interviews. Inasmuch as the host's role was to "do life," these issues were treated as legitimate therapeutic content for problem solving and cognitive-behavioral interventions. The parts containing traumatic material waited, usually patiently, for their turn. Occasionally Anger would express indignation about the host using up too much therapy time, and then the host would accommodate the parts' needs, with a little prompting from the therapist.

During rape processing, aspects of memories of childhood trauma came to mind. Those were consistent with the emotional theme of the material and the function of the part of the self "looking through the eyes" (present) during the processing.

The treatment consisted of fifteen double sessions over four months. Shelley appeared to achieve mastery of developmental milestones, including having an adult perspective on her early molestation experiences. Significantly, she chose to write a magazine article about her rape experience and reported achieving additional mastery in so doing. She began to have better judgment in her selection of male companions. In the last two weeks of treatment, the ego states spontaneously resolved, reporting that they no longer needed to be separate. Shelley terminated treatment upon relocating to Dallas as part of the job she acquired during treatment. On six-months follow-up, her gains are continuing, with no setbacks or uses of dissociation. Shelley is currently in a relationship with a boyfriend—a relationship that she describes as serious and healthy, the first of its kind in her life.

This case represents an ideal and optimal EMDR treatment outcome for a highly dissociative client. It illustrates how rapidly even significant

PTSD and dissociative symptomatology can be resolved with EMDR and ego state therapy. Although the client originally was just over the line into DID, amnesia was present as were different modes of operating, although with little investment in separateness. There were no problems of looping that could not be solved using a dissociative table, ego state, or cognitive intervention.

Ronald: DID with No Red Flags

Ronald came into treatment with complaints of depression, anxiety, and significant dissociation. There was amnesia in present time that occurred when Ronald was out on shopping expeditions with his wife, during which he would find himself in toy stores feeling upset and deprived. Presently employed as a paramedic, he had a prior career as a firefighter. His DES score was 42. He barely qualified for a diagnosis of DID based on occasional amnesia in present time and overt switching in and outside of session.

Ronald was amenable to an ego state approach from the beginning. Immediately available in the conference room were Ronnie, Toddler, and Teen. Within about six weeks of treatment, introjects of the mother and grandmother were both available in the conference room. Although initially they believed themselves to be the external mother and grand-mother, upon concretely demonstrating to them that they were in the same body (by having them look through the eyes at the body and attire of the adult male client) they accepted that they were part of Ronald. Both introjects were amenable to changes in their job descriptions to move Ronald toward health, upon the therapist expressing appreciation of their role as protectors.

Ronald was able to tolerate about one standard EMDR session every two weeks with no disorganization or flooding. The EMDR sessions were all focused on Ronald's strict and neglectful upbringing. He had been expected to have no needs or feelings, so all needs and feelings were dissociated. EMDR enabled these bottled-up feelings to be evacuated. EMDR was also conducted on Ronald's traumatic memories of being a firefighter, which had not been debriefed.

Ronald experienced a reduction in time loss and other symptoms of depression and anxiety at a steady pace over the course of treatment. As he became current in his emotional processing, energy became available to dedicate to creative art and writing, activities that had been considered "sinful" by his mother and grandmother. At the end of treatment, those introjects had no power in the system, and Ronald was free to have and express needs and feelings in his marriage and at work. At the end of a year's worth of treatment, when the therapist left Ronald's area, he was able to engage in artwork for the first time in his life, and his quality of life was much improved. He continued therapy with a subsequent therapist but no longer meets criteria for a dissociative disorder.

Both Shelley and Ronald were easy to work with, compliant with treatment, reliable reporters, and absent of borderline pathology. These two cases contrast starkly with the following more difficult case.

Georgina: Severe DID with Red Flags and Extreme Ambivalence

Georgina, now in her fourth year of treatment with me, is a forty-eight-year-old homemaker, mother of four, and a ceramic artist. She is highly intelligent and creative, and in those life domains functions well, considering the extent of her symptomatology. She carries diagnoses of DID, borderline personality disorder, bulimia, and bipolar disorder. In her initial visit, she spent nearly the entire session in a fetal position, rocking, as the therapist attempted to provide reassurance and acceptance. It was not possible to conduct a standard structured interview or administer a test of dissociation for months. Attempts at inquiry about Georgina's life history would result in rapid switching, including the presentation of an angry protective alter, George, who would interrupt abruptly and deride the therapist's questions and competence. George explicitly reported that no therapist should be trusted, and recounted experiences with prior therapists that, if true, indicated severe boundary violations by the therapists.

The host, Georgina, would appear depleted and overwhelmed, describing herself as a helpless victim of everyone in her environment. Her arms and legs commonly evidenced signs of recent cutting or other self-mutilation, but she had had no recent suicide attempts. Hospitalizations had been frequent but have been reduced in frequency over the course of treatment with the author.

Georgina frequently projected her certain belief that I hated her and that she was loathsome. Her psychiatrist and I were able, as a team, to keep our perspective on her many behaviors that invited splitting, as she frequently described each of us to the other as angry, cruel, abandoning, incompetent, and uncaring. These statements were coupled with imperceptions about the mood states, motives, and other aspects of others.

Child states would appear at interviews, asking if I was their new mother, in spite of my repeated attempts to define the nature of an appropriate therapeutic relationship. The host had almost complete amnesia for childhood, and the child alters struggled with flashbacks and nightmares. Georgina resisted my attempts at containment and affect regulation with condescending and arrogant remarks and behavior.

When the child states appeared in interview, they commonly recounted sadistic pseudomedical procedures administered by Georgina's father and overlooked by her mother, who was apparently alcoholic and given to rages.

Many sessions were spent with my describing the nature of appropriate therapeutic boundaries for various alters, none of whom took limits very well. Over time, Georgina gradually absorbed rudiments of containment skills, taught through cooperative alters. One angry protective alter described discarding the office policy handout, saying it only applied to the host.

If Georgina detected subtle body leakage of frustration from me in the face of extreme distortions and accusations, she engaged in exaggerated compliance and trembling, as if I were a perpetrator in present time.

In sum, none of the prerequisite conditions for proceeding to use any abreactive procedure, least of all EMDR, were met for this client in the first three years of treatment. Rapport was intermittent. Red flags, including self-mutilation, were present. Georgina could not be counted on to report on her internal state and said whatever was needed to get out of an uncomfortable moment. She did not allow me consistent access to her internal system until the third year. Indeed, she did not embrace the notion that therapy involved hard work on her part. The client worked hard in therapy, but rarely on what I recommended, so frightened was she of not having complete control.

In short, none of the prognostic signs of successful therapy outcome were present (Kluft, 1994). Ironically, Georgina's family reported that she was doing better under treatment with her current team than in many prior years of treatment! This may have been in part because of firm insistence and reeducation about boundaries, attempts at consistency in spite of projective identification in the transference field, and a few successful attempts at resource development and rudimentary self-soothing.

Resource development was conducted by means of very brief BLS (approximately two or three sets of six taps) in the form of the client tapping her own legs (I modeled those on myself) while I described positive images: planting seeds for healing and beginning to take steps on a pathway leading to a healing white light. Self-soothing skills development was initiated using BLS, again in the form of self-tapping, while reminding Georgina of her long-standing belief in Cosmic Consciousness, another ego state that promised to assist therapy with "every fiber in my being." She also found that she could calm herself with her favorite hymns, which pulled forward her spiritual ego states.

At about the three-year mark in therapy, Georgina began to remember to turn to this state for self-soothing, but still more commonly needs to be prompted to do so. Child states began to develop the necessary conditioned response to contain and close at the end of a session. Ten-minute phone calls to finish tucking them in occur about once a week, with crisis calls being much rarer than in prior years.

A cadre of positive internal resources have begun to work together for certain limited goals, such as keeping Georgina out of the hospital. That cadre includes George in his capacity as protector, Cosmic Consciousness in her self-soothing capacity, a good-natured teen, and an organized administrator called Georgie II. That cadre is now meeting in an internal conference room, and recently, outside of the therapy session on their own. Interestingly, it is George who is most cautious about doing so.

This case supremely illustrates the kind of client with whom early EMDR for trauma work should not be attempted. Georgina required years of ego state work before being ready for abreactive trauma work.

The first interventions using BLS were not standard protocols, but very brief interventions. In one session, I was chatting with the maternal introject about the external mother and the fact that the internal mother was part of Georgina, and not the external mother. After about thirty seconds of BLS, the maternal introject, which previously had denied that the external mother did any harm to the client, suddenly remembered the deliberate harm that the external mother had done. This caused her great sadness and a new awareness, which caused a shift in internal dynamics. This was a turning point in the treatment, with the introject more or less being on board with the treatment and allowing the therapy to slowly progress on a surer foot than previously.

At the time of this writing, Georgina is three and a half years into treatment and three fractionated EMDR treatment sessions using the ARCHITECTS approach have been conducted with good results, though each one precipitated a brief wave of some destabilization because of the large impact on the internal self-structure. In the most pivotal of the three sessions, there was considerable planning to ensure both that there were no current red flags contraindicating proceeding and that the majority of the system consented to EMDR. I also ensured that any concerns of alters had been addressed and that a safety plan was agreed to in the event of destabilization. An extended session was scheduled to ensure adequate time to complete the procedure. The work was planned to address a disturbing memory of the client's mother torturing the young child, Little Georgina.

The beginning of this extended session was dedicated to hypnotically arranging the system as follows: The host, Georgina, went for a walk in a forest; the perpetrator introjects (four of them) went off on a cruise; the positive resource team (four alters) stood around in a circle holding hands to strengthen the client for the work; and the other parts not related to the memory being targeted were all tucked into a church where they knew they could be safe, even if the EMDR caused them to be buffeted a bit. One of the positive resources, Earth Mother, held Little Georgina on her lap to give her strength, and the EMDR was conducted using tapping.

Little Georgina was the subject of the EMDR, and she abreacted a memory of being burned deliberately by her mother. Not surprisingly, though the maternal introject had been tucked in ahead of time and had agreed to the work, the abreactive work of the EMDR pulled forward the maternal introject, who was herself suffering at this point, whereas Little Georgina had achieved relief. Upon reminding the introject that she was not the external mother who had actually done the harm, I reeducated and appreciated the introject for containing the toxic mother energy all these years and for keeping the little one under her thumb, which served to keep her out of trouble as much as possible from the real external mother.

At the end of the ninety-minute session, half of which had been spent on a fractionated abreaction using EMDR, Georgina was exhausted. For closure, we secured residual BASK elements in a Tupperware container, which we put into a hypnotic vault, and then appreciated all participating alters and tucked them away in fluffy white clouds. Georgina made crisis calls in the days that followed as the introject herself shrunk into a very small child in a mother costume, a child feeling herself bereft and abandoned. This caused the system as a whole to feel startled that the world had changed so. For the first time, they were not under the thumb of the mother (external or internal).

Georgina's family continues to report that she is improving. She is moving toward realistic acceptance of the reality of her childhood experiences. I moved to another city, but I conducted a follow-up call with the concurrence of Georgina's present therapist. Georgina reported that the EMDR sessions were turning points in her treatment, after which she knew and accepted what had happened to her. She grieved her misspent life and the loss of her therapist simultaneously, and, appreciative of the follow-up call, said that now the walls were coming down to her self, so that there was only "one pair of toes" now. Georgina, her family, and her present therapist note her greatly increased stability.

CONCLUSION

EMDR and ego state therapy are natural complements to each other, and both serve in the treatment of DID, with the exception of those clients with DID who do not meet criteria for proceeding with the abreactive work. The skillful use of the two, in sequence and in combination, allows the clinician to adjust the tension on both the therapeutic and abreactive processes. This enables the appropriate rhythm of ego strengthening and painful insight, containment, and uncovering, which leads slowly to integration.

REFERENCES

American Psychiatric Association. (1994). *Diagnostic and statistical manual of mental disorders* (4th ed.). Washington, DC: Author.

Bernstein, E. M., & Putnam, F. W. (1989). Development, reliability and validity of a dissociation scale. *Journal of Nervous and Mental Disease, 174,* 727–733.

Braun, B. G. (1988). The BASK model of dissociation. Part II: Treatment. *Dissociation, 1*(2), 16.

Dell, P. F. (2001). Why the diagnostic criteria for dissociative identity disorder should be changed. *Journal of Trauma and Dissociation, 2*(1), 7–37.

Fine, C. G. (1991). Treatment stabilization and crisis prevention: Pacing the therapy of the MPD patient. *Psychiatric Clinics of North America, 14,* 661–676.

Fine, C. G. (1993). A tactical integrationist perspective on the treatment of multiple personality disorder. In R. P. Kluft & C. G. Fine (Eds.), *Clinical perspectives on multiple personality disorder* (pp. 153–153). Washington, DC: American Psychiatric Press.

Fine, C. G. (1999). The tactical integration model for the treatment of dissociative identity disorder and allied dissociative disorders. *American Journal of Psychotherapy, 53*(3), 361–376.

Fine, C. G., & Berkowitz, A. S. (2001). The wreathing protocol: The imbrication of hypnosis and EMDR in the treatment of dissociative identity disorder and other dissociative responses. *American Journal of Clinical Hypnosis, 43*(3/4), 275–290.

Foster, S., & Lendl, J. (1996). Eye movement desensitization and reprocessing: Four case studies of a new tool for executive coaching and restoring employee performance after setbacks. *Consulting Psychology Journal: Research and Practice, 48*(3), 155–161.

Fraser, G. A. (1991). The Dissociative Table Technique: A strategy for working with ego states in dissociative disorders and ego state therapy. *Dissociation, 4*(4), 205–213.

Fraser, G. A. (1993). Special treatment techniques to access the inner personality system of multiple personality disorder clients. *Dissociation, 6* (2/3), 193–198.

Klein, M. (1975). *Love, guilt and reparation and other works, 1921–1945* (M. Masud R. Khan, Ed.). London: Hogarth Press.

Kluft, R. P. (1990a). The fractionated abreactive technique. In D. C. Hammond (Ed.), *Handbook of hypnotic suggestions and metaphors* (pp. 527–528). New York: Norton.

Kluft, R. P. (1990b). The slow leak technique. In D. C. Hammond (Ed.), *Handbook of hypnotic suggestions and metaphors* (pp. 526–527). New York: Norton.

Kluft, R. P. (1990c). A fusion ritual in treating multiple personality. In D. C. Hammond (Ed.), *Handbook of hypnotic suggestions and metaphors* (pp. 339–341). New York: Norton.

Kluft, R. P. (1990d). Another fusion ritual. In D. C. Hammond (Ed.), *Handbook of hypnotic suggestions and metaphors* (pp. 341–342). New York: Norton.

Kluft, R. P. (1993a). The initial stages of psychotherapy in the treatment of multiple personality disorder patients. *Dissociation, 6*(2/3), 145–161.

Kluft, R. P. (1993b, June/Sept). The treatment of dissociative disorder patients: An overview of discoveries, successes, and failures. *Dissociation, 6(2/3)*, 87–101.

Kluft, R. P. (1994). Clinical observations on the use of the CSDS dimensions of therapeutic movement instrument (DTMI). *Dissociation, 7*, 272–283.

Korn, D. L., & Leeds, A. M. (2002). Preliminary evidence of efficacy for EMDR resource development and installation in the stabilization phase of treatment of complex post-traumatic stress disorder. *Journal of Clinical Psychology, 58*(12), 1465–1487.

Lazrove, S., & Fine, C. G. (1996). The use of EMDR in clients with dissociative identity disorder. *Dissociation, 9*, 289–299.

Levine, P. (1997). *Waking the tiger*. Berkeley, CA: North Atlantic Books.

Nijenhuis, E .R. S., Spinhoven, P., Van Dyck, R., van der Hart, O., & Vanderlinden, J. (1996). The development and the psychometric characteristics of the Somatoform Dissociation Questionnaire (SDQ-20). *Journal of Nervous and Mental Disease, 184*, 688–694.

Paulsen, S. (1995). Eye movement desensitization and reprocessing: Its cautious use in the dissociative disorders. *Dissociation, 8*(1), 32–44.

Paulsen, S. L. (2004a, September). *Ego state therapy and EMDR: Activating, modifying, and containing dissociated neural nets*. Invited Masters Series Lecture presented at the EMDR International Association Annual Conference, Montreal, Quebec, Canada.

Paulsen, S. L. (2004b, November). *Softening the perpetrator introject*. Paper presented at ISSD International Conference, New Orleans, LA.

Paulsen, S. L. (2006a, November). *ACT-AS-IF and ARCHITECTS approach to utilizing ego state therapy, somatic psychotherapy, and EMDR with highly dissociative clients*. Paper presented at the 23rd Annual Conference of the International Society for the Study of Trauma & Dissociation, Los Angeles.

Paulsen, S. L. (2006b, April). *Giving the body a voice with EMDR, ego state therapy and somatic psychotherapy*. Workshop presented at the Northwest Regional Trauma Conference, Lake Chelan, WA.

Paulsen, S. L., & Golston, J. C. (2005, September). *Taming the storm: 43 secrets of successful stabilization*. Workshop at the EMDR International Association Annual Conference, Seattle, WA.

Paulsen, S. L., & Stanley, S. A. (2005, November). *Giving the body a voice: How EMDR, ego state therapy, somatic experiencing, and indigenous healing methods can cure somatic dissociation*. Workshop presented at the Fall Conference of the International Society for the Study of Dissociation, Toronto, Ontario, Canada.

Paulsen, S. L., & Watkins, J. G. (2003a, November). *Ego state therapy: EMDR and hypnoanalytic techniques*. Workshop presented at the Society for Clinical & Experimental Hypnosis, Chicago.

Paulsen, S. L., & Watkins, J. G. (2003b, November). *Comparing ego state therapy and EMDR techniques*. Workshop presented at the 20th Annual Conference of the International Society for the Study of Dissociation, Chicago.

Paulsen, S. L., & Watkins, J. G. (2005, November). *Best techniques from the armamentarium of hypnoanalytic, EMDR, somatic psychotherapy and cognitive-behavioral methods*. Workshop presented at the Fall Conference of the International Society for the Study of Dissociation, Toronto, Ontario, Canada.

Paulsen Inobe, S. (2000, September). *EMDR for executive performance enhancement and strategic visioning*. Workshop presented with Sandra Foster & Jennifer Lendl at the EMDR International Association Annual Conference, Toronto, Ontario, Canada.

Paulsen Inobe, S. (2001, December). *Integrating EMDR, ego state therapy, and dissociative table: A cartooning psychologist's glimpse into the mind's eye*. Workshop presented at the Annual Conference of the International Society for the Study of Dissociation, New Orleans, LA.

Paulsen Inobe, S. (2003, March). *EMDR and ego state therapy across the dissociative continuum.* Invited faculty presentation at the First World Congress on Ego State Therapy, Bad Orb, Germany.

Phillips, M. (2000). *Finding the energy to heal: How EMDR, hypnosis, imagery, TFT and body-focused therapy can help restore mind-body health.* New York: Norton.

Phillips, M., & Frederick, C. (1995). *Healing the divided self: Clinical and Ericksonian hypnotherapy for post-traumatic and dissociative conditions.* New York: Norton.

Putnam, F. W. (1989). *Diagnosis and treatment of multiple personality disorder.* New York: Guilford Press.

Ross, C. A. (1997). *Dissociative identity disorder: Diagnosis, clinical features and treatment of multiple personality* (2nd ed.). New York: Wiley.

Ross, C. A., Heber, S., Norton, G. R., Anderson, D., Anderson, G., & Barchet, P. (1989). The Dissociative Disorders Interview Schedule: A structured interview. *Dissociation, 2*(3), 169–189.

Shapiro, F. (1995). *Eye movement desensitization and reprocessing: Basic principles, protocols, and procedures.* New York: Guilford Press.

Shapiro, F. (2001). *Eye movement desensitization and reprocessing: Basic principles, protocols, and procedures* (2nd ed.). New York: Guilford Press.

Siegel, D. J. (1999). *The developing mind: How relationships and the brain interact to shape who we are.* New York: Guilford Press.

Spiegel, D. (2001). Deconstructing the dissociative disorders: For whom the Dell tolls. *Journal of Trauma and Dissociation, 2*(1), 51–57.

Steinberg, M. (1994). *Interviewer's guide to the Structured Clinical Interview for DSM–IV Dissociative Disorders (SCID-D).* Washington, DC: American Psychiatric Press.

Twombly, J. H. (2000). Incorporating EMDR and EMDR adaptations into the treatment of clients with dissociative identity disorder. *Journal of Trauma and Dissociation, 1*(2), 61–81.

van der Kolk, B. A., & van der Hart, O. (1989). Pierre Janet and the breakdown of adaptation in psychological trauma. *American Journal of Psychiatry, 146,* 1530–1540.

Watkins, J. G., & Paulsen, S. L. (2004, March). *Abreactions in EMDR and hypnoanalytic therapies.* Workshop presented at the American Society of Clinical Hypnosis, Anaheim, CA.

Watkins, J. G., & Watkins, H. H. (1997). *Ego states: Theory and therapy.* New York: Norton.

CHAPTER 6

Loving Eyes

Procedures to Therapeutically
Reverse Dissociative Processes While
Preserving Emotional Safety

Jim Knipe

ONE FOOT IN THE PRESENT, ONE FOOT IN THE PAST

A client with a history of severe traumatization and a fragmented sense of self recently said to me, "This time, therapy has worked for me, because now I can come back and be present here in the room. Previously, feelings would get stirred up, and then I would dread the next session. In the past, I've had no trouble going into my memory of what happened. It's been way too easy. It's been like sliding down a slippery slope. The hard part has always been coming back. In here, I've been able to come back."

Dual attention (simultaneous awareness of both the disturbing material and a neutral or safe aspect of the present situation) is an essential element of the effectiveness of EMDR (Shapiro, 2001). That is, in EMDR therapy, the therapist assists the client in keeping "one foot in the present, one foot in the past." Metaphorically, "two feet in the past" would simply be emotionally reliving the trauma, and not therapeutic. For those clients with highly dissociated and intense affect, there is a danger with standard EMDR that uncontrolled emotion may intrude into consciousness in a way that undermines this important balance between present and past. In this chapter, several methods are described that seem to be useful in empowering clients with dissociated ego states to stay oriented to the present while processing unfinished disturbing memories. Specifically, these EMDR variations seem to enable the client to maintain the balance between emotional safety and the controlled emergence of unresolved affect, so as to avoid dissociative abreaction and make possible the healing and eventual integration of separate parts of the self.

For many client situations encountered in clinical practice, the concepts of ego state therapy seem to be a natural adjunct to the EMDR Adaptive Information Processing model (Forgash & Knipe, 2001). In 1871, the poet Walt Whitman expressed a truth of the human condition in his *Song of Myself* when he wrote, "I am multitudes." In general (and to varying degrees between people), different and distinct "states of mind" often coexist with a single individual's personality, and these different ego states may have separate histories and be experienced subjectively as distinct from one another.

Another variable is one of experiential distance between separate ego states. Different ego states may either be relatively co-conscious (Watkins & Watkins, 1998) or be so dissociated from one another that there is very little mutual awareness between these states. If these parts of the self are repeatedly in conflict, or working at cross-purposes, the result can be an ongoing experience of dysphoria and low self-esteem. For example, an adult ego state might be highly motivated to block and avoid the activation of a child ego state that carries the fear, horror, and other affects associated with a traumatic event.

When posttraumatic disturbance is triggered by a present-day situation, the intrusive images and feelings from the memory tend to have a "right now" quality—a sense of living the trauma again—that can give the adult feelings of disorientation and loss of control. If the adult self strongly identifies with the wish to escape from, disown, or obliterate the unpleasant affect, then the problem tends to remain locked in place, with an ongoing experience of helplessness and depression. The memory material is pushing for expression in awareness; the adult self is blocking this expression. This type of self-defeating deadlock can lead to ongoing shame and depression: "What is wrong with me?! I should be able to just get over this!" For clients who are at cross-purposes with themselves in this way, I will often tell the following story (with the child the same sex as the client).

> Imagine a little girl who falls down and skins her knee, and it hurts. Her knee is bleeding and she runs into the house. A loving parent sees her and says, "Oh, it hurts, doesn't it? Come over here. Let me wash it off. Yes, it hurts! I'll put a bandage on it. Come sit in my lap for a little while." It is easy to see that after a few minutes, for this little girl, this lap will become pretty boring, and she will want to go back out and play again. If the parent asks her if her knee still hurts, she is likely to

say, "No," as she bounds out the door. Now think of another little girl just down the street who also skins her knee in the same way, and runs into her house, but instead either has no adult available to soothe her, or has an adult who says, "Stop crying right now! If you don't stop crying I'm going to give you something to cry about. I won't help you until you stop crying." This second child now has two problems. Her knee still hurts, and also, now she is bad if she cries. If in the future she falls down and hurts herself again she is not very likely to go into the house looking for help. She may wonder, years later, following a sad event in her life, why she is unable to cry about it. Or she may wonder why she cries so easily, as if there is always this reservoir of tears ready to spill out.

EMDR AND DISSOCIATION

There is clearly an element of dissociation in posttraumatic stress disorder. Even in the case of single-incident PTSD, there are two relatively dissociated ego states: one that is aware of present safety, and another that has a sense of felt reality about intrusive flashbacks or hyperarousal associated with the traumatic event. Generally, the purpose of therapy for PTSD is to reverse this mild dissociation, integrate the two ego states, and transform the disturbance into a completed declarative (narrative) memory (van der Kolk, 1994). The trouble is that the standard EMDR protocol, much more than other psychotherapy methods, tends to invite dissociated memory experience into present consciousness (Lipke, 1994; Paulsen, 1995). This, of course, can be a very good thing if the individual is able to maintain orientation to the present safety of the therapist's office while the disturbing material comes into consciousness.

But for a client with severe dissociation between separate ego states, the abrupt emergence of dissociated affect has the potential to be startling, disorienting, and retraumatizing. For example, in the story above, what if the little girl now grown up had put out of awareness all of the times that her feelings had been invalidated by that parent, in order to preserve in her mind a highly valued and positive picture of a loving and nurturing home environment? What if this little girl's story had also included even more extreme abuse and neglect? These factors increase the risk of uncontrolled and nontherapeutic abreaction.

In these situations, then, it is very important to counter this risk with an increased emphasis on safety and containment of affect. The client and therapist, in partnership, "go fast by slowing down." In other words, the more traumatized and dissociative the client, the more important it is that concerns of emotional safety and affect containment be an integral part of the treatment process. This concern regarding safety has many implications in the overall planning of treatment for a dissociative individual, and the implementation of that treatment (Forgash & Knipe, 2001; Kluft & Fine, 1993; Putnam, 1989).

This chapter presents three cases, all of which show a method of containing affect and reconciling conflicted ego states through what I term "loving eyes." The second case illustrates a method of targeting avoidance defenses, and the third example shows the procedure of Constant Installation of Present Orientation and Safety (CIPOS; Knipe, 2002) as well as the Back of the Head Scale (BHS; Knipe, 2002), a measurement tool that is useful in assessing a client's moment-to-moment level of dissociation. All of these session transcripts are derived from video recordings that were made as EMDR training tapes. In all three instances, the clients have generously given their permission for their session to be described in this chapter. The dialogue here is repeated verbatim except for minor editing for clarity and alteration of identifying information.

LOVING EYES: SEEING THE TRAUMATIZED CHILD

Active visualization, guided and contained by the therapist, may be used to create an emotionally safe connection between dissociated ego states. Often, just as in normal daily interactions between people, the language of visualization is a part of the expression of mutual understanding. One friend might convey concern and acceptance to another by simply saying, "I see. I see what you mean." To "see" the troubles of another person is to provide comfort for the troubled individual; it is a connection and a sharing of experience. In addition, the word "seeing" also connotes a certain distance—a buffer of separation for the one who is empathizing. Those clients with dissociated ego states who are able to "see," from one state to another, can experience a sense of protective separation from their own disturbing affect, a grounding in emotional safety, while also connecting, reconciling, and resolving disturbing memory material.

In addition, it seems that for many clients with extensive childhood histories of abuse and neglect, a major element of their dilemma was that their deepest needs and feelings were not "seen." That is, their inner experience was not lovingly acknowledged, and thus validated, by a caretaker. This lack of validation of inner experience is hypothesized (Linehan, 1993, pp. 51–52) to contribute to the emotional pathology of adults who have difficulty regulating their own affect (as with borderline personality disorder and other related conditions).

The EMDR treatment methods described below are based in part on the speculation that the "loving eyes" of an adult are often an essential element in the process of healing from childhood trauma. It is certainly a necessary element of therapy that the clinician view the client with positive regard (Truax & Carkhuff, 1967). One hypothesis (Schore, 2000) is that the therapist's positive regard is not only necessary, but also sufficient to heal the damage caused by childhood abuse and neglect. It is often the hope of a client who experienced neglect that the therapist will be the mother or father the client never had. Indeed, for many such clients, the reparative work that occurs in the transference is, in fact, a primary element of their healing. But for clients with intense dissociative processes, it seems an additional step is necessary. For these clients, it is often useful for the therapist to assist the client in strengthening the part of the self that is oriented to present reality, and then assist that present-oriented ego state in witnessing the painful affect held in a dissociated child ego state. Oftentimes, the affect within a child ego state has never been compassionately observed, either by another person or by another part of the self within the personality system.

In working with clients who have this particular difficulty, I have found it useful to use a procedure that I call Loving Eyes. Years ago, a client with a dissociative disorder asked a peculiar and provocative question: "How do most children grow up from four to five?" (This client suffered horrible abuse and neglect at age four.) "When I was four, I wanted to grow up to be five, but I couldn't do it, so I made a 'box,' with the real me inside, and a happy face on the outside of the box so that everyone would think I was normal. But now the part of me that is still four wants to grow up. How do other children grow up to be five?"

We focused on this important question for several sessions, and finally a principle became clear—a principle that has since been confirmed with many other clients—that the reliable loving eyes of an adult seem to be important, perhaps essential, for the emotional growth of a child and the maturation of that child's identity. In contrast, a child who grows up in a world that is devoid of loving eyes (a neglectful, emotionally unresponsive environment) will be compelled to focus awareness on the fragile thread of connection to that environment. That is, the child will place all importance on adaptation, at the expense of inner needs and emotions. The child's sense of self may split into an adaptive "box" that faces the world and attempts to "look normal," and another little secret self inside that holds the feelings that the child's environment cannot tolerate.

If, within a disinterested and neglectful world, the child also experiences specific trauma, that is very likely to make the dissociative split much worse. A child in these unfortunate circumstances may grow up with an overemphasis on adaptation and a sense that many internally experienced needs and feelings are unwelcome and ego dystonic. Of course, this can result in many emotional difficulties in that individual's adult life.

For adult clients who come to therapy with this type of background, the Loving Eyes intervention has frequently been useful. The steps in the procedure are as follows:

Step 1. Find a visual image, preferably an actual memory, that represents the ego-dystonic affect. The adult client, reminded of being an adult, sitting in a therapist's office, is asked to visually witness the childhood event, *as a separate person from the child.* Usually a memory image can be identified with a simple question such as, "When you were a child, were you ever afraid?"

Step 2. If the client has trouble clearly accessing an actual memory, the therapist can speak to the client in way that identifies a memory via an affect bridge (Watkins & Watkins, 1997), by saying, "When you notice where that fear feeling is in your body, and take that back to when you were a kid, what do you get? Just take whatever you get." Most clients will then begin to form a memory picture. This picture can then be clarified with specific questions such as, "Is this child inside or outside?" "How old is he?" "What room is he in?" "What is he looking at, when you see him right now?" It is important to ask these questions in a general way (that is, not leading the client to respond in a particular way).

Step 3. Ask the client, "Sitting in this chair, the adult you are today, can you just look at that child?" If the client says "yes," the therapist initiates eye movements, with words that are open and permissive, such as, "Just see this child. When you see this child, *just see whatever you see.*" The therapist's wording conveys acceptance of the child, without judgment. This type of unconditional acceptance is probably what the child needed at the time of the original traumatic event. It frequently occurs at this point that the adult ego state begins to experience the feelings of the child, and so the therapist must take care to ensure that these feelings are contained within the adult's sense of present safety. Sometimes it is necessary to pause in this process, so that the client will stay oriented to present safety.

Step 4. It often occurs that the adult client initially has a nonaccepting reaction to this image of the childhood self. For example, as in the first case below, there may be a lecturing or scolding reaction, or, as in the second case, a reaction of embarrassed avoidance. These negative reactions to the child represent defense, which remains in place in order to maintain dissociative distance from the painful affect that is held within the separate, frightened, child ego state. Because the negativity is a defense, it will generally process with eye movements if the client is asked to focus on the positive feelings (relief, containment) associated with the avoidance defense. For example, in such instances, the therapist might ask, "What's good about not looking at that child?" In response to this question, the client might say something like, "If I look away, I don't have to feel those feelings," or "If I don't look, I don't have to see how awful it was." Often, disgust with the childhood self is an adaptation that was necessary at the time of the trauma, a way of allying with a powerful perpetrator in order to not be totally abandoned. Whatever the client's response, the therapist can then respond, "Think of that" accompanied by bilateral stimulation. Very frequently, the avoidance urge lessens and the resistance to compassionately seeing the child is very likely to diminish. This procedure is described and illustrated in the second session transcript, below.

Step 5. When the client is able to freely see the child, the therapist may then ask, "When you look at that child, can you see the child's feelings?" Usually, the client will acknowledge that the child's feelings can now be seen, and at this point the client notices beginning to share the feelings of the traumatized child. As sets of bilateral stimulation continue, with sufficient continuing orientation to present safety, the fear will dissipate and positive feelings of connection and compassion for the child are likely to increase.

Step 6. As the client begins to speak of the child compassionately, the therapist can ask, "When you look at that child, how do *you* feel about the child?" The client may be surprised to discover the possibility, as an adult, of viewing this child with love and respect. The child part can then begin to experience this love and validation. Another question for the client might be, "Is there anything that you know, as an adult, that would be helpful to that child? Something that child doesn't know?" Whatever the client answers to these questions, the therapist can respond by saying, "Stay with that," and apply additional sets of eye movements. This internal dialogue typically continues to a point of healing resolution.

Step 7. If the client says that the child is "scared that we see him," or "is worried that we will criticize him for being afraid," then the shift should be back to the adult self with questions like, "Do you in fact, as an adult, looking at the child, feel critical of the child for having that fear?" It may be necessary to go back to Step 5, above. Interweaves of cognitive information about the realities of the child's life circumstances are often useful in softening the harshness of the critical adult's perspective (for example, "Do you think that child has it rough?").

MEHMET: DISSOCIATED AFFECT DUE TO CHILDHOOD DEPRIVATION

The first case illustrates the use of the Loving Eyes procedure. In 1999, following a series of catastrophic earthquakes in Turkey, the EMDR Humanitarian Assistance Program (HAP), in coordination with the Istanbul branch of the Turkish Psychological Association, began a project of EMDR trainings for Turkish therapists who were voluntarily providing services to people suffering from PTSD following the quakes. The following transcript is from a therapy session with Mehmet, a forty-three-year-old man who was horribly traumatized when his apartment building nearly collapsed during the initial earthquake in August 1999. For a seemingly never-ending period of forty-three seconds, in the middle of the night, he felt certain he was going to die. He was able to escape to the street, but then reentered the dangerous and totally dark apartment building to rescue members of his family. In the hours after the quake, he learned of the deaths of several friends and acquaintances. In October 1999, Mehmet volunteered to undergo EMDR with a member of the HAP training team (with the help of a translator), and he generously agreed to allow his sessions to be videotaped to provide a demonstration of the method to the Turkish trainees.

At the time of his first EMDR session, he reported very disrupted sleep since the night of the quake. (He actually said he had "not been able to sleep at all.") Whenever he would close his eyes, he would begin to relive the worst moments of that night. After two sessions of EMDR, his nightmares and his waking visual flashbacks had significantly diminished, and he reported that he no longer experienced any emotional disturbance during daytime hours. However, at bedtime, he was still experiencing hyperarousal with spikes of panic in response to unexpected environmental sounds such as a door shutting in his apartment building, a refrigerator coming on, and sounds in the street below. He then would have difficulty going to sleep, as well as a racing heartbeat and sweaty palms. Because the initial sessions of standard EMDR had been only partially successful in helping him, he requested an additional session.

It was not surprising that Mehmet was continuing to have trouble at nighttime, since the initial earthquake had occurred at night. When I met with him, it was late afternoon, and he insisted that at that hour, he was not having even a trace of fear, that he was completely free from disturbance of any kind. In spite of this absence of present disturbance, he stated that his difficulty at night was a desperate problem, and he hoped that EMDR could somehow help him get over it, as it had helped previously with his flashbacks and nightmares. His affect in our session was very depressed, and he would spontaneously express his frustration and disgust with himself, that he couldn't "just get over it" and rid himself of this ongoing dilemma. He said, "I hate this fear! I say to myself, 'There is no reason for it. I shouldn't have it.'" For me, these statements raised the question, Who is the hater and who is the hated? In other words, his statements suggested an ego state conflict between a part that continued to hold posttraumatic fear from the earthquake, and another part that had hatred for this ongoing fearful response.

The following excerpt shows the EMDR work with these conflicted ego states. First, visual imagery is suggested to clarify the origins of this problem, and then the Loving Eyes method is used to facilitate communication, mutual understanding, and reconciliation between these parts of the self in order to help Mehmet resolve his depression and his specific bedtime problem.

THERAPIST: When you hear the sound of the refrigerator starting up in the night, and it startles you, what thoughts are you thinking?

CLIENT: I want to throw away this feeling of fear inside me. I want to be relaxed; I don't want to bring these things back into my mind. No matter how much I try, all of a sudden a small something brings it back to my mind again. Inside, I feel this fear has not yet come to an end. I talk to my mind. I talk to myself, and say, "Am I just making this up? Why can't I get rid of it?"

THERAPIST: Do you talk to yourself harshly like that?

CLIENT: Yes, naturally. Why do I put these things into my brain?

THERAPIST: So you have the fear and then you say to yourself, "Why do I still have this fear?!"

CLIENT: Yes.

Finding the Dissociated Ego State

In order to access and clearly differentiate the ego state holding the fear, I help Mehmet remember a childhood experience of fear.

THERAPIST: When you were a little boy, were you afraid sometimes?

CLIENT: When I was a little boy...we grew up without a mother and father. I never met my father. I was born after he was dead. My mother died when I was nine and we were in poverty. My brothers and I, we are six all together. I am the youngest.

THERAPIST: Can you remember a time, when you were a child, when you were afraid? Most children have fear at one time or another. Was there a time when you were afraid?

CLIENT: [*Long pause*] In our country place, I had to take the cattle out to the field, and when I was bringing them back, and it was getting dark, I saw on the body of the animal a figure, a long something.... But later on I didn't have these things, these feelings.

THERAPIST: Are you able to think of that right now, when you saw something on the cow?

CLIENT: I see it often, and it's like a giant...like something that is dead. It's like a giant figure.

THERAPIST: As you see it now, is it uncomfortable for you?

CLIENT: No. It is nothing. It doesn't affect me, but in my childhood I had fears like this.

We might say that Mehmet cannot allow himself, as an adult, to experience the irrational fears of his childhood. But he is able to *observe* the fear, in the present, and he states, "I see it often," suggesting that this fear memory remains unresolved, though dissociated.

Reversing the Dissociation

To help Mehmet begin to make a connection with his unresolved fear, I ask him to visualize his frightened childhood self.

THERAPIST: Try to use your imagination right now to see this little boy who is bringing the cattle back, and it's dark now, and he has fear. Can you see this little boy right now?

CLIENT: I do.

THERAPIST: How old is he?

CLIENT: Ten, twelve.

THERAPIST: Can you see his clothes?

CLIENT: I do.

THERAPIST: Can you see how his hair is?

CLIENT: I do. His clothes are torn and he is not well groomed.

THERAPIST: See this boy right now, and just see him while you watch my fingers go back and forth. [*Very slow eye movements, while I continue speaking*] And when you see him, see whatever you see, right when he is frightened and sees the cow. He sees something big on the side of the cow. And just look at him. That's good. Can you see his feelings?

CLIENT: I do.

THERAPIST: Just think of that. And see whatever you see when you look at him. [*Eye movements, while I continue speaking*] That's good. When you see this child, if you could go back in time, the man you are today, and go to that boy and tell him something that would help him with his fear, something you know that he doesn't know, that would really help him, what would you say to him?

CLIENT: I could have told him there is nothing there, don't believe in these things, don't be afraid.

THERAPIST: Stay with that. [*Set of eye movements*]

Even though these first words from Mehmet to his childhood self are somewhat judgmental and not very validating of the child's fears, it is a step in the direction of increased communication and reconciliation. In other words, he is slowly and safely reversing the dissociation that was necessary during his childhood to contain his fear. We can assume that the bleakness of his circumstances as a young boy made it impossible for him to fully experience and process his childhood anxiety.

THERAPIST: Good, think of that and in your mind, tell him now. [*Set of eye movements*] And what if this boy said back to you, "But it seems like there is something that's so scary?" What would you say to him then?

CLIENT: Don't believe in these things. There is nothing there. I would try to persuade him. [*Eye movements*]

The word "persuade," while still connoting a difference of opinion, also contains a recognition that the child's fears do in fact exist.

Activating the Nurturing Response of the Adult Ego State

The next question I pose to Mehmet is very important, in that it requires him to decide whether to continue to disown this child ego state, or begin to lovingly reconnect with this part of himself.

THERAPIST: When you look at this boy, how do *you* feel about him—the boy in your mind—when you think of this?

CLIENT: I pity him when I look at him because he is without a mother and father. [*Begins crying*]

THERAPIST: Think of that. [*Set of eye movements*]

CLIENT: He has reasons to be afraid.

THERAPIST: Think of that. [*Set of eye movements*]

CLIENT: If I could go back in time I would hug him and kiss him with love and make him get rid of this fear.

THERAPIST: That's right, think of that. [*Set of eye movements*] If you could, would you like to take this boy away from this place and bring him into today with you?

CLIENT: Yes.

THERAPIST: So, you would know how to take care of a boy like this?

CLIENT: Yes, I would make him grow without making him sad or afraid, not in the slightest bit.

THERAPIST: And if this boy sometimes heard a refrigerator sound or heard a door slam in the night because he is still scared, because of where he has been, would you get mad? Would you get angry with him?

CLIENT: No.

THERAPIST: Think of that. [*Set of eye movements*] You know, the truth is that this boy no longer exists...because he grew up into you, into being you. But in another very real way, perhaps he is still with you, right now in this room, and at night when there are sounds. Is this boy with us here today, as we talk about these things?

CLIENT: Yes, he is.

THERAPIST: So, if tonight there is the sound of a refrigerator or a door slamming, or a sound in the street, and there is fear, and your heart is pounding, try to remember what you learned here today. What will you want to remember?

CLIENT: I will remember myself as a boy.

At the end of this session, Mehmet said that he no longer felt anger at himself. In the weeks that followed, he was seen by his regular therapist, and it was reported that Mehmet found it very comforting to return to the image of the frightened boy and realize his own ability to soothe the feelings of his childhood self. This image, of a moment of childhood fear, was now a positive resource for him. Several months later, his therapist relayed the information that he was "sleeping like a baby" and was no longer troubled by his previous depression or emotional reactivity. When I was able to talk with him one year later, Mehmet reported that his previous symptoms remained resolved.

In this example, a memory image from childhood served as a point of access to the ego state containing the fear, but if no such memory had been accessible, another image from Mehmet's adult life (for example, of being frightened during the worst moment of the earthquake) could probably have been used. The main criterion is that the image somehow includes the affect that the individual is resisting or has pushed out of awareness. However, because these patterns of ego state conflict are usually set in motion during childhood, the most potent images would generally be of childhood fear or loneliness. For Mehmet, there was no place in his childhood world for fears, so these fears, when they nevertheless naturally occurred, had no place of acceptance within himself. Thus, he had to dissociate his fear as a last-resort method of regulating this affect. When this dissociation was reversed, with emotional safety, he was able to discover a new and more effective way of soothing his fear.

VERONICA: TARGETING AN AVOIDANCE DEFENSE

The above procedure created what Mehmet originally needed as a child— an accepting adult witness to his fears. Mehmet initially had a mildly negative reaction to the image of his traumatized childhood self. His judgmental attitude lessened and dissolved as processing continued, but this result does not always occur. Sometimes, in contrast, the client's adult self will persist in a strong negative reaction toward the image of the child in the trauma. The traumatic memory material is threatening to the stability and functioning of the adult, and in spite of the client's strong wishes to heal a particular traumatic memory, there may also be simultaneous and very intense avoidance urges when the person attempts to think of the childhood traumatic events.

When this situation occurs, the individual's avoidance defense may be the best point of access to healing the traumatic material. An avoidance impulse may be the front door into the client's dysfunctionally stored memory network, and as such it is an aspect of the client's experience that can be targeted using the Adaptive Information Processing model (Knipe, 1995, 2005). The therapist asks questions that direct the client's attention, not to disturbing affect, but to positive affects (typically relief or containment) associated with the avoidance. Specifically, the client may be asked, "What is good about not thinking of that memory?" Or, "When you realize we could use this session to talk about what occurred when you were a child, how much, right now, zero to 10, do you not want to? How much would you rather think about something else?" Many clients have the attitude, "I don't want to think of it. But I *want to* want to think of it." Of course, if a client truly does not wish to access traumatic material, this method is inappropriate, but generally this is not the case. The more typical picture is one of a strong motivation to address and resolve the disturbance, and the avoidance impulse is experienced as a frustrating barrier to that resolution. In these types of situations, when avoidance is targeted, the typical result is that the defensive process weakens, and the underlying disturbing traumatic material can then be addressed successfully using standard EMDR procedures.

The following transcript illustrates this approach. Veronica, a fifty-eight-year-old woman in weekly therapy sessions, had benefited from previous EMDR treatment for her phobia of certain foods, and in these sessions she had become increasingly aware of a separate child ego state, while also becoming aware of previously dissociated details of sexual abuse by her father while she was between the ages of one and five. The adult had a strong avoidance impulse regarding this traumatic material, out of fear of being embarrassed and overwhelmed by what the child might tell her about the abuse. The following are verbatim segments from video recordings of three successive therapy sessions.

THERAPIST: Last time we started to talk about what happened with your father. We could go back to that again today.

CLIENT: [*Frowns*] After last time, I don't know what she [the child part] is going to say. I really have this feeling of "I don't want to!" I know it would help, but it just feels like I don't want to.

THERAPIST: Okay, then, just be honest. On a scale of zero to 10, how much do you not want to think of it right now?

	How strong is that urge or impulse to just think of anything else?
CLIENT:	Not how much I don't want to want to but just how much I don't want to. Okay. I don't want to, about a 9.
THERAPIST:	Notice where that feeling is, physically, that feeling of "I don't want to."
CLIENT:	I don't want to feel yucky. But... I want to get better. And, if that's what I have to do to get better, I'm going to do it.
THERAPIST:	So scan through your physical sensations. Where is that 9 of "I don't want to"?
CLIENT:	It's kind of a queasiness in here, and my throat.
THERAPIST:	Stay with "I don't want to." I'm turning on the sounds. Stay with that. [*Set of alternating sounds for about 10 seconds*] Stay with how much you don't want to go back into it.
CLIENT:	But I *do* want to because I want to get better.
THERAPIST:	Stay with that. [*Set of alternating sounds*] Now, stop and just take a deep breath. Look around the room. Just be here. Let yourself pause and take a break from all this. Take a rest.
CLIENT:	You know, it starts making that little girl inside think she did something wrong when I act like this. [*Set of alternating sounds*]
THERAPIST:	Given all that, right now, use the numbers to really look at the issue. How much do you just not want to, right now? The urge might still be there. It's okay if it is, but how much, right now, do you just not want to?
CLIENT:	Half and half, about a 5.
THERAPIST:	Okay, is that different from when it was a 9?
CLIENT:	Yes, because I really want to get through this stuff. I really want to progress. I really want to get better. I really *want* to be able to do the things I've always wanted to do, like eat normally, you know.
THERAPIST:	Good. Stay with that. [*Set of alternating sounds*] Do this: Go back and ask yourself the same question

again. Zero to 10, how much do you *not* want to think of it right now? It might be more.

CLIENT: Not want to think about what happened? I'm *thinking* about it!

THERAPIST: Stay with that.

CLIENT: It's just happening.

THERAPIST: Stay with that. [*Set of alternating sounds*]

CLIENT: It's like that little kid's not going to let me shut her up anymore.

THERAPIST: Stay with that. [*Set of alternating sounds*]

CLIENT: I wish I were as brave as my insides. I wish my outsides were as brave. [*Set of alternating sounds*]

THERAPIST: What are you getting now?

CLIENT: Smells, how I don't like smells.

THERAPIST: Stay with that. [*Set of alternating sounds*]

For the next several minutes, Veronica tells specific details of the sexual abuse. Then, after a brief break to rest and return to present orientation, she once again returns to directly observe the child in the trauma situation, and comes to a realization regarding her previous feelings of shame regarding the abuse. This insight, in turn, helps her overcome her avoidance of seeing her childhood self with "loving eyes."

CLIENT: She's not ashamed to talk about it. I don't understand why. I'd think she would be. Oh, it's because *she's* not following *Mom's* rules. She is herself.... All she knows is what happened, and how it made her feel, and she doesn't know the rules yet. So she isn't ashamed.

THERAPIST: Just think of that. Stay with that. [*Set of alternating sounds*]

CLIENT: [*From the child ego state*] I used to feel so scared when he came home.

THERAPIST: Stay with that. [*Set of alternating sounds*]

With her avoidance defense now much reduced, the adult ego state is able to allow the child ego state to speak directly:

CLIENT: [*From the child ego state*] There wasn't anybody there to help me then.

THERAPIST: Stay with that. [*Set of alternating sounds*]

CLIENT: [*From the child ego state*] And that is why *I* want to talk so much, because there's someone here to help me. For so long it hurt to know all that stuff, and feel so bad about myself. And no one was there to talk to me, and nobody understood me, and nobody understood. [*Set of alternating sounds*]

THERAPIST: I have a question for the adult right now.

CLIENT: What?

THERAPIST: You let her talk today. Was that something you're glad you did?

CLIENT: Glad. I'm glad.

During the next session, one week later, the child tells, and the adult compassionately hears, many more details about the worst parts of the sexual abuse. Toward the end of that session, the following interaction occurs between the therapist and the client's adult self:

CLIENT: I was afraid of him when he smelled like beer.

THERAPIST: Stay with that. [*Set of alternating sounds*]

CLIENT: I'm not afraid of him anymore.

THERAPIST: Stay with that. [*Set of alternating sounds*]

CLIENT: It feels good to not be afraid anymore. I've been afraid a long time.

THERAPIST: How much disturbance do you have right now, zero to 10?

CLIENT: It's a different kind of feeling now. I don't like what happened, I *hate* what happened, but I don't feel so paralyzed by it. It's further away.

THERAPIST: Good. [*Set of alternating sounds*]

CLIENT: Right now, I want to do for my little girl—inside— what my mom was not able to do for me. I comfort...I hold. I feel like going out and buying her a toy! [*Laughs*] That sounds weird, doesn't it? That sounds weird, but I feel like rewarding this inner kid inside of me that was so much braver than I was. Golly! She had a lot of guts.

Toward the end of the next session Veronica showed a new understanding that her trauma was in the past and no longer triggered such strong feelings of fear.

CLIENT: I feel more powerful today.

THERAPIST: That's good. It shows. So, just to check, go back and think of it again. And what do you get now?

CLIENT: I feel, like... it happened. And it's over. Does that make sense?

THERAPIST: It sure does.

CLIENT: It's like, I remember. It's like looking at a picture, but not being in the movie.

THERAPIST: Stay with that. [*Set of alternating sounds*]

CLIENT: I know, I know it happened. I used to *not know* it happened. I know it happened, and I'll always know that. But, I'm not afraid of him anymore. And I want to try to start looking at things I put in my mouth in a different way.

THERAPIST: What have you figured out today, and over the last few weeks?

CLIENT: I think I figured out that it's not too late to be the person that I want to be. And that I've been awfully hard on myself. And I'm going to try not to do that anymore. She is no longer shut away in the little part. It's me. I'm me. She is me.

I call the procedure illustrated above, which helps the client work through avoidance, the Level of Urge to Avoid (LOUA) method. It consists of the following steps:

1. Ask the client a question that accesses the positive affect, relief, or containment that is associated with the avoidance defense: "What is good about not thinking about that?" or "Zero to 10, how much do you not want to think about that, right now?"
2. Ask, "Where do you feel that in your physical sensations?"
3. Initiate sets of bilateral stimulation. When the target is reaccessed, ask, "How much, right now, zero to 10, would you rather not think of it?" Allowing the client to keep the avoidance defense during processing is typically "softer" and less stressful for the client, and in some instances, is the only available point of access to traumatic material.

ENHANCING PRESENT ORIENTATION

In Mehmet's case, there was only a moderate degree of dissociation between separate ego states, and the amount of negative affect contained
in the child ego state was not potentially overwhelming to the adult part.
In the case of Veronica, there was initial avoidance of the experience of
the child, which then dissipated as that defense was directly targeted,
leading to a constructive dialogue between adult and child ego states and
therapeutic processing of traumatic information. However, in many other
cases—farther out on the dissociative spectrum—this type of adult-child
connection has much greater potential for causing out-of-control feelings
and extreme emotional vulnerability. If disturbing memory material has
been deeply dissociated, the emergence of that material during therapy
can potentially overwhelm the client's sense of being safe in the present.
The memory can feel more real than the real situation the client is in, and
the experience can be one of nontherapeutic retraumatization.

The Back of the Head Scale

Given these considerations, it is important for therapist and client alike
to know when the client is drifting into derealization, that is, losing a
felt sense of the reality and safety of the present situation. For clients
who are potentially dissociative, the degree of orientation to the present situation can be assessed through the use of the Back of the Head
Scale (Knipe, 2002). This procedure is introduced to the client during
the preparation phase, before any desensitization of trauma is begun.
The therapist says, "Think of a line that goes all the way from here
[the therapist holds up one index finger about fifteen inches in front
of the person's face], running right from my finger, through your face to
the back of your head. Let this point on the line [therapist wiggles index
finger] mean that you are completely aware of being present here with
me in this room, that you can easily listen to what I'm saying, and that
you are not at all distracted by any other thoughts. Let the other point
on the line, at the back of your head [therapist points] mean that you are
so distracted by disturbing thoughts, feelings, or memory pictures that
you feel like you are somewhere else. Your eyes may be open, but your
thoughts and your awareness are completely focused on another time,
place, or experience. At this very moment, show with your finger where
you are on this line."

The therapist should check to make sure the client gets this idea.
Most clients who have dissociative experience will quickly recognize this
procedure as a way of measuring and expressing a familiar aspect of
their mental life. The assumption is that the more the person points toward the "most present" endpoint of the line, the safer it is to do trauma

work with eye movements. Clients seem to be able to easily assess the full range of dissociative experiences, pointing to either a place in front of the face, or to a place parallel with the eyes, or to the temple, or to an area further back in the head, according to what they are experiencing. As a rough rule of thumb, I have assumed that it is necessary for the person to point to a position at least three inches in front of their face in order for trauma-focused work to proceed, although this may vary from client to client. Using the BHS throughout a therapy session can be very helpful in ensuring that the client is staying present while reprocessing disturbing memories.

Constant Installation of Present Orientation and Safety (CIPOS)

The CIPOS method (Knipe, 2002; see Figure 6.1) is used in conjunction with the BHS, and basically consists of using eye movements to strengthen or install in the client's awareness a clear subjective sense of being present in the immediate real-life situation of the therapy office. This method may be used in the preparation phase, prior to the desensitization work, or during the actual desensitization of a particular highly disturbing traumatic memory. By constantly strengthening the person's present orientation through eye movements, processing of the memory can proceed more safely; that is, with much less danger of unproductive, dissociated reliving of the traumatic event. The CIPOS steps are as follows:

Step 1. Obtain full permission from the client to work on the highly disturbing memory in a gradual and safe way, with ample time in the therapy session to complete the work regardless of whatever unexpected traumatic material may emerge during processing. With clients who have dissociated ego states, it is necessary to also ask for and obtain permission from "any other parts that are involved in this memory."

Step 2. Ensure that the client is aware of the objective reality of the present situation in the therapist's office, including the safety of that place. If the client seems unsure of the physical safety of the present situation, this issue should be addressed directly. Sometimes it is necessary, through observations, questions, and discussion, to help the client see that the fears that are being experienced in the present actually are the direct result of a past event, one that ended long ago and often took place far away. This cognitive orientation to present reality does not have to be accompanied by feelings of safety, but it should be clearly established in the client's intellectual understanding.

Back of Head Scale (BHS) Assessment Method
Constant Installation of Positive Orientation and Safety (CIPOS) Method

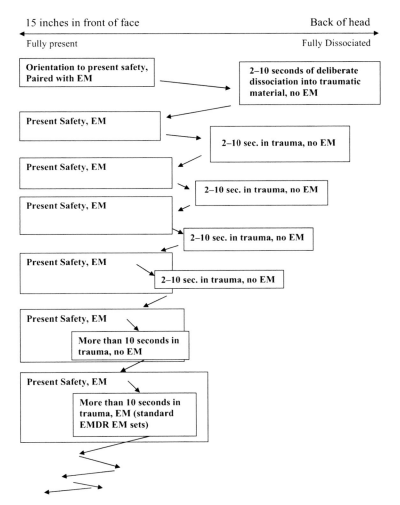

FIGURE 6.1   Flow chart for the BHS and CIPOS methods for
assessment of dissociation and grounding in EMDR sessions. With
the BHS, the client indicates the degree of dissociation, moment-to-
moment, in the session. The session protocol alternates back and forth
between orientation to present safety and exposure to the traumatic
memory. Trauma exposure is at first very brief (with no paired eye
movements) and increases gradually until the client can tolerate
standard pairing of traumatic material with eye movement sets.

Step 3. To further strengthen the person's sense of present orientation, the therapist may ask a series of simple questions relating to the client's present reality in the therapist's office, with each client answer followed by a short set of eye movements. Examples include "What do you think of that picture over there?" or "Can you hear the cars going by outside?" or "Can you see the design in this rug?" or "How many tissue boxes do I have in this room?" When the client responds to these "dumb questions," the therapist says, "Think of that," and initiates a short set of eye movements. In addition, the client's subjective sense of being present can then be strengthened by asking, "What's good about being here right now, instead of somewhere else?" Of course, it is much better to be in the relatively safe present than to be reliving a traumatic event, so (usually without much direction) the client is able to say something like, "I'm comfortable here" or "I know I'm safe here," and this positive information can then be strengthened with additional eye movements. If the client is confused about why the therapist is asking these simple questions, the purpose can be explained—a firm grounding in present reality is an essential precondition for the use of EMDR to resolve old disturbing memories.

One particularly useful method of assisting the client in orienting to present time is to engage in a game of catch with a pillow or a tissue. It seems that it is just about impossible to be dissociated from present reality while tossing an object back and forth. Playing catch is an easily performed task, and seems to require the individual to neurologically activate the orienting response in order to follow the trajectory of the tossed object. This procedure seems to reciprocally inhibit (Wolpe, 1958) the activation of excessive traumatic material, which in turn allows the client to be more aware of the actual safety of the therapist's office.

Thus, with the simple questions, the therapist is directly guiding the client to an awareness of these present stimuli, which automatically carry with them feelings of relief and safety.

Step 4. Through the use of the BHS, the therapist is able to assess the effectiveness of the CIPOS interventions. In this way, it can be ensured that the client is remaining sufficiently grounded in the present, so that reprocessing of the trauma can occur. Children growing up near water sometimes receive some wise advice: "Don't jump into water if you don't know how deep it is." If a client wades into an old memory, without one foot on solid ground, it is likely to be retraumatizing, not therapeutic. The BHS is a way of making sure the client remains safely in shallow water.

Step 5. When present orientation is sufficiently established, ask if the client is willing to go into the memory image for a very brief period of time (two to ten seconds), with the therapist keeping track of the time. This is essentially a carefully controlled dissociative process. Immediately following the end of this period of seconds, the therapist instructs the client, using soothing but repetitive and emphatic words, to "Come back into the room now, okay, now come back here. Just open your eyes, find your way back here now. That's right. Just open your eyes," and so on until the client's eyes open and the client is looking out into the room again.

Step 6. At this point, the therapist gives words of encouragement like "good," or "that's right," and then resumes the CIPOS interventions with questions like, "Where are you right now, *in actual fact?*" with the answers followed by short sets of eye movements. The CIPOS interventions are continued until the client is able to report, using the BHS, orientation toward the present reality of the therapist's office. At this point, Step 5 can be repeated.

Step 7. As this process continues, the client develops increasing ability to stay present as well as greater confidence and a sense of emotional control in confronting the disturbing memory. This opens the door to the use of the standard EMDR desensitization procedures, that is, directly pairing bilateral stimulation with traumatic material.

CHRIS: DISSOCIATIVE IDENTITY DISORDER RESULTING FROM CHILDHOOD SEXUAL ABUSE

In the following case example, the Loving Eyes method is combined with the CIPOS procedure to contain potentially overwhelming unresolved affect in order to assist a fifty-four-year-old man in resolving a very early and severe childhood trauma. Although Chris has had various diagnoses in connection with past treatment episodes, his *DSM–IV* diagnosis since 1992 has been dissociative identity disorder (DID). I started seeing Chris in therapy in February 1999. At that point he had been receiving mental health services intermittently for twelve years. He was receiving social security disability income for his emotional disorder. His treatment within the mental health system had been successful in that he was no longer at risk for hospitalization, and he was no longer imminently suicidal. However, his waking hours were filled with free-floating anxiety, and, as he would express it, he continued to be frequently "dis-suicidal"—his invented word that allowed him to talk about self-destructive ideation while avoiding rehospitalization. In spite of this ideation, his actual suicide risk appeared to be low throughout the time of therapy, which has now concluded successfully.

Chris's case was complex, and the following excerpt from a session does not describe this complexity in full. Instead, the purpose of this transcript is to illustrate the use of the CIPOS and BHS methods, in the EMDR treatment of an individual highly susceptible to dissociation.

Preparation Prior to This Session

At the time of this session, Chris had been in therapy with me for sixteen months. The first six to eight months of our work were spent developing ego-strengthening resources (Kiessling, 2003; Leeds, 2002), helping Chris become generally more comfortable in therapy with me, and putting together, as much as we could, a narrative history of his life experience as well as several maps of the internal structure of his dissociated parts.

This work was guided by established methods of providing treatment to individuals with DID (Kluft & Fine, 1993; Putnam, 1989). Within this model, there are basically three stages to treatment: stabilization, trauma resolution, and integration. Chris had actually been able to attain a relatively high level of stability in his life—he owned his own house, had a circle of friends, and was not engaged in substance abuse or self-injurious behavior. With regard to past trauma, he was able to report, in a kind of dreamy, dissociated way, that sexual abuse had begun at an early age. The clearest of these memories were from ages four to ten and involved violent sexual encounters with adult males in the neighborhood where he grew up. He said, "I try not to remember that, but some of the little ones remember it all, and it still bothers them a lot." He reported that he had been aware for many years of the different parts within his personality system.

Our initial use of EMDR with disturbing material was done very cautiously, with clearly visualized, present-day, low-SUD targets such as not wanting to clean up his kitchen and frustration about not being able to drive his car on a snowy day. We also worked on several more disturbing targets from childhood, for example, a clearly remembered incident of being frightened by a drunken man encountered on the way home from school. For the sake of increased emotional containment and control, we initially used the EMD procedure (Shapiro, 1989), which is different from EMDR in that the client is asked to return to the initial visual image after every set of eye movements. In these sessions, we began using the CIPOS and BHS methods, and Chris reported that this work was very helpful to him.

Difficulties with Self-Assertion and Their Origin

Chris's previous successful sessions became resources as we began to address targets that held more disturbance. In particular, as we began working on a present-day problem, we found that this problem had its origins in an incident of violent childhood sexual abuse. As is often the case with a person with a severe history of traumatization, Chris had considerable difficulty with self-assertion. He reported that it was often terrifying for him to say "no" to another person, especially if that person was in a position of power or authority. This of course was a significant issue, because the ability to say "no" is often crucial in establishing appropriate interpersonal boundaries.

Initially, several sessions of therapy were focused on the ways that this injunction was manifested between Chris and myself. In these sessions we focused through discussion on transference issues and the importance of truth telling in our sessions, with the outcome that Chris was able to express his real feelings much more easily and give priority to accurately reporting his inner experience. This shift, from adaptation to truth-focused therapeutic alliance, was an essential precondition that had to be in place before we could use EMDR with the highly disturbing core memories that remained unresolved.

As we were discussing this issue, Chris told me of several current troubling situations with other people in which this inability to say no was a major problem. We worked with one of these specific situations with EMDR, using the Dissociative Table Technique (Fraser, 1991), with the result that Chris's VOC rating rose from a 2 to a 4 for the positive cognition "I am easily able to say 'no' in a way I feel good about." He felt an increase in confidence following this work, but he also stated that he was aware that this issue remained highly disturbing "to all the little ones."

On the evening prior to our next session, Chris called me to say he had had a very disturbing dream that he was sure was actually a memory of a real event. He was able to contain the affect of the memory dream by making a drawing of it, and the next day in our session he described his drawing in the following way:

> I think I was about four or five years old when this happened. I was walking down by the river in a place where there was tall grass. Some men—they were kind of like bums—jumped out and grabbed me and told me they wanted me to do some things. They took me over to the top of the cliff going down to the river. They put me in a big oil barrel, and they put the lid on it, and then they told me they were going to throw it over the cliff. Here's the drawing I made last night after we talked. When I had the dream, I got these pictures in my mind and these feelings that I'm about to die...or I really wish I would die.

Chris went on to say that this thought was just an impulse, not an actual suicidal danger, but it was nevertheless clear that he was experiencing intense emotion in connection with this memory material. This incident was one that he had alluded to in a previous session, but it was clear now that previously blocked-off visual imagery and affect had broken through his protective dissociation, leaving him vulnerable to an intense reliving of the original event.

Preparing to Work through the Traumatic Memory

In view of Chris's distress in the current session and his success with previous EMDR experiences, we proceeded, with his permission, to make this memory the focus of this session. In this transcript, Chris refers to Little Terri, the dissociated child ego state that holds the unresolved traumatic memory—"the child it happened to."

THERAPIST: [*Looking at the drawing*] So, this is Little Terri, with all the awful feelings on this side of his head.

CLIENT: Yeah, his head split, his mind split from fear, fear and terror.

THERAPIST: And these are the men?

CLIENT: Three of them.

THERAPIST: [*Reading words on the drawing*] "We will kill you if you don't do what we want." "I'm so scared—scared to death. Help, help, help—Jesus!"

CLIENT: He's praying to Jesus.

THERAPIST: "I will always do whatever you want." It's like Little Terri made a promise to them but it was almost like a decision in his life about how he had to be, how he had to live in the world. So, you drew this last night. Chris, let's use our time today—if you think it's a good idea, and if Little Terri thinks it's a good idea—to see what we can do to free him from where he is. I want to be sure, before we begin that though.... Now, how are we going to be sure?—because he'll agree to anything. Does he know that we really want to know if it's okay with him? He does have a right with you and me to say "no" if it's too scary for him to let us try to save him from this place.

CLIENT: Yeah. From what I've experienced the last few days, I don't think it's Little Terri's fear of exploring it so much as...mine. I got this from flashbacks, years back, and one time recently—I don't know if it was a year ago or something—it flashed back again and I had the awesome terror and panic and fright. In the flashback, the barrel was there, and they took him and there was a big cliff. When he looked down, it was just frightening, it was so far down.

THERAPIST: So, you, Chris, have more fear about this than even Little Terri does. Is that what you're saying?

CHRIS: I think so. When I felt that last night, it was just overwhelming...fear and panic. The greatest fear and panic. Well, they told him, they threatened him, they were going to kill him, 'cause apparently he wasn't doing exactly what they wanted, or something. They had a lid for that barrel and put it on. And it was total blackness in there. And, last night, when *I* got the feelings...it was just unbelievable, I probably wept for an hour, hard, and felt the fear and panic and it was awful, it was just terrible. So frightening, so frightening to have the lid put on. I think children somehow are aware of what death is. And to be scared to death, even for a child, is just traumatic and totally freak-out frightening.

THERAPIST: It had to be way, way beyond your ability as a child, when you were a child, to contain it, to understand it. It probably was so overwhelming that all you could do is just what you did.

I used a distancing interweave to help Chris achieve a greater sense of present-day safety:

THERAPIST: Chris, here's something to think about. We're talking about this today, in a room, just about two thousand miles away from where this happened, and just about fifty years, far away from when it happened. And I'm saying this so that you'll include that information in what you're experiencing right now, not to invalidate your feelings, because your feelings are so strong when you think of this, but to give you a perspective that the source of the feelings that you are having right now, at this moment—and this is rather strange when you think about it—is something that happened two thousand miles and nearly fifty years away. And there's that distance which actually creates a lot of real safety for you. Now, that won't make the feelings go away in itself. It's just a perspective to have.

I made sure to obtain permission from the system to work on the memory:

THERAPIST: Is it okay with you, Chris, the grown-up, if we work with this today, and see if we can do something to help it feel better? Along the way it might be very frightening, but the end result would be, I think, that it would feel better.

CLIENT: I think that would be good.

THERAPIST: So you the grown-up say that it's okay to work with this? And does Little Terri say that it's okay?

CLIENT: Yeah.

THERAPIST: Now, check inside and see if it's okay with the other little parts that we work with this today. They don't have to be part of it; if it's too frightening for them they don't have to be part of it. What I'm asking is, are they okay with allowing you and Little Terri to work with this today to see if something good can happen?

CLIENT: They say, "Okay."

I now used CIPOS interventions to make sure that Chris was clearly present in the setting of my office:

THERAPIST: Good. Now before we begin to work on this memory, let me ask you some of my dumb questions. Look around and just say where you are. Where are you right now, in actual fact?

CLIENT: I'm here in your office.

THERAPIST: That's right. Think of that. [Set of eye movements] And notice what's good about being here instead of somewhere else. Notice whatever the answer is right now, today, when you think of that. What's good about being here, in this office, today, instead of somewhere else?

CLIENT: I like being here.

THERAPIST: That's right. Okay.

At this point, Chris closed his eyes and appeared to be beginning to dissociate into the memory experience, in a way that risked upsetting the therapeutic balance between past and present. In order to help him shift back to the present, I use an additional CIPOS method.

THERAPIST: Now open your eyes again if you can, because that helps you stay grounded here. [*Chris opens his eyes.*] But now notice the pull of the memories; they want you to notice them. So let them know, we'll get to you in a minute, we won't forget you. But before we go there, here is another question: Can you catch a pillow with one hand?

CLIENT: I don't know if I can catch with one hand.

THERAPIST: Try and see if you can. Catch this pillow. [*Gently tosses a small pillow.*] Good. Okay, now, can you throw it with one hand? Now see if you can catch it again. Good. [*Chris smiles.*] Are you more back here now? Notice that you are more back here now?

CLIENT: Yes.

THERAPIST: That's good.

Controlled Accessing of the Memory Material

Initially, I ask Chris to think of the memory for only a short interval of a few seconds, without eye movements. Then I ask him to return to being oriented to the therapy room, to acknowledge that he is objectively safe in the present situation, and then we pair this awareness of present safety with eye movements. In this way, Chris is able to continuously strengthen his awareness of safety and maintain the necessary balance in his dual awareness of past and present.

THERAPIST: And now notice when you close your eyes, just let the memory come, let the memory come like it wants to. And let yourself go down into the memory. That's good. And notice how that feels and notice whatever you notice. [*Three-second pause*] Okay, now, Chris, open your eyes and come back here. We'll go back there in a minute, but right now, open your eyes and come back here. [*Chris opens his eyes.*] Are you in my office right now in actual fact?

CLIENT: I am.

THERAPIST: Okay, just think of that. [*Short set of eye movements*] That's good. That's good. Now when I stop moving my fingers, let yourself go back into the memory again. [*Chris closes his eyes.*] That's good. Just take whatever you get and just be there and realize whatever you realize about it when you're there. Notice whatever you notice when you're there. Okay, now, Chris, come back again. Come back here. [*Chris opens his eyes.*] That's good. Are you here?

CLIENT: Yes.

THERAPIST: Good. So just think of that and watch my fingers again. [*Another set of eye movements*] Just realize you're here and nowhere else. Okay now, when I stop moving my fingers again, just let yourself go back there again. [*Chris closes his eyes.*] Good. And maybe notice even more this time when you go back there again, notice whatever there is for you to simply observe. That's right, okay. Now, Chris, open your eyes again and notice now, when you do this, is it easier to come back?

CLIENT: Yeah.

THERAPIST: Good. Notice that; notice that it's easier to come back now. [*Additional set of eye movements*] That's good. That's right. Okay, now this time when I stop moving my fingers, keep your eyes open so you can just simply be here without the eye movements but just know you're still here. Just keep your eyes open. That's good. What are you noticing right now with your eyes open?

CLIENT: It's hard to keep them open.

THERAPIST: It pulls very strongly, doesn't it? The urge to go back there.

CLIENT: Yeah. Like last time I went in, Terri is not just sitting in that barrel. He's really struggling and struggling

> to get out... panicked to get out and... it's like a
> life-and-death struggle rather than... just putting
> a kid in a barrel and putting the lid on. Panicked,
> panicked, panicked...

THERAPIST: Yes, it's understandable that he's feeling a lot of panic. Now, before we go back there again, just return in your mind to the room here. Okay? Just realize you are here, nowhere else than here. You've been here the whole time we've been talking. We're just talking about old stuff, things that happened a long time ago, a long, long time ago. You're really here right now.

CLIENT: Yeah, it's kind of hard. I don't think I fully come out anymore. I kind of stay in it.

Because Chris is indicating some difficulty in maintaining his orientation to the present situation, I assess for the degree of his dissociation using the Back of the Head Scale. He is familiar with the BHS from our work in previous sessions.

THERAPIST: Yeah, that's what can happen when we talk about these things. Show me with your finger: on a line from the back of your head to right out here [*I hold one finger about fifteen inches in front of his face.*], how far out are you?

CLIENT: Maybe in here. [*Points about three inches in front of his face.*] I'm out enough to help but I can't really get away from it.

THERAPIST: It's not necessary to come all the way out for this to work. Just come out enough so you know that in reality you're out here. You are, in fact, here.

CLIENT: I noticed that helps. Kind of like you said, one foot in and one foot out.

THERAPIST: One foot in the present and one foot in the past.

CLIENT: Yeah, I notice that a lot, that it helps. [*Long pause*] It wouldn't be so bad if people just had sex with children... but when they threaten them and terrorize them, then sex is almost a pleasure, you know, compared to that. Big deal, have sex, who cares, just don't kill us.

THERAPIST: Chris, that is exactly the manipulation that they were planning, I think, so that sex with them would look like good news compared with death.

CLIENT: Perps are smart, very smart. They think of everything.

THERAPIST: You know, what we're trying to do here, and I think you can see that it is already happening, is to undo the damage that was caused by that. Can you see that this is already moving in a positive direction?

CLIENT: Yeah, I noticed last week that it helped a very lot, very much.

THERAPIST: Good.

CLIENT: Yeah, but last night the pain and fear was so much that it kept drawing me back in. So, I would go in and find it and then, dwell in it a little bit and then try to talk to the little parts and then try to come back out of it, but, man, I noticed there is so much pain and fear!

THERAPIST: I know there is more than you thought. But do this now: show with your hand, how far out you are right now.

CLIENT: I'm a little farther out. [*He points about eight inches in front of his face.*]

THERAPIST: Good. So what's different from when—I'll show with my hand—you were here [*I point to three inches in front of his face.*] and now you're here [*I point to eight inches in front of his face.*]. What's different?

CLIENT: I am not as...I don't feel so much in the back of my brain as I did a few minutes ago.

THERAPIST: [*Initiating slow eye movements*] Think of that. Just notice that difference. That's good.

What does Chris's statement mean, that he doesn't feel so much in the back of his brain? It is not important that I, the therapist, know the exact meaning to him of these words. Rather, it is sufficiently clear that Chris is describing some kind of positive shift in his experience, toward increased orientation to the present, as measured on the BHS. Thus, my response is to simply strengthen this resource with eye movements, with the result that he is further empowered in his confrontation of the trauma memory.

Accessing the Traumatic Memory for a Longer Interval

As Chris showed increasing ability to return to present orientation from a state of dissociation, he was now ready to remain with the memory longer so we could process it.

THERAPIST: Good. Now when I stop moving my fingers, let yourself go back into it, whenever you're ready. Just close your eyes whenever you're ready [*Chris closes his eyes.*], and go back in for about ten seconds. I'll keep track of the time. You can still hear everything I'm saying just fine. If you want to talk to me from there, you can and I'll hear you. Is there anything you want to say to me, from there?

CLIENT: It hurts a lot. [*Begins crying*]

THERAPIST: Okay now, Chris, open your eyes and come back out again now. [*He opens his eyes.*] Come all the way back out. Find the way back out. Be here. Here's some Kleenex.

CLIENT: Thank you.

THERAPIST: Now remember, keep the eyes open. That helps a lot. Keep the eyes open because then you know where you are. Is it better to be here or there? You want to remember it so you can resolve it, but where would you rather be? Which place would you rather be?

CLIENT: I think I'd really rather be here, but I'm more drawn there. Some days in the past I would be drawn in all day long. I used to go inward and stay there.

THERAPIST: Yes, and when you go all the way in and stay there, it tends to not be therapeutic; it doesn't heal. It's like reliving it. What we're doing here is therapeutic because you're going back and forth, and back and forth. It's a world of difference between that and going completely into it, and being much more there than here. Can you see that?

CLIENT: I kind of caught onto that last week.

THERAPIST: That's good. As we continue this, you're likely to get better and better at staying here at the same moment you go there, almost like a split screen in your mind. Just see if that's possible for you now. Just try it out right now and see.

CLIENT: Yeah, it is.

THERAPIST: Now when you're ready, just go back into it. What do you get now when you think of it?

CLIENT: Fear and pain inside us. Panic and nausea. [*Begins to close his eyes*]

At this point, Chris is feeling a strong sense of being pulled into the memory, and so I begin to talk more actively as a way to maintain his connection with me and the safety of my office.

THERAPIST: Now, keep your eyes open; keep your eyes open. [*Chris opens his eyes.*] Take a good deep breath and look around at the sunshine shining on the carpet here in my office...and see out the window...and just do whatever you need to do to really remind yourself that you're here; you're not there. You're really here. You're in a place where you are safe. You're just remembering things. That's all these are; they're just memories. They feel like relivings, but they're just experiences that are stored in your mind in kind of an unfinished way. That's all they are. They're stored in your neurology, somehow. And we're just working it all out so you can be free of these old memories, from all the disturbance of them. You'll still remember what happened; it just won't tear you up anymore.

CLIENT: Yeah, the mental and physical disturbance, that is horrible, because it keeps us stirred up all the time, and the fear and anxiety we feel, just nausea in our stomach...mental disturbance in our brain...that draws us there and draws us there...to the fear, being very afraid of things. [*Closes his eyes*]

Chris appears to be more able now to access a sense of present orientation and safety, so in order to help him recognize this positive change, I ask the following question:

THERAPIST: Right now, this may be a hard question but, how much are you drawn to be there right now, zero to 10, with 10 the most?

CLIENT: Right now about 5.

THERAPIST: Okay, what was it before?

CLIENT: Probably 10.

THERAPIST: Is something changing? Open your eyes again and notice how easy it is to come back. [*Chris opens his eyes.*] Is that a relief to you?

CLIENT: Yeah, it is.

THERAPIST: Good, think of that. [*Another set of eye movements*]

With his increased ability to come out of the dissociated trauma ego state, Chris is now more able to go back into the memory in a way that is therapeutic. He is learning that he is bigger than this memory.

THERAPIST: Okay, in a few moments, I'm going to stop moving my fingers, so be ready now to go back into it, give into being drawn into it again. [*Chris closes his eyes again.*] There you go. Just let yourself be drawn into it. Kind of satisfy that part of you that wants to just go back and think of it again. . . . That's good.

CLIENT: God, we've got to get out of that barrel. I've got to get Little Terri out of there.

Chris now has a greater awareness of his adult self as experientially separate from his Little Terri ego state. In order to increase the healing connection between these present and past ego states, I ask him the following question:

THERAPIST: Can Little Terri tell that we know about him and that we're trying to save him? Can he tell that's happening?

CLIENT: He does.

THERAPIST: Okay. Now, how does he feel about us trying to save him?

CLIENT: He hopes we will.

THERAPIST: Okay, that's good. Does that help him just a little bit, to know that we are on our way, trying to save him?

CLIENT: It helps even knowing that we know he's in there. He's all alone.

Loving Eyes Intervention

To further enhance the healing connection, I suggest that Chris see his childhood self with eyes of acceptance.

THERAPIST: Chris, can you look right at Little Terri right now and see him in there? Even though he's totally in darkness, you can see him in there, can't you? [*Chris nods.*] Look into his feelings. See into his feelings. Can you see into his feelings? [*Chris nods.*] Stay with that and watch my fingers because this will help a lot. [*Set of eye movements*] Just see whatever you see when you look at him right now and see how scared he is, right after the lid has gone on the barrel. Stay with that.

CLIENT: Let me out! Let me out!

Chris's tone of voice suggests that he is mirroring the words he sees in Little Terri, not dissociating into becoming Little Terri. Nevertheless, to keep the process emotionally safe, I ask him to come back to a clear awareness of present reality.

THERAPIST: Open your eyes now. Open your eyes. [*Chris slowly opens his eyes.*] We'll get back to Little Terri in a minute, but right now come back out of it again. Come back out of it, coming back now. Keep your eyes open; that helps. Just be here. Look around. It's hard to stay here, I know. Isn't it interesting, when you come back here to the safety of this room, how strong the pull is? [*Chris nods.*] Okay, when you're ready, close your eyes and just be drawn into it again. [*Chris nods.*] Let yourself be sure to stay partly here. Little Terri needs so much to know that there are some adults that are on the way. Do you see how that's connected to the pull of being drawn back into it? Little Terri has always needed that. He's always needed to have an adult who sees him with acceptance, who wants to help him be safe, who can know what he's going through. So there's a pull. He needs for us to come back and help him. But before we can do that, it's important to be aware of being safe and being here. So open your eyes now. Is this room a safe room?

CLIENT: Yes, it is.

THERAPIST: Just think of that, Chris. [*Another set of eye
               movements*] I'm really glad you know it's a safe
               room. That's good. That's right. Now, are you ready
               to go into it again? [*Chris nods and his eyes stay
               open.*] Okay, let yourself go back into it. I'm going
               to keep moving my fingers and when you're ready,
               just close your eyes and go back into it. What do
               you get when you go back into it right now?

CLIENT: I don't go back in as far.

THERAPIST: Just notice that. What's different when you go back
               into it now?

CLIENT: It's kind of weird. I feel actually kind of calm, like
               Little Terri's going to be okay.

THERAPIST: How's he feeling right now?

CLIENT: He actually feels a little better, but he's scared.

[Note the differentiation in affect between the two ego states. Chris,
the adult, is calm, while Terri is "better, but scared."]

THERAPIST: Sure he is. I wonder if what you're experiencing
               right now, Chris, is something that's a little bit
               surprising for you. Just notice how that is. Go back
               into it again now. Close your eyes. What do you get
               when you go back into it now?

CLIENT: Little Terri wants out. He's screaming and kicking
               and swinging and praying. Please, please, let me
               out.

Shift to Standard EMDR Desensitization/Reprocessing

At this point, Chris has sufficient orientation to present reality and safety
to use the standard EMDR desensitization procedures, that is, to combine eye movements directly with disturbing material from this memory.

THERAPIST: Okay, open your eyes and think of that. [*Eye
               movements resume and continue while Chris and I
               are speaking.*] And notice how much fear he has in
               his body.

CLIENT: It's terrifying.

> THERAPIST: Just notice that when he's screaming and kicking. Notice all the fear he has. Where does he have that fear, in his body? Where is that fear located in his body?
>
> CLIENT: In his stomach. His mind is shattered.

The word "shattered" implies an irreversible degree of damage to Little Terri's mind. However, in this context, I suspect this word is being used differently, to simply express the intensity of unprocessed disturbance. Therefore, we focus on the experience associated with this word. I ask Chris to be aware, with acceptance, of Little Terri's shattered mind, and he is able to continue the processing. Also, an informational interweave is added—the idea that the shattering of Little Terri's mind may be reversible.

> THERAPIST: Notice how it feels for him when his mind is shattered, how awful that is for him. Just notice that because—you know what?—when you notice how it is for him when his mind is shattered, that begins to heal his mind.
>
> CLIENT: Childhood fear and panic is so awful.
>
> THERAPIST: Yes. So notice how his mind is shattered again now; just notice that. See what happens when you direct your attention to how his mind is shattered. Notice what happens with his mind when he knows that you're seeing that, and you are paying attention to that, and you care about him. Notice what happens. What would you say happens in his shattered mind when he notices that?
>
> CLIENT: It helps him, even though the fear and panic is so great that his mind is just messed up and gone.
>
> THERAPIST: Okay, now keep your eyes open. Stay here, and just notice how disturbing it is for you now. How disturbing is it for you now when you think of it, zero to 10? That's it, go into it and just check it out. How disturbing is it?
>
> CLIENT: It feels quite a bit less. I feel better.

Little Terri's Rescue

The emotion associated with this memory is significantly less than when we started. There is a healing process under way that is proceeding at its own pace and with its own direction. In order to facilitate this process, I remind Chris of our goal at the beginning of the session:

THERAPIST: Chris, just notice that difference. Remember when we started today, the goal was to rescue Little Terri from that barrel. Do you see that that's what we are doing?

CLIENT: I need to get him out.

THERAPIST: How can we get him out of there?

CLIENT: I think a great big adult, like Jesus, that has powers, could come and take that lid off and pull him out of there.

Taking Chris's lead, I add to his imagery.

THERAPIST: Is it okay if you and I and Jesus come right now?

CLIENT: That would be great.

THERAPIST: Let's do that. Just let that happen now. You, I, and Jesus are here. And notice the three perpetrators; notice how they are when they see Jesus.

CLIENT: They fall on the ground and can't move.

THERAPIST: So what do we do now? Let's go ahead and do whatever needs to be done now.

Chris always brought a backpack to our sessions. He hands it to me.

CLIENT: If this were Little Terri, could you reach in and pull him out? [*He cries.*]

THERAPIST: Yeah, here he is. [*Handing back the backpack*] Here, you hold him, okay? You hold him tight. And while you hold him, just move your eyes now and enjoy holding him tight. That's right. Is it okay if he cries? It's okay, isn't it? It's okay if he cries and cries. He probably needs to cry and cry a lot. You won't get mad at him for crying, will you? [*Chris shakes his head "no."*] That's right. [*Set of eye movements*] I'm going to stop moving my fingers in just a moment. Let yourself go back into it again.

Rechecking the Work

Even though the memory has now been largely processed, I ask Chris to go back to it to see what disturbance may remain and to enhance the positive associations he is making.

THERAPIST: Go all the way back into it now. When you go back into it, what do you get now?

CLIENT: I'm so relieved to be out of that barrel. It's like a miracle. I didn't think I'd ever get out. [*Set of eye movements*]

THERAPIST: Now go back into this memory again. What do you get now?

CLIENT: I feel so much relief.

THERAPIST: Notice when you feel that nice feeling of relief in your body, notice where that is. Let yourself breath into it and enjoy it; enjoy that relief. Open your eyes and follow my fingers and just enjoy that relief. Finally. I'm so glad. [*Set of eye movements*]

CLIENT: It feels so good that it's over. [*Chris closes his eyes with relief.*]

THERAPIST: Chris, open your eyes and come back here. Open your eyes and notice how it's different now when you come back here. Remember when you, just an hour ago, went into it and tried to come back out. What's different now?"

CLIENT: I feel kind of *normal*! I feel okay.

THERAPIST: Normal is kind of nice, isn't it?

CLIENT: Yeah, very nice.

Since the scheduled time for the session is winding down, I ask a question to help Chris recognize the shift in his memory, as a way to consolidate what he has gained in this session.

THERAPIST: Let's do this now. Look over across the room and see that picture that you drew. Just remember how scary that was. Look at that now. What do you get?

CLIENT: That was very scary and terrorizing—mind shattering. Fear, panic.... What perps can do to a child's brain and mind is incredibly evil and horrible, but now that Little Terri is out of there,...that picture can be just what it was like at one time.

THERAPIST: Think of that and watch my fingers. And notice any feelings that are still there, anything that's still part of this whole incident. Just notice whatever there is.

CLIENT: There's still fear. That was only like the beginning of the problems, but that was actually the worst part.

THERAPIST: This was the beginning but it was also the worst one. There were others incidents that came later, and on another day, you and I can talk about those other times. Today was a major, major piece of work you've done. Chris, go back again and think of the worst part—when the lid is going on the top of the barrel. What do you get when you think of that? It still may be disturbing to you. Just notice if it is.

CLIENT: That was the worst part. [*Set of eye movements*]

THERAPIST: Just be with that now. Notice whatever you notice about that now.

CLIENT: It's one of the worst things you can do to someone. [*Set of eye movements*]

THERAPIST: When you go back and think of it again. What do you get now?

CLIENT: The lid is off.

That evening, following this session, Chris left a message on my answering machine, saying, "I can't believe this, but since our session, for a few hours tonight, I've still felt normal." In subsequent weeks, he reported with great satisfaction that this particular memory remained resolved. There were other incidents of severe abuse in his history; however, in later sessions, when we were about to work on other difficult memories, he would spontaneously remind himself that "Little Terry is still out of the barrel."

CONCLUSION

The CIPOS method, in combination with the Loving Eyes procedure, seems to be useful not just with clients with DID, but with any clients who are afraid of being overwhelmed by their own posttraumatic affect. With some clients, this method can be a safe and useful preparation for full desensitization of a highly disturbing memory using the standard EMDR protocol. This procedure seems to significantly increase the accessibility of EMDR to clients who are vulnerable to dissociative abreaction. However, it is very important that such clients be informed that unpleasant affect may emerge, in a controlled way, and that full permission of the ego state system be obtained before proceeding. It is also important that the client have sufficient reality contact. That is, the client must have a factual understanding that the current emotional disturbance is a residue of the past—the original trauma is over, and the present situation is one of objective safety. It is not necessary for this understanding to feel true, but it is important that the client know that it is true, in objective reality.

The reader may have noted that the standard EMDR assessment procedural steps (representative visual image of the traumatic event, negative cognition, positive cognition, VOC score, emotion, SUD score, and associated physical sensations) are either absent or modified in the above transcript. Usually in standard EMDR these steps are important as a means of bringing all experiential elements into the processing. Indeed, with nondissociative clients, processing often begins or is accelerated by the assessment questions. In contrast, clients who are potentially dissociative typically do not need this extra acceleration in accessing dysfunctionally stored affective information (Hartung & Galvin, 2002). For these clients, the main issue is how to slow the process down so they are not overwhelmed by their own posttraumatic emotion. A metaphor (useful for clients I see in Colorado) is of coming down a steep mountain road, where acceleration is not a good idea. The main issue is knowing how to slow down, how to steer, and even how to stop when necessary. One element of the standard assessment steps—the 0 to 10 scale—was used in the session to ask Chris how much he was drawn into the memory material, but the purpose of that question was to assist him in decelerating, that is, consciously recognizing and containing the ongoing pull of his dissociation.

In a later session, Chris and I went back and used standard EMDR procedures to resolve the remaining disturbance connected with this incident. Revisiting the event in this way was important because Chris's initial resolution involved a fantasy, not what really occurred, and it was therefore important to go back to recover, process, and resolve all aspects of the real events.

In general, an underlying assumption of the CIPOS method is that the therapist is alert to any positive shift in the client's experience of the traumatic memory, and is constantly strengthening these shifts as resources through eye movements. For example, at one point in time Chris reported that he was still "way back in my head." At another point, a few minutes later, he reported that on the BHS he had shifted to about six inches in front of his nose. The question "What's different now?" focused Chris's awareness on something positive he had just accomplished, and so his response to this question may be regarded as a resource, which then became even stronger and more positive with a short set of eye movements. As another example, a client might say, "I see now how alone I was as a child." These words express a very sad fact of the client's life, but this realization may nevertheless be a positive step in coming to an adult understanding of the childhood events. Therefore, the therapist might then ask, "Is it good you can see that now?" If the client says, "Yes," the therapist can assume that the new information is experienced as helpful and install it as a resource with an additional set of eye movements.

Throughout the CIPOS procedure, the client's answers to the simple orienting questions may reflect the reality of the therapist's office, but may also express information regarding the trauma itself. For example, the therapist may ask, "What do you like about being here right now in this office?" The client may respond, "You aren't hurting me." Such an answer is clearly more about the trauma than about the therapist's office, and when these types of answers are paired with eye movements, desensitization of traumatic material occurs, but in a way that feels softer and safer to the client.

The BHS can also be useful with clients who present in therapy with depressed affect and an emotionally detached interpersonal style. Oftentimes, the depression partially originates in social anxiety and difficulty in engaging in satisfying interpersonal interaction. The BHS gives therapist and client a language to discuss the issue of being comfortably engaged with others. In addition, long-term goals of therapy, and within session positive cognitions, can be defined in the context of the BHS, for example, "Would you like it if you could easily be out here on the line, and easily enjoy talking with other people?"

The effective use of the BHS is based on the assumption that the individual is able to experience some degree of safety in the therapist's office. For most dissociative clients, a sufficient sense of relative present safety can be developed over repeated experiences of being understood and accepted by the therapist. However, for some people with extensive histories of distrust (originating in betrayal of that trust by others), this will not be possible early in therapy. Even if trust in the therapist is established at a later point, the client may still have an abiding sense that subjective safety is an experience that is unattainable. For such clients, all parts of the system live in vigilance and anxiety, even the ego state that has the function of interacting with other people. Some of these clients, after a period of time, can develop a feeling of being *safe enough* to slowly and cautiously access traumatic material. For other clients, very early preverbal traumatic experiences may be dysfunctionally stored, not as recognizable memories, but as a negative coloration to present perceptions. This type of transferential distortion can take many forms, but is usually evident in the interaction between client and therapist. For example, a child who is repeatedly hurt or frightened in interaction with caregivers during infancy may perceive present relationships as intrinsically unsafe, without having clear memories of the events that set this attitude in motion. Such clients are likely to be confused when the therapist presents the concept of the BHS and talks about how the client is "here in the present safety of this room," and thus for these individuals, the BHS is not likely to be useful until later in the therapy process.

However, these dissociative clients appear to be the exception. To date I have used the BHS procedure with approximately forty to fifty clients. It appeared to be helpful on all but a few occasions. One exception was a situation with a client with DID on a day of particularly high stress. In this instance, the eye movements paired with an awareness of present surroundings increased the client's disturbance, and so the procedure was immediately discontinued and other methods of self-calming and self-control were utilized. With this same client, on less stressful days the procedure has been very helpful. This illustrates a principle worth repeating: with this client population, neither this nor any other procedure is an adequate substitute for appropriate training, experience, and accurate attunement to the client. But, with this important caveat, the BHS and CIPOS interweaves seem to be useful tools in enabling individuals with dissociative conditions to reconnect with their full life experience and view their childhood selves with compassion and "loving eyes."

REFERENCES

Forgash, C., & Knipe, J. (2001, September). *Safety-focused EMDR/ego state treatment of dissociative disorders.* Workshop presented at the EMDR International Association Annual Conference, Austin, TX.

Fraser, G. A. (1991). The Dissociative Table Technique: A strategy for working with ego states in dissociative disorders and ego state therapy. *Dissociation, 4*(4), 205–213.

Hartung, J., & Galvin, M. (2002). *Energy therapy and EMDR.* New York: Norton.

Kiessling, R. (2003, September). *Integrating resource installation strategies into your EMDR practice.* Workshop presented at the EMDR International Association Annual Conference, Denver, CO.

Kluft, R. P., & Fine, C. G. (1993). *Clinical perspectives on multiple personality disorder.* Washington, DC: American Psychiatric Press.

Knipe, J. (1995, Winter). Targeting avoidance and dissociative numbing. *EMDR Network Newsletter, 5* (3), 4–5.

Knipe, J. (2002, June). A tool for working with dissociative clients. *EMDRIA Newsletter, 7*(2), 14–16.

Knipe, J. (2005). Targeting positive affect to clear the pain of unrequited love: Codependence, avoidance, and procrastination. In R. Shapiro (Ed.), *EMDR solutions: Pathways to healing* (pp. 189–211). New York: Norton.

Leeds, A. (2002). A prototype EMDR protocol for identifying and installing resources. In F. Shapiro (Ed.), *Part two training manual*. Pacific Grove, CA: EMDR Institute.

Linehan, M. M. (1993). *Cognitive-behavioral treatment of borderline personality disorder*. New York: Guilford Press.

Lipke, H. (1994, August). *Survey of practitioners trained in eye movement desensitization and reprocessing*. Paper presented at the American Psychological Association Annual Convention, Los Angeles.

Paulsen, S. (1995). Eye movement desensitization and reprocessing: Its cautious use in the dissociative disorders. *Dissociation, 8*(1) 32–44.

Putnam, F. W. (1989). *Diagnosis and treatment of multiple personality disorder*. New York: Guilford Press.

Schore, A. N. (2000, June). *The neurobiology of attachment and the origin of the self: Implications for theory and clinical practice*. Paper presented at the EMDR International Association Annual Conference, Toronto, Ontario, Canada.

Shapiro, F. (1989). Efficacy of the eye movement desensitization procedure in the treatment of traumatic memories. *Journal of Traumatic Stress, 2*, 199–223.

Shapiro, F. (2001). *Eye movement desensitization and reprocessing: Basic principles, protocols, and procedures* (2nd ed.). New York: Guilford Press.

Truax, C. B., & Carkhuff, R. R. (1967). *Toward effective counseling and psychotherapy*. Chicago: Aldine.

van der Kolk, B. A. (1994). The body keeps the score: Memory and the evolving psychobiology of posttraumatic stress. *Harvard Review of Psychiatry, 1*, 253–265.

Watkins, J. G., & Watkins, H. H. (1997). *Ego states: Theory and therapy*. New York: Norton.

Wolpe, J. (1958). *Psychotherapy by reciprocal inhibition*. Stanford University. Stanford, CA: Stanford University Press.

CHAPTER 7

Hidden Selves

Treating Dissociation in the Spectrum of Personality Disorders

Uri Bergmann

> In spite of the long tradition of emphasis on the self as a conscious entity in philosophy and psychology, there is a growing interest in a broader view of the self, one that recognizes the multiplicity of the self and emphasizes distinctions between different aspects of the self, especially conscious and non-conscious aspects.... When viewed in terms of memory, the multiplicity of the self becomes less mysterious and, in fact, becomes approachable through the brain.
>
> —Joseph LeDoux, *"The Self: Clues from the Brain,"*
> *Annals of the New York Academy of Sciences*

For Hippocrates (460–400 BC), personality consisted of four traits, referred to as the "humors." The disorders of personality originated in their excesses or imbalances. An excess of yellow bile resulted in irritability; an excess of black bile in melancholia; an excess of blood in an overly optimistic nature; and an excess of phlegm in apathy (Erdberg, 2004). The early Egyptians speculated on the link between the uterus and emotional disorders, passing this fascination on to the Greeks, who, borrowing from their words *hystero* ("placenta" and "embryonic hymens") and *hystera* ("womb"), named them *hysterias* (Babiniotis, 1882/1998). Centuries later, Freud (1915/1925) dealt with the same question, the basic dimensions of personality, positing that "our mental life as a whole is governed by three polarities, namely, the following antitheses: Subject (ego) vs. Object (external world), Pleasure vs. Pain, and Active vs. Passive" (pp. 76–77). Frustration of one or reinforcement of another resulted in maladaptive personality styles skewed toward either actively impacting on the environment versus passively accommodating to it, or seeking new experiences versus avoiding all threat, or focusing on self versus concentrating on the welfare of others. The clinical syndrome of hysteria became the major focus of study on the etiology of maladaptive personality traits by Charcot and Janet, in Paris, and the impetus in the development of Freud's psychological understanding of the personality, in Vienna. Each of them formulated theories on the relationship of personality, traumatic experiences, and dissociative phenomena.

The integration of EMDR with ego state therapy will be presented in this chapter as a comprehensive approach to the treatment of a wide spectrum of personality disorders. These diagnostic categories include individuals manifesting character pathology, narcissistic personality, borderline personality, antisocial and sociopathic tendencies, as well as addictive behaviors. These clients have often been seen as poor candidates for psychotherapy, as well as EMDR, or even nonresponders. They are often mandated for treatment or come at the behest of others. Their histories often include early repeated experiences of abuse, deprivation, abandonment, and parental coldness.

The hallmarks of personality disorders are rigid, intractable defenses and difficulty relating to and empathizing with others. The defensive balance for these individuals has swung more to the pervasively rigid characterological than the overtly dissociative, although dissociative phenomena and defenses are found in those with personality disorders. This presentation will propose, therefore, that the symptoms of personality disorders be viewed as aspects of dissociation that remain hidden and untreated when traditional theory is applied. Central to this approach is the conceptualization of self and object representations, self-objects, and schemas as ego states. Oftentimes, personality-disordered clients present difficulties in both forming and responding to EMDR targets as they often evidence limited results and little or no change in desensitization or reprocessing.

This chapter will examine the applications of the ego state concepts and techniques to all phases of the EMDR process in order to facilitate the treatment relationship—especially with the lonely, vulnerable ego states—as well as identify and strengthen the more developed self-aspects. Treatment is usually long-term EMDR, interweaving the activation of fear-based, aggressive, infantile ego states necessary to facilitate, deepen, and accelerate desensitization and reprocessing. Case examples will be offered of the treatment of passive-aggressive and narcissistic personality disorders.

HISTORICAL AND CONTEMPORARY CONCEPTUALIZATIONS OF EGO STATES

In order to understand and appreciate the main tenet of this chapter—that the most thorough treatment of personality disorders requires the direct and comprehensive targeting of dissociative processes—it is imperative that the history of the positing of dissociation as a normative developmental phenomenon be examined in at least some detail.

In the 1930s, with the theories of Charcot, Janet, and Breuer and Freud long in disrepute, an idea—implied by Janet—began to germinate. In an autobiographical essay published in 1930 at age seventy-one, Janet wrote the following regarding his ideas of dissociation:

> These studies have been somewhat forgotten today because of the discredit thrown on observations relative to hysteria since the death of Charcot in 1895. Hysteria patients seemed to disappear because they were now designated by other names. It was said that their tendency toward dissimulation and suggestibility made an examination dangerous and interpretations doubtful. I believe these criticisms to be grossly exaggerated and based on prejudice and misapprehension, and I still am under the illusion that my early works were not in vain and they have left some definite ideas.... From the medical viewpoint, I still believe that one will eventually be compelled to return to interpretations of neuropathic disorders similar to those which I have proposed in regard to hysteria. (p. 127)

Throughout his writing about dissociation in traumatic hysterias, Janet (1907/1920, 1919/1925, 1930) appeared to imply that the personality patterns that he observed in his trauma patients existed subconsciously in others, although not overtly, and were available to conscious observation. He therefore appears to be the first to describe covert personality segments in nontraumatized people (Bromberg, 1998; Watkins & Watkins, 1997).

Reik (1936), in a work decades ahead of its time, anticipated the issues that we struggle to understand today when he wrote,

> The root problem of neuroses is not fear, but *shock*. In my opinion, that problem remains insoluble until fear is brought into connection with the emotion of shock.... Shock is the prime emotion, the first thing that the little living creature feels.... I hold that shock is in general

a characteristic of a traumatic situation, fear only one of danger. (pp. 267–268)

This appears to be the first explicit writing to connect traumatic feelings and the neuroses and to imply that dissociation, albeit less severe, be considered in the treatment of mainstream psychoanalytic patients.

Federn (1943, 1947, 1952), apparently the first writer to systematically apply the concept of ego states in the psychodynamic understanding of behavior, posited that normally as well as pathologically, ego states are repressed—successfully in "normal" people and unsuccessfully in "neurotics and psychopaths." He viewed ego states as organized entities of the ego, writing, "I conceive of the ego as not merely the sum of all functions, but as the cathexis (energy) which unites the aggregate into a new mental unity" (1952, p. 185). He echoed Janet's ideas of covert "personality segments," stating, "It would be simple to say that the ego feeling is identical with consciousness, yet there are ego states which are not conscious because they are repressed, and there are conscious object-representations which do not belong to the ego" (1952, p. 212). The last part of this statement and his exploration of ego cathexis and object cathexis illustrated, for the first time, the difference between introjection and identification, concepts that were left vague by the brilliant elaborations of Hartmann (1939/1958, 1964) and anticipated the refinements of Jacobson (1964).

John Watkins (1949) described the treatment of an army officer with a phobia of the dark, noting that the successful resolution of the treatment involved more than one ego entity. He wrote further that in contrast to true multiple personality disorders, the two subpersonalities did not emerge spontaneously but could be activated hypnotically. Watkins viewed this experience as "our first direct acquaintance with those covertly segmented personality structures we, now, call ego states" (Watkins & Watkins, 1997, p. ix).

Eric Berne (1957a, 1957b, 1961) extended psychodynamic thought with his elaboration and application of Federn's concept of subdivisions of the mind, predating many of the ideas of Mahler, Kohut, Kernberg, and those of Watkins and Watkins (Erskine, 1997). He described the states of the ego, phenomenologically, "as a coherent system of feelings related to a given subject, and operationally as a set of coherent behavioral patterns; or pragmatically, as a system of feelings which motivates a related set of behavioral patterns" (1961, p. 17). Berne described ego states as child, adult, or parent, conceptualizing them as phenomenological manifestations of the psychic organs. These psychic organs were designated as "archeopsyche," "neopsyche," and "exteropsyche," respectively. Berne considered this as the conceptual model and used these terms and the term "ego states" interchangeably to denote states of mind and their related patterns of behavior (Erskine, 1997). He also stated, in elaborating on the complexity of ego states, that at times a child state could behave as an exteropsyche or a parent state as an archeopsyche. As the model increased in detail, in tune with observations of ego state complexity, Berne (1964, 1972) and his followers described further subdivisions of the child, adult, and parent states, conceptualizing them as the Structural, Functional, and Second-Order Structural models. This allowed for the observations that any one ego state (child, adult, or parent) could have any and all characteristics of another (Trautmann & Erskine, 1997).

John Watkins and Helen Watkins (H. H. Watkins, 1978; J. G. Watkins, 1977; J. G. Watkins & Johnson, 1982; Watkins & Watkins, 1979, 1997), drawing from the ideas of Janet, Breuer and Freud, Reik, Federn, and Berne and from the implicit allusions to personality multiplicity in the writings of Fairbairn, Ferenczi, Glover, Guntrip, Searles, Sullivan, and Winnicott, proposed that the self was comprised of ego states, which they defined as "an organized system of behavior and experience whose elements are bound together by some common principle and are separated from other such states by a boundary that is more or less permeable" (Watkins & Watkins, 1997, p. 25). They viewed the formation of ego states on a developmental continuum, theorizing that personality was segmented into self-states as a result of normal differentiation, introjection, or trauma (H. H. Watkins, 1978; Watkins & Watkins, 1997).

Psychoanalytically oriented developmental infant studies (Beebe & Lachmann, 1992; Emde, Gaensbaure, & Harmon, 1976; Sander, 1977; Stern, 1985; Wolff, 1987) began to suggest that the psyche does not start as an integrated whole, but is unitary in origin: a mental structure that begins and continues as a multiplicity of self-states that maturationally attain a feeling of coherence that overrides the awareness of discontinuity. This was seen to lead to the experience of cohesion and a sense of one self (Bromberg, 1993, 1994, 1996, 1998). Much of this was spurred on by the writings of Ferenczi (1930), Glover (1932), Sullivan (1940), Fairbairn (1944, 1952), Winnicott (1945, 1949, 1965, 1971), Searles (1977), and Lampl-de-Groot (1981), each of whom, either implicitly or explicitly, accorded the phenomenon of multiplicity of the self to be important in their work.

Gazzaniga and LeDoux (1978), renowned for their split-brain research, noted that research and clinical observations (Gazzaniga, 1970, 1976; Gazzaniga, Bogen, & Sperry, 1963, 1965; Gazzaniga, LeDoux, & Wilson, 1977; LeDoux, Wilson, & Gazzaniga, 1977) indicate that in normal people there may well exist a variety of separate memory banks, each inherently coherent, organized, logical, and with its own set of values. These memory banks do not necessarily communicate with one another inside the brain. They note further that these data require us to consider the possibility that multiple selves exist, each of which can control behavior at various moments in time, and that

> the person is a conglomeration of selves—a sociological entity. Because of our cultural bias for language and its use, as well as the richness and flexibility that it adds to our existence, the governor of these multiple selves comes to be the verbal system [the adult self]. Indeed, the case can be made that the entire process of maturing in our culture is the process of the verbal system trying to note and eventually control the behavioral impulses of the many selves that dwell inside of us. (Gazzaniga & Ledoux, 1978, p. 161)

Putnam (1988), then director of the Dissociative Disorder Research Unit of the National Institutes for Mental Health, explored "nonlinear state changes" as a developmental paradigm, stating,

> States appear to be the fundamental unit of organization of consciousness and are detectable from the first moments following birth. . . . [They] are self-organizing and self-stabilizing structures of behavior. When a transition (switch) from one state of consciousness to another occurs, the new state acts to impose a quantitatively and qualitatively different structure. . . . The new structure acts to reorganize behavior and resist changes by other states. . . . Switches between states are manifested by nonlinear changes in a number of variables (Wolf, 1987). These variables include (1) affect; (2) access to memory, that is, state-dependent memory; (3) attention and cognition; (4) regulatory physiology; and (5) sense of self. . . . Changes in affect and mood are, however, the single best marker of state switches in normal adults. (p. 25)

Bromberg (1998) writes that "self-experience originates in relatively unlinked self states, each coherent in its own right. . . . The experience of being a unitary self is an acquired, developmentally adaptive, illusion" (p. 273). He echoes Young's (1988) developmental view of dissociation, stating that "under normal conditions, dissociation enhances the integrating functions of the ego by screening out excessive or irrelevant stimuli. . . . Under pathological conditions. . . the normal functioning of dissociations becomes mobilized for defensive use" (1998, pp. 35–36).

Ramachandran (1995; Ramachandran & Blakeslee, 1998), known for his research on phantom-limb pain and the syndrome of anosognosia (a condition in which an individual is unaware of impairment following a brain injury, or denies being impaired), observed that when confronted with an anomaly or discrepancy, the coping styles of the two cerebral hemispheres are fundamentally different. The left hemisphere tends to smooth over these discrepancies by engaging in denials, confabulations, rationalizations, and even delusions, whereas the right hemisphere appears to be the reality-checking mechanism, more anchored in the truth. Regarding the structure of personality, Ramachandran and Blakeslee (1998) write that the "self may, indeed, be a useful biological construct based on specific brain mechanisms; a sort of organizing principle that allows us to function more effectively by imposing coherence, continuity and stability on the personality" (p. 272). They continue that various parts of the brain create a useful representation of the external world and generate the *illusion* of a coherent and monolithic self that endures in space and time.

LeDoux, an eminent neuroscientist, wrote, "In spite of the long tradition of emphasis on the self as a conscious entity in philosophy and psychology, there is a growing interest in a broader view of the self, one that recognizes the multiplicity of the self and emphasizes distinctions between different aspects of the self, especially conscious and non-conscious aspects" (2003, p. 296). For LeDoux (2002), the self is "synaptic" and to the extent that the self is a set of memories, the particular patterns of synaptic connections in an individual's brain and the information encoded by these connections are the keys to who that person is. Regarding memory, LeDoux writes,

> Because you are a unique individual, the particular multifaceted aspects of the self that define you are present in your brain alone. And, in order for you to remain who you are from minute to minute, day-to-day, and year-to-year, your brain must somehow retain the essence of who you are over time. In the end, then, the self is essentially a memory, or more accurately, a set of memories. That one word, "memory," is the key to our ability to begin to understand the self in terms of how the brain works.... If the self is encoded as memories, then we have a way of beginning to understand how the self is established and maintained in the brain. (2003, pp. 298–299)

LeDoux continues, "It was once thought that memory was a single capacity mediated by a single brain system. We now know that many different systems in the brain are able to learn during experience and store information about different aspects of the experience" (p. 298), echoing recent discoveries that memory is indeed fragmented (Eichenbaum, 2002; LeDoux, 2002; Squire & Kandel, 1999). LeDoux writes further,

> While some aspects of the experience are stored in a system that makes it possible to consciously recall the experience, most of the learning occurs in systems that function unconsciously or implicitly. When viewed in terms of memory, the multiplicity of the self becomes less mysterious and, in fact, becomes approachable through the brain. (pp. 298–299)

Michael Gazzaniga and his associates (Cooney & Gazzaniga, 2003; Funnell, Johnson & Gazzaniga, 2001; Gazzaniga, 1985, 1989, 2000; Gazzaniga & LeDoux, 1978; Gazzaniga & Smylie, 1983; Metcalf, Funnell, & Gazzaniga, 1995; Phelps & Gazzaniga, 1992; Turk et al., 2002; Turk, Heatherton, Macrae, Kelly, & Gazzaniga, 2003) explored the mechanisms by which the brain creates a unified sense of self. Echoing the work of Ramachandran, they noted that split-brain research has identified different cognitive-processing styles for the two cerebral hemispheres. The right hemisphere appears to process what it receives and no more, while the left hemisphere appears to make elaborations, associations, and searches for logical patterns in the material, even when none are present. In lateralized memory experiments, the right hemisphere retains a veridical representation of each to-be-remembered item, tends to recognize previously viewed items, and correctly rejects new items (seen after the experimental sequence), even when they are similar to the target material. The left hemisphere tends to elaborate and make inferences about the material presented, often at the expense of veracity (Metcalf et al., 1995; Phelps & Gazzaniga, 1992). Gazzaniga (2000) has argued that this difference in processing style between the two hemispheres is adaptive and represents an underlying role for the left hemisphere in the generation of a unified consciousness experience. Turk et al. (2003) address the question "How does the brain-mind unify many distinct and distributed mental modules and their content into a coherent self?" by concluding that "the mind just makes it up" (Moss, 2003, p. 3). They posit, from the studies mentioned above and many others, the existence of an "interpreter" module in the left hemisphere whose purpose is to unify the multiplicity of experience and function into a single self-constituting narrative. They write,

> This interpretive function of the left hemisphere takes available information from a distributed self-processing network and creates a unified sense of self from this input. When information from the entire network is available, a realistic interpretation can be made, but when portions of the network are disconnected, the interpretation verges on fantasy. (p. 76)

Therefore, in many of the schools of human behavior theory, psychological and neurobiological, there appears to be a palpable shift with regard to the understanding of the human mind—a shift from the monolithic view of the self to one of the self as decentered and the mind as a "configuration of shifting, nonlinear, discontinuous states of consciousness, in an ongoing dialectic with the healthy illusion of unitary selfhood" (Bromberg, 1998, p. 270).

THE DEFINITION AND SPECTRUM OF PERSONALITY DISORDERS

The current diagnostic system, the *DSM–IV–TR*, defines personality disorders as "an enduring pattern of inner experience and behavior that deviates markedly from the expectations of the individual's culture, is pervasive and inflexible, has an onset in adolescence or early adulthood, is stable over time and leads to distress or impairment" (American Psychiatric Association, 2000). In the general literature, which is more reflective of clinical realities, the overall description of a personality disorder is the presence of serious and chronic interference in cognition and emotion regulation that affects functioning in the domains of work and interpersonal relations. Thus, chronic dysfunction in relationships and work is the hallmark of personality disorders (Clarkin, 2004).

Vaillant and Perry (1985) traced the articulation in the history of clinical psychiatry of the notion that personality itself can be disordered back to work in the 19th century on "moral insanity." By 1907, Kraepelin had described four types of psychopathic personalities. The psychoanalytic study of character pathology began in 1908 with Freud's *Character and Anal Eroticism*. This was followed by Franz Alexander's distinction between neurotic character and symptom neuroses and by Reich's psychoanalytic treatment of personality disorders (Clarkin & Lentzenweger, 1996). Throughout the 1900s, theories of personality development, psychopathology, and treatment have evolved from the cognitive, psychoanalytic, family systems, interpersonal, evolutionary, and neurobiological schools of thought.

The spectrum of personality disorders, according to *DSM–IV–TR*, is clustered into the following three groups: Cluster A: Paranoid, schizoid, and schizotypal personality disorders; Cluster B: Antisocial, borderline, histrionic, and narcissistic personality disorders; and Cluster C: Avoidant, dependent, and obsessive-compulsive personality disorders. A new cluster is being proposed for passive-aggressive and self-defeating personality disorders. Although very descriptive, this classification tends to be rigid and does not allow for the blends of personality traits and disorders that are seen in the real world of clinical practice.

The symptoms of personality disorders, as described in the literature, are seen to be ego syntonic and are therefore reflective of a marked inability at self-observation and introspection. This then leads to the inability to take responsibility for oneself and the need to see all responsibility falling on others. Accordingly, the treatment of personality disorders is characterized in the general literature as more complicated, slower, and less effective than the treatment of symptomatic clients without personality disorders (Clarkin, 2004; Clarkin & Lentzenweger, 1996). Anecdotally, many therapists describe traditional treatment modalities as "impossible" or only minimally effective.

It should be noted that the terms "character" and "personality," and "ego state" and "self-state" are used interchangeably, in the literature and in this chapter.

THE TREATMENT OF PERSONALITY DISORDERS WITH EMDR

Shapiro (1995, 2001) states that personality characteristics are rooted in childhood memories that have left these clients in "child perspectives" and affect states. Their characteristics and symptoms will therefore be ego syntonic, given their lack of appropriate development. She recommends the processing of pivotal experiences as well as categories of experiences to facilitate the elimination of overt symptoms. She writes that experiential processing may allow the client to respond more adaptively to psychosocial stressors, thereby decreasing overt symptoms and potentially increasing future resiliency.

Grand (1998), citing Herman (1992), notes that individuals who have suffered repeated trauma are often misdiagnosed as having personality disorders. He echoes Herman's warning that treatment can be effective only if directed at healing the effects of the traumatic events. He notes that many experienced EMDR practitioners have reported difficulty in accomplishing meaningful growth with clients who manifest rigid ego-syntonic defenses and symptoms and recommends modifications of techniques derived from psychodynamic treatment, such as dynamic interweaves and dream processing. Additionally, he recommends markedly longer sets of bilateral stimulation (BLS) and extensive somatic processing.

Knipe (1998) describes the treatment of a client with an apparent narcissistic personality disorder. He states that the focus of treatment was on the identity structure of the client, not "the relatively isolated damage caused by a specific event" (p. 250). Knipe cogently notes that a great deal of preparation was needed, with the focus on relationship building and empathic mirroring. What is also implied in his writing is the gradual exploration of this client's tendency to demand mirroring and to perceive people—including the therapist—in either a markedly idealized or devaluated manner. Had this preparation not been done, in this way, any future EMDR work would have likely failed.

Manfield (1998) discusses a case that began with a focus on a "bathroom problem" and difficulty with public urination, but quickly got bogged down with characterological defenses and rigidity. This necessitated an elaboration of the preparation phase, which focused on an empathic exploration of the approach and avoidance behavior, within and without the treatment. This allowed for the eventual confrontation of the withdrawal and the material that evoked it, as well as facilitating the use of EMDR. Manfield concludes by noting that the use of EMDR with highly defended clients is a creative endeavor, with the interweave as the central feature of the work. He stresses the importance of understanding characterological issues and the use of skilled and thoughtful innovations. Particularly interesting is his use of the "reparenting protocol," implying the targeting of dissociative processes.

Manfield and Shapiro (2004) state that the utilization of the basic eight-phase approach can be used "straightforwardly" with personality-disordered clients as long as the target is insulated from the characterological issues. They note that when processing the actual character disorder, the treatment is much longer and more complex, requiring extensive preparatory work before, during, and after EMDR targeting. They conceptualize this as (1) stabilization, (2) working in the past, (3) working in the present, and (4) working in the future. Stabilization and preparation are described to take the form of the therapeutic relationship, safe-place imagery, and resource-development techniques (Korn & Leeds, 2002; Leeds, 1998; Leeds & Shapiro, 2000; Linehan, 1993). Manfield and Shapiro note that when traumatic memories are accessed, clients often revert to "a dissociated child state . . . in which the powerlessness of childhood is reexperienced as if still valid for the adult" (p. 321) and stress that these "memories must somehow be linked up to a more mature reality-based adult perspective to be metabolized" (p. 322). They observe that the use of BLS and dual awareness causes a rapid oscillation of attention and awareness between the present and the past perspectives, facilitating a swift integration of the two.

These examples illustrate attuned and dynamically sophisticated modifications, which are paramount if the EMDR targeting is to succeed in its use with personality-disordered clients. My experience, however, has been that they are in general, incomplete, in that underlying dissociative processes and defenses, although recognized and, to some degree, addressed, are not targeted and treated, explicitly or comprehensively.

DISSOCIATION: A DEVELOPMENTAL LINE OF PERSONALITY

Phyllis Tyson (1998), in a special volume of the *Journal of the American Psychoanalytic Association* that was dedicated to developmental theory, commented on the upheaval in the field of developmental psychoanalysis, noting a new emphasis on the plurality, multiplicity, uncertainty, and ambiguity that have come from a recognition of the complexity of nature and of how little we really know about it. Psychoanalytic developmental theory has not escaped this challenge and this scrutiny. Indeed, the very nature of developmental theory has been challenged. Tyson credits Nobel laureate and cytogeneticist Barbara McClintock for this shift in attitude about our methods of study. McClintock recommended that we "always question how we know what we know" and discovered that when she shifted her orientation in this manner, she could see things she had not seen before (Keller, 1983).

It is proposed, therefore, in keeping with the work of John Watkins and Helen Watkins, that dissociation be viewed as another developmental line (A. Freud, 1963), in addition to psychosexual maturation, drive taming, object relations, adaptive function, anxiety level, defensive function, identity formation, and internalization. Accordingly, as in the other developmental lines, dissociation will be viewed as a dynamic continuum, from healthy/adaptive to pathological, and will be present, at some level, in all diagnostic categories.

Therefore, the symptoms of personality disorders will be viewed as aspects of dissociation that remain hidden and untreated when traditional theory is applied, and, accordingly, these dissociative processes will need to be addressed directly and comprehensively. This recommendation is made in contrast to approaches that either target dissociation indirectly or directly only when it is so rampant as to derail treatment or threatens to cause the client to decompensate.

Central to this approach is the conceptualization of character traits, dynamics, and symptoms as ego state driven. Accordingly, for example, from a cognitive-behavioral approach, early maladaptive schemas, aspects of schema maintenance, schema avoidance, and schema compensation are considered ego states, as are their respective beliefs and behavioral patterns. So, for example, the early maladaptive schema of "I'm incompetent" is seen as an ego state with that belief as its core. The schema maintenance and the self-defeating behavior that it produces are seen as an ego state that behaves in that manner. The same holds true for schema avoidance and schema compensation. From a psychodynamic perspective, aspects of psychosexual development, drive derivatives, object-relations (self and object representations, self-objects), adaptive function, anxiety level, defensive function, identity, and internalization (superego function) are considered ego states and their respective beliefs and behavioral patterns. For example, in the realm of object relations, the self-representation of "I'm bad" is seen as an ego state with that belief. In the realm of identity, the fear of engulfment or abandonment is seen as an ego state with that fear. The same holds true for the other developmental lines.

From the perspective of self psychology, all self-configurations are conceptualized as ego states. For example, the grandiose self (Kohut, 1971, 1977) is conceptualized as an ego state.

Ego-syntonic traits are conceptualized as unconscious ego states. That is, there is no co-consciousness. As the ego state exploration commences and these ego states emerge from hiding, so to speak, they become conscious, as do their beliefs and behaviors. Once this is accomplished they become increasingly ego alien (ego dystonic).

TREATMENT GOALS

The goal of treatment in traditional psychotherapy is to make the pathological, ego-syntonic trait dystonic or alien to the client. This is done by exploration and properly dosed confrontation designed to facilitate an increase in anxiety. If this anxiety is generated at an optimal level, the client is rendered sufficiently anxious to be motivated to explore change. The problem with this theory is that personality-disordered clients become either too anxious or not anxious enough and, in either case, are unable to move ahead with their treatment, which either bogs down or terminates prematurely.

Ego state work, in contrast, focuses on discovery of the self (or selves). This inquiry entails constantly focusing on the client's experience of affect, motivation, beliefs, or fantasy and not on behavior or problems alone (Erskine, 1997). It is grounded in a genuine interest in the client's subjective experience. As the exploration of different self-states ensues, co-consciousness of different selves increases. In the process of the exploration, the feelings, fears, issues, and adaptive traits of the self-states are explored. This renders them increasingly dystonic. Within this process, the therapist articulates the understanding that these selves, no matter how angry or apparently maladaptive, are serving a function that is in some way adaptive. This is accomplished by the explanations regarding the adaptiveness of these functions in childhood and of their origin, as creations of children, given the limitations of children. The product of this exploration and explanation is attunement and empathy, the likes of which the client has usually never before experienced.

This is in stark contrast to the anxiety that traditional treatment creates. The client generally experiences this attunement once the therapist gently moves past the defenses that protect the client from awareness and makes contact with long-forgotten parts of the self. It is this empathic sense of safety that is required for these clients to slowly but surely begin to examine their traumatic experiences and shed their character armor (Reich, 1933). It is also the introjection and eventual identification of the therapist's empathy that over time allows these clients to develop their own sense of empathic awareness of others.

INTEGRATING EGO STATE TREATMENT INTO THE EIGHT-PHASE PROTOCOL

Phase 1: History

A careful history is taken on a number of dimensions to identify critical targets for processing. Regarding the three-pronged approach, an exploration is undertaken to identify (1) past experiences that underlie the dysfunction, (2) present situations that act as triggers, and (3) future templates that target anxiety vis-à-vis future behaviors and functioning. A developmental assessment is also paramount in that the fears and beliefs generated by the developmental level that the client is functioning at will reflect targets that may or may not be explicitly articulated during the ego state exploration or the ego state work proper. For example, if a client is manifesting borderline personality organization, self-states will be struggling with fears of engulfment, abandonment, and annihilation, reflecting, in this example, the developmental lines of object relations, drive taming, and anxiety level, respectively. This may not be articulated, if at all, until months or years into the treatment. The awareness of these themes by the therapist will facilitate developmentally attuned interweaves during the ego state work and targeting, which will be experienced by the client as profoundly empathic.

It is also extremely important, before embarking on EMDR, to either screen for or assess the level of dissociation. In order to ensure accuracy, it is recommended that a structured interview, such as the Dissociative Disorders Interview Schedule (DDIS; Ross et al., 1989) or the Structured Clinical Interview for DSM–IV Dissociative Disorders (SCID-D; Steinberg, 1994), be utilized.

Phase 2: Preparation

In this phase, ego state work is explained to the client. The existence of ego states as a normal developmental phenomenon is articulated until the client finds an understanding and comfort. This often goes rather quickly, with many clients claiming that this notion had occurred to them instinctively. The next step is to explain and prepare the client for EMDR. The process in this model is identical to the standard preparatory phase for all EMDR, with one exception. The therapist explains to the client that the EMDR targets that are generated will at times be ego state specific.

With this in place, the ego state exploration can begin with the development of the imagery. My preference is to explain the Dissociative Table Technique (Fraser, 1991, 2003), also known as the "conference room," so that the client understands the underlying concepts. The Dissociative Table Technique is a straightforward method to gain access to a client's inner world without engaging in formal hypnotic inductions. It is easily accomplished in the patient's normal waking state by asking a patient to imagine a pleasant internal "conference room" in which there is comfortable furniture for all aspects of the self. At the center of the room is a large conference table with comfortable chairs surrounding it. Fraser (1991) suggests that the shape of the table be oval so as to preclude arguments as to who sits at the head of the table. I often suggest a round table because even an oval table can be seen as having a head. There may be various equipment (for example, a microphone, spotlight, remote control, or movie screen) and adjacent facilities as needed for any given self. For example, there may be a waiting room with or without speakers and a one-way mirror so others can hide but observe (Paulsen, 1995). This explanation allows the client to visualize the table or conjure any other imagery that feels safe or more "resourceful." Other examples of places where ego states can gather are a meadow adjacent to a forest; a beach surrounded by caves; a large, open living room with closed rooms around it; or the stage of a theater, complete with the seats and the backstage area.

What is most important in this imagery is the allowance for an open (exposed) area and an area for hiding, to respect the needs of the ego state system as the client becomes familiar with the "internal cast" (Fraser, 2003). For clients with borderline personality organization, the conference room may be more suitable, since their level of dissociation can be expected to be high. The detailed features of the room supplant the need for either switching or formal hypnosis and therefore save time and enhance co-consciousness (Paulsen, 1995). Some clients may come to treatment already able to hold dialogue with self-states and may not need this imagery. The reader is referred to Fraser (1991, 2003), Twombly (2000), and Paulsen (1995) for detailed descriptions and suggested language for this technique.

Once the imagery is set up, the client is asked to assume the role of the adult ego state, either at the conference table or in the open area of the chosen imagery. This self-state has been referred to in the literature by a multitude of names, including the "adult self," the "presenting personality," the "executive personality," the "host personality," and, most recently, the "apparently normal part" (ANP) of the personality (Nijenhuis, van der Hart, & Steele, 2004b; Steele, van der Hart, & Nijenhuis, 2001). The latter designation was originally coined by Myers (1940) and resurrected by Nijenhuis, Steele, and van der Hart in their recent articles (Nijenhuis, 2004a).

The adult self is then asked to invite any and all other selves to come into the open area if they wish to be included in the discussion. The client is invited to be the voice for the self-states and communicates their experiences to the therapist (Paulsen, 1995). Although the aim of the treatment was articulated by the therapist during the preparation for the table technique, it is helpful to again state that all of the ego states are part of the system and that the aim of the treatment is the elimination of the dissociative barriers and the facilitation of harmony and cooperation. The assumption is that self-states are listening and many are suspicious. Movies and many therapists have suggested that the aim of this type of treatment is the fusion of ego states into one cohesive state. One should assume that a realistic paranoia exists internally and should continually, throughout the treatment, remind the adult self (or any other self that is active) that ego states are not eliminated or "killed," not even the most virulent and angry ones. Anger and hate should be explained to contain the energy and assertiveness that was channeled into defense. Borrowing from systems theory, the context and function of these self-states needs to be explained as having been adaptive at one time. In a language that can be understood by children, the therapist needs to explain that all the selves can keep their jobs (even if we don't yet know what they are) and need only to retool, that is, learn another way to do them. This will need to be continually articulated throughout the treatment, as other ego states will come out of dissociative zones and enter the treatment for the first time.

When the adult self sees or in any other way senses the selves around the table or in the room (or whatever other open area the client has chosen to imagine), the therapist guides the client to "just notice what happens." The appearance of other selves may occur within moments or may take many sessions. A delay may indicate uncertainties about trust, a lack of belief in the normality of ego states, or fear of exposure by the ego states in control. In any case, additional assurances regarding the normality and the safety of the ego states will be required. Issues of trust and transference may also need to be explored.

Upon reporting the presence of other ego states, the client is asked to give some description of them, such as age, gender, and emotional state. There may be some confusion in these self-states as to where they are, who the others are, and so forth. This is an opportune time to orient them, if necessary, to the date, the place, and the identity of the other states. Their relation to the adult state will also need to be explained. The adult self may also be surprised by the physical manifestation of the other ego states. For example, the gruff voice that was so feared may actually belong to a young child ego state, some ego states may be of a different gender than expected, or some may look like the presenting personality did at a younger age. What needs to be explained at this point is that what appears at the table is not the interpretation of the adult self, but rather each ego state's own perceived identity. The various ego state presentations may represent ages from the time that these states were formed or may be symbolic of their roles, for example, a tough-looking persona or a seductive one.

Now that the initial group of selves has come to the table or the opening, the next step is to set up a way to communicate with these ego states in an organized manner. It should be remembered that until this point, these ego states generally have made only unexpected and spontaneous appearances, at times to the distress of the adult state. Just as likely, some have been operating internally, triggering affective and somatic experiences. For some clients, however, there may never have been any previous dialogues with the internal states or co-conscious awareness until this point.

In the ensuing sessions, different ego states will show themselves at different times. This becomes a good opportunity not only for exploration but also for self-soothing and resourcing. This is accomplished by making use of the client's dissociative abilities and allowing the adult ego state to act as a parent and soothing agent for the other ego states. Very often ego states will present themselves as angry, anxious, or extremely frightened. The adult ego state can ask these selves what their experiences are and what they need to feel better. The adult self can then soothe the younger selves or ask another more adaptive and helpful self to do the soothing. This soothing can be accomplished by explaining away confusion, holding, and comforting and continuing to explain that the adult self is there as a permanent ally—something that these selves did not have in their childhood or adolescence.

Angry and critical ego states can also be expected to appear, and initially will not allow themselves to be soothed or cajoled. The most useful response by the therapist is to continue to ensure them that the therapist and the adult ego state will continue to be available when these selves feel the need. When this happens, the therapist or the adult self can take the opportunity to explain to the other selves that underneath the angry, critical, and punitive expression of these selves is fear and shock, which are expressed as anger and criticism.

Regardless of the reaction of these angry and punitive selves to these comments, the therapist should be aware that all communications have been heard and have at some level been registered as empathic. It should be understood that any communication made by the therapist is also assumed to be heard by any and all other ego states because there can be no way to ascertain if other ego states are lurking within hearing or in some dissociative zones during any given session. This parenting, soothing, and enlisting of other ego states constitutes an internally ecological resourcing that becomes the mainstay of the preparation phase.

When the ego state system has become comfortably accustomed to this pattern of communication with the therapist, the time for an EMDR target is at hand. The therapist needs to again explain the process of EMDR to the ego state system and, when the system appears to understand, obtain permission to proceed with EMDR from the self-states. If permission is not obtained, the following can be expected: clients with borderline personality organization, whose level of dissociation can be expected to be high, may deteriorate, and clients with more adaptive personality organization may not process properly, or may begin looping at the onset. My experience, from using this approach for the past seven years, is that obtaining permission is experienced internally as a courtesy and as such garners a great deal of internal cooperation and results.

Phase 3: Assessment

At this juncture, the client and therapist, utilizing what both have learned from the history taking, work at formulating an overarching EMDR target. For most personality-disordered clients, this entails the negative cognition that comes as close as possible to the core of their dysfunction. For clients with borderline personality organization or low-functioning, narcissistic personality organization, a global target would be contraindicated. This is due to their high level of dissociation and the potential for maladaptive affect bridging. For clients such as these, EMDR targets need to be fractionated (Fine, 1991) by formulating and processing these targets by individual ego states. The overall procedures for treating borderline and low-functioning narcissistic personality disorders should follow the guidelines for the treatment of dissociative disorders with ego state work and EMDR.

Since in most personality disorders there are rarely profound or defining traumas, the targets for EMDR processing tend to be characterological, for example, schemas, self-representations, or other developmental lines, which are easily formulated into standard EMDR targets. Let's take, for example, a client whose main characterological issues revolve around a fear of inadequacy. As in the standard protocol, the client is asked to bring up a picture that goes with this fear. The therapist should be mindful that other sensory modalities may also be involved and inquire about sounds, smells, and so forth. The client is then asked to generate a negative cognition ("I'm inadequate"), a positive cognition ("I'm okay"), a VOC rating, affective state, SUD level, and sensory location of discomfort.

Phase 4: Desensitization

Processing of the target begins in the usual manner. The client is asked to "just notice" and give the therapist feedback when asked. As long as the processing continues in the expected manner, the therapist follows standard procedure and stays out of the way. When the process begins to loop, an ego state interweave is utilized by asking, "Is any self in the system experiencing difficulties with this process?" In most cases, one or any number of selves will communicate their distress. The therapist can then explore the particulars of the problem and enlist the adult or any of the other ego states to solve the problem. In many cases, these selves will report fears of the affect, or the fear of being alone while this affect is being generated. The explanations, assurances, and soothing by the adult or other self-states will often ameliorate the problem.

When this is done, the therapist returns the client to target. There is generally a noticeable reduction in anxiety and the processing continues in standard fashion until the next looping, where the same ego state interweave is utilized. If the interweave is again successful, the client is returned to target and the level of disturbance can be expected to be reduced.

There are times, however, when this type of interweave will not be successful due to some form of blocking belief, resulting from either a schema or a characterological dynamic. For example, a young self-state may not allow itself to be soothed and will articulate, "I don't deserve to be soothed." It can be expected that no cajoling or soothing by other ego states will have an effect. The therapist can, however, inquire if this ego state would like to be helped. If the ego state answers, "Yes," or even, "You can try to help, but nothing is going to work," the therapist can then suggest and formulate an ego-state-specific target, utilizing either "I don't deserve to be soothed" as the negative cognition or, depending on the exploration, something more global, such as "There's something wrong with me." A complete target is then formulated and the standard EMDR instructions are given to this self-state.

These ego-state-specific targets tend to process rather quickly, often taking from twenty minutes to two sessions for desensitization down to a SUD of 0, installation up to a VOC of 7, and a clear body scan. Upon completion of this target, the therapist utilizes ego state work to make the transition from this state to the adult state and to the return to target (the original target). As before, the level of disturbance will be reduced and processing will continue.

This kind of looping, conceptualized as the dissociated feeder memories, can be expected to occur continually, with many different self-states interrupting the process as they become triggered. At times ego state work alone will be sufficient and at other times, these ego states will require their own targets to work through their blocks. Conceptually, what is required to treat dissociation, at its most comprehensive level, are these ego state interweaves and target-within-target interweaves. This to-and-fro movement—from the main target, to ego state work, to ego-state-specific targets, to return to the main target—is carried out in the required sequences until the original or main target has been desensitized to a SUD of 0.

Phase 5: Installation

As in the standard protocol, the installation phase is used to facilitate the full integration of the positive cognition with the targeted information. The adult self-state pairs the positive cognition with the target and processes it until the VOC rating reaches a level of 7 (or perhaps a 6, if ecologically valid) and does not increase in strength with additional sets.

Phase 6: Body Scan

When the VOC rating reaches a level of 6 or 7, the adult ego state is asked to hold both the target and the positive cognition in mind while mentally scanning the entire body to identify any lingering feelings of tension or tightness or any other unusual sensation. If the adult ego state reports any unusual physical sensations, they are targeted with further sets. The sensations will usually clear uneventfully with a few successive sets. On the other hand, although not as frequent, focusing on body sensations at this point can open other channels of information triggered by ego states that are emerging from deep dissociation and are becoming conscious. When this does happen, the dynamics or schemas of these ego states are explored by the therapist and the adult self-state. As was done previously, this is either repaired with standard ego state work or ego-state-specific targets to process the blocking beliefs or feeder memories. Upon full resolution, the adult ego state is again asked to pair the original target with the positive cognition and, again, perform a body scan. At this point, a clear body scan can be expected.

Phase 7: Closure

The closure to any session is carried out in the therapist's standard manner and involves imagery or other stabilizing and containment techniques. Afterward, a safety assessment is made, followed by some form of debriefing.

Phase 8: Reevaluation

This is done in the standard manner of the therapist at the outset of the next session.

CASE PRESENTATIONS

Arnie: Treatment of Passive-Aggressive Personality Disorder

Arnie was a forty-eight-year-old, extremely successful married man with two children. He was the youngest of three children, being two years younger than his sister and four years younger than his brother. He began his treatment with me in 1995, following seven and a half years of thorough psychoanalytic treatment. His father had died four months prior to Arnie's entering treatment. Arnie reported what appeared to be substantial growth in his previous treatment. He stated that he began treatment at his wife's insistence and related that she complained of his being aloof, withdrawn, passive-aggressive, and critical. He acknowledged that he still struggled with these symptoms, although they were much improved, and stated that he hoped that EMDR would finish what his psychoanalysis had left undone.

Arnie was extremely successful in his work and prospered financially. He spoke of his two adolescent children with great tenderness and empathy and related that although he loved his wife, he felt unable to experience this tenderness and safety with her. Arnie experienced her as controlling and as the "enemy," and felt unable to assert himself and articulate his beliefs.

Arnie described his father as self-centered, narcissistic, and a workaholic. He said he was impatient, critical, and often angry and emotionally labile. When describing his father's narcissism, he noted that his father's view of Arnie was contingent, on any given day, on how Arnie had made him feel that day. Arnie felt that his needs were never considered. If Arnie's school grades were high and his tennis game of the highest level, his father would interact with him. Arnie's siblings were neither excellent students nor tennis players and were therefore devalued and generally abandoned by their father.

Arnie experienced his mother as narcissistic, critical, and clinging. Although gratified by Arnie's performances, she always pressed for more. Like his father, she viewed tennis as the supreme social sport. Arnie felt that she was subservient to his father and never defended him.

Arnie's siblings, reacting to their felt neglect by their parents, were envious and resentful of Arnie. This continued into their adult lives and was often acted out at family gatherings.

Arnie's developmental assessment revealed the following: Psycho-sexual maturation tended to be moderately complete, evidencing mild regressions during interpersonal difficulties with his wife. His difficulties in asserting himself with his wife, other than in a passive-aggressive manner, evidenced incomplete neutralization of aggression. Self and object representations were conflicted and led to his experiencing himself as inadequate and his wife as narcissistic and untrustworthy. When he was able to be introspective and to utilize an observing ego, he noted that these were fantasies and were not based on her behavior. His capacity for self/object differentiation was well developed, with appropriate boundaries in the majority of his relationships. His overall function evidenced superior synthetic and integrative functioning. Signal anxiety was fully intact, with his patterns of anxiety tending to revolve around feeling emasculated and inadequate. Defenses were relatively high functioning, with dissociation at the more adaptive end of the spectrum. His overall sense of identity was moderately well established, tending toward regressions in his interactions with his parents and his wife. With respect to overall levels of internalization, he appeared overly identified with his father's punitive perceptions. Diagnostically, Arnie appeared to display a passive-aggressive personality disorder, and his level of dissociation, assessed by the DDIS, appeared to be at the low end of the spectrum.

Because Arnie's treatment began prior to my utilization of ego state work with clients who functioned at his level, his preparation for EMDR was standard. Arnie reported a number of positive experiences with hypnosis and asked if he could utilize it as his resource and safe place. This was accomplished with an induction, utilizing progressive muscular relaxation and guided imagery. With his resource in place, Arnie was also taught the eye-roll technique for hypnotic induction and appropriate imagery to be used between our sessions for self-soothing.

The next phase of his treatment (Phase 3) began with the standard EMDR targeting his fear of assertiveness. When asked for an image Arnie said, "I see myself as a worm ground into the floor." His negative cognition was "I can't assert myself without rage." His positive cognition was "I can assert myself without rage," with a VOC of 2. Affectively, Arnie became aware of "an awful inner pain," with a SUD of 6. Somatically, he experienced a tightening of his muscles and slight nausea.

The processing started (Phase 4) and continued for months, with extensive cognitive and dynamic interweaves. An audio CD designed for EMDR was utilized, with continuous stimulation. Arnie's experience of EMDR was extremely emotional and dramatic, and he felt an intensity of affect that was very new for him. He felt that the dynamic interweaves "went deeper" than any of his previous analyst's interpretations, and he was very hopeful.

However, as the next three months passed, he noticed very little change and became increasingly frustrated. To his credit, Arnie, a veteran of seven years of psychoanalysis, continued to press forward. Although still frustrated by his lack of symptomatic change, he began to notice an intrapsychic change as he began to feel safer and "cared for" in the therapeutic relationship. Unlike his analysis, which dealt with the same issues but was unemotionally verbal, Arnie experienced EMDR as intense and emotionally moving.

During the beginning of a session approximately nine months into the treatment, after processing for approximately ten minutes, Arnie said, "The problem isn't that I can't assert myself without rage; it's that I feel inadequate as a person...and realizing this frightens the hell out of me." When he was ready, we reassessed the target and found it was similar to the previous one. When asked for an image Arnie said, "I still see myself as a worm ground into the floor." His negative cognition changed to "I'm inadequate." His positive cognition was "I am adequate," with a VOC of 2. Affectively, Arnie continued to feel "an awful inner pain," with a SUD of 7. Somatically, he continued to experience the muscular ache and the queasy feeling in his stomach. He realized that despite the lack of symptomatic change, his ability to experience his fear of inadequacy was a dramatic piece of growth, and he felt gratified.

In the spring of 1996, I began to notice, both in Arnie and in other high-functioning clients, a variety of subtle self-state shifts. To me, these were subtle variations of the kind of switching that I observed in my extremely dissociative clients. Since at that time I had only been treating highly dissociative clients for approximately a year and a half, it didn't surprise me that I had been "blind." When I mentioned this to colleagues who were experienced in the treatment of dissociative disorders, I was informed that there was a small body of literature that addressed the existence of dissociation across all diagnostic categories. This of course led me to the writings of Federn, Berne, Watkins and Watkins, Erskine, and Bromberg. As I was reflecting on my observations and the ideas expressed by the aforementioned authors, it occurred to me that the mainstream psychoanalysis that Arnie had undergone and my use of the standard EMDR protocol, including dynamic interweaves, were limited in their scope in that the presence of dissociation, albeit mild, was not being directly addressed.

Arnie's treatment shifted to a new preparation phase as we began to explore and identify his ego states. As I explained this shift to Arnie, he was simultaneously frightened and fascinated. My understanding of Arnie made me aware of the fact that he would have to grasp this concept cognitively prior to being able to embrace it emotionally. Arnie had related to me, in his history, that he had read a fair amount of the psychoanalytic literature in the beginning of that treatment. He was extremely bright and had achieved a good understanding of developmental diagnosis and the concept of developmental lines. When I suggested that he add dissociation to that list of developmental lines and just conceptualize what that meant to him, he understood and his anxiety dissipated.

We spent the next few sessions utilizing the dissociative table, exploring and listing the ego states that became apparent to him. Arnie became aware of the following self-states: an inadequate four-year-old; a frightened three-year-old; a "wormlike" five-year-old; an enraged eleven-year-old; his adult self; his professional self; a number of adaptive adolescent selves; a paternal introject; a maternal introject; and his paternal self. His treatment now took the form of exploration and self-soothing. Arnie utilized his adult and other adaptive selves in the soothing and comforting of the younger selves who were frightened and confused. One of Arnie's most adaptive roles was that of a father, and he was able to utilize this strength, mobilizing his paternal self, in the reparenting of his younger, fragile selves.

After a few sessions of this exploration and soothing, as Arnie was becoming comfortable with his multiplicity, we asked permission to return to the previous target, which dealt with his fear of inadequacy. We reentered the assessment phase (Phase 3) to check if the previous target was still valid and if so, to check the levels of distress. All aspects of the target remained unchanged except the SUD level, which had now risen to an 8. The rise in the SUD level indicated to me that although permission was given for this processing, not all the selves were involved and some future sabotage could be expected.

We reentered the fourth phase of desensitization and restarted the target. As Arnie began processing, he noticed that he was becoming slightly agitated and frightened. I suggested that he stay with the material and "just notice." This continued for the next twenty minutes with no change. Utilizing an ego state interweave, I asked, "Who is afraid to proceed with this?" Arnie reflected for a moment and said, "Someone is huddled in the dark....It's the frightened ten-year-old. He's saying that he's scared and has to stop this." I asked why and Arnie answered, "He says it's too dangerous." I suggested that Arnie's adult and the other adaptive self-states might try to soothe and comfort that self. This was attempted for approximately ten minutes, to no avail. Arnie was becoming more agitated and wondered what else we could do. I asked if this self-state wanted some help. Arnie reflected for a moment and answered, "He says he wants help, but nothing will work."

It occurred to me to try an interweave using an ego-state-specific target, since this would link the treatment of dissociation and its inherent fragmentation of neural networks (ego states) to the main (overarching)

EMDR target, ensuring the proper targeting of memory networks. I explained that the frightened self needed only to focus on his feelings and "just notice." Arnie reluctantly agreed. When asked for an image, the frightened self said, "I see nothing." His negative cognition was "Anger is dangerous." His positive cognition was "Anger is okay," with a VOC of 2. Affectively, the frightened self felt "scared," with a SUD of 9. Somatically, he experienced upper chest and abdominal tightness. The frightened self began processing the target, sitting in the adult self's lap.

The entire target processed in approximately forty minutes (SUD of 0, VOC of 7, and a clear body scan) and required no interweaves. An ego state interweave was utilized to return to the adult self and to the original target. The adult self reported that the SUD level was down to a 6 and that he felt "looser."

This process of weaving back and forth from the original target, to ego state interweaves, to ego-state-specific target interweaves continued for the next year. At one point, as the main target began to loop again, an ego state interweave revealed a four-year-old frightened self. When asked about his fear, he stated, "I'm getting angry. . . . I'm scared. . . . Dad won't love me if I get angry." I chose not to process this first, in the hope that I could engage the paternal introject that was causing this dilemma. I asked the adult state if he could find and engage his paternal introject. This required an exploration between myself, the adult self, and the paternal introject as to the origins of his need to stifle the emotions of others.

What is crucial when dealing with introjects is an explanation, in the most simplistic terms, that identification with the aggressor is the genesis of their beliefs. When this is accomplished, the therapist can then utilize a Socratic interweave and ask how this introject felt when the original parents acted in this way. When the introject expresses the pain felt at that time, the therapist can explore this and eventually make the empathic link as to how the introject's behavior is making the other self-states feel.

At times, this type of extended ego state interweave can change the behavior of an introject. In Arnie's case, it didn't, but it did induce a sufficient amount of ambivalence, which allowed me to ask if he needed some help. Fortunately, there was sufficient ambivalence and he answered, "Yes." A target was established for this introject.

When asked for an image, the paternal introject said, "I see nothing." His negative cognition was "I can't let anyone become angry at me." His positive cognition was "Their anger is okay," with a VOC of 2. Affectively, he felt "scared," with a SUD of 9. Somatically, he experienced upper chest and abdominal tightness.

This ego-state-specific target took four ninety-minute sessions to process to a SUD of 0, a VOC of 7, and a clear body scan. The four-year-old frightened self was then engaged and an ego state-specific target was formulated with "Dad won't love me if I get angry" as the negative cognition. As a result of the work with the paternal introject, this target took only thirty minutes to process completely. An ego state interweave was utilized to return to the adult self and to the original target. The adult self reported that the SUD level was down to a 4 and that he felt better.

This process continued into the summer of 1997, at which time the SUD level had reduced to a 0. We began the installation (Phase 5) and very quickly reprocessed to a VOC of 7 and a clear body scan (Phase 6). Arnie felt slightly euphoric and there appeared to be no need for formal closure (Phase 7).

For the next few sessions, we reevaluated (Phase 8) and Arnie began reporting a reduction in the symptoms that brought him into treatment. When Arnie and I returned from our summer vacations in September, he reported that these symptoms were gone. We explored this for a few sessions, and I suggested that a couples' session might be in order for a more complete evaluation vis-à-vis the changes in Arnie's relationship with his wife. Arnie agreed, and the conjoint session confirmed all the changes. We proceeded with termination and ended treatment at year's end.

Marina: Treatment of Narcissistic Personality Disorder

Marina was a thirty-year-old married woman who entered treatment with complaints of anxiety and marked difficulties with self-esteem and extreme jealousy. Although she related that her husband had always been loving and faithful, she continually found herself plagued with extreme jealousy. Although well trained and credentialed in her profession, any minor criticism by coworkers or clients would bring painful doubt about her competence. In her late teens, Marina had undergone two years of cognitive-behavioral treatment, which she described as helpful but incomplete. In her twenties, she entered psychoanalytic treatment and remained for three years. She described this as "very growth promoting," but also incomplete.

Approximately nine months prior to entering treatment with me, she began EMDR treatment with another clinician. From her description and from my knowledge of that clinician, the treatment consisted of standard EMDR processing. She experienced this treatment as "frustrating" and at times slightly destabilizing. Her description of the destabilization was that for approximately three days following her session, she would become extremely anxious and fatigued, requiring a massive effort to function. After approximately three days, she would begin to feel better, only to restart the cycle after her next session. Her friend, a psychotherapist, referred her to me for EMDR and ego state work.

Marina's history was replete with parental inconsistency, unreliability, and emotional abandonment. Her parents divorced when she was three years old, an event that she described as a "mixed blessing." Although Marina had few clear memories of her father, she related that the thought of him always made her anxious. From her mother's stories, she was aware that he had been verbally abusive to both her and her mother.

Marina experienced her mother as anxious, phobic, and emotionally unreliable. She recalled that her mother was very attached to her after her parents' divorce. However, when she was six years old, her mother began dating the man who would eventually become her stepfather. She recalled that suddenly her mother turned her total attention to this man, abandoning her completely.

When her future stepfather moved into their home and eventually married her mother, Marina began to experience affection from her mother as her mother reattached herself. Within a year of this remarriage, her mother became pregnant. When Marina's new brother was born, she again experienced her mother's emotional abandonment, as her mother turned her entire attention to her newborn.

Abandoned by her mother, Marina turned increasingly to her stepfather, whom she described as interested and caring. He became her emotional haven and "knight in shining armor." As a result of his tumultuous divorce, he had become completely estranged from his daughter and turned to Marina for the affection that he had lost.

Although Marina's mother had ostensibly abandoned her emotionally, Marina described her as becoming increasingly jealous, as Marina was developing a warm relationship with her stepfather. Marina remembered her shock at this turn of events, as her mother became increasingly critical and punitive.

When Marina was eleven years old, her stepfather reconciled with his daughter, who had come to him when her mother, in a fit of rage, had thrown her out of their home. Overjoyed at his daughter's return, and reacting to her crisis, he arranged for her to move in. Initially Marina was happy, hoping to have found a new friend and sister. Her joy, however, soon turned to shock and sadness as her stepfather began to emotionally gravitate away from her and increasingly turned to his daughter. Marina recalled that thereafter, she felt neglected and an "outsider" in her own family and looked to her friends and boyfriends for affection.

Marina's developmental assessment revealed the following: Psychosexual maturation tended to be moderately complete, evidencing moderate regressions during interpersonal difficulties with her husband and coworkers. Her jealousy and insecurity vis-à-vis her husband reflected conflicted libidinal functioning. Self and object representations were conflicted and led to her experiencing herself as inadequate and others as critical and rejecting. The narcissistic wounds inflicted from her childhood experiences left her with a constant need for approval and mirroring from others, experiencing them as self-objects (Kohut, 1971). Her overall function showed adequate synthetic and integrative functioning. Signal anxiety was generally intact, with her patterns of anxiety tending to revolve around feeling unloved and unappreciated. Defenses were moderate in functioning, with dissociation at the more adaptive end of the spectrum, except during periods of extreme interpersonal stress. Her overall sense of identity was moderately well established, tending toward regressions in her interactions with her parents and husband. With respect to overall levels of internalization, she appeared overly identified with her mother's critical dynamics. Diagnostically, Marina appeared to display a midfunctioning narcissistic personality disorder, and her level of dissociation, assessed with the DDIS, appeared to be in the middle of the spectrum.

As we entered the preparation phase of her treatment, we began by constructing her resource or safe place. My intention was to utilize a somatic resource, very much in keeping with Levine's (1997) recommendations. I asked Marina to scan her body and to find a comfortable and quiet place. When she stated that she had, I asked her to "just notice" and to allow that somatic experience to become as strong as possible. As Marina continued to do this, I noticed that her breathing became slower and deeper. Her facial muscles relaxed and a half smile formed on her face. I recognized this as a signal that her resource was in place and turned on a mechanical tapping device in order to enhance this experience for her. We continued in this manner until Marina noted that this experience was no longer increasing and had indeed reached a plateau.

The next part of the preparation phase was utilized to explain dissociation and the nature of ego states. The process of dissociation was normalized and explained as a developmental phenomenon. Given that Marina's educational background was in biology and physiology, the conceptualization of ego states as neural networks, manifested by state-dependent memory, made the most sense to her. We used the dissociative table to facilitate the ego state exploration.

Although Marina fully understood and believed the previous explanation of dissociation and ego states, she struggled for weeks, unable to sense or identify any aspect of her self-states. Initially, this did not alarm me because clients had often shown varied rates of delay in accessing their ego states. However, as the weeks turned into two months, I began to wonder what I had missed clinically that could cause such a struggle and delay.

Then, it occurred to me that I had not treated a client with a narcissistic personality disorder in more than six years. As I began to reflect on this disorder and the unique challenges that it brought to treatment, it dawned on me that I had not been fully cognizant of the nature of her narcissistic strivings, defenses, and modes of communication. What was lacking was my full awareness of her need for mirroring by an idealized self-object (Kohut, 1971, 1977) and her concomitant fear of exposing aspects of herself that could elicit feelings of shame and humiliation—her "keystone affects" (Broucek, 1982). I had not given sufficient consideration to her need for a defensive use of a false self, which sought to live, not for herself, but for the unending, never satisfied need to gain parental approval and acceptance (Winnicott, 1965). I then understood that on a transferential level, my lack of awareness vis-à-vis the unique needs for mirroring of narcissistically disordered clients had caused Marina to believe that my clinical agenda was more important than her needs.

Accordingly, I explained to her that something in the therapeutic situation was missing for her and was keeping her from feeling safe. I suggested that we set the ego state exploration aside for the moment, and that we take the time to learn what she needed. That seemed to immediately relax her, and she began to talk about her fears and the lack of attunement by significant people in her life. Now that I was attuned, awake, and listening, I was aware that these descriptions were also indicative of what she experienced with me. This continued for approximately three months, and I remained in the background, listening and understanding. This was what she had needed at the outset: quiet, empathic mirroring.

Then, one beautiful spring morning, Marina walked into my office, picked up my tapping device, and said, "Let's try this inner child business, again." We again used the dissociative table and began our exploration. We used the tapping device, with continuous stimulation. This time, the results were immediate, as she became aware of the following ego states: a four-year-old anxious girl; a four-year-old angry girl; a critical six-year-old boy; a critical maternal introject; an anxious paternal introject; a critical six-year-old girl; an adult maternal self; and two adaptive adolescent girls.

Her treatment now took the form of exploration and self-soothing. Marina utilized her adult self and maternal self to orient these self-states to time, place, and their relationship to the adult self. This self-soothing led to a great deal of internal relief and discharged much of what she called "the terrors." Given the magnitude of her narcissistic character structure and the level of her dissociation, I concluded that an overarching target could trigger marked affect bridging. I chose instead to let the ego state work generate state-specific EMDR targets, which would in effect fractionate them. In addition, we utilized her resource in the form of pendulation. Throughout this ego state work, I would regularly ask her to utilize the resource, often after approximately ten to fifteen minutes of ego state work. After utilizing the resource for approximately two minutes, I would steer her back to the processing. In this manner, we pendulated back and forth from processing to resourcing. Although I believe that the ego state work alone would have been sufficiently stabilizing, my inclination, given her previous EMDR experience of destabilization combined with my initial mistake in the treatment, was to not take any chances.

As everything was now progressing smoothly, Marina was focusing on the extreme anxiety she experienced at work. As mentioned previously, although she was well trained and credentialed in her profession, any minor criticism from coworkers or clients would bring painful doubt about her competence. Although she realized the absurdity of these fears, that knowledge did little to mitigate against them.

I suggested that we explore this with ego state work. It became quickly apparent that the four-year-old anxious girl state was experiencing the anxiety and that the punitive maternal introject was being mercilessly critical and punitive. I chose to try to engage the maternal introject that was causing this dilemma. I asked the adult state to find and engage this maternal introject. This required an exploration between myself, the adult self, and the maternal introject as to the origins of her constant need to be critical and punitive.

Marina, like Arnie, needed to understand that her negative self-beliefs stemmed from identifying with her rejecting mother. When I asked how her maternal introject had felt when she experienced her mother's constant critiques, she said, "Hurt and mad," speaking through the adult self. As we continued to explore this, her maternal introjects began to empathically perceive the others' experience of her rejection. I suggested that the adult self explain to this introject that she was no longer alone, that she now had the adult ego state as an ally, and that she could choose to redefine herself. The introject was not completely ready to abandon her critical stance, but she did accept my offer of help. We now used the standard EMDR preparation. I explained to Marina that in contrast to her previous EMDR treatment, this processing would be targeted for her maternal introject self only, thereby preventing any destabilization because the introject was willing.

We now moved into the third phase, assessment, and an ego-state-specific target was established for this introject. When asked for an image, the maternal introject said, "I see her cold eyes." Her negative cognition was "I have to be critical to do my job." Her positive cognition was "There are other ways to do my job," with a VOC of 3. Affectively, she felt "scared," with a SUD of 6. Somatically, she experienced discomfort in her stomach.

We now entered the fourth phase, of desensitization. For the remainder of the session, Marina was able to process the target very well. We processed this target for approximately fifty minutes. As the session was coming to an end. Marina stated that she felt fine and was noticing none of the destabilization that she experienced earlier. When I brought her and the maternal introject back to target, the SUD level had decreased to 4.

In the next session, except for some initial conversation about the week, the majority of the ninety minutes was spent processing this target. A few ego state interweaves were utilized for soothing, combined with resource pendulation. At the session's end, when Marina and the introject returned to target, the SUD level had reduced to 2. She felt fine.

When Marina returned to the next session, she reported a change, noting that she had felt more relaxed during the week, especially at work. Within ten minutes of starting target processing, the SUD level had reduced to 0. We began the fifth stage, installation, and within five minutes she reported that the VOC rating was a 7. We instituted the body scan (Phase 6), which was clear for Marina and the maternal introject.

We used an ego state interweave as a closure (Phase 7) to the target and to reevaluate (Phase 8) the emotional and functional status of the maternal introject. Marina related that the introject was calm and no longer felt "like having my mother in my head." She reported that she was becoming aware of the four-year-old anxious self.

As Marina and this ego state explored her fears, it became apparent that this was the self that had been reacting to the previously critical maternal introject. I suggested that the maternal introject might want to become involved in the needed soothing and reassurances. The introject agreed, and the remainder of the session consisted of the adult state, a number of other adaptive self-states, and the maternal introject soothing and reassuring the four-year-old anxious self. At the session's end, the four-year-old self no longer felt anxious. We ended the session with approximately ten minutes of resourcing.

Marina returned for the following session in better spirits and reported that for the first time ever, she had felt confident and assured in her work. She related that for this session, she "just wanted to talk." I recognized this communication as her need for mirroring and for me to remain in the background. From the perspective of self psychology (Kohut, 1971, 1977), I understood this to be her grandiose self needing me to act as a mirror for her "greatness," a mechanism designed to protect her from experiencing the narcissistic wounds inflicted on her by her parents. Although I was aware that she now still needed me to be in background, I knew that at some point this would have to be dealt with an ego state level. So she talked and I listened.

In the next session Marina related that she had become aware of another self-critical ego state. We reentered the preparation phase (Phase 2) by orienting the ego state to time, place, her relationship to the adult ego state, and what had transpired in the previous ego state work. Since this ego state was motivated to change, but felt unable to do so, an ego-state-specific target was formulated. When asked for an image, as we reentered assessment (Phase 3), the self critical ego state said, "I see nothing." Her negative cognition was "I have to be extra careful, because there's something wrong with me." Her positive cognition was "I'm okay as I am," with a VOC of 3. Affectively, she felt nervous, with a SUD of 6. Somatically, she experienced discomfort in her stomach. We began the desensitization (Phase 4) and started to process. A number of resource pendulations were required to modulate her affect. After approximately sixty minutes, the SUD was reduced to 0 and we began installation (Phase 5). Within five minutes the VOC rating had risen to 7 and her body scan (Phase 6) was clear. We spent a few minutes resourcing to close the session down.

In the next session (Phase 7) Marina reported increased improvement in her work. Our work has continued in the same pattern, weaving back and forth from ego state work, to ego-state-specific targets, to mirroring sessions. In recent sessions, focusing on the relationship, Marina has become able to explore her tendency to experience others and me in either an idealized or devaluated manner. This exploration will eventually allow her to process this with ego state work, targeting aspects of grandiose selves and parental introjects that are experienced as omnipotent. This is imperative if the unique aspects of her narcissistic personality disorder are to be worked through thoroughly and comprehensively (Kohut, 1971, 1977).

Discussion

The cases of Arnie and Marina illustrate two different aspects of a particular variation on the standard EMDR protocol. Each was chosen as much with regard to the assessed level of dissociation as to the diagnostic category itself.

Arnie's case was chosen because it was the first case that required me to transition from standard EMDR targeting (utilizing cognitive and dynamic interweaves) to the integration of ego state work into the standard protocol and, finally, the use of ego-state-specific target interweaves, which were then integrated into the standard protocol. In addition, Arnie's high level of psychic functioning presented a wonderful opportunity to illustrate the use of the standard EMDR targeting as the cornerstone of the treatment, as well as the modifications necessitated by the presence of dissociation that were required to make it robustly successful.

Marina's case was chosen because my experience in over twenty-four years of practice has been that with the exception of cases of outright psychopathy and sociopathy, clients with narcissistic personality disorders are the most difficult to treat. As a result of the wounds to their healthy narcissism and the resulting pathological narcissism, the clinician is required to be exquisitely attuned to the mirror transference that is created by their needs. This requires the clinician to remain empathically in the background initially and function as a mirror by listening and understanding only. Failure to do so, either by mistake, ignorance, or refusal to gratify this demand, invariably leads to stalled or prematurely terminated therapies. In order for these clients to perceive the therapist as a true object (independent and autonomous), they need to first experience the therapist as a self-object, utilizing the relationship to grow. In addition, their dynamics (ego states) manifest themselves as grandiose selves and introjected omnipotent selves, which causes them to perceive themselves and others in an either highly idealized or highly devaluated manner.

Another reason for choosing Marina as an illustrative case was her diagnostic and dissociative assessment. My observation has been that most clinicians are aware that clients at Arnie's level of functioning can utilize the standard protocol without any problems. Most clinicians are also aware that clients diagnosed with formal dissociative disorders and borderline personality disorders are prone to massive affect bridging and therefore cannot utilize the standard protocol without formal modifications that are designed to address their dissociation. In addition, the literature has consistently recommended that when EMDR targets are used in such cases, they be fractionated (Lazrove & Fine, 1996; Paulsen, 1995; Twombly, 2000).

I believe that narcissistic personality disorders fall somewhere in the middle of the two extremes noted above. However, given these clients' inherent level of dissociation and moderately severe dynamics, it has been my experience that they also require special modifications and fractionated targets. My impression is that this is not well known, or sufficiently appreciated.

Additionally, both cases presented above were chosen because they involved challenges, transitions, and mistakes. It is rather easy and tempting to present cases that proceed smoothly and easily. I believe however that it is more instructive to present cases that have been fraught with difficulties.

CONCLUSION

Finally, some thoughts about the need to make such major modifications in the standard protocol come to mind. In 1989, following the San Francisco Bay Area earthquake, Francine Shapiro discovered that when the standard protocol was utilized to reprocess the most traumatic part of a recent incident, clients still experienced disturbances when bringing up other parts of the incident. She concluded based on these observations that on some level of information processing, the memory had not had sufficient time to consolidate into an integrated whole (Shapiro, 1995, 2001). She estimated that approximately two to three months was required for the consolidation of these memories into a cohesive narrative. Accordingly, she developed the Protocol for Recent Traumatic Events as a modification of the standard protocol to allow the fragmented neural network to be comprehensively reprocessed.

As mentioned previously, the notion of dissociation as a normal developmental phenomenon has been suggested since the 1930s by renowned clinicians and developmental researchers. In recent years, the most renowned neuroscientists have also begun to suggest this quite explicitly. The modifications suggested in this chapter are designed solely to target memory and normal personality fragmentation and fragmented neural networks more comprehensively. The preparation phase is only modified to include ego state work, which is the graphical user interface for targeting dissociation. This also allows the ego state work to be used throughout the treatment as an interweave. In the case of Arnie, where the EMDR targets and memories were too fragmented to be processed, the use of the ego-state-specific targets allowed for the processing of memory and personality fragments. In the case of Marina, where the overall level of dissociation was already moderate, the use of the ego-state-specific targets allowed for fractionation and the prevention of dysfunctional affect bridging, as well as allowing the processing of inherent memory and personality fragmentation.

REFERENCES

American Psychiatric Association. (2000). *Diagnostic and statistical manual of mental disorders* (4th ed., text revision). Washington, DC: Author.

Babiniotis, G. D. (1998). *Lexicon of the new Hellenic language.* Athens, Greece: Lexicology Centre. (Original work published 1882)

Beebe, B., & Lachmann, F. (1992). The contribution of mother-infant mutual influence to the origins of self and object representations. In N. J. Skolnick & S. C. Warshaw (Eds.), *Relational perspectives in psychoanalysis* (pp. 83–117). Hillsdale, NJ: Analytic Press.

Berne, E. (1957a). Intuition v. The ego image. *Psychiatric Quarterly, 31,* 611–627.

Berne, E. (1957b). Ego states in psychotherapy. *American Journal of Psychotherapy, 11,* 293–390.

Berne, E. (1961). *Transactional analysis in psychotherapy: A systematic individual and social psychiatry.* New York: Grove Press.

Berne, E. (1964). *Games people play: The psychology of human relationships.* New York: Grove Press.

Berne, E. (1972). *What do you say after you say hello? The psychology of human destiny.* New York: Grove Press.

Bromberg, P. (1993). Shadow and substance. *Psychoanalytic Psychology, 10,* 147–168.

Bromberg, P. (1994). Speak! That I may see you. *Psychoanalytic Dialogues, 4,* 517–547.

Bromberg, P. (1996). Standing in the spaces. *Contemporary Psychoanalysis, 32,* 509–535.

Bromberg, P. (1998). *Standing in the spaces: Essays on clinical process, trauma and dissociation.* Hillsdale, NJ: Analytic Press.

Broucek, F. (1982). Shame and its relationship to early narcissistic developments. *International Journal of Psychoanalysis, 63,* 369–378.

Clarkin, J. (2004). Foreword. In J. Magnavita (Ed.), *Handbook of personality disorders: Theory and practice* (pp. viii–ix). New York: Wiley.

Clarkin, J., & Lentzenweger, M. (1996). *Major theories of personality disorders.* New York: Guilford Press.

Cooney, J. W., & Gazzaniga, M. S. (2003). Neurologic disorders and the structure of human consciousness. *Trends in Cognitive Sciences, 7*(4), 161–165.

Eichenbaum, H. (2002). *The cognitive neuroscience of memory.* New York: Oxford University Press.

Emde, R., Gaensbaure, T., & Harmon, R. (1976). Emotional expressions in infancy: A biobehavioral study. *Psychological Issues, 10,* Monograph 37. New York: International Universities Press.

Erdberg, P. (2004). Assessing the dimensions of personality disorder. In J. Magnavita (Ed.), *Handbook of personality disorders: Theory and practice* (pp. 78–91). New York: Wiley.

Erskine, R. (1997). Inquiry, attunement, and involvement in the psychotherapy of dissociation. In R. Erskine (Ed.), *Theories and methods of an integrated transactional analysis: A volume of selected articles* (pp. 37–45). California: TA Press.

Fairbairn, W. R. D. (1944). Endopsychic structure considered in terms of object-relationships. In *Psychoanalytic studies of the personality* (pp. 82–132). London: Routledge & Kegan Paul.

Fairbairn, W. R. D. (1952). *Psychoanalytic studies of the personality.* London: Routledge & Kegan Paul.

Federn, P. (1943). Psychoanalysis of psychosis. *Psychoanalytic Quarterly, 17,* 3–19, 246–257, 480–487.

Federn, P. (1947). Principles of psychotherapy in latent schizophrenics. *American Journal of Psychotherapy, 1,* 129–144.

Federn, P. (1952). In E. Weiss (Ed.), *Ego psychology and the psychoses.* New York: Basic Books.

Ferenczi, S. (1930). Notes and fragments II. In M. Balint (Ed.), *Final contributions to the problems and methods of psychoanalysis* (pp. 219–231). New York: Brunner/Mazel.

Fine, C. G. (1991). Treatment stabilization and crisis prevention: Pacing the therapy of the MPD patient. *Psychiatric Clinics of North America, 14,* 661–675.

Fraser, G. A. (1991). The Dissociative Table Technique: A strategy for working with ego states in dissociative disorders and ego state therapy. *Dissociation, 4*(4), 205–213.

Fraser, G. A. (2003). Fraser's "Dissociative Table Technique" revisited, revised: A strategy for working with ego states in dissociative disorders and ego state therapy. *Journal of Trauma and Dissociation, 4*(4), 5–28.

Freud, A. (1963). The concept of developmental lines. *The psychoanalytic study of the child, 18,* 245–265.

Freud, S. (1935). Instinets and their vicissitudes. In J. Riviere (Ed.), *Collected papers* (Vol. IV, pp. 60–83). London: Flogarth Press. (Original German version published 1915.)

Funnell, M. G., Johnson, S. H., & Gazzaniga, M. S. (2001, March). *Hemispheric differences in egocentric and allocentric mental rotation: Evidence from fMRI and a split-brain patient.* Paper presented at the 8th Annual Meeting of the Cognitive Neuroscience Society, New York.

Gazzaniga, M. S. (1970). *The bisected brain.* New York: Appleton-Century Crofts.

Gazzaniga, M. S. (1976). The biology of human memory. In M. Rosenzweig & M. Bennet (Eds.), *Neural mechanisms of learning and memory* (pp. 57–66). Cambridge, MA: MIT Press.

Gazzaniga, M. S. (1985). *The social brain.* New York: Basic Books.

Gazzaniga, M. S. (1989). Organization of the human brain. *Science, 245,* 947–52.

Gazzaniga, M. S. (2000). Cerebral specialization and interhemispheric communication: Does the corpus callosum enable the human condition? *Brain, 123,* 1293–1326.

Gazzaniga, M. S., Bogen, J. E., & Sperry, R. W. (1963). Laterality effects in some thesis following cerebral commissorotomy in man. *Neurpsychologia, 1,* 209–215.

Gazzaniga, M. S., Bogen, J. E., & Sperry, R. W. (1965). Observations on visual perception after disconnexion of the cerebral hemispheres in man. *Brain, 88,* 221.

Gazzaniga, M., & LeDoux, J. (1978). *The integrated mind.* New York: Plenum Press.

Gazzaniga, M. S., LeDoux, J., & Wilson, D. H. (1977). Language praxis and the right hemisphere: Clues to some mechanisms of consciousness. *Neurology, 27,* 1144–1147.

Gazzaniga, M. S., & Smylie, C. S. (1983). Facial recognition and brain asymmetries: Clues to underlying mechanisms. *Annals of Neurology, 13,* 536–540.

Glover, E. (1932). A psycho-analytical approach to the classification of mental disorders. In *On the early development of the mind* (pp. 161–186). New York: International Universities Press.

Grand, D. (1998). Emerging from the coffin: Treatment of a masochistic personality disorder. In P. Manfield (Ed.), *Extending EMDR: A casebook of the innovative applications* (pp. 65–90). New York: Norton.

Hartmann, H. (1958). *Ego psychology and the problem of adaptation.* New York: International Universities Press. (Original work published in German, 1939)

Hartmann, H. (1964). *Essays on ego psychology: Selected problems in psychoanalytic theory.* New York: International Universities Press.

Herman, J. L. (1992). *Trauma and recovery: The aftermath of violence—From domestic abuse to political terror.* New York: Basic Books.

Jacobson, E. (1964). *The self and the object world.* New York: International Universities Press.

Janet, P. (1920). *The major symptoms of hysteria.* New York: Hafner. (Original work published 1907)

Janet, P. (1925). *Psychological healing* (Vols. 1–2). New York: Macmillan. (Original work published in 1919)

Janet, P. (1930). Autobiography. In C. A. Murchinson (Ed. & Trans.), *A history of psychology in autobiography* (Vol. 1, pp. 123–133). Worcester, MA: Clark University Press.

Keller, E. (1983). *A feeling for the organism: The life and work of Barbara McClintock.* New York: Freeman.

Knipe, J. (1998). "It was a golden time…": Treating narcissistic vulnerability. In P. Manfield (Ed.), *Extending EMDR: A casebook of the innovative applications* (pp. 232–255). New York: Norton.

Kohut, H. (1971). *The analysis of the self.* New York: International Universities Press.

Kohut, H. (1977). *The restoration of the self.* New York: International Universities Press.

Korn, D. L., & Leeds, A. M. (2002). Preliminary evidence of efficacy for EMDR resource development and installation in the stabilization phase of treatment of complex post-traumatic stress disorder. *Journal of Clinical Psychology, 58*(12), 1465–1487.

Kraepelin, E. (1907). *Clinical psychiatry* (A. R. Diefendorf, Trans.). New York: Macmillan.

Lampl-de-Groot, J. (1981). Notes on "multiple personality." *Psychoanalytic Quarterly, 50,* 614–624.

Lazrove, S., & Fine, C. G. (1996). The use of EMDR in patients with dissociative identity disorder. *Dissociation, 9,* 289–299.

LeDoux, J. (2002). *Synaptic self: How our brains become who we are.* New York: Viking.

LeDoux, J. (2003). The self: Clues from the brain. *Annals of the New York Academy of Sciences, 1001,* 295–304.

LeDoux, J., Wilson, D. H., & Gazzaniga, M. S. (1977). Manipulospatial aspects of cerebral lateralization: Clues to the origin of lateralization. *Neuropsychologia, 15,* 743–749.

Leeds, A. M. (1998). Lifting the burden of shame: Using EMDR resource installation to resolve a therapeutic impasse. In P. Manfield (Ed.), *Extending EMDR: A casebook of the innovative applications* (pp. 256–282). New York: Norton.

Leeds, A. M., & Shapiro, F. (2000). EMDR and resource installation: Principles and procedures for enhancing current functioning and resolving traumatic experiences. In J. Carlson & L. Sperry (Eds.), *Brief therapy strategies with individuals and couples* (pp. 469–534). Phoenix, AZ: Zeig & Tucker.

Levine, P. (1997). *Waking the tiger.* Berkeley, CA: North Atlantic Books.

Linehan, M. M. (1993). *Cognitive-behavioral treatment of borderline personality disorder.* New York: Guilford Press.

Manfield, D. (1998). Treating a highly defended client: Reworking traditional approaches. In P. Manfield (Ed.), *Extending EMDR: A casebook of the innovative applications* (pp. 217–231). New York: Norton.

Manfield, P., & Shapiro, F. (2004). Application of eye movement desensitization and reprocessing (EMDR) to personality disorders. In J. Magnavita (Ed.), *Handbook of personality disorders: Theory and practice* (pp. 304–330). New York: Wiley.

Metcalf, J., Funnell, M. K., & Gazzaniga, M. S. (1995). Right hemisphere memory superiority: Studies of a split-brain patient. *Psychological Science, 6*(3), 157–164.

Moss, H. (2003). Implicit selves: A review of the conference. *Annals of the New York Academy of Sciences, 1001,* 1–30.

Myers, C. S. (1940). *Shell shock in France, 1914–1918.* Cambridge, England: Cambridge University Press.

Nijenhuis, E. R. S., van der Hart, O., & Steele, K. (2004a). Strukturelle dissoziation der persönlichkeitsstruktur: Traumatischer ursprung, phobische residuen [Structural dissociation of the personality: Traumatic origins and phobic residues]. In L. Redemann, A. Hoffmann, & U. Gast (Eds.), *Psychotherapie der dissoziativen störungen* [Psychotherapy of dissociative disorders] (pp. 47–69). Stuttgart, Germany: Thieme.

Nijenhuis, E. R. S., van der Hart, O., & Steele, K. (2004b). *Trauma-related structural dissociation of the personality: Traumatic origins, phobic maintenance.* Retrieved June 28, 2007, from http://www.trauma-pages.com/nijenhuis-2004.htm

Paulsen, S. (1995). EMDR: Its cautious use in the dissociative disorders. *Dissociation, 8*(1), 32–41.

Phelps, E. A., & Gazzaniga, M. S. (1992). Hemispheric differences in mnemonic processing: The effects of left hemisphere interpretation. *Neuropsychologia, 30,* 293–297.

Putnam, F. (1988). The switch processes in multiple personality disorder and other state-change disorders. *Dissociation, 1,* 24–32.

Ramachandran, V. S. (1995). Anosognosia in parietal lobe syndrome. *Consciousness and Cognition, 4,* 22–51.

Ramachandran, V. S., & Blakeslee, S. (1998). *Phantoms in the brain.* New York: Quill/HarperCollins.

Reich, W. (1933). *Character analysis.* New York: Orgone Institute.

Reik, T. (1936). *Surprise and the psycho-analyst*. London: Kegan Paul.

Ross, C., Heber, S., Norton, R., Anderson, D., Anderson, G., & Barchet, P. (1989). The Dissociative Disorders Interview Schedule: A structured interview. *Dissociation, 2(3),* 169–189.

Sander, L. (1977). The regulation of exchange in the infant caretaker system and some aspects of the context-content relationship. In M. Lewis & L. Rosenblum (Eds.), *Interaction, conservation, and the development of language* (pp. 133–156). New York: Wiley.

Searles, H. F. (1977). Dual and multi-identity processes in borderline ego functioning. In P. Hartocollis (Ed.), *Borderline personality disorders* (pp. 441–455). New York: International Universities Press.

Shapiro, F. (1995). *Eye movement desensitization and reprocessing: Basic principles, protocols, and procedures.* New York: Guilford Press.

Shapiro, F. (2001). *Eye movement desensitization and reprocessing: Basic principles, protocols, and procedures* (2nd ed.). New York: Guilford Press.

Squire, L. R., & Kandel, E. R. (1999). *Memory from mind to molecules.* New York: Scientific American Library.

Steele, K., van der Hart, O., & Nijenhuis, E. R. S. (2001). Dependence in the treatment of complex posttraumatic stress disorder and dissociative disorders. *Journal of Trauma and Dissociation, 2(4),* 79–116.

Steinberg, M. (1994). *The Structured Clinical Interview for DSM–IV Dissociative Disorders—revised (SCID-D).* Washington, DC: American Psychiatric Press.

Stern, D. (1985). *The interpersonal world of the infant: A view from psychoanalysis and developmental psychology.* New York: Basic Books.

Sullivan, H. S. (1940). *Conceptions of modern psychiatry.* New York: Norton.

Trautmann, R., & Erskine, R. (1997). Ego state analysis: A comparative view. In R. Erskine (Ed.), *Theories and methods of an integrated transactional analysis: A volume of selected articles* (pp. 99–108). California: TA Press.

Turk, D. J., Heatherton, T., Kelley, W. M., Funnell, M. G., Gazzaniga, M. S., & Macrae, C. N. (2002). Mike or me? Self-recognition in a split-brain patient. *Nature Neuroscience, 5(9),* 841–842.

Turk, D. J., Heatherton, T. F., Macrae, C. N., Kelly, W. M., & Gazzaniga, M. S. (2003). Out of contact, out of mind: The distributed nature of the self. *Annals of the New York Academy of Sciences, 1001,* 65–78.

Twombly, J. H. (2000). Incorporating EMDR and EMDR adaptations into the treatment of clients with dissociative identity disorder. *Journal of Trauma and Dissociation, 1(2),* 61–81.

Tyson, P. (1998). Developmental theory and the postmodern psychoanalyst. *Journal of the American Psychoanalytic Association, 46(1),* 9–15.

Vaillant, G. E., & Perry, J. C. (1985). Personality disorders. In H. I. Kaplan & B. J. Sadock (Eds.), *Comprehensive textbook of psychiatry* (4th ed., Vol. 1, pp. 958–986). Baltimore: Williams & Wilkins.

Watkins, H. H. (1978). Ego states therapy. In J. G. Watkins (Ed.), *The therapeutic self* (pp. 360–398). New York: Human Sciences Press.

Watkins, J. G. (1949). *Hypnotherapy of war neuroses.* New York: Ronald Press.

Watkins, J. G. (1977). The psychodynamic manipulation of ego states in hypnotherapy. In F. Antonelli (Ed.), *Therapy in Psychosomatic Medicine, 2,* 389–403.

Watkins, J. G., & Johnson, R. (1982). *We, the divided self.* New York: Irvington.

Watkins, J. G., & Watkins, H. H. (1979). The theory and practice of ego states therapy. In H. Grayson (Ed.), *Short-term approaches to psychotherapy* (pp. 176–220). New York: Human Sciences Press.

Watkins, J. G., & Watkins, H. H. (1997). *Ego states: Theory and therapy.* New York: Norton.

Winnicott, D. W. (1949). Mind and its relation to the psyche-soma. In *Collected papers* (pp. 243–254). London: Tavistock.

Winnicott, D. W. (1958). Primitive emotional development. In *Collected papers* (pp. 145–156). London: Tavistock.

Winnicott, D. W. (1965). Ego distortion in terms of true and false self. In *The maturational processes and the facilitating environment* (pp. 37–55). New York: International Universities Press.

Winnicott, D. W. (1971). Dreaming, fantasizing and living: A case history describing a primary dissociation. In *playing and reality* (pp. 26–37). New York: Basic Books.

Wolff, P. (1987). *The development of behavioral states and the expression of emotion in early infancy.* Chicago: University of Chicago Press.

Young, W. C. (1988). Psychodynamics and dissociation. *Dissociation, 1,* 33–38.

EMDR in Couples Therapy

An Ego State Approach

Barry K. Litt

NATALIE AND ROGER: ONE COUPLE, MANY SELVES

"I can't win!" said an exasperated Roger. "If I do what she wants, then I'm too dependent on her. If I have my own opinion, then I'm fighting with her. Even if I do the same thing that she does, it's wrong. She's never satisfied. I give up!" Thoroughly frustrated, Roger threw up his hands in a gesture of helplessness.

At my urging, he continued. "First, she's all over me because I don't get projects done fast enough. Then she's screaming that all I do is projects and I'm avoiding her and the kids." Roger wiped his eyes and went for another round. "I'm a criminal because I let the kids eat in the family room. Then I come in the next day and there she is, eating in the family room with the kids! 'But that's different,'" he mocked, his whiney tone a caricature of hers. "I give up," he repeated, shrugging in defeat.

I watched Natalie. Shaking her head, she looked at her husband of sixteen years contemptuously, exclaiming, "That's great, Roger! You give up. It's always about you. While you're giving up, I'm trying to raise a family and make our marriage work. I try to communicate with you and all you can do is yell or run away. I approached you last night as nicely as I could and said, 'Honey, it's going to be too hot to work outside tomorrow and the town pool is opening, so let's take the kids swimming during the day and work outside when it cools down.' And you said, 'Go to hell!' and stormed off. It's called 'communication,' Roger. Why don't you tell Barry what a terrific job you did of communicating last night when I asked if we could talk about the weekend?"

Natalie was quite deft at using me to shame her husband, but I knew better than to play into her hands. Just the same, I could understand her desire to level the playing field with her uncooperative husband by pulling me into her corner. How could he be such a jerk?

As my sympathies began to go out to her, I was struck by that very fact. She's done it again, I thought to myself. In a kind of interpersonal sleight of hand, Natalie had conjured up a tableau in which she was the well-meaning victim of her lunatic husband's imperious rage. Serene, almost triumphant, she sat quietly at the unspoken request of my upraised hand. I was a traffic cop; Roger was a volcano. Goaded by his wife's taunt, it appeared he might erupt at any moment.

This was escalating much too quickly, and I had the distinct feeling that I was being pulled into the vortex of this couple's unconscious drama—that somehow my next move had already been determined and that time alone awaited my complicity. I had been at this place many times with them, helplessly trying to untangle the Gordian knot of their interminable argument. Assigning blame or determining who started what is rarely therapeutic. But I at least wanted to get a handle on what actually happened between these two. Why couldn't I see her the way he did?

Because my instinct, and therefore my countertransference, was to look at Roger for an explanation, I resisted the temptation and stayed with Natalie. In stating that it was always about Roger, she was making it all about herself. It was her misdirection that commanded my attention. It's what the magician does not want you to see that lays bare the secret, and I thought it was this secret that was driving the couple's dynamic.

"What does it do to you when he talks to you that way?" I asked. Natalie pressed her attack on Roger, but I persisted with my inquiry. "What feelings does it bring up in you? What happens inside you?" My questions at first annoyed, then confounded, and then finally disarmed her. In what Johnson, Makinen, and Milliken (2001) call a "softening event," Natalie's tone changed as she revealed her pain at being treated like a nuisance, her fear that Roger no longer loved her, and finally her secret shame: that she couldn't see how anybody could love her.

Natalie began weeping. Roger was touched by his wife's vulnerability, which normally was invisible to him. He handed her a tissue and caressed her arm. She calmed herself and, wiping her eyes, asked, "What now?" This was the moment I had been waiting for. Now I could reconcile the discrepancies between what I saw, heard, and sensed. Natalie was receptive in a way I hadn't seen previously; her guard was finally down.

Turning to her now, I said softly, "The trouble, Natalie, is that there are three of you."[1]

INTRODUCTION: EGO STATE THEORY, EMDR, AND CONTEXTUAL THERAPY

The ego state therapy of John Watkins and Helen Watkins (1997) has come into increasing use among hypnotherapists (Toothman & Phillips, 1998) and, as this book indicates, EMDR practitioners. Like its psychodynamic siblings, ego state therapy has been primarily described as a treatment approach for individual psychotherapy. There is little written on its application in couples therapy. Indeed, the literature on the use of EMDR in couples therapy is novel; the bulk of it can be found in a recent text edited by Shapiro, Kaslow, and Maxfield (2007). EMDR is unequivocally an individual intervention, aimed at transforming intrapsychic processes.

However, family therapists have observed that couples and families present with emergent dynamics that cannot properly be understood as the mechanistic summation of each member's psychology. Such "the whole-is-greater-than-the-sum-of-its-parts" thinking has given rise to systemic constructs to describe the functioning of multiperson groups.

In order to combine the explanatory power of ego state theory with the healing power of EMDR in the treatment of couples and families, an overarching theory of relationships is needed. Such a theory should be sufficiently complex to integrate the intrapersonal (intrapsychic), the interpersonal (couple), and the systemic (family) domains of human experience. A theoretical approach that satisfies this criterion is the contextual therapy of Ivan Boszormenyi-Nagy and colleagues (Boszormenyi-Nagy & Krasner, 1986; Boszormenyi-Nagy & Spark, 1973).

While it is beyond the scope of this chapter to discuss the contextual approach in detail, certain of its theoretical underpinnings that serve to assimilate ego state therapy and EMDR in the treatment of couples will be described. I will use the case of Natalie and Roger—composites of actual clinical experience—to illustrate the manifestations of ego state phenomena and contextual principles, and to demonstrate the application of EMDR in couples therapy.

CONTEXTUAL THEORY: THE RELATIONAL SELF

In their discussion of contextual therapy, Boszormenyi-Nagy and Krasner (1986) describe four dimensions of "relational reality" that constitute the relevant parameters of the therapeutic spectrum of inquiry and intervention. These are *objective facts, individual psychology, systems of transactional patterns,* and *relational ethics.*

Dimension One, facts, refers to historical and demographic factors that constitute each individual's life story. This is the type of data clinicians gather in a thorough history and genogram.

Dimension Two, individual psychology, refers to psychological dynamics and processes: the stuff of individual psychotherapy.

Dimension Three, systems of transactional patterns, includes widely known systemic formulations of relational functioning, including homeostasis, isomorphism, double binds, and recursive patterns, plus constructs that are unique to contextual therapy.

Dimension Four, relational ethics, is concerned with the balance of give and take in relationships, and the obligations and entitlements that accrue over time as a result. Relational ethics describes an irreducible realm of social reality predicated on the inescapable fact that how we treat others has consequences, and those consequences affect future generations. This dimension both encompasses and supersedes the first three, and constitutes a unique contribution of contextual therapy.

To better understand the integrative power of contextual therapy, I will first describe the dialectic nature of relationship: why we need each other. Then I will discuss the ethical dimension of relationship: how we use each other. These ideas form the bridge between psychodynamic formulations of development and behavior and systemic manifestations of relational impasse.

The Dialectic of Relationship

We need each other. This simple truism encompasses more than our functional interdependence, or even our biological imperative. Fundamental to contextual theory is the recognition that the self relies on a transactional field in which the subject is dialectically related to the object. Self exists only as figure to the ground of a not-self, or other (Boszormenyi-Nagy, 1965). The resistive pressure of the uterine wall against the fetus's kicking foot may be one of the earliest sensate experiences of a self/not-self boundary. Our ontic interdependence (interdependence that is deeply rooted in the structure of being itself) finds expression in the powerful attachment bond and its attendant emotions even in highly conflicted couples like Natalie and Roger. But to whom or what is Natalie actually attached?

Experiences with early attachment figures are encoded, or introjected, as a running simulation of mental representations of self and others (Dicks, 1967; Horner, 1979). Describing these representations, Framo

(1965) points out that "a whole family system—its emotions, its codes, its style—is sometimes introjected" (p. 158). Object constancy denotes the individual's capacity to rely, temporarily, on internalized relationships as a self/not-self resource in the absence of an intimate Other, rather than suffer the anomic void of depersonalization (Boszormenyi-Nagy, 1965).

Boszormenyi-Nagy refers to these representations as a "relational need template" (1965, p. 46). The need template is a structural patterning of instinctual needs plus relational obligations and entitlements derived from early attachment figures and family transactions. Placing an emphasis on need (as opposed to drive), Boszormenyi-Nagy highlights the subject's ontic dependence on the other as ground for self-delineation. The dynamic structure of the need template determines what behaviors and attributes are sought in an attachment relationship as complementation to the self's requirement of a consistent not-self referent. As such, the need template influences one's choice of partner and the transactional patterns that evolve (Boszormenyi-Nagy, 1965). From the standpoint of ego state theory (Watkins & Watkins, 1997), this need template can be construed as an ego state system.

The Ethical Dimension of Relationship

We use each other. The fact that we use other relating partners to meet our own needs is a nonnegotiable fact of our ontic interdependence. *How* we use others qualifies this inescapable ethical dimension of relational reality and is of paramount clinical importance, both as it informs pathology and as it offers leverage for growth.

Borrowing from Martin Buber's work, Boszormenyi-Nagy recognized that "using" one's partner as an object to reinforce or complement one's internal need template (for example, through projective identification or idealization) or to discharge toxic psychic energy (externalizing, splitting) would lead to unfairness and exploitation. By contrast, Boszormenyi-Nagy reasoned that the self-serving ontic need for a sustainable relationship is best achieved through the reciprocal exchange of subject and object roles (Boszormenyi-Nagy, 1965; Boszormenyi-Nagy & Krasner, 1986). Generally speaking, the object is the one who responds to the subject.

It is in my own long-term interest to provide my partner with an incentive to care about my welfare (and thereby remain an available object). The most sustainable incentive I can provide is to be an available object myself, such that subject and object roles are shared to mutual satisfaction. This is the ethical foundation of trust. The psychological need for self-sustaining trust is inextricable from trustworthy relating.

Put differently, the capacity for I-thou dialogue, due consideration for the relational consequences of one's actions, and commitment to mutually satisfying give-and-take with significant others are the sine qua nons of a healthy ego structure (Litt, 2007). The seminal contribution of Boszormenyi-Nagy cannot be overstated. His articulation of this ethical dimension to relational reality is a perspective that bridges psychodynamic concepts with relational theories.

THE INTERIOR LIFE OF THE COUPLE

With each retail adventure, Roger was convinced that he had found the perfect gift for Natalie and he beamed in anticipation of her gratitude and praise. His eagerness was surprisingly untainted by the fact that in sixteen years he had rarely scored a hit. In all likelihood, Natalie would rebuke Roger for his ill-considered purchase, his impulsive spending, and his childish need to be praised. "This gift is really for you!" she would protest, and rightly so. Roger's humiliation would activate his angry ego state and he would rage and tantrum for a few days. Things would settle down, and then the two would go at it again as if doing it once more they might yet get it right.

Roger and Natalie's predicament begs for obvious, commonsense solutions. But as most experienced couples therapists can attest, they will resist. Clearly, there is more here than meets the eye. That two intelligent grown-ups can reenact the same drama for years without solution is a testament to the limits of a strictly cognitive solution to the problem and hints at the deep structure of interlocking needs that dominate the transactional field. This section will examine our fundamentally relational nature and how early relational experience shapes both our psychic structure and our transactional behavior.

The Postponement of Mourning in Individuals

In the latest example, Roger's apparent generosity belies a deeper ethical reality. Rather than trying to cultivate self-worth through a self-validating act of genuine concern for Natalie as a subject, he relies instead on attempting to extort validation from her by manipulating her into the role of good object. Natalie intuits this and rejects his attempt to parentify her. Despite repeated failures, Roger clings to an idealized view of his marriage in which he can receive validation as the thoughtful husband of an adoring wife. Moreover, in this "good boy" ego state, he compulsively reenacts a relational configuration from a much earlier time in his development in which his narcissism was indulged and rewarded.

Healthy individuation requires one to surrender the unconscious regressive urge to experience unconditional parental love and acceptance. The reciprocal to this is the wish to correct the giving capacity of our parents (Boszormenyi-Nagy, 1965). This involves mourning—and thereby letting go of—idealized objects: the idealized family, my parents as I wish they could be.

The trouble is that mourning is painful and human beings are only variously adept at tolerating the loss of an idealized would-be parent or family. To the extent that I do not mourn, I not only project my internal world onto others but, in fact, try to induce others to play their part in my intrapsychic drama through projective identification (Dicks, 1967; Framo, 1982). Put differently, by relying on externalizing (Middleberg, 2001; Wynne, 1965) my psychic conflict onto my interpersonal context, I will be drawn compulsively and unsuccessfully into trying to solve an intrapsychic problem with a relational solution (Humphrey & Stern, 1988).

The Postponement of Mourning in Families

Incomplete mourning not only influences the relational attitudes and behavior of the individual, but reciprocally influences those with whom that individual is in close relationship, especially children. Boszormenyi-Nagy (1965) reasoned that growth per se induces a painful sense of loss that all family members would experience and would unconsciously collude to avoid. For example, rather than embracing their own individuation, parents may transfer their dependency needs onto a child and groom that child to perform a quasi-parental role (Boszormenyi-Nagy & Krasner, 1986). Such parentification of the child is not a one-way street, but a mutual arrangement in which the child gains (pathological) self-validation by attempting to meet the parents' needs. In contextual terms, the child exhibits "invisible loyalty" to the parents (Boszormenyi-Nagy & Spark, 1973). In ego state terms, the child develops one or more ego states whose function is to offer care, validation, and security to needy parents. Such ego states embody the function of a "counterautonomous superego" (Boszormenyi-Nagy, 1962); that is, they inveigh against developmentally appropriate autonomous strivings—or ego states—that would threaten the parents' internal need template.

Intersubjective Fusion: When Self and System Become One

The reciprocal processes of collusive postponement of mourning, reliance on projective identification, captive role assignment, bilateral transference, and others give rise to systemic constructs variously termed "intersubjective fusion" (Boszormenyi-Nagy, 1965), "undifferentiated family ego mass" (Bowen, 1965), and "pseudomutuality" (Wynne, 1965). Each of these authors, in his own way, is describing a family system characterized by individuals with poor ego boundaries who collusively and unconsciously work together as if to create a singular personality structure (Framo, 1982; Humphrey & Stern, 1988). In so doing, family members not only dissociate unwanted feelings and impulses across the system (Wynne, 1965), but also take on roles and functions for the group. Thus, the object relations approach provides a working definition of pathological dependency as a predilection to displace autonomous ego functions onto one or more relating partners. Autonomous ego functions should not be confused with instrumental functions typified by the mutually agreed upon division of labor in most households. There may be many autonomous ego functions, but I will mention three that bear directly on the use of EMDR.

The Superego Function. The superego is the executive function of the self. In our case study, Roger acquiesces, displacing his superego function onto Natalie. At one level, his deference is a futile attempt to seek validation in the form of her approval: he can play out the role of the good son to the good (internalized) mother—a scene from his past. At another level, his behavior can be understood as an attempt to pacify his controlling and anxious wife. Unable to tolerate the anxiety state she activates in him, Roger cannot create a holding environment in which Natalie might ultimately soothe herself. Instead, drawing from his internal world, he plays the compliant but ineffective father to her needy child ego state. In either role—good son or ineffective father—the actions of Roger's self are centripetal, that is, geared toward eliciting care (being the subject). Put differently, Roger offers a needy, anxious subject in reaction to Natalie's attachment-hungry ego state.

From her perspective, Natalie's demanding behavior stems from an introjected critical ego state derived from part of her own mother, and a relational template that mirrors her parent's marriage. By projecting the critical demands of this ego state, Natalie purchases temporary relief from her inner critic. But in so doing, she elicits anxiety, anger, and ultimately withdrawal from Roger. His reactions validate her inner critic's view of herself as unlovable, and Natalie reacts by becoming more controlling.

Looked at collectively, the couple can be described as fitting a pursuer/avoider pattern. However, this characterization of their transactions does not do justice to the interlocking dynamics and frustrated needs that trap these two in what amounts to a repetition compulsion of past failed relationships. Examining the "inherent paradoxes" (Schnarch, 1991) in the relationship reveals covert conflicts. Consciously, Natalie cannot respect a man who does not have a mind of his own, yet she cannot tolerate being challenged. At a deeper level, Natalie's desperate need for an attuned, approving attachment relationship ironically gives rise to the very behavior that pushes Roger away. Still, she would rather provoke Roger's angry ego state and elicit negative attention than endure the aloneness of his withdrawal. For Natalie, inciting marital conflict is trading up from the depersonalizing effects of feeling alone.

Similarly paradoxical is Roger's compliance, which has the appearance of caring—even doting—but stems from his own insecurity. His actions are not motivated by authentic concern for his wife, but are rather an attempt to contain her anger or garner praise. Unable to engage Natalie in genuine dialogue, Roger is left to settle for "as-if" relating. His "I'm not good enough" schema triggers Natalie's "I'm unlovable" schema, and vice versa. The resource orientation of the contextual approach points to the couple's colliding entitlements. Natalie and Roger, each shortchanged by their own parents and in need of soothing, simultaneously look to the other to press a claim for compensatory parenting.

The implications for EMDR interventions in this cycle are made apparent when the underlying schemas and their respective origins are uncovered. In keeping with Shapiro's (2001) three-pronged protocol, Roger's "not good enough" negative cognition can be isolated from the current marital interaction. Its family of origin context can be identified and targeted, followed by its contemporary manifestation and finally a future template of the same triggering interaction. The same can be said of Natalie's negative cognition, "I'm unlovable."

The Self-Soothing Function. In the most general sense, self-soothing is the ability to calm oneself down. The banality of this definition belies the fact that the capacity for affect regulation is arguably at the heart of adaptive functioning. It is certainly a prerequisite. In their discussion of the related, albeit more refined, concept of "integrative capacity," Steele, van der Hart, and Nijenhuis (2001) explain why this is so:

> High levels of integrative capacity enable use of the available level of mental energy to produce reflective thought and action, leading to adaptation, integration...and modulated levels of dependency....Low levels result in poor and inconsistent activation of daily life emotional systems, with reflexive action based on emotionality and impulsivity, avoidance, and lack of critical thinking, with lack of integration in one's life (the "classic" borderline or DID presentation). (p. 90)

The phenomenon of dysregulated affect is indicative of limbic system functioning, which tends to inhibit the neocortex. Individuals in this state are prone to fall back on autonomic (unconscious) behaviors

(Steele et al., 2001). Self-soothing, therefore, is the ability to tolerate affect or distress and maintain conscious, self-reflective neocortical functioning.

From an object relations perspective, "The ability to tolerate the simultaneous gratifying [libidinal] and frustrating [antilibidinal] aspects of a parent (or partner) is the substance of self-soothing" (Schnarch, 1991, p. 192). Faced with perceived threats to an attachment bond (for example, marital conflict or rejection), the anxious individual will fall back on archaic relational modes with defenses formed in childhood. In Natalie's case, the anxiety brought on by her unresolved insecure attachment elicits the ego state that is introjected from her mother—the very person to whom she is insecurely attached. Natalie's self-soothing function is displaced onto Roger, who feels responsible for his wife's happiness.

The Self-Nurturing Function. Self-nurturing is the capacity to maintain positive self-regard in the face of conflict, rejection, or disruptions in attachments. In psychodynamic theory, this is the role of a healthy superego, and it most certainly requires both the neurophysiological and the object integration attributes of self-soothing. Due to its importance in psychotherapy, I have chosen to distinguish it as a function in its own right.

I refer to this ego function as "self-nurturing" to emphasize that the validation of self-worth that normally comes from a nurturing primary caregiver in childhood comes from the self in a differentiated adult. People often resist self-nurturing, despite its obvious advantages of reliability and portability, as it requires mourning. The natural tendency to postpone mourning inclines individuals to hold out for external validation (Schnarch, 1991) through transference-based relating.

EGO STATE CONFLICT IN THEORY AND PRACTICE

A Basic Ego State Configuration

I realized that Natalie presented with what I have come to experience as a "classic" or "basic" ego state configuration when there is early attachment injury. Fairbairn (1954) coined the terms "libidinal ego" and "antilibidinal ego" to describe self-representations that contain attachment strivings and the pain of attachment disruptions respectively. For many, these representations have the qualities of discrete, often covert, ego states. I see Natalie acting out of each of those ego states in turn, with an important addition. Like Fairbairn's "central ego," the third ego state might be considered a host personality or part—what Steele et al. (2001), in their "structural model of dissociation," call the "apparently normal personality" (ANP). The ANP maintains equanimity through the mechanism of dissociation to avoid the painful, dysregulated affect associated with past trauma or relational failures. The ANP operates in a relatively narrow emotional bandwidth, however, which gives way to "emotional personalities" (ego states) when the subject's attachment injuries are triggered (Steele et al., 2001).

I told Natalie, "There is a young part of you that desperately seeks closeness with Roger, that feels alone and invisible and fears she's unlovable. This is the part that wants to do things together, that becomes anxious when Roger is away and wants to be held. This is also the part that felt abandoned by your mom, not good enough for your parents, and constantly in need of acceptance and approval."

"There is another part of you that's angry at your mom or Roger when you feel mistreated or unloved. This is a fierce protector part that says, 'I don't need you.' This is the part that makes mincemeat out of Roger to punish him for being aloof. This is the part that wants Roger to know what it's like to feel the hurt of aloneness. Sadly, this is also the part that, I suspect, beats up on you for being needy. This part probably thinks the other part is a sucker. Then, of course, there is your adult-most self who goes to work, talks with friends, and shows up here most of the time."

I paused to let the information sink in. I held my gaze on Natalie to signal that it was now her turn to talk. Natalie did not take long to respond: "What's weird," she said, "is that I've always known that about myself. I'm just kind of freaked out that you know it!"

In the next section, I will describe family processes that contribute to ego state conflict. Readers are invited to reflect on the interconnectedness of systemic family patterns and ego structure, which can be invaluable in both assessment and treatment. To witness these patterns in conjoint work is to suspect ego state conflict in one or more family members, and to observe ego state conflict in individual psychotherapy is to suspect pathogenic family processes like those described below in the client's family. For EMDR practitioners, an understanding of these family dynamics can lead to the generation of process targets, that is, the targeting of pathogenic transactions as opposed to discrete traumatic events.

Pathogenesis of Ego State Conflict

Some intergenerational family processes are sufficiently pathogenic to result in fragmentation of the ego into conflicting and often covert (unconscious) ego states (Watkins & Watkins, 1997). Dissociation and ego fragmentation are often associated with prolonged childhood abuse (van der Kolk, van der Hart, & Marmar, 1996). However, it is increasingly being recognized that pathogenic family processes are as important as and possibly more important than trauma to the etiology of tertiary dissociation (Gold et al., 2001). An incomplete list of these putative mechanisms includes transgenerational coalitions, parentification (Boszormenyi-Nagy & Krasner, 1986), projective identification, family secrets or collusive denial, split loyalties (Boszormenyi-Nagy & Spark, 1973), and the double bind (Watzlawick, Beavin, & Jackson, 1967). I will address the latter two.

In a *split loyalty* configuration, the child is forced to choose one parent's affiliation at the cost of betraying the other parent. The child can solve the problem of mutually exclusive attachments by forming separate ego states to bond with each parent individually. Parental conflict becomes internalized in the form of ego state conflict. The trauma of split loyalty can be sufficient to lock the ego states in a perpetual state of antipathy even if the parents eventually reconcile. The victim of split loyalties may seek to discharge the anxiety state attendant upon the intrapsychic split by externalizing the conflict onto other relating partners.

A *double bind* occurs between two interdependent partners when one authors contradictory injunctions and obviates the means by which the other can reconcile the contradiction (Watzlawick et al., 1967). Beyond the communicational paradox, there is a deeper ethical conflict that the double bind invokes. Consider the man who asks his son, "Do you think I'm a good father?" Let us assume, for the sake of this example, that the father is seeking validation from his son. Presumably, a good father would not do this, as that would parentify the boy. The ethical question is this: Is the boy obligated to meet his father's needs by denying his own reality (that is, become the good object to his father's needy subject), or is the boy entitled to speak his own truth (press his claim to remain a subject over and against the parentifying action of his father)?

Should this transactional pattern become a dominant feature of the attachment relationship between the child and parent, the child's ego may solve the paradox by splitting into covert ego states. For example, one ego state, containing forbidden knowledge of the father's failure, might remain in a perpetual state of striving for nurturance and validation. Another, counterautonomous ego state would form to collude with the father's need to perceive himself as good. Isomorphic with the structure of the double-binding relationship itself, the first, libidinal ego state would be denied or repressed just as the family denies the father's neediness. The antithetical, collusive ego state would dominate the child's cognitive interpretation of the family as "good." He would interpret his despair and rage as decontextualized defects in his own character.

Above I posed the query, to whom or what is Natalie actually attached? The reality to which Natalie is wedded has more to do with her own internalized need template than with Roger and her kids as separate, autonomous subjects. In my experience, most people lack the diabolical mind required to author a really effective double bind as a consciously conceived plot to torment their partners or avoid responsibility. A simpler explanation is that separate ego states are making separate but conflicting demands that represent the unresolved ambivalence of attachment.

AN INTEGRATIVE TREATMENT APPROACH

To my relief, Natalie was refreshingly open to my assessment of her own ego state system in action. Herself a product of double-binding relationships, she was predisposed to deny her unmet dependency needs. But at this moment, she was ready. I continued, saying, "You're at war with yourself, Natalie, and until you can heal the conflict inside you, you're doomed to play it out with Roger and also with your kids." At this, Natalie became alarmed. "What do the kids have to do with it? I'm a good mother!"

Parental devotion and obligation are powerful sources of therapeutic leverage, as children are the greatest bearers of relational consequences. As a contextual therapist, it is axiomatic that I include them in the treatment even if I never lay eyes on them.

I made my explanation to both parents, saying, "This applies to you, too, Roger, because you're a lot like Natalie in this way. When you two are duking it out you're both triggered into childlike emotional states. It's like a reflex; it's automatic. Natalie, you want Roger to make you feel lovable, and you, Roger, want Natalie to tell you you're a good boy. In a real sense, you're both acting young—real young, even younger than your kids. So with both of you competing to get parented by the other, who is doing the real parenting in the family at that moment?"

Reflecting on this, Roger was quick to agree. "That makes sense," he conceded. "Our son has started to play referee when we argue."

"That's right," Natalie joined in. "Just yesterday, he said to me, 'Mommy, why don't you try to be the bigger person and make up with Daddy?'"

The session was ending and I took this moment to propose a treatment contract. "Okay," I said, "can we agree that (a) you didn't do such a lousy job in choosing a partner after all and that the problem does not lie entirely with the other person; (b) that the issues have more to do with the past than the present; and (c) that each of you needs to do some work on those issues so you can hold onto the wisdom and integrity you've accumulated over the years without turning into a pumpkin whenever you're challenged?"

The couple agreed, and thus the treatment focus could now shift to the intrapsychic work each partner needed to overcome reliance on archaic patterns of relating. This is a pivotal transition in which the therapy can move beyond short-term symptom reduction ("decrease marital conflict") or alteration of superficial transaction patterns ("improve communication"). With each partner beginning to accept responsibility for a heretofore unconscious role in the conflict, I gain leverage to add psychological assessment and intervention strategies to an otherwise here-and-now, transaction-focused couples treatment contract. That is, I move from referee to therapist.

The approach I have been describing transcends traditional boundaries of individual versus couples therapy. The contextual therapist must be able to assess and intervene fluidly between the intrapsychic, interpersonal, and systemic realms. The following sections will describe general treatment goals, the overall structure of the therapy, and specific therapeutic methods.

Contextual Goals in Couples Therapy

Above all, contextual therapy is concerned with the long-term consequences of relational behavior. Accepting responsibility for one's behavior, commitment to mutuality, and the reliance on dialogue to establish trust through fairness are the gold standards for mature, differentiated relating.

These relational goals both require and support a healthy ego structure. Therefore, for therapy to realize its grandest possibilities, psychological (intrapsychic) objectives must be incorporated into the therapy. Psychic wounds from trauma and attachment injuries must be healed, affect regulation must be improved, integrative capacity (for example, the healing of ego state conflicts) must be enhanced, and the mourning process must be facilitated. These objectives are instrumental in developing autonomous ego functions such that clients rely on the self-validating behaviors of offering due care and thereby relieve the relationship of the burden of being the solution to intrapsychic conflict.

Structuring the Therapy

While individuals presenting for couples therapy differ in their agendas and readiness for therapy, a general structure can nonetheless be described that illustrates the integration of psychological and relational treatment domains in actual practice. The proposed model suggests three phases of treatment: alliance and assessment, contracting, and therapeutic intervention. In the discussion of the latter phase, I will present a structure for incorporating EMDR into couples therapy. The following is offered as a basic outline, not as an immutable sequence, as these phases are likely to overlap or even coincide.

Phase 1: Alliance and Assessment. Beginning with the first contact with the couple and typically encompassing three to five sessions, the objectives of this phase are (1) forming a therapeutic alliance with each partner, (2) initial assessment of individual and interpersonal dynamics, and (3) assuring the stabilization of each client individually and of the relationship as a whole. Forming an alliance is done through the practice of "multi-directed partiality," a central tenet of contextual therapy defined by Boszormenyi-Nagy and Krasner as the "sequential siding *with* (and eventually *against*) member after family member. The therapist tries to empathize with and credit everyone on a basis that actually merits crediting" (1986, p. 149). This can be contrasted with therapeutic neutrality.

Drafting a genogram is an efficient, structured way to gather history about developmental issues, traumas small and large, intergenerational legacies, and pathogenic transaction patterns in the family of origin. This process, usually completed in one to three sessions, is invaluable in ascertaining the etiology of negative cognitions and ego state conflicts, and aids the therapist in understanding each partner's contribution to the relational dynamic. Significantly, it is also a vehicle for helping each partner recognize and take ownership of individual issues. This is vital in contracting for change, discussed below.

Assuring the stability of each partner individually as well as the couple relationship as a whole is a routine activity in any therapy practice. Relevant to this discussion is the flexibility of moving from conjoint to individual therapy sessions while still retaining the couple's relational goals. On occasion I have chosen to work with partners individually for a definite period of time before resuming conjoint treatment when I determined that one or both partners were too reactive to use conjoint sessions constructively. I have also recommended therapeutic separations when it was clear that partners were damaging the relationship at a faster rate than it could be repaired through therapy alone.

Phase 2: Contracting. In my view, contracting—that is, cultivating the motivation and willingness to work toward change—is an art that taxes all the therapist's interpersonal skills. The last entry on Roger and Natalie gives a flavor of this; more will be said below under "Methodology." Therapists need to recognize that clients with ego state conflicts may exhibit ambivalence about a willingness to change. For some, one or more ego states may have a strong investment in the symptom and sufficient influence over the self system, and specialized ego state techniques must be used to cultivate a readiness for healing and change (for example, Fraser's Dissociative Table Technique; Fraser, 2003).

Because contextual goals are both psychological and interpersonal, the assessment yields goals for each partner individually, plus the couple (and possibly the family unit and the children). Generally, I will identify some key issues for each partner and describe how those issues affect the relationship (and family).

Accordingly, I offer an individual treatment plan to each partner and a relational plan to both. I introduce EMDR at this stage as I use it extensively. If the partners concur with the assessment and are motivated to change, the next step is to negotiate the who, what, and when of therapeutic intervention. For example, one partner may wish to begin working on individual issues, including EMDR or family-of-origin work, while the other partner wants to work on the relationship conjointly. Each partner contracts with me individually for the desired services.

Phase 3: Therapeutic Intervention. Interventions can be classified as interpersonal (relational) or intrapsychic (individual), although clearly these domains intertwine. Clinical judgment and client motivation combine to determine the priority and timing of interventions. However, because relational work can trigger negative cognitions and ego state conflicts, it may be more efficient to do some preliminary individual therapy preparatory to having conjoint sessions with a partner, parent, or sibling. With improved ego strength and integrative capacity, relational work is far more constructive.

If both partners contract to use EMDR in attaining individual goals, as is often the case in my practice, then the next consideration is who should go first and how and when to involve the other partner. I use EMDR with one person at a time, and, unless it is contraindicated, I prefer to use EMDR with one partner (the *working partner*) while the other—the *witnessing partner*—bears witness to the other's affective experience, gaining insight and empathy along the way (Litt, 2000).

Dissociated material that has been externalized onto the observing partner is often taken back and put in its proper place, giving the observing partner a sense of relief at no longer being burdened with the other's projections. The rapid insight that EMDR fosters in clients can be revelatory to both partners and opens the door to greater intimacy (see Protinsky, Sparks, & Flemke, 2001). As the working partner undergoes sometimes intense emotional release through EMDR, I have often been moved by the compassion that is shown by the observing partner. In these instances, I am also relieved that the observer is present to comfort the working partner and do the driving home, if needed.

Doing EMDR conjointly is contraindicated in the following circumstances:

1. The working partner is unable to freely emote in the presence of the partner.
2. The working partner is not ready to disclose personal history or issues to the partner.
3. The observing partner is likely to use the working partner's revelations in retaliation.
4. The observing partner is unlikely to tolerate the working partner's affect or disclosures.
5. The observing partner is unable or unwilling to let the working partner have all the therapist's attention (and, for example, interrupts the processing with comments or questions).

Note that conjoint sessions may be suitable for one partner but contraindicated for the other. A man may be uncomfortable emoting in front of his wife, or a woman may need to process fear of her husband in private, yet the spouse prefers to do EMDR conjointly. Respecting the wishes of the individuals, versus imposing an arbitrary quid pro quo, models mature relating and has worked well in my practice.

Deciding which partner should go first, if both are candidates for EMDR, is best a mutual decision. If one partner's acting-out is destabilizing the relationship, then I recommend EMDR with that person first. If EMDR is conducted with one partner in the other's absence, options for the excluded partner to contact the therapist and remain involved in the therapy should be discussed. Naturally, the option of referring out for EMDR should be raised with the couple if either expresses discomfort with sharing the same therapist.

Methodology

Treatment guided by principles of contextual therapy seamlessly combines interpersonal and intrapsychic interventions. Nowhere is this more evident than in conjoint sessions in which interlocking need templates are teased apart, loyalty expectations from the family of origin are made visible, and claims of entitlement in the present relational context are differentiated from those of the past. Intrapsychic interventions, such as EMDR and ego state therapy, whether conducted conjointly or in individual sessions, are enriched and road tested by the conjoint work.

Conjoint Interpersonal Interventions: Identifying the Pattern. As I observe couples interact, I monitor both the content of their concerns and the process by which their issues are transacted. As I listen to the content, I scan for statements that reveal displacement of ego functions, parentification of the partner, and reliance on blame. I listen for "we" and "you" statements (for example, "We need to decide what to do," or "You make me feel stupid")—pronoun usage that denotes a diffusion or displacement of personal responsibility and ego function. I also listen for contradictions in relational attitudes that hint at ego state conflict.

In the opening section of this chapter, I could hear Roger abdicate his own terms of relating and express his need for Natalie's approval, thus parentifying her. I also observed that Natalie did not challenge the double standards she authored, but punished Roger for calling her on it, creating a double bind. When I see a destructive transaction pattern repeat itself (for example, Roger giving Natalie a gift only to be rejected), I make a point to explore it as a possible repetition compulsion (Gleiser, 2003), or reenactment from one or both partners' early family life.

As I observe process, I watch for each client's ability to be attuned to the other, especially in the face of criticism—a marker of ego strength. I assess how verbal and nonverbal behavior functions to structure give-and-take in the relationship. I also watch for affect tolerance and how each client reacts to the other's increasing emotional arousal.

I noticed that Natalie met Roger's claim for validation with a counterclaim for being a good object: a real-time competition for parenting. I also observed Natalie's double-binding operations and discrete changes in character that were suggestive of conflicting ego states. I considered the function of each partner's behavior and relational attitude in the structure and emotional tone of the couple and family system. A familiar recursive pattern began to emerge in which Natalie pursued Roger by placing demands on him, and Roger distanced himself by placating and fleeing, which stimulated Natalie to make more demands.

Eliciting the Negative Cognition. I had met with Roger individually three times prior to the present couples session. The family history was revealing, especially to Roger. He came to see his emotional caretaking for his alcoholic mother and his vain efforts to impress his critical father. Now he was trying to explain how this affected his behavior with Natalie: trying to placate her and avoiding conflict. "That's your opinion," she retorted. "I see it differently."

"That's what I mean!" Roger exclaimed, grabbing his gut as if in spasm. He looked pleadingly at me, then at Natalie. His speech was halting, as if he both desperately wanted to protest and wished he had kept his mouth shut at the same time. Natalie wanted urgently to intervene, but I signaled to Roger to continue. I could sense that our alliance was stronger and he was taking a risk because of it. He said, "Just hearing her say that—'It's your opinion'—I can feel myself tighten up. I know

I'm going to be wrong no matter what I say. Normally I just walk away. I don't want to argue."

Natalie wanted to defend herself and asked if she could explain what she meant. But there was no need and I reassured her of this. I stayed with Roger: "Can I explore this with you right now? This reaction you're having?" Roger agreed, and in response to my questions, explained that he felt a tightness in his stomach, like a knot, a SUD of about 7 out of 10. " 'I'm always wrong'—does that fit the sensation in your gut?" I asked. Roger concurred.

A high degree of emotional arousal and its correlate, affect intolerance, are clues to core negative beliefs about the self. A well-timed question such as, "When your partner does that, what does that make you believe about yourself?" can often reveal a negative cognition in operation. As illustrated in the case study above, negative cognitions are reciprocally embedded in pathological transactions. One client's negative cognition initiates behavior that triggers the negative cognition of the other. By mapping the recursive flow of negative cognitions and their corresponding behaviors, the clinician can begin to surface the unconscious need templates and perceive just how they interlock. Identifying and labeling the negative cognitions educates clients about their own triggers and sets the stage for EMDR.

In my experience, most negative cognitions fall into one of three domains of self experience, depicted in Figure 8.1 as they inform the threat to ego integrity.

Within each domain, I have listed negative cognitions typical of their category. Note that negative cognitions that relate to the most central domain, "Being vs. Nothingness," are indicative of depersonalization and derealization and reflect an unstable Self/Not-Self relational configuration consistent with an early attachment failure. It may be surprising to some readers to find "Safety" listed as less central than "Merit" or "Being" in importance to ego stability. Experience shows, however, that clients will sacrifice safety in order to matter to another (for example, battered wives), and people would rather be bad than not be at all. Consequently, processing a target that has multiple negative cognitions will be more successful, in my experience, if I begin working with the negative cognition closest to the core of the personality structure and work outward (that is, from Being vs. Nothingness, to Merit, and then to Safety).

Contextualizing the Transaction. Once I have identified a rigid pattern and the negative cognitions that maintain it, I explore the history and meaning of the transaction for each client. A high degree of affective reactivity and a reduction in the capacity to consider the partner's perspective (and offer compassion) are additional indicators that suggest

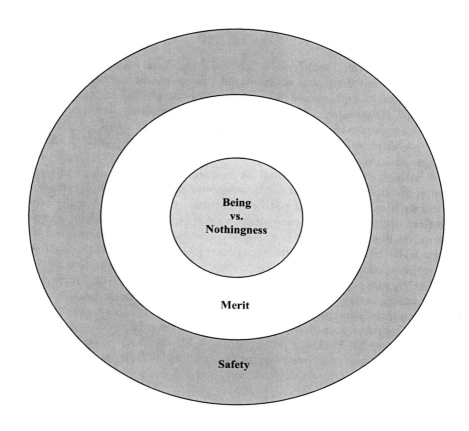

Being vs. Nothingness	Merit	Safety
• I don't exist	• I don't matter	• I'm not safe
• I'm invisible	• I'm not good enough	• I'm going to die
• I'm not real	• I'm a failure	• I'm trapped
	• I don't measure up	

FIGURE 8.1   Negative cognitions and their relationship to the self.
Being vs. Nothingness is at the core of self-experience. A result of secure
attachment, the experience of being "real" is the foundation upon
which the successive domain rest. *Merit*—or worth to relating
partners—is more central to self-experience than *safety*: many would
risk their very lives to belong to another person, family, or group.
Listed are representative negative cognitions that correspond to each
layer of self-experience.

that the source of the client's wounds is not anchored in the current relational context, but rather in the family of origin.

At my request, Roger kept his hand on his gut. I asked for another intensity rating while I repeated the phrase, "I'm always wrong." "It's still about a five," he said. I asked him, "Would you be willing to do an experiment?" He agreed, and I asked him to close his eyes and picture his mother. I repeated the negative cognition "I'm always wrong." "Do the feeling and the phrase fit the picture?" I asked. "No," he said. "With her, it's more like 'I'm not good enough.' It feels different."

"Now picture your dad and think of the phrase 'I'm always wrong.'" Roger reacted instantly. "Oh yeah, it's him—definitely him. He always had something to say that made me think I was stupid." "Give me a number now," I said. Roger closed his eyes again. "Six," he said. Natalie eagerly validated Roger's experience of his father. "He's a bastard," she affirmed. "I don't mean to offend you, honey," she said, turning to Roger, "but no matter how hard you tried, he always had to find fault."

This had been a productive sequence, and I summarized for the couple. "That was a very loving thing you just said to Roger, Natalie. You seem to really understand how Roger tried to please his dad but learned that it was no use. We all carry our family issues into our relationships, and this is a piece that you, Roger, carry into these situations with Natalie. It seems that as soon as you sense conflict, that part of you that 'knows' it's no use gets activated and you're giving up before you begin. Now I don't know if it's any use arguing with Natalie, but I do know you don't give her much of a chance."

Roger was listening attentively and nodding. I turned to Natalie. "And I'll bet that when he gives in and walks off, that triggers that part of you that feels all alone, and you get madder and start chasing right after him!" Both were chuckling now. In this light, they could see the absurdity of their pattern. "That's right," Natalie said, thoughtfully. "I feel like I don't matter and I want him to feel the pain I feel."

Surrendering the Acting-Out Behaviors. When behaviors and negative cognitions are contextualized, often the couple's relationship is relieved of the burden of being perceived as both the source of the problem and the means to its solution. Potentially, each client is more accepting of the need for individual growth and less reliant on trying to change the partner. This step in the therapy sets the stage for simultaneously moving the focus to individual intrapsychic therapy and for giving up acting-out behaviors that adversely affect the relationship.

At this juncture, Natalie was readily offering up possible solutions to the problem Roger identified. "Maybe I can be nicer in how I disagree," she proffered. But this solution was relational, where an individual solution was required. Though Roger liked the idea, I jumped in. "That's very considerate," I said, "but it won't do in the long run. It would just mean that Roger is dependent upon you to say the right thing, in just the right way. You have a bad hair day and he's jumping out the window. No, I think a more sustainable solution is that we use EMDR to make you, Roger, about as bulletproof as we can so Natalie can say whatever is on her mind and you won't get overwhelmed."

Both Roger and Natalie appeared to like the idea, so I continued. "In the meantime, Roger, you would do well to resist the temptation to run away when there's a conflict. I know it's easier said than done, but if you can stay bolted in place and just breathe for a few minutes, you'll both probably calm down and maybe you can settle your differences." Roger looked dubious, and I can't say I blamed him. He had had a lifetime of feeling overpowered compared to a moment's inspiration. I acknowledged this and lamented with him that it was going to take a lot of work, but it could be done. "Besides," I added, "the alternative is more of the same: you keep building up resentment, you're emotionally absent for the woman who agreed to spend her one and only lifetime with you, and the kids wind up parenting you both."

Roger was starting to get it, so now I turned to Natalie. "You said that you want him to feel the pain that you feel when it seems you're being ignored or dismissed?" She nodded and began to defend herself, but I continued before her angry defender ego state could get charged up again. "That's the angry part of you that bites back when the lonely part of you is triggered." She reflected for a moment, calmer now, then concurred. "Well," I continued, "he's feeling your pain all right and he's running away from you to avoid it. Now I just told Roger to stay bolted in place even when he feels overwhelmed, and maybe he will sometimes and maybe he won't. But the pain of your feeling alone and unlovable can't be solved by Roger acting in a particular way. That problem lies between your left ear and your right ear and that's where you have to find the solution."

Natalie was restless at this suggestion, and I could tell it was going to be hard for her to accept. Intuitively she knew that I was telling her that she had to parent herself, and I've yet to meet anyone who actually likes this idea. Her young ego states, who were also listening, were predisposed to hear my message in all-or-nothing terms. They would need reassurance that I was not prescribing a life of solitude, or passive complicity vis-à-vis a distancing spouse. We had a short dialogue differentiating between the healthy, responsible adult-to-adult relating that she was entitled to expect, and the ego soothing from Roger that she was not.

She shifted uneasily in her seat, but, maintaining executive control over her ego states, she was receptive. I ventured an initial contract with her to give up the acting-out symptom, just as I did earlier with Roger.

"Natalie," I began, "I'm talking to your adult-most self when I offer this suggestion. The angry and lonely parts of you are young, and it won't do any good to let your child parts conduct your marriage for you. If you want to have a sustainable relationship then you have to make it a policy that no matter what he does, you're not going to get demanding or controlling or verbally abusive, but instead you'll take the time to calm yourself down and eventually ask for what you need. That means you have to do a lot of talking to those younger parts of yours and not let them take over." Natalie's challenge was a formidable one, and my sympathetic gaze told her that I knew it, but that we were off to a good start.

Because the acting-out behaviors serve such an important psychic function by masking issues with the family of origin and mitigating intra-psychic conflict through externalization, clinicians need to be mindful of how symptoms function and what the client is being asked to give up. Surrendering these behaviors can increase symptoms of anxiety and depression, even as behavioral and relational improvement is apparent to all. The intensified anxiety can lead to regression and an inertial pull to recapitulate earlier dynamics. Clinicians are wise to anticipate this and advise clients of the possibility of this phenomenon. Clients need healthier means of self-soothing and adaptive ways of using the relationship as a resource.

Intrapsychic Interventions: EMDR and Ego State Therapy. To review, contextual goals for the individual therapy component include healing traumas and attachment injuries, reducing reactivity (increasing affect regulation), enhancing integrative capacity, and facilitating the mourning process. Consistent with the relationally based theory of personality development that I have described is a developmentally based method for structuring EMDR.

Processing and resolving pathogenic family transactions (for example, split loyalty and double binds) can have a profound healing effect on clients' experience of themselves as worthy, whole, and safe. Resolution of the "Merit" domain of ego integrity vis-à-vis one's parents yields a working-through process that humanizes and thereby deparentifies them. Thus, with the mourning process accelerated, clients are able to surrender archaic modes of relating.

By the time the client and I are ready to begin EMDR, I have observed the couple's relational dynamics and obtained both a family history and a chronological history of traumas small and large. Consistent with Shapiro's (2001) recommendation for starting with early targets, I develop a chronological sequence for processing targets. I have found that an effective and efficient sequence is one I learned from Maureen Kitchur (2005). Typically, I first target conflict in the parents' marriage, followed by the relationship with each parent in turn. Then specific family conflicts, disturbing dynamics, and nodal events can be targeted, also in chronological order.

I use clinical judgment about amending the order and when to introduce other traumas (for example, nonfamilial abuse) into the sequence. I also use discretion about using the "recent events protocol" (Shapiro, 2001) to target current conflicts with the partner. These targets usually feed back to family of origin experience, so it is more efficient to start with early targets. Nonetheless, selecting the partner as the target image, or a recent conflict with the partner, has at least two advantages: it can provide relief in the current situation, and it offers proof to clients that their reactivity is truly anchored in the past.

As mentioned earlier, some negative cognitions are the result of repetitive, pathogenic family processes as opposed to discrete traumatic experiences. With such process traumas, clients may not be able to identify a first or worst example of the target dynamic. Clients also may not register the dynamic as being especially affect laden upon recollection, and client and clinician alike may believe that the family dynamic chosen is a poor choice for EMDR—a dud.

However, my experience has shown me that what *should* be clinically salient according to the theories described here most often responds well to EMDR and produces significant results. Clinicians should anticipate that clients whose families exhibit the pathogenic processes described above may experience ego state conflict that may be blocking access to the material. Ego state techniques can be invaluable in overcoming resistance and processing to full resolution.

Shapiro (2001) describes EMDR as a three-pronged protocol in which disturbances are processed starting with their antecedents, their present manifestations, and their anticipated future occurrence ("future template"). Accordingly, EMDR applied to relational therapy follows this model, with the future template work acting as an imagined practice session for on-the-fly self-soothing, ethical negotiating, and attunement in the presence of high arousal. EMDR and ego state techniques aimed at increasing integrative capacity should also take advantage of this imaginal practicing, such that clients become aware of and in control of their ego state system in the face of triggering situations.

EMDR augmented with ego state therapy techniques can be used to heal attachment injuries, leading to cooperation between, or eventually integration of, ego states. Developmentally structured processing facilitates mourning and efficiently resolves negative cognitions that wreak havoc in the contemporary relational domain. As affect tolerance is enhanced, partners are better able to make use of conjoint relational therapy to learn how to dialogue, negotiate conflicts, and remain attuned in the face of each other's individuality.

CONCLUSION

Contextual therapy is an intergenerational, differentiation-based model that integrates psychological and systemic understanding into a coherent theory of relationships. The approach incorporates ethical, systemic, and psychodynamic elements to describe the recursive confluence of intrapersonal experience and interpersonal transaction.

Tracing a path from the dialectical nature of self to the generativity that flows from parent to child, contextual theory argues for our basic human need for sustainable relationship and offers a model for its attainment. Boszormenyi-Nagy and colleagues show us that genuine dialogue, rooted in the mutuality of commitment for the equitable give-and-take of subject and object roles, is a pinnacle achievement in human development.

Ego state theory and therapy are an important refinement of object relations theory and offer diagnostic clarity and a rich vein of clinical interventions. Some degree of ego state separateness may be universal, but ego state conflict can lead to crippling personality disorder and refractory symptoms and behavior. An awareness of ego state dynamics can make a client's baffling behavior suddenly make sense, and explains that good therapy can go nowhere if the whole ego state system is not cooperating. Nowhere is this more true than in couples therapy, as ego states are especially activated within the context of attachment relationships.

EMDR is a stand-alone, trauma-based model of psychotherapy. For reasons that are still poorly understood, EMDR allows the brain to adaptively process information and heal emotional wounds to an unprecedented degree. By using the power of EMDR to resolve trauma and facilitate the healing of attachment wounds, and structured by the knowledge of developmental issues illuminated by ego state and contextual theories as described here, therapy moves beyond trauma and symptom resolution into fostering mature, sustainable relationships.

The treatment of Natalie and Roger illustrates the integration of psychodynamic and relational theories. The impact of pathogenic family processes in each partner's family of origin is uncannily played out in their present relationship. The immaculate interlocking of each partner's relational need template informs the intractability of the couple's conflict. Therapy that aspires to something more than superficial change must address the unconscious loyalty to the family of origin and heal the wounds that perpetuate ego state conflict.

Therapists treating clients both individually and conjointly enjoy the rich opportunity to both deepen their assessment of clients through live observation and evaluate the effectiveness of the therapy. Client self-reports of progress, remissions, and impasses are augmented by direct observation of behavior in conjoint sessions. Clients are generally very appreciative of the advantages of "one-stop shopping," and I have experienced remarkably few complications in over twenty years of practice. By incorporating the tools of EMDR and ego state therapy into my contextual work, I have been able to shepherd more rapid and profound change with couples and families. Finally, I have the satisfaction of knowing that generations yet to be born will reap the benefits of therapy grounded in an ethic of responsible care within and between the generations.

NOTE

1. This case illustration is a composite of several different clinical cases.

REFERENCES

Boszormenyi-Nagy, I. (1962). Concept of schizophrenia from the point of view of family treatment. *Family Process, 1*, 103–113.

Boszormenyi-Nagy, I. (1965). A theory of relationships: Experience and transaction. In I. Boszormenyi-Nagy & J. Framo (Eds.), *Intensive family therapy: Theoretical and practical aspects* (pp. 33–86). New York: Harper & Row.

Boszormenyi-Nagy, I., & Krasner, B. (1986). *Between give and take: A clinical guide to contextual therapy.* New York: Brunner/Mazel.

Boszormenyi-Nagy, I., & Spark, G. (1973). *Invisible loyalties.* New York: Brunner/Mazel.

Bowen, M. (1965). Family psychotherapy with schizophrenia in the hospital and in private practice. In I. Boszormenyi-Nagy & J. Framo (Eds.), *Intensive family therapy: Theoretical and practical aspects* (pp. 213–243). New York: Harper & Row.

Dicks, H. V. (1967). *Marital tensions: Clinical studies toward a psychoanalytic theory of interaction.* New York: Basic Books.

Fairbairn, W. R. D. (1954). *An object-relations theory of the personality.* New York: Basic Books.

Framo, J. L. (1965). Rationale and techniques of intensive family therapy. In I. Boszormenyi-Nagy & J. Framo (Eds.), *Intensive family therapy: Theoretical and practical aspects* (pp. 143–212). New York: Harper & Row.

Framo, J. L. (1982). Symptoms from a family transactional viewpoint (1970). In J. L. Framo (Ed.), *Explorations in marital and family therapy: Selected papers of James L. Framo* (pp. 11–57). New York: Springer Publishing.

Fraser, G. A. (2003). The Dissociative Table Technique revisited, revised: A strategy for working with ego states in dissociative disorders and ego state therapy. *Journal of Trauma and Dissociation, 4*(4), 5–28.

Gleiser, K. A. (2003). Psychoanalytic perspectives on traumatic repetition. *Journal of Trauma and Dissociation, 4*(2), 27–47.

Gold, S. N., Elhai, J. D., Rea, B. D., Weiss, D. Masino, T., Morris, S. L., et al. (2001). Contextual treatment of dissociative identity disorder: Three case studies. *Journal of Trauma and Dissociation, 4*, 5–36.

Horner, A. J. (1979). *Object relations and the developing ego in therapy.* New York: Aronson.

Humphrey, L. L., & Stern, S. (1988). Object relations and the family system in bulimia: A theoretical integration. *Journal of Marital and Family Therapy, 14*(4), 337–350.

Johnson, S. M., Makinen, J. A., & Milliken, J. W. (2001). Attachment injuries in couple relationships: A new perspective on impasses in couples therapy. *Journal of Marital and Family Therapy, 27,* 145–155.

Kitchur, M. (2005). The strategic developmental model for EMDR. In R. Shapiro (Ed.), *EMDR solutions: Pathways to healing* (pp. 8–56). New York: Norton.

Litt, B. (2000). *Trust, intimacy, and sex.* Symposium conducted at the EMDR International Association Conference, Toronto, Canada.

Litt, B. (2007). The child as identified patient: Integrating contextual therapy and EMDR. In F. Shapiro, F. W. Kaslow, & L. Maxfield (Eds.), *Handbook of EMDR and family therapy processes* (pp. 306–324). Hoboken, NJ: Wiley.

Middleberg, C. V. (2001). Projective identification in common couple dances. *Journal of Marital and Family Therapy, 17,* 341–352.

Protinsky, H., Sparks, J., & Flemke, K. (2001). Using eye movement desensitization and reprocessing to enhance treatment of couples. *Journal of Marital and Family Therapy, 27,* 157–164.

Schnarch, D. M. (1991). *Constructing the sexual crucible: An integration of sexual and marital therapy.* New York: Norton.

Shapiro, F. (2001). *Eye movement desensitization and reprocessing: Basic principles, protocols, and procedures* (2nd ed.). New York: Guilford Press.

Shapiro, F., Kaslow, F. W., & Maxfield, L. (Eds.) *Handbook of EMDR and family therapy processes.* Hoboken, NJ: Wiley.

Steele, K., van der Hart, O., & Nijenhuis, E. R. S. (2001). Dependency in the treatment of complex posttraumatic stress disorder and dissociative disorders. *Journal of Trauma and Dissociation, 2*(4), 79–116.

Toothman, D., & Phillips, M. (1998). Coming together: Working with couples from an ego state perspective. *American Journal of Clinical Hypnosis, 41*(2), 175–189.

van der Kolk, B. A., van der Hart, O., & Marmar, C. (1996). Dissociation and information processing in posttraumatic stress disorder. In B. A. van der Kolk, A. C. McFarlane, & L. Weisaeth (Eds.), *Traumatic stress: The effects of overwhelming experience on mind, body, and society* (pp. 303–327). New York: Guilford Press.

Watkins, J. G., & Watkins, H. H. (1997). *Ego states: Theory and therapy.* New York: Norton.

Watzlawick, P., Beavin, J., & Jackson, D. (1967). *Pragmatics of human communication.* New York: Norton.

Wynne, L. (1965). Some indications and contraindications for exploratory family therapy. In I. Boszormenyi-Nagy & J. Framo (Eds.), *Intensive family therapy: Theoretical and practical aspects* (pp. 289–322). New York: Harper & Row.

CHAPTER 9

The Integration of the Internal Family Systems Model and EMDR

Joanne H. Twombly and Richard C. Schwartz

Although EMDR can be used successfully with the majority of clients, there are times when its effectiveness is limited, and clients for whom it simply doesn't work. Often this occurs when affect is partially or completely unavailable and the flow of the processing becomes partially or completely blocked. The Internal Family Systems Model (IFS; Schwartz, 1995) is an elegant, efficient, and powerful ego state treatment modality that, when used with EMDR, can increase its range of effectiveness. This chapter will provide an introduction to IFS and describe ways of using it to enhance or enable EMDR processing.

THE UNTARNISHED HEALING SELF

The Internal Family Systems Model was developed by Richard Schwartz and is based on family systems theory and practice. The focus of IFS is on working within the network of internal relationships in which each ego state or part is embedded. This parallels the way family therapists work to understand and intervene within the family system, based on the realization that for anyone to change, the whole family system must change.

Like other ego state modalities, IFS emphasizes the normal multiplicity of the mind. It can be differentiated from them by its belief in the universal presence of an undamaged Self that exists in everyone. The IFS concept of the Self is analogous to the spiritual concepts, present in many of the world's religions, of a soul, a transcendent state of compassion and calm.

Through Schwartz's work with hundreds of clients, many severely abused, he came to believe that everyone has an untarnished, healing Self despite the fact that many people have very little access to it initially. The Self is the most authentic essence of a person—the person's strongest, most resourceful, and wisest core, enfolding the individual's most important values. This Self contains the qualities of compassion, confidence, curiosity, and perspective—that is, qualities of good leadership in any human system—making it best equipped to lead the family system.

The belief in the existence of the Self has been difficult for many therapists because it requires trusting that an inherent healing wisdom exists in clients, even those with severe symptoms. Often therapists learn this kind of trust only after repeatedly witnessing the healing power of the client's Self. Our observation, however, is that therapists who come to IFS trainings with EMDR experience already have witnessed clients' innate healing abilities. As Shapiro (2001) states,

> The natural tendency of the brain's information-processing system is to move toward a state of mental health. However, if the system is blocked or becomes imbalanced by the impact of a trauma, maladaptive responses are observed. If the block is removed (here, through the use of EMDR), processing resumes and takes the information toward a state of adaptive resolution and functional integration. (p. 32)

The concept of innate healing is well known to EMDR therapists, so for them, the idea that clients have the capacity to heal themselves is familiar and comfortable, and leads to an easier acceptance of the existence of the Self.

THE INNER ECOLOGY: DYNAMICS OF THE SELF AND PARTS IN IFS

Central to IFS is creating access to the Self, and then working through the Self to heal the parts of the mind, which results in clients becoming able to live more fully in a state of self-leadership. Rather than dealing with a client whose Self is obscured and blended with parts, or dealing directly with a client's parts, the IFS therapist works as a partner to the client's Self, and the client's Self becomes the compassionate therapist or leader with the parts. This decreases the possibility of the therapist developing a parentlike or hierarchal relationship with the client.

Along with the idea of the Self, IFS holds the belief that parts are multidimensional, each having feelings and beliefs. In other words, each part is a distinct personality, with a full range of emotions, desires, temperaments, talents, and varying perceptions of age and gender. For example, a sad part is not conceptualized as just a cluster of melancholy emotions and negative thoughts, but is seen as a childlike part that is sad because it carries the burden of sadness from unresolved traumatic childhood experiences. Along with sadness, the part also has the capacity to experience the range of normal emotions, and has a large degree of autonomy in the sense that the part might think, say, and feel things independently from the person in which the part exists.

Most parts carry extreme beliefs and emotions or burdens that entered the person's system from the outside world during charged or traumatic events and became lodged within the parts. Thereafter, these burdens govern the way the parts feel or behave, as if they are embedded viruses or computer programs. It is the burdens that parts carry, not the parts themselves, that cause problems. These burdens need to be expelled from the client's inner system in order for healing to begin.

Because IFS grew out of systems thinking and family therapy, the focus has not been on getting to know and change each part individually, but instead on working within the network of internal relationships in which each part is embedded. This parallels the way a family therapist does not try to understand and work with a child outside the context of the child's family, but rather, realizes that for the child to change, other family members may have to change first or simultaneously. In IFS, symptoms are viewed as the result of traumatic life experiences that cause the Self to become blended with and obscured by parts that carry the burden or impact of the experiences.

In working with internal families, it quickly becomes clear that parts are as highly polarized as the external families in which they developed. Many parts never relate directly to one another and hold extreme views of what others are like. For example, in many bulimic clients, the part that drives them to binge is polarized with an inner critic that harshly scolds them for bingeing. The more the inner critic attacks the part that binges, the more that part binges, and vice versa.

Like families, parts also form alliances and coalitions and will interrupt one another with impunity. As is true in family therapy, long-standing polarizations often melt once two parts are encouraged to communicate directly and without interference from other parts. Finally, just like parentified children in families, some parts protect other more vulnerable parts or protect the inner system in general. These protectors will resist intrusions by well-meaning therapists if their fears are not respected and addressed. This phenomenon is what leads EMDR processing to become blocked at times.

Thus, IFS views a person as containing a Self and an ecology of relatively discrete, autonomous parts, each with qualities that want to play a valuable role within. The goal of IFS is for people to operate primarily from self-leadership with parts being informed and guided by the Self. Negative life experiences can cause parts to be forced out of their valuable roles as the system becomes reorganized to make survival and functioning possible. Through this reorganization, the Self becomes submerged and blended with parts that lose confidence in the Self, and lose their ability to learn and evolve on their own.

A good analogy is that of an alcoholic family in which the children are forced into protective and stereotypic roles by the dynamics of their family. Although similar roles are found across alcoholic families (the scapegoat, parentified child, lost child, and so forth), these roles do not represent the essence of the children. Instead, all children are unique individuals and, once released from their role by therapy, can find out who they are, distinct from the demands of their chaotic family. The same process seems to hold for internal families in which parts are forced into extreme roles by external circumstances, and then continue functioning that way even when the external circumstances have passed. By learning about and respecting the inner ecology, IFS avoids power struggles with protective parts, releases the constraints that bind parts in their roles, and enables parts to transform into valuable inner family members.

The therapist's job is to help clients reach and maintain a state of self-leadership in which they can heal themselves. Once a person has been hurt, parts lose trust and respect for the leadership of the Self and, like parentified children, believe they have to take over to protect the system.

The initial step in the IFS treatment process is to differentiate the parts from the Self or to unblend parts from the Self. Access to the Self can often be accomplished with remarkable speed and efficiency using IFS techniques. This is true for all clients, even those who have experienced complex abuse or neglect, although for some of these clients, parts must often be accessed directly to facilitate access to the Self.

THE THREE PRIMARY CATEGORIES OF PARTS

To begin to understand the tasks of helping the client unblend parts from the Self, the therapist must understand the functions of the parts. Parts are divided into three categories (Schwartz, 1995): *exiles*, who, having experienced the trauma or neglect directly, hold the burden of unresolved negative feelings; *managers*, who act as protective gatekeepers and not only protect the system from becoming overwhelmed by burdens carried by exiles, but protect the exiles from situations that might add to their burdens; and *firefighters*, who react reflexively to bring the system back to its original balance whenever managers get overwhelmed and overridden, resulting in the exiles' feelings being experienced on the surface. When that happens, firefighters do whatever they need to restore balance as quickly as possible.

Exiles are most often vulnerable child parts that carry many of the emotions, sensations, memories, and beliefs (that is, the burdens from experiences of being abused, shamed, neglected, or terrorized). This means that if they take over the system, the person will reexperience some or all of those burdens. Symptoms indicative of the presence of exiles include flashbacks, anxiety, depression, somatic pain, and affect storms.

Managers come in a number of familiar guises. They are at times inner critics who protect by using criticism to inhibit or motivate; codependent parts who decrease the possibility of abandonment by helping and pleasing everyone around them; workaholic parts who by overworking distract from any internal pain; parts who blunt affect, numb, or provide an obstructive blanket of confusion; and so forth.

Incomplete resolution of EMDR targets and treatment failures are often the result of therapists not recognizing and dealing with the client's managers, who are at times wrongly seen as manifestations of a client's "resistance." Managers are often exhausted by their task of protecting exiles and very much want the system to heal. However, they will work to maintain the status quo and work against any interventions undertaken before their concerns are fully understood and addressed. It is important for therapists to note that overriding the concerns of managers may result in the client going into crisis, as some negative-appearing symptoms protect clients from worse symptoms or from the system becoming unbalanced. Indications of manager interference include superficial processing, intense processing with no resolution, or the failure of EMDR. For managers to be willing to shift their roles, they must develop enough confidence in the Self, the therapist, and in the proposed treatment process.

When managers become overwhelmed and are unable to function, exiles are triggered and firefighters go into action. Firefighters often act impulsively, frantically, or reflexively to find stimulation that will override or help dissociate from the overwhelming danger of the exile's feelings. Bingeing on drugs, alcohol, food, or sex and self-destructive behaviors are common examples of firefighter activities. When a client has a history of dangerous firefighter activity, it is necessary for the therapist to focus on the firefighters first to develop agreements and cooperation before working with exiles. These parts are often tired of the restrictive roles they have been forced into and will welcome treatment that helps exiles unburden and gives them other behavioral options and the chance to move into a healthier mode of being.

IFS STEPS TO HEALING

In IFS treatment, the client's Self is accessed and begins to relate to the parts in loving ways that lead to their unburdening the emotions and beliefs that they accrued from negative life experiences. As that happens the internal family system reconfigures in new, more harmonious and adaptive ways. IFS treatment consists of the following seven steps:

Step 1: Accessing the Self. Accessing the Self, or at least a critical mass of the Self, is accomplished through the process of unblending it from the parts. The presence of the Self is recognized when it exhibits qualities such as compassion and curiosity toward the parts. If the Self appears to be present, but has, for instance, no feelings toward a part, or feels angry or afraid of a part, it is a sign that a "Self-like" part is present and must be unblended from the Self.

Step 2: Witnessing. Once the Self is accessed and a part has been identified who is willing to work with the Self, then other parts are asked if they have any objection to the proposed work. Once the objections (if any) are dealt with, witnessing takes place. The goal is for the part to feel and trust that the Self knows and fully understands whatever the part needs the Self to know. This might include information about burdens the part holds, feelings it suffers, feelings it has toward the Self, beliefs it holds, and so forth.

Step 3: Retrieval. At times, before further work is possible, the part must be retrieved. As most parts believe they are still living in the past, it can be necessary to retrieve them from the past and bring them into the present before healing work can be done. As long as parts are living in the past, they tend to react as if the conditions in the past still exist in the present. First, the Self checks with the part to see if this is necessary, and if it is, the Self goes to where the part is (usually in the past), and brings it to the present. Note that sometimes retrieval is done after the unburdening phase.

Step 4: Unburdening. Once the first steps are accomplished, the parts are asked if they are willing to unburden feelings or beliefs they have been carrying. Twombly conceptualizes clients' burdens as being held as tangled webs of energy. Once barriers to the burden being released are dealt with, the burden is released and energy returns to its normal state; that is, the toxic material is transformed. Any concerns the parts have about this process must first be addressed. Frequent concerns include the fear that the part is the burden and will disappear without it, or that the burden will

be released and pollute the world. The parts are given suggestions as to how they can release the burdens; for example, into
the air, wind, light, water, fire, or earth. Sometimes one of these
suggestions will feel right to a part or the suggestions will enable
the parts to come up with their own ideas. Keep in mind that at
times, the unburdening may need to be done in small increments
as the parts feel safe and ready to manage the process.

Step 5: *Replacing burdens with positive qualities.* As burdens are released, space opens up and the part is invited to notice what positive qualities are coming into that space. Qualities often noticed
include energy, peacefulness, hope, trust, and possibility.

Step 6: *Integration and reconfiguration of the system.* Parts who have
unburdened may merge with other parts, develop a new position
in the system, or need a new function.

Step 7: *Checking for questions and concerns.* At the end of an IFS session, the therapist asks the Self to check and see if there are any
parts that have concerns or comments. Each concern and comment needs to be heard and addressed.

OPTIMIZING THE THERAPIST'S ACCESS TO THE SELF

An important aspect of IFS practice is to help therapists develop their own
access to the Self. Richard Schwartz strongly recommends that therapists
be in their own Self as they work with clients. This recommendation is in
fact useful when working in any treatment modality. All therapists have
clients whose dysfunction or personality style pushes their buttons or
whose issues touch on their own in such a way that countertransference
takes on a presence in session or in the treatment relationship. This presence can be diagnostic, providing important information, as well as potentially damaging to the effectiveness of the treatment process. I recommend
that therapists spend a few minutes before each session first noticing what
parts get activated by their next client, and second noticing any parts of
the therapist not connected to the client that are activated. The third step
is to negotiate with the parts to step back and allow the therapist (in Self)
to handle the session. The Self elicits the Self, so the therapist who works
from the Self will facilitate access to the Self in the client.

The following case study will illustrate how the seven steps of IFS
treatment are carried out. The emphasis in this case is on working with
the dynamics of the internal family system. A further case study later
in the chapter will show how IFS treatment and EMDR can be used
together.

JACK: RICHARD SCHWARTZ USES
IFS TO RESOLVE RAGE

Jack came to treatment to deal with his rage, which had resulted in his being fired from several jobs. To begin the first step of the IFS process, I asked Jack to focus on where he felt rage in his body, which helped him connect with the part holding the rage. At this point, Jack's Self was blended with the part. To facilitate presence of the Self (Step 1), I asked Jack to ask the part to separate himself from Jack. Note that communication with parts is almost always done through the client to support access to the Self. Sometimes this process is visualized as the part actually stepping back or out in front of the Self. I ascertained the presence of the Self by asking Jack what he felt toward the part. Jack's answer, "compassion and curiosity," indicated the presence of the Self. As the part holding rage felt the Self's compassion and curiosity for him, the process of healing was well on its way.

To begin witnessing (Step 2), Jack asked the part to tell Jack everything he wanted Jack to know about him. Jack learned that the part functioned to protect Jack from situations that would activate child parts, the exiles that carried burdens of terror and sadness left over from Jack's childhood. In other words, the part holding the rage was a protective part that shielded Jack from becoming overwhelmed with old terror and sadness carried by the exiles or child parts. At work, Jack's rages occurred when he felt taken advantage of by his bosses and colleagues. As Jack listened to the protective part, he learned that there was another part, a manager, who avoided conflict by approval seeking, which led to Jack's taking responsibility for tasks that others would have normally done. Exiles became activated and triggered as Jack felt taken advantage of and as his own needs were not being met. When the exiles became triggered, the system became flooded with old feelings of exploitation, terror, and sadness, and the protective part, a firefighter, would rage in an attempt to correct injustices. As Jack understood more about how and why the firefighter operated, he developed more appreciation and respect for that part. Jack was surprised to learn that the firefighter was tired of raging and needing to be vigilant, and wanted Jack to stop the managers from their approval-seeking behavior so he could relax.

As Jack continued to witness, he discovered that the firefighter had assumed this extreme role at a time when Jack was a child being bullied every day on his way to school. The firefighter was one of several parts who helped Jack deal with this, each in its own unique way. The approval-seeking manager dealt with the bullies by doing anything he could to get their approval. When this didn't work, the firefighter flew into a loud, fearless, fighting fury, which earned Jack the respect of bullies much bigger than he. The child/exile parts ended up carrying the actual feelings of humiliation, vulnerability, and terror.

As do all parts burdened with old roles and unresolved trauma, these parts functioned in the present as if it were the past. The approval-seeking manager sought approval because he thought that doing anything else would endanger Jack; the vulnerable child parts/exiles felt traumatized; and the protective firefighter flew into rages, all in the service of protecting Jack and managing unresolved feelings from the past.

This illustrates the basic assumption of IFS that each of one's parts is performing an important role and is an important element in the psyche. Once Jack (in Self) witnessed the firefighter, he found that this part—whom he had always thought of as a curse—was actually working hard to protect him from unresolved terror and sadness held by child parts. The approval-seeking parts were also working hard, albeit in a different way, to manage situations in which they felt overpowered and at risk.

In Step 3, Retrieval, I asked Jack to check with the protective firefighter and we learned that he was indeed living in the past. Retrieving the firefighter and bringing him into the present brought him some cautious relief, as he could then begin to see possibilities in the present that had been unavailable in the past. The firefighter was asked what he would like to do if he no longer had to fly into rages to protect the child parts, and he told Jack that he would like to help him judge who was safe to trust and who was not.

The firefighter was burdened with old rage, which led to Jack becoming excessively angry in the present. For any part to unburden (Step 4), it needs to feel connected to and be fully witnessed by the Self in whatever way is necessary for that part to feel comprehensively known. For some parts, this includes the Self experiencing some or all of the affects and learning some or all of the experiences that engendered the burdens. Other parts may need much less, and unburdening can happen quickly.

The firefighter felt fully witnessed by Jack, but before he felt safe enough to unburden the old rage and become the internal advisor he wanted to be, the approval-seeking manager had to stop putting Jack in positions where he was exploited. When I had Jack check with the approval-seeking manager, he found the manager unwilling to stop because he used approval-seeking behavior to prevent confrontations that triggered child parts into flooding the system with their burdens of old terror and sadness. As is often the case, the exiles needed to be worked with before systemwide change could take place.

When Jack initially turned his attention to the exiles, he said he felt contempt for them because they were so weak. This indicated that a part holding contempt was blended with Jack. I asked Jack to identify this part and ask it to step back and let Jack (in Self) deal with the exiles.

After the part holding contempt stepped back, Jack spontaneously reported that he felt compassion toward the exiles and was curious to learn about them.

Jack was silent as he witnessed the exiles. These parts showed Jack scenes from his childhood in which he was terrorized on his way to school. Once they felt fully witnessed, they realized that Jack now had many resources that were unavailable during his childhood. They allowed Jack to bring them into the present and were eager to unburden. As Jack watched, he saw "black balls of terror and sadness" leave their abdomens and float away into a stream of light.

As the burdens floated away into the stream of light, the exiles were asked to notice that space and energy were being freed up, allowing them to receive important qualities (Step 5). Jack reported that during the process, the exiles became older boys who reported a new sense of lightness and now wanted to go and play. Jack noticed he too felt lighter and more positive.

As parts no longer need to function as they did in the past, they gain awareness and their roles shift (Step 6, Integration and reconfiguration). In Jack's case, once the exiles became unburdened, they became older boys who could relax and play. Once that happened, the approval-seeking manager felt his job was easier and realized that confrontations at work weren't the same as being bullied. The firefighter let go of most of the old rage but wanted to watch how Jack managed things at work. A plan was made to check in with him in the next session.

In Step 7 (Checking for questions and concerns), the firefighter wondered if he was as important as before and if Jack (in Self) would pay attention when he noticed things about people they met. Jack assured him this would happen, and it was decided that Jack would check with him at least twice a day until the next session.

Jack's progress illustrates a segment of the IFS process. As parts were witnessed and unburdened, Jack no longer experienced the rage he had been troubled by. He became able to advocate for himself and found himself generally happier.

USING IFS WITH EMDR

Before we look more closely at integrating IFS and EMDR, a brief cautionary note is in order. Through our family therapy experience, we have developed a view of the inner family as a delicate ecology, which therapists must enter carefully and respectfully. Like several other powerful psychotherapy techniques, EMDR can sometimes override managers and access exiles before the system is ready to handle them. This results in what IFS calls "backlash," in which managers or firefighters punish the client or the relationship with the therapist for violating their rules. Backlash can consist of reactions ranging from managers distancing from the therapist, threatening to stop therapy, numbing out, or dissociating, to firefighters responding with self-destructive behaviors, suicidal ideation, or substance or habit disorders.

This is, in our opinion, one of the reasons why at times EMDR processing does not work, and explains occasions when apparently successful processing is followed by some kind of self-destructive behavior. Our experience is that EMDR therapists who understand the network of relationships among clients' parts and know how to work respectfully and sensitively with these inner ecosystems will have greater success and fewer complications when using EMDR than those who use EMDR without regard for the inner terrain of multiplicity (Twombly, 2000).

EMDR appears to activate a very similar healing process in many clients in which scenes from their past are witnessed and parts are unburdened spontaneously. Specifically, Shapiro's (2001) hypothesis of Adaptive Information Processing states that there "is an innate physiological system that is designated to transform disturbing input into an adaptive resolution and a psychologically healthy integration" (p. 54). Thus, EMDR therapists learn to trust the innate physiological healing system released by the EMDR process, similarly to IFS therapists learning to trust the existence of the Self and the natural healing wisdom of their clients' inner systems. This abiding trust in clients' inner resources and the possibility of healing is an essential and fundamental commonality that EMDR shares with IFS.

The search for efficient, comprehensive healing that resulted in many clinicians learning EMDR also has resulted in many clinicians learning IFS. Joanne Twombly came to learn IFS after working extensively with EMDR and with clients with ego state and dissociative disorders. In spite of (as one client put it) "knowing lots of tricks," she encountered a few clients for whom EMDR did not work and processing stalled out or appeared to be occurring, but only at a superficial level. She also worked with several clients who appeared to have processed everything but still had symptoms. With these clients, the addition of IFS to the EMDR process has proved to be extremely useful.

The Internal Family Systems Model can be used in partnership with EMDR in many ways. Some therapists combine it all the time, and some use it only when there is a problem with EMDR processing. IFS has been used with EMDR in the following ways:

1. To check to see if there is any objection to using EMDR. Before EMDR is initiated, clients can be asked if they have any inner

sense of an objection to doing EMDR. If they do, IFS can be used to determine the specific nature of the objection and figure out what needs to be done to allow processing. This process can be used to identify resources needed and reduce the possibility of failed processing.

2. To access the Self before processing is begun. This has the advantage of beginning the processing with attributes of the Self present (compassion, curiosity, and so forth) and ensures maintaining duality (Harper, Ortiz, & Radke, 2003). Once the Self has been accessed, its presence can be strengthened and reinforced with bilateral stimulation (BLS). For example, one man found that in Self he could think clearer and understand better, and that there was a "cleanness" to the way he felt. These feelings were installed. Using IFS to prepare a client for EMDR treatment can strengthen the relationship between the Self and parts, and make the EMDR treatment go more smoothly (J. Britta, personal communication, September 26, 2005).

3. Sometimes it is helpful to have the Self and one or more managers observe the exile using EMDR to process traumas and burdens. If the manager gets too uncomfortable with the material or the feelings, the Self asks the manager to step back a little further, as with regular IFS (N. Robinson, LICSW, personal communication to J. Twombly, September 26, 2005).

4. If there is difficulty in identifying parts, BLS can facilitate identification and communication among parts in clients with dissociative disorders (Twombly, 2005).

5. An IFS-informed cognitive interweave can be often used effectively to intervene when there is looping by prompting the client to "Ask the part who's blocking the processing to step back." IFS can also be used to identify managers who have some concern and are not allowing processing (D. Korn, personal communication, September 9, 2005).

6. To explore the underlying cause of firefighter activity when an apparently successful EMDR session is followed by acting out. For example, after a session that Joanne Twombly thought had gone well, the client reported that he had spent the next three days surfing the Internet and eating excessively. Using IFS, it was discovered that the target processed had caused one manager to relax, at which point two exiles got activated. A different manager used Internet surfing and eating as a way to calm the exiles.

7. To identify targets not apparent on the surface. For example, after much successful EMDR processing, a woman felt she had completed treatment but wished that some somatic symptoms

had been resolved. IFS was initiated and a manager was found who used somatic symptoms to keep an exile at bay. This exile was burdened from the impact of very early neglect and abandonment. Once the concerns of the manager were heard and the manager was retrieved from the past, EMDR was used to process the abandonment and neglect. This resulted in the somatic symptoms being reduced significantly.

8. The unburdening process can be used in partnership with EMDR trauma processing. For example, a man with a history of chronic and severe child abuse used EMDR successfully until targeting a particularly bad trauma. Managers refused to consider allowing processing until the trauma was contained in a vault and only 10 percent of the trauma was accessed at a time. Even that small portion seemed excessive to the managers until it was agreed that EMDR processing would be combined with IFS unburdening into "a light that shone down from heaven."

9. To wrap up an incomplete session, IFS can be used to identify parts that can help contain unprocessed traumatic material, and to identify parts willing to help others who do not feel safe or need extra support (Harper et al., 2003). For instance, parts can be asked if they are willing to contain unprocessed material until the next session. It also helps to ask what parts need from the Self between sessions. Often it helps if the Self agrees to check in with parts every day, answer questions, or just to show an interest.

10. To check parts' concerns and questions following a completed EMDR process. At the end of IFS sessions, any managers and firefighters who gave permission for work with exiles are asked if they have any concerns or questions about the process (Schwartz, 1995). Therapists who combine IFS and EMDR can also check back with parts to see if they have concerns and questions. Sometimes parts need new jobs, or have questions about how to now connect with the world as the processing shifts the old relationship. For example, the day after successful EMDR processing a client called to report that since the session she had been fine but completely unproductive. It turned out that an exile was feeling much better and the manager who had been working so hard to protect her was now out of a job and had absolutely no idea what to do. Checking with this manager before the end of the session would have prevented this problem.

11. There appears to be a subset of clients for whom EMDR does not work but who have been able to use IFS effectively. These clients are often those with many managers who effectively stop any attempts to process in service of protecting the client. It is possible

that once IFS has been used to connect and negotiate with managers, EMDR may be used to clear remaining targets.

The following composite case study will clarify the use of IFS to facilitate EMDR processing.

LUCY: JOANNE TWOMBLY USES IFS AND EMDR TO RESOLVE MEMORIES OF ABUSE AND NEGLECT

Lucy was a thirty-seven-year-old woman with a history of long-term neglect and emotional and sexual abuse. Her therapist of fifteen years referred her to me for EMDR, reporting that the client had made much progress but remained stuck on various issues, including relationship problems, difficulties with work, and transient substance abuse. Lucy agreed with the therapist's assessment. A safe-space resource was developed (Twombly, 2001, 2005), and targets were identified.

As Lucy began to process the first EMDR target, affects that had been readily available during the setup vanished and processing immediately stalled out. I attempted a number of strategies, including cognitive interweaves, exploring blocking beliefs, and returning to target, all to no avail. I gave a simplified explanation of IFS: "Everyone has parts and our parts are set up both to protect us and to hold unresolved feelings. It seems like a part of you does not agree with us doing EMDR. If it's okay with you, I'd like you to tune into where in your body you feel your feelings are being blocked, and ask that part of you if it would be willing to relax and sit next to you so we can find out what's going on."

Lucy replied that all she got in her head was a loud "No!" I asked her to ask that part what it thought would happen if the part relaxed and gave her some space. The part explained that if any feelings were gotten rid of, no one would ever remember or believe how much she had been hurt. The part's function was to hold tightly to feelings, which effectively stopped the processing. I asked Lucy to tell the part we would not do any EMDR without its permission. With this condition in place, the part was again asked if it could relax and step away from her for just a few minutes, which would help us to figure things out. The part was reassured that if it felt something dangerous was going to happen, it could move right back in. With that understanding, the part was willing to sit next to Lucy, allowing Lucy to begin to access the Self.

I then asked Lucy how she saw the part. She replied that she saw the part as a tenacious little girl who wouldn't give up no matter what. I asked Lucy how she was feeling toward the part, and she said, "Frustrated because she won't let me do what I need to do!" I asked Lucy to turn her attention to where she felt frustration in her body, and ask that part if it was willing to step back and let her work with the part that was blocking. Once the frustrated part stepped back, Lucy turned her attention back to the blocking part and noted she now felt grateful for the part's toughness, and sad that it had to work so hard. This ability of the client to feel sadness and compassion and to be grateful to the blocking part indicated the presence of the Self. I then asked Lucy to let the part know that she felt sad about how much work the part had been doing, and how grateful she felt to her. As she did that, the part began to relax.

Witnessing was initiated by having Lucy ask the part to tell her whatever the part wanted her to know about the past. The part reminded Lucy of all the times bad things had actually happened that her parents "totally forgot about" and then acted like she was making things up if she said anything. As a little girl she vowed to never forget, and the blocking part said her job was to keep the feelings because if she lost them, there would be no proof. I asked Lucy if it made sense to her that under those circumstances the blocking part would want to continue blocking the loss of the old feelings. She agreed it made sense and she let the part know that, but she admitted that she was tired of feeling anxious and depressed.

Psychoeducation was provided to the part through the client/Self to help her realize that the only thing we wanted to unburden was painful stored up feelings. Getting rid of them would help her have more energy and feel better, and we would certainly not be getting rid of anything important like information about what happened and how awful it was. The part acknowledged that she was tired of holding the feelings, and that without all of them, she could get some rest and her job would be easier.

With that assurance, the part consented to EMDR processing. I then asked Lucy to ask all parts of her mind if anyone had any other objections to doing EMDR. There was no objection and EMDR processing was begun. This time the processing flowed and the initial target was cleared.

After several sessions, processing again stalled out around beginning to work on targets related to physical abuse by Lucy's mother. I again asked Lucy to tune into the part that was blocking the processing. With the assurance that no processing would be done, the part was willing to "sit next to her" so Lucy could find out more about this blocking part. She was asked what she felt toward the part, and she reported that she was afraid of it. This fear indicated that the Self was blended with at least one other part that held fear. I asked Lucy to tune into where she felt fear in her body and to ask that part if it would be willing to step back and allow her to work with the part doing the blocking. The fear part refused until the Self agreed to work with her first. Once the fear part relaxed and stepped out of Lucy, she could feel compassion for her (indicating the presence of the Self). She communicated that to the part, and the part began to relax.

The part explained that she feared that if the traumatic material was accessed and worked on, she would lose her love and connection to her mother, the only parent who had given her any attention. This part was living in the past and felt that without the love and connection to her mother she might die. Again that information made sense to Lucy. Her understanding and compassion for the part, plus her willingness to listen, created the trust and connection that was necessary for the part to allow Lucy to retrieve her from the past and bring her into the present. Retrieving this part allowed the part to attach to Lucy in the present. This made it possible for the part to detach from the past dysfunctional relationship she had had with her mother.

Once the part was retrieved, I asked Lucy again if she or any other parts had concerns about resuming the EMDR processing. Two concerns were voiced. The part that had been blocking much of the affect was concerned that it would disappear if all the material got processed, and the part holding the burden of the traumatic material was afraid it would be too overwhelming. The part was told through Lucy that no one is born holding traumatic material, that parts and people get stuck with it as a result of circumstances. Sometimes a part might think that all there is to the part is traumatic material, but it isn't true! This explanation partially relieved the part, although not enough to allow processing. After Lucy negotiated that the traumatic material would be placed in a container and processed 10 percent at a time, processing was resumed.

IFS was again used when Lucy came to a session reporting increased substance abuse. In this case, a firefighter had become activated when EMDR processing inadvertently opened up access to a pool of unbearably painful affects. This part acknowledged using alcohol to "numb things out" and was angry at the therapist for letting things get out of balance. After this session, IFS was used to check with the parts to see if they had any questions, concerns, or comments at the end of each session. This was done after both incomplete and completed processing in order to avoid further problems after sessions.

This case is a good example of how a manager blocked EMDR processing until its concerns were dealt with. The addition of IFS to EMDR enabled this client to successfully complete her treatment.

CONCLUSION

It is clear that EMDR and IFS are in and of themselves each powerful, comprehensive treatment modalities that have helped many clients heal.

Many EMDR therapists have found that the addition of IFS can extend and facilitate EMDR processing, while some IFS therapists report that the addition of EMDR has extended and facilitated their work with IFS. The multiplicity of the mind resembles patterns of woven threads in a complex tapestry. The challenge for therapists is to tease this tapestry apart, shedding light on the multidimensional parts that exist within in order to heal the entire system. One way to do this is with the combined use of EMDR and IFS.

Many questions remain to be answered. For example, are there occasions when, or client populations for whom, EMDR or IFS would be the sole treatment of choice? If so, what are they? Does one modality do something that the other does not do, or is the combination of the two ideal? These questions will continue to be a focus for therapists who work in both modalities.

For more information on the Internal Family Systems Model of psychotherapy, visit the Center for Self Leadership at http://www.selfleadership.org/

REFERENCES

Harper, J., Ortiz, T., & Radke, M. (2003, August). *Expanding the IFS frontier through EMDR*. Workshop presented at the Internal Family Systems Twelfth Annual Conference, Mundelein, IL.

Schwartz, R. C. (1995). *Internal Family Systems therapy*. New York: Guilford Press.

Shapiro, F. (2001). *Eye movement desensitization and reprocessing: Basic principles, protocols, and procedures* (2nd ed.). New York: Guilford Press.

Twombly, J. H. (2000). Incorporating EMDR and EMDR adaptations into the treatment of clients with dissociative identity disorder. *Journal of Trauma and Dissociation*, 1(2), 61–81.

Twombly, J. H. (2001, December). Safe place imagery: Handling intrusive thoughts and feelings. *EMDRIA Newsletter* [Special edition] 35–38.

Twombly, J. H. (2005). EMDR for clients with dissociative identity disorder, DDNOS, and ego states. In R. Shapiro (Ed.), *EMDR solutions: Pathways to healing* (pp. 88–120). New York: Norton.

Applying EMDR and Ego State Therapy in Collaborative Treatment

Carol Forgash

INTRODUCTION: REVIVING STALLED TREATMENTS THROUGH COLLABORATIVE THERAPY

Most therapists are familiar with the frustrating phenomena of stalled treatments, impasses, and apparent negative therapeutic effects. Therapists who are vigilant of their clients' progress and well-being are alert to changes in the client's emotional and functional status that arise as the therapy unfolds. Those changes may indicate new needs that require accommodation in new ways. This is particularly the case in the treatment of trauma, where the client's growing awareness of past traumas may produce new symptoms that can be unsettling for both client and therapist. If not addressed effectively, these can undermine the therapeutic relationship itself.

A therapist who lacks specific training in trauma treatment may feel inadequate to the task of dealing with the symptoms and destabilization associated with trauma. This challenge to a therapist's insight and technical skills may be expected to occur frequently, given the ubiquity of trauma in our contemporary society.

It is under these circumstances that a therapist may consider using collaborative therapy to meet the client's specialized needs that lie beyond the therapist's expertise. *Collaborative therapy* is the concurrent treatment of a client by two therapists: the primary therapist, and a specialist who provides adjunct treatment of specific conditions. The adjunct therapy is time limited, and the client continues to work with the primary therapist during and after the adjunct therapy.

This chapter will describe the application of the collaborative treatment model to clients who undergo EMDR and ego state therapy with a specialist in addition to their regular therapy. EMDR and ego state therapy specialists are uniquely positioned to assist primary therapists in resolving stalled therapies and enhancing the treatment provided by the primary therapist.

We will explore in this chapter the issues that become problematic over time in a course of therapy, which clients are good candidates for collaborative EMDR and ego state treatment, how to develop an effective working relationship with the primary therapist, and how to avoid problems that may arise out of this dual relationship. A detailed case study will illustrate each step of the treatment, from the initial contact with the primary therapist through the conclusion of the adjunct therapy.

SARA: A STALLED TREATMENT
IN NEED OF REPAIR

Laurel Roberts, a psychotherapist in Suffolk County, Long Island, specializing in substance abuse and depression, found herself at an impasse in her treatment of Sara, a thirty-five-year-old physician diagnosed with depression. After a year and a half of successful work with Laurel, Sara had begun to lose ground. Her depression and anxiety had worsened; she was experiencing nightmares that contained vivid memories of childhood trauma; and she felt unable to cope with the demands of her roles as physician, wife, and mother. Laurel felt herself at a loss to understand the dramatic decline in her client's functioning or to identify strategies to reverse it. Having been introduced to EMDR at a conference, Laurel contacted me to discuss whether EMDR treatment could be helpful to Sara and provided me with a brief history of her background and progress in therapy.

Sara was a married mother of three daughters ages six, three, and eighteen months. Shortly after the birth of her last child Sara had entered therapy for treatment of her postpartum depression and generalized anxiety. For over a year she appeared to make good progress in therapy, but in the three months prior to her referral for EMDR treatment she experienced a recurrence of the symptoms that had led her to seek therapy. She appeared to be in a fatigued and numb state, with little affect—a significant change from her energetic demeanor prior to this setback.

Sara had grown up in a chaotic family environment in which she had witnessed her parents' frequent verbal and physical altercations. Their confrontations were lengthy and dramatic, and Sara herself was also subjected to her father's anger and his demeaning criticism. Sara had been troubled by memories of these events periodically throughout her adult life, but she did not accord great significance to them, nor was she aware of their relation to her current difficulties, though the connection was unmistakable. Her nightmares revolved around images of the family violence that had deeply frightened her as a child. Her disturbed sleep was leaving her exhausted. The nightmares intruded into her daytime thoughts as well, preventing her from focusing on her work.

As the nightmares continued Laurel also noted a change in Sara's self-concept. She expressed feelings of worthlessness and a return to a childlike state: "I feel very small," she told her therapist, "sometimes like a little kid." I hypothesized that Sara was reexperiencing the fears, help-lessness, and loss of self-worth associated with her abusive father and her parents' violent relationship that were held as traumatic memories by a child ego state. Lacking resources to neutralize and integrate those feelings and memories in the present (as had been the case in childhood as well), Sara was possibly experiencing dissociation along with other symptoms characteristic of chronic posttraumatic stress disorder. She was overwhelmed by the flashbacks in her nightmares and was shutting down emotionally. She expressed a fear of collapse that in fact seemed well grounded.

Laurel Roberts lacked experience working with posttraumatic stress disorder related to childhood trauma and felt unable to assist Sara. She was unfamiliar with affect containment techniques and stress management strategies that her client would need prior to working with traumatic material. She was unable to recognize the range of dissociative phenomena and had no awareness of ego states or how to respond to them.

Laurel feared that Sara would remain in this regressed state unless she received treatment to help her resolve these major past traumas. She contacted me to discuss whether her client could benefit from a collaborative treatment model that would allow Sara to continue working with Laurel as her primary therapist while undergoing EMDR and ego state treatment with me to address her trauma issues.

OFFERING SPECIALIZED EMDR TREATMENT THROUGH COLLABORATIVE THERAPY

Sara had a well-established therapeutic relationship with Laurel, and their work had proven successful over a period of fifteen months. Clearly

Laurel had been working effectively with Sara in some respects and was deeply committed to the welfare of her client, and yet Sara encountered difficulties that required specialized treatment beyond the training of her primary therapist. In a case such as this, the collaborative treatment model can be a powerful tool for making specialized treatment like EMDR available to the client. The client is able to continue working with the primary therapist, with whom there is an established, secure relationship, while at the same time receiving treatment from an EMDR practitioner.

Concurrent treatment has long been used by psychotherapists who refer clients to psychiatrists for evaluations, to specific types of group therapy, or for couples counseling (Bradley, 1990; Lustig, Smrz, Sladen, Sellers, & Hellman, 2000). While a relatively new treatment approach, collaborative EMDR therapy has been supported by recent research (Forgash, 1997; Lovett, 1999).

As a clinician trained in EMDR and ego state therapy, and with over twenty years of experience treating clients with PTSD and dissociative and Axis II disorders, I frequently receive referrals for clients such as Sara for consultation and possible collaborative treatment. Clinicians are most likely to refer clients who are not making gains in conventional treatment or who are presenting symptoms outside the therapist's area of expertise. Primary therapists seek assistance from EMDR specialists in treating a wide variety of conditions that they find problematic, including panic disorder, early or current trauma, child abuse, substance abuse and other compulsive disorders, long-standing depression, psychosomatic disorders, personality disorders, PTSD, dissociative disorders, performance anxiety, and phobias (Forgash, 1997). Many therapists also lack training in treating clients with serious medical illnesses such as cancer, AIDS, lupus, and Parkinson's disease and terminal illnesses. These illnesses are traumatic for the client, who needs assistance in therapy to learn to cope with the illness and to work through fears of limitations imposed by the illness or even fears of death.

The field of traumatology has shed light on the deep impact of events such as childhood sexual abuse, war, natural disasters such as fires and tornadoes, early losses of primary caregivers, and accidents. These major traumas, which have been termed "big-T" traumas (Shapiro, 2001), are likely causes of PTSD and dissociative disorders (Herman, 1992; Shapiro & Forrest, 1997; van der Kolk & van der Hart, 1991). It has also become evident in clinical practice that a large segment of the population suffers from aggregates of lesser traumas, termed "small-t" traumas (Shapiro, 2001), that hamper current functioning. These include sporadic emotional neglect or abuse in childhood, negative experiences in school such as peer bullying, chronic employment problems, and ongoing financial stresses. Like big-T traumas, these lesser traumas are stored as negative memories and have negative emotional and physical associations.

The number of clinicians trained in EMDR and ego state therapy is relatively small compared to the large number of clients who require treatment for trauma. The collaborative therapy model allows the limited resources of this EMDR-trained group of clinicians to be used most effectively to reach the greatest number of clients. While the primary clinician may be effective in treating part of the client's presenting issues, the addition of EMDR and ego state therapy results in successful resolution of trauma that may not be obtained, or that takes longer to achieve, through conventional therapy. As clients treated with EMDR learn better affect management and the frequency of overwhelming flashbacks and other distressing phenomena diminishes, their response to conventional therapy is enhanced while the length of treatment may be reduced (Forgash, 1997, 2005).

A NEW EXPERIENCE FOR CLIENTS: BENEFITS AND OUTCOMES OF COLLABORATIVE THERAPY

Many of the approximately twenty clients I have treated with integrated EMDR and ego state therapy in a collaborative treatment model have reported that this approach was a new experience for them, significantly different from what they had experienced in prior therapy and resulting in changed perceptions, beliefs, and conceptions of relationships.

Many of the changed perceptions result from seeing the primary therapist in a new light. The therapist is humanized when it is recognized that not all of the needs of the client can be met by a single individual and that the therapist is not invested in being the client's only resource. Rather than feeling abandoned by the therapist, the client comes to realize that the proposal for additional specialized treatment is being made out of a genuine concern for the client's needs, a degree of attunement that most likely has not been experienced by the client who grew up in a dysfunctional family. The therapeutic triad models for the client a collaborative relationship based on open communication without secrets, power sharing, and concern for the client. This can be a new experience that is very different from the dysfunctionally triangulated relationships in the client's family of origin. A lack of trust in authority figures, often developed as a result of the abuse of parental power, evolves into a new view of relationships as productive and satisfying encounters that meet the participants' needs and goals (Gold, 2000).

Many clients with a history of trauma have attachment and abandonment issues. These may be aggravated when the primary therapy arrives at an impasse and the client feels that the therapeutic relationship is in jeopardy. The therapist clarifies that the referral to a collaborative EMDR therapist is for the purpose of furthering the client's progress and that the primary relationship will continue during and after the specialized treatment. The client is thus able to experience the continuity of a relationship in spite of difficulties: the therapist is not giving up on the client but in fact proposing a way to improve and continue the treatment.

The double format of the collaborative therapy model appeals to many clients. As targeted issues are resolved through EMDR and ego state therapy, the client has the opportunity to practice new skills in both treatment settings. The two treatment modalities complement and reinforce each other, allowing the client to focus on specific targeted problems and ego state issues in the specialized treatment setting while continuing to explore the feelings, dreams, and so on that are the essence of their work with the primary therapist; those in turn may provide further targets for EMDR work. New issues, memories, and body sensations are likely to emerge from the EMDR and ego state work, resulting in increased concerns that can be addressed by both therapists. Clients appreciate the ongoing safety of the familiar primary therapy while undertaking the new EMDR and ego state work. This continuing safety and the additional level of support and encouragement are especially important for clients with security issues.

The collaborative therapy approach offers a new model for personal empowerment. As a client-centered approach, the EMDR protocol provides many opportunities for the client to exert significant control regarding the length of the sets of eye movements, audio tones, or tactile stimulation and to choose traumatic events or situations to work on as targets. The interest that the primary therapist expresses in the EMDR experiences and the therapist's support of those experiences is empowering for the client as well. The success of the experiences results in feelings of mastery and inner security for the ego state system.

In addition to these changes in perceptions, beliefs, and ways of conceiving relationships, which are apparent to the client, EMDR and ego state integrated treatment leads to deeper internal changes to the ego state system and response to trauma. The family systems approach (a reference to both the treatment triad and the internal family system) used in ego state therapy results in the evolution of the internal system from a conflicted, noncooperative model to one that is functionally adapted to present experience (Watkins & Watkins, 1997). Extensive preparation for the trauma-processing phases of the EMDR protocol is necessary for dissociative clients (Parnell, 2007; Paulsen, 1995; Phillips, 1993). This preparation involves ego state work, affect management, and bilateral stimulation (BLS, also known as *dual attention stimuli*, or DAS).

This phase also includes individualized psychoeducational work such as information about EMDR, trauma, and PTSD. These stabilizing interventions and new information all help the client to cope more effectively with traumatic material. EMDR itself emphasizes reprocessing body sensations (such as pain, tension, and muscle spasms), normalizing them for the adult client and the ego states; the client subsequently becomes less fearful of processing these sensations and the memories to which they are tied (Forgash & Knipe, 2001).

IDENTIFYING CLIENTS WHO MAY BENEFIT FROM EMDR AND EGO STATE THERAPY

Combined EMDR and ego state therapy may be used to treat a varied group of trauma survivors.

Untreated survivors of childhood sexual abuse: These clients, like Sara, have undiagnosed symptoms of posttraumatic stress disorder. When these individuals are subject to further trauma in adulthood—assaults, illness, accidents, and so on—they are particularly vulnerable to developing acute complex PTSD and dissociative disorders. Conventional treatment may not be sufficient to help them restabilize (Bergmann & Forgash, 1998, 2000).

Clients who grew up in family environments with conditions of chronic instability and violence: Again, these clients have preexisting PTSD and developmental deficits that compromise their ability to deal successfully with crises in adulthood such as sexual assault, marital issues, job loss, or children leaving home. A family that abounds in violence and instability fails to provide the sequential experiences that children and adolescents require in order to develop productive stress-response skills, thus setting the stage for chronic PTSD in adulthood.

Clients with somatic problems that may be psychogenic in origin: Somatic problems may be symbolic representations of body memories of trauma. These problems are manifested in a variety of ways, including muscle spasms, chronic pain, and sleep disorders. Many sexual abuse survivors experience severe and painful menstrual cycles. An individual who was subjected to chronic stress in a chaotic household may develop digestive tract problems such as colitis. Other somatic problems arise from injuries suffered as a result of physical or sexual abuse, risk-taking behaviors subsequent to the abuse, or severe medical problems in childhood. Often these clients are misdiagnosed, as the trauma origin of their somatic symptoms is not recognized. They may have spent years seeking relief through unsuccessful medical treatment, stress-reduction training, or pain-management treatment. While at times the symptoms of these clients are minimized by medical practitioners and psychotherapists, they are distressing and interfere with functioning.

Clients who have experienced a large number of small-t traumas: The failure of these clients to make progress in conventional therapy may not be recognized as stemming from an accumulation of lesser traumas, entrenched negative core beliefs, cognitive distortions, and chronic anxiety. These and other symptoms of PTSD may be present, even though the client does not meet all of the *DSM–IV* criteria for the PTSD diagnosis. These problems can make the client resistant to change, blocking progress.

THE CHALLENGE OF TREATING
TRAUMA SURVIVORS

Trauma survivors bring with them a complex array of treatment challenges that require the therapist to be well versed in the dynamics of the ego state system and the manifestations of PTSD, including its dissociative aspects. These challenges often perplex the primary therapist, but they must be anticipated by the EMDR and ego state therapist (Forgash & Knipe, 2001).

The ego state system (also called the "internal family system") includes many parts that have developed throughout the life span in response to life experiences, both negative and positive. Some of the states developed long ago in response to the original traumas or crises. Since they are oriented toward conditions that existed in the past, they are likely to be particularly maladaptive in the present; in fact they may not be oriented at all to present time and place. Other states that have not been subjected to trauma may be better adapted to functioning in the present. It is particularly characteristic of chronic PTSD that ego states of varying capacity and maturity coexist in the same client, resulting in an uneven pattern of development, achievement, and coping skills.

All of the ego states, whether adaptive or maladaptive, are important to the client: each plays a specific role in the system as a whole and seeks to be preserved. The states perceive that to give up that role would result in their annihilation—this is especially true of states that developed initially as system protectors. The ego state system of the trauma survivor is troubled by conflicts among them as they compete for recognition and preservation and each one, with its individual needs and characteristics, strives to be recognized and maintained.

In addition to the challenge presented by the complexity of the ego state system and its conflicts, clients with chronic PTSD experience problematic responses to treatment ranging from impasses to dissociative episodes and destabilization. The primary therapist often experiences these responses as a frustrating resistance to treatment but may not recognize their true nature and their origin in trauma. For example, the therapist may find the client reluctant to discuss past events, but may not realize that underlying this apparent resistance are one or more ego states that fear exposure or are unable to violate family taboos against telling the truth. Clients who have been subjected to abuse or other family trauma often have experienced threatened or actual punishment for disclosure of family secrets; they anticipate that disclosure in therapy will also result in punishment. The feared or actual punishment may have included abandonment by parents, siblings, or relatives and is extrapolated to abandonment or rejection by the therapist. In fact an ego state that discloses abuse may even come under attack or be abandoned by another state that has a stake in maintaining the family secrecy. A further consequence of childhood abuse is overwhelming shame, guilt, and distrust, all of which intrude on the therapy and the therapeutic relationship.

Clients may be aware, either partially or acutely, of their past trauma, but not anxious to explore it in therapy. They realize that difficult work lies ahead, and they fear reexperiencing their traumas. They are particularly fearful of being flooded by memories and the associated feelings, which they believe will result in a loss of control and ability to function similar to the lack of control associated with the original trauma.

At times trauma survivors take comfort in familiar responses to emotional overload. Memories, flashbacks, and nightmares may produce dissociative freezing, a state of immobilization and emotional withdrawal or numbness designed to protect the individual from further harm. This return to a survivor mode that was utilized at the moment of trauma may feel familiar and therefore comforting to the client, providing a sense of pseudosafety. It becomes an obstacle to treatment if symptoms persist or escalate to higher levels of distress, resulting in increased frustration, feelings of defeat, depression, anxiety, and loss of faith in the efficacy of treatment.

DEVELOPING A SUCCESSFUL COLLABORATIVE THERAPY RELATIONSHIP

The objective of the collaborative treatment model is to create a cooperative triad of client, primary therapist, and EMDR therapist. The transition to a triadic relationship presents a number of challenges that do not arise in the typical dyadic relationship. An awareness of these issues prior to making the decision to enter into a collaborative agreement along with careful planning and preparation of the client will help to minimize difficulties (Bradley, 1990; Lustig et al., 2000).

The best working team is composed of two practitioners who trust each other's professional skills, judgment, and working methods (Forgash, 1997). Clear communication between the two therapists as well as with the client is the cornerstone of the collaborative approach (Goin, 2001).

Before the decision to implement collaborative treatment is made, its advisability must be assessed by way of a risk/benefit analysis of EMDR for the client. The client's present functioning and readiness for trauma work are evaluated, allowing the purpose of the work—whether for restabilization or resolving trauma—to be defined.

Consideration must be given to how the client is likely to respond to a major change in the current dyadic team. Above all, the client needs to be reassured of the continuity of the relationship with the primary therapist. Clients may feel rejected and anxious if they believe they are being referred away from the primary therapist because they are in some way defective or inadequate or because the therapist no longer has interest in them or time to work with them. Although the work pattern of collaborative therapy is individually determined for each case, it is important for the client to know that continuity of treatment with the primary therapist will be maintained.

Primary therapists may also need reassurance if they express feelings of inadequacy or helplessness in their inability to meet all the client's needs. Once the therapist's self-doubts are recognized and assurance is given that the decision to seek consultation and specialized help is a mark of competence and concern for the welfare of the client, the primary therapist will likely feel relief that help is at hand. Thus, both actual and potential transference and countertransference issues between the therapists need to be addressed to smooth the way for collaborative treatment.

The first step in the assessment process is for the EMDR and ego state therapist to elucidate the course of the client's therapy to date, including success that has been achieved and problems that remain, and the reason for the referral at this point in the treatment. I inquire about the primary therapist's knowledge and expectations of EMDR and how the client feels about the referral as well. I explain how EMDR and ego state therapy will fit in with the work already in progress.

If the client is found suitable for EMDR work, the specific goals and nature of the collaborative treatment arrangement and how it will be implemented are established. A treatment contract will clarify the presenting problems to be addressed, the approximate length of the treatment, a schedule for formal case conferencing, and provisions for informal discussions for clarification and problem solving. At this point it is time for the first meeting between the EMDR therapist and the client.

To continue with our case study, before bringing Sara into our discussion, I needed to address Laurel's unresolved feelings of inadequacy at having to ask for assistance from another therapist. I congratulated her for being able to transcend those feelings and act in the best interest of her client by seeking additional treatment for her. I emphasized the progress that Sara had made in her work with Laurel, and the trust in her that Sara showed when revealing to her the traumatic nightmares and their connection to childhood events. Laurel, as well as Sara, needed to know that their working relationship was solid and would continue after the EMDR treatment. When reassurance of her skills and Sara's attachment to her were provided, Laurel was able to release some of the stress she had been experiencing in her work with Sara.

Sara expressed some initial anxiety when Laurel first proposed collaborative therapy to her. She was concerned that working with me would be disloyal to Laurel. When in a later session she realized that she was not being sent away and would continue working with Laurel, she began to cry with relief, revealing for the first time the depth of her attachment to Laurel.

I met once with Sara to discuss the work I proposed to do with her and to allow her to ask questions. Subsequently Sara decided to proceed with the collaborative therapy.

Once Sara's agreement to participate in EMDR therapy was obtained, Laurel and I set the parameters of our work. Sara would see each of us during alternate weeks. We contracted for ten sessions, meaning that the EMDR and ego state component of Sara's therapy would be time limited, although it could be extended by mutual agreement. Sara signed releases to allow us to discuss her case by telephone. As the primary therapist, Laurel would retain decision-making responsibility but would discuss with me in advance any major decisions such as recommending medication. These parameters were discussed with Sara as well.

Laurel and I agreed that Sara was not ready to begin the trauma work immediately because she was so easily overwhelmed by her nightmares and other triggers; she would need to stabilize first and learn techniques for affect regulation and stress reduction. We discussed some of the potential challenges that might arise in Sara's trauma treatment, including her perception that she could be punished for revealing what had occurred in her family, the legacy of the excessive secrecy imposed by her parents.

The remainder of this chapter will describe the actual collaborative work carried out with Sara.

CASE STUDY

Session 1: History Taking

In the initial interview Sara was able to recall a great deal about her childhood and told me in detail about the "horror house," as she termed it, that she lived in. She believed that her gestation and birth were normal, although there was a family myth that her mother was very stressed by the pregnancy, possibly reflecting her mother's ambivalence about womanhood and motherhood. Her mother often complained about being restricted because she was a woman—she greatly disliked being confined at home and felt that she could have been productive and successful in the work world. She professed to not want children, but eventually she produced three daughters, of whom Sara was the oldest. Her maternal limitations and resentments were apparent soon after Sara was born: she refused to nurse her infant daughter after feeling ineffective on her first attempt. "I even failed as a newborn to get her to love me," Sara lamented.

Sara's mother also resented her marriage into an uneducated family when she herself came from an educated family. The rivalry between Sara's parents, centering on their competition to establish superiority, was expressed in violent altercations from as early as Sara could remember. Although she scorned her husband, Sara's mother feared his volatile temper. From the age of six Sara took on the role of peacemaker in order to protect her mother from injury. (I noted that Sara's oldest daughter was also now six years old and wondered if that played a role in triggering her nightmares at this particular time in her life.)

Sara painted a picture of narcissistic parents whose only focus was their thwarted need for recognition from each other. They appeared disinterested in their children and had no involvement in their education.

Sara's parents were strict disciplinarians who used verbal and sometimes physical abuse and harsh punishments to exact obedience from their children. Both parents were very controlling. Sara became socially isolated as a result of her father's excessive screening of her friendships and his demeaning treatment of her in front of friends. She had no experience with relationships with the opposite sex as dating was not allowed. Her father permitted no moments of relaxation such as reading or daydreaming. The atmosphere in the home under his control was one of constant tension; Sara always felt anxious and on guard when her father was at home. Her mother, well aware of her husband's temper, exhorted Sara to be quiet and avoid upsetting him when he came home from work. Sara had no actual or perceived safety at home and, as might be expected, became a poor sleeper.

Sara's mother micromanaged all aspects of her daughters' lives to such an extent that their individuality was lost to her preferences in decorating their bedrooms and choosing their clothing until they went to college. Her refusal to allow them to wear the same clothing as their peers further deepened their social isolation. Not surprisingly, Sara's mother was unable to show genuine warmth and caring toward her children unless they were injured or ill, the only times when she would cuddle them and read to them.

The control that Sara's parents exerted over their children extended even to the children's emotional lives. The parents were unable to tolerate any expression of anger or other negative emotions other than their own, which dominated the family dynamic. Such an overwhelmingly negative family environment inevitably impacted the relationships among the siblings as well. They were unable to develop a supportive or protective bond among themselves, instead retreating into self-protective individual isolation and loneliness. Their lack of closeness continued in adulthood such that when Sara came to work with me she had no close relationship with any family member. The sense of lack of belonging, of being outsiders, that began in childhood as a result of both abuse within the family and intentional social isolation imposed by the parents continued in adulthood.

Sara's one haven away from home where she was able to receive some nurturing was school, where she excelled and was well liked by her teachers. In spite of her success in school, she had no internal sense of her worth and abilities and felt like a fraud. The encouragement she received from her teachers was not enough to compensate for the disinterest of her parents and their deliberate efforts to undermine her individuality, sense of self, and self-esteem.

As a child Sara was very anxious to grow up and move away from her controlling mother and her violent father. She found relief from the present in her fantasies about the future and in reading. Her opportunity to make good on her resolve to escape from her parents came when she was accepted at an Ivy League college. She graduated in the top 10 percent of her class and was accepted into medical school, where she also received high honors. In spite of this sure evidence of her abilities and worth, Sara was still troubled by her feeling of fraudulence, that she wasn't really good enough to be in medical school. To compensate for her feelings of inadequacy she overapplied herself in college and medical school, avoiding social activities and dating as had been required in her adolescence.

It was not until she became a physician that Sara began to establish a secure identity for herself, and she reported that she loved her work. During her residency she met her husband, who was also a physician.

This was her first extended relationship. Her husband came from a family background that was very different from Sara's, and she described him as a warm and loving father. She herself however felt inadequate to the task of raising her three daughters because she feared being unnurturing and controlling like her own mother.

Session 2: Assessment and Introduction to EMDR and Ego States

At the second session I learned more about Sara's work with Laurel Roberts. After the birth of her third child Sara began to experience depression, worry, anxiety, dissociation, and loss of libido. She started treatment with Laurel almost immediately after the birth. She reported that she had an excellent relationship with Laurel and that they had been making good progress in their work together until she started to feel like a small child and to "trance out," as she expressed it, in session and sometimes in moments of relaxation. Along with these experiences, which she understood as dissociation, she found herself withdrawing emotionally in her marriage and in her work with Laurel.

The symptoms that Sara reported to me at the beginning of our work included depression, anxiety, hypervigilance, loss of concentration, a lack of spontaneity and enjoyment of life, inability to relax, and disturbed sleep. She expressed concern about her ability to parent her new daughter due to her emotional state and fear of what was happening to her. Sara had little insight into the cause of her dissociation and was confused by the turn of events.

I noted several strong personal qualities in Sara, including her sense of humor, intelligence, and motivation. She applied her intelligence to the task of learning about the sequelae of chronic stress and trauma and EMDR from books that I recommended to her. This helped her to realize that her symptoms were an expectable response to her early trauma and that we would be able to resolve them through our EMDR work.

In this session Sara was able to make a connection between her family of origin and her current family. Like her parents, she had three daughters. She recognized that it was when she was six years old, the current age of her own oldest daughter, that she began to intervene in her parents' arguments to protect her mother. She began to cry as she realized that her nightmares were flashbacks to early traumatic experiences triggered by this association between her former and current families. She stated her resolve that although her parents had ruined her childhood, she would not allow them to sabotage the rest of her life or her children's lives.

Sara was now able to identify more clearly her goals for herself: to be able to feel contentment again; to be rid of anxiety and be able to relax; to regain her libido; to be free of the nightmares; to have conscious control over dissociation; to end her parents' cruel reign over her self-esteem so she would no longer fear criticism and scrutiny of her actions; to end her own negative self-criticism; and to be able to enjoy her children and offer them the nurturing she had never received herself.

Some of Sara's core beliefs about herself, primarily negative, emerged in this session: "I'm not safe." "I'm worthless." "I'm not lovable." "I'm just a fraud." "I'm an appendage." "I'm useless in relationships." To help her understand the origin of these beliefs, I introduced her to the idea of ego states, describing them as parts of our emotional selves that we all possess, like an internal family. The concept made intuitive sense to her and helped her to understand that her recent feelings of smallness were an expression of a child ego state and that getting in touch with that state was a positive development. The idea of ego states helped Sara to understand the relationship between her early traumas and her dissociative experiences.

Despite her intellectual understanding of these concepts, Sara needed further preparation for our trauma-related work in order to attenuate the emotional flooding that overwhelmed her at times. I explained to her that we would be working with the parts of her ego state system and would teach them to deal with stress, learn to relax, and identify their own needs so that they could learn to understand and interact with one another.

Given that Sara was already experiencing flashbacks and nightmares, at this point in our work I did not want to subject her internal family system to any further stress and I also hoped to avoid having to have recourse to medication; my plan therefore was to begin with some relatively easy relaxation work to give Sara the time to get to know me in a nonthreatening setting.

Session 3: Stabilization Phase

A series of sequential readiness activities is used to help the client create stable internal structures, learn to manage stress and affect in therapy and in daily life, and become acquainted with the ego state system in a safe environment. The therapist begins by identifying the client's preferred learning style as visual, auditory, or tactile. Sara was a visual learner, which would prove very helpful in our work. She began this phase by visualizing safe and relaxing spaces to which she could retreat should she feel overwhelmed during the trauma work.

Once the client has established a safe place of retreat, BLS is explained and introduced in very short sets. This trial serves an important diagnostic function as an indicator of the client's tolerance for BLS, that is, whether BLS is likely to be a positive experience or whether it might cause the client to dissociate or become flooded. I asked Sara to visualize her safe place, and I began short sets of BLS. She tolerated these initial sets very well, and she noted that they increased the positive emotions and body sensations such as warmth and muscle relaxation associated with the scene of her safe place. I then asked her to practice going to her safe place without the aid of the BLS. She again experienced pleasant relaxation. I recommended that she take a few minutes each day to practice safe-space work between the sessions.

When the client has the ability to return to the internal safe space in times of distress and has been successfully introduced to BLS, it is time to begin accessing the ego state system. Being a visual learner, Sara wanted to "see" her ego state system; she was in fact able to visualize a few shadowy figures. Despite their lack of clarity at this stage, Sara was comfortable with the idea of their existence and was willing to work with them. She referred to the states as "parts"; other clients are more comfortable with the terms "states of mind" or "selves." Sara chose my office as a safe workplace for the system, holding the image of the office in her mind when she wanted to think about her ego states or speak to them in session. I used BLS to help her strengthen the image.

We then worked to create a metaphorical home base for Sara's ego state system. She visualized a cabin on the shores of a lake in the mountains, with a large front porch with gliders and rocking chairs, and she introduced her ego states to their new home. This image was also reinforced with BLS.

When Sara expressed interest in the trauma-processing phases of EMDR I explained that we would not start that portion of our work until her ego state system felt safe enough. This was an appropriate time, however, to describe to her the standard EMDR protocol in preparation for the work to come. I told Sara that she would describe a problem or troubling event that she had already selected, visualize a target (a component such as an image, thought, feeling, or memory related to that traumatic event), and describe her initial beliefs and feelings about the target. She would also develop both a negative cognition that best described her belief about herself in regard to that trauma (for example, "I'm not good enough") and a positive cognition identifying what she would prefer to believe about herself ("I'm okay"), even though this traumatic event had occurred. She would use the Validity of Cognition (VOC) Scale to rate the positive cognition from 1 (not at all true) to 7 (completely true). Then, using the Subjective Units of Disturbance (SUD) Scale, she would describe the emotions she felt while viewing the target scene and rate the distress associated with the scene from 0 (no distress at all) to 10 (maximum possible distress). Finally she would identify any body sensations she noticed as we went through the above steps. I explained to Sara that

BLS would be used to help her process the target scene, negative cognitions, emotions, and body sensations associated with the trauma until the SUD reached 0, and then to enhance the positive cognition.

We discussed the concept of present orientation. I asked whether Sara's ego states knew what year it was, who Sara was, where she lived, and that she was a doctor, wife, and mother. It emerged that some of the states were indeed aware of all of these present phenomena, while others were unaware of them. Some of the states expressed anxiety when questioned in this way; they preferred to not know that anything had changed in Sara's life because they felt anxious about potential future changes. Sara, however, responded with her belief that life is all about change; she reassured her ego states that she would try to negotiate change at a pace that would be comfortable for everyone. I explained that present orientation and change were difficult concepts for the ego states and that they would need time to come to terms with them.

Finally, Sara agreed to use a hand signal and the word "stop" to indicate moments when the EMDR protocol felt too overwhelming.

Session 4: Beginning to Work with the Ego State System

By the fourth session, Sara was able to look inside herself and invite individual ego states to join her and get acquainted. She discovered a very rich internal world and was pleased with the complexity and variety of the states she found. While these ranged from infants to adults, she often referred to all of them as "kids." Different parts—some that she could see and some that she could only sense—appeared at each session. They included a terrified child, a competent, problem-solving adult, an efficient worker, a popular and attractive girl, a compassionate physician and healer, a stubborn and rigid perfectionist, an awkward girl, an excellent doctor, and a peacemaker. The emotions and personalities of these parts varied greatly; they were approval seeking, creative, very critical of themselves and others, thorough and detail oriented, emotionally distant, angry and defiant, self-hating, defensive, and unintelligent. Sara realized that some of her ego states resembled her parents, and she expressed discomfort with those parts.

Sara demonstrated increasing ability to work with her ego state system. In our work we employed the metaphorical language that is used in the treatment of dissociative identity disorder. Using this metaphorical language Sara was able to admit her states into consciousness and give them a voice in communicating with both her and me. I explained to her that all of the states could be present and listening to our conversation even if they were not visible to her, reinforcing the concept of the individual states constituting a whole. To avoid overwhelming Sara I encouraged her to focus on only a few states at a time while reassuring her that the others continued to be present.

Before beginning any exploratory work, it is necessary to obtain the consent of the ego states. The states should be reassured that they will retain control over their participation in the work. I always tell the ego state system that no state is obligated to participate in each session. They can stay at the home base, listen in, choose not to speak, and so forth. Most importantly, whether they participate or not, they need to agree not to sabotage the work. This may take many sessions in order to work out a consensus. In Sara's case her ego states were most anxious about making errors.

At this point Sara expressed some negative thoughts about Laurel. A part of her that idealized Laurel felt that Laurel should have been able to "make everything better by now." Her nightmares were seen as evidence that Laurel was not entirely competent and undermined Sara's trust in Laurel. Now, however, she was able to recognize that her idealization and expectations were not realistic.

It must be kept in mind that some ego states play an important role in keeping the client safe. While they may carry out this task in a manner that is maladaptive, their function must still be honored by the therapist.

To further enhance her ability to manage stress and affect, Sara was participating in a breathwork class. She was including positive affirmations ("I have self-worth"; "I deserve self-care") in the breathing exercises practiced in the class. As she told me about this class, she reported soreness in her head and neck. To understand the cause of this discomfort, she consulted with her ego states and found that they were experiencing a mixture of fear and anger toward both her and me.

I was unable to foresee the response of the protective states—which in Sara's case were the child states that protected her from her parents—to our relaxation work. In their role as protectors it was necessary for them to be on guard at all times, although their primary belief was "I'm not safe even when I'm on guard." The goal of our relaxation work was to diminish this anxiety, which left the protectors feeling threatened—they believed that if they let their guard down they could be harmed.

In fact some of Sara's ego states perceived me to be dangerous and pressured Sara to end her work with me. They further expressed their loyalty to Sara's parents, their resistance to change and new ideas, and even their discomfort with Sara's positive affirmations. All of these aspects of Sara's work with me were experienced as threatening to the status quo of the ego state system, which did not want to be deprived of its parts, functions, and manifestations, no matter how maladaptive. The system blamed not only me but also Sara for not being mindful of the existence and needs of the protectors.

I realized my error in not taking care to obtain the permission of these ego states before beginning our relaxation work. I apologized for not including the protectors in our visualization work that created safe places and a home base for the system and promised to include them in our future work and to make sure they understood the nature and purpose of the work.

With those reassurances we were able to continue developing specific relaxation strategies, including sensory awareness. Sara learned to locate and focus on the most relaxed part of her body. As she held onto her awareness of the physical sense of relaxation, the feeling would spread to the rest of her body, resulting in a relaxed state throughout the body. We then worked to teach this strategy of finding the positive, stress-free part of the body to the ego states. When some anxiety about returning to full alertness arose, I reminded Sara that as the mother of young children she always awoke from sleep if she heard the sound of a child and would go to locate the source of the sound. I asked her to reassure the anxious ego states that she would also be able to "awaken" from her relaxed state if they sensed that her full alertness was required. To demonstrate that relaxation does not diminish present orientation, we practiced the exercise again and Sara noted that the ego states were aware of a clock ticking and cars passing by my office.

Finally in this session I introduced the concept of containment to Sara so that she could manage her anxiety at home. I reassured her that I was not asking her or any ego state to repress important feelings, as had been necessary in childhood, but that sometimes, in order to remain calm and be able to work or be an effective parent, it was important to be able to put feelings or thoughts away until they could be examined safely. I proposed journaling and drawing as ways of externalizing feelings and using an imaginary object to contain negative affect. Sara chose to visualize a piggy bank into which she could deposit upsetting feelings; the feelings would be held safely in the bank until she could process them in our work and empty the bank.

Session 5: Reprocessing Parental Anger and Control

At the beginning of the fifth session Sara reported that she had been successful in practicing at home the relaxation strategies she had learned with me and that she had been able, through internal dialogue, to reassure her ego state system of the benefits and safety of relaxation. However, as she described her successful experiences with relaxation to me, she once again experienced soreness in her neck. Continuing to use our metaphorical language, Sara summoned her ego states to the meeting room to discuss what was distressing them. She discovered that her relaxation work was bringing back memories of her tense and chaotic childhood home, where relaxation was impossible, and of her father, who insisted that she be continually engaged in productive work. There was no quiet, relaxed refuge away from his control and his anger.

Continuing to explore this theme, Sara discovered that some of her ego states held her responsible for failing to protect them from her father. They believed that since Sara's mother was ineffectual in protecting them, Sara herself should have taken on the protective role, in effect becoming a parent to her own ego states. In her present adult state Sara was stunned by this. I asked to her to explain to her younger ego states why she could not have protected them from her father. She told them that she could not have been there for them because she (the adult) did not exist at that time. She explained that she was now their grown-up self. She said she wished she could have been there to protect them, adding, "But I'm your protector now." As she cried she was able to release some tension in her body. I noted during this conversation with her ego states Sara's shift from a negative cognition ("I'm a wimp for not protecting myself in the past") to a positive cognition ("I can protect myself now").

I felt that this was an opportune moment to focus on the disturbing memory of her father's anger and control that Sara was currently experiencing. This became our first target. Sara agreed to try to work with the target but cautioned me that her ego states did not want to get too close to her father. I offered Sara a visualization strategy that would allow her to control the image of her father shouting at her. I asked her to imagine herself sitting in a screening room similar to a theater with very comfortable seats. I directed her to project the image onto the screen at a comfortable distance. She practiced using an imaginary remote control to turn the image on and off, make it fade from dark to light, and change from color to black and white.

Before we could begin working with the target it was necessary to reassure a six-year-old child ego state that what we were about to do would not be upsetting to Laurel and would not cause Laurel to reject Sara or terminate their work. This ambivalent child was simultaneously angry at Laurel for not having referred Sara for further treatment a long time ago, when she first started having nightmares. A thirteen-year-old ego state supported this child, and both expressed not feeling strong enough to participate in the EMDR. I invited them to join us as observers, telling them that the work we were about to do might make them stronger.

We continued by reviewing the target (Sara's father shouting at her) and the negative cognition "I'm a wimp." Sara rated her belief in the positive cognition "I'm a protector" as a 4 out of 7 on the VOC Scale. She reported that a preschool-age part was very upset because they had to go through the horrible shouting sessions with Sara's father all alone, with no one to protect them. Sara felt upset, fearful, and angry. She rated her distress as a 6 out of 10 on the SUD Scale. I asked about her body sensations and she reported that her shoulder hurt and her chest was tight, but there was no discomfort in her neck. I asked her to focus on the image of her father shouting at her when she was alone with him, and to be aware of the negative beliefs, emotions, and body sensations she felt.

Sara wanted to reassure her ego states who felt unprotected. She told them, "It's okay with me if you're angry. I'm not angry with you and I'm right here if you need me." As we had practiced during our preparatory sessions, she was able to provide a safe container for her own strong affect and the shoulder pain receded. Her affect management was an indication that she was ready to provide the empathy and soothing needed by the ego states who had been subjected to her angry father. Though no one had protected and soothed her in childhood, she could provide this for herself now with therapeutic assistance.

In session 3 I had presented Sara with the modalities she could choose from for our EMDR work: a light bar or tracking my fingers for eye movements, music with alternating tones, or a tactile device to be held in each hand. She expressed a preference for bilateral music, and in this session she chose a CD track that mixed music with ocean sounds and she put on the headphones.

Very quickly Sara felt a fear of being angry that she recognized as stemming from her family dynamic, in which she was not allowed to express any discontent and there was room only for her parents' anger and control. She identified her fear as being expressed by the preschooler. She turned the music off and said, "One part says I want to be angry and tell. Another says if you're angry, someone big will be angry at you." I wondered to myself whether she was referring to her father or to me.

As Sara noticed her feeling of dread and verbalized it, it first grew stronger and then receded. She turned the music on again and found that her fear again intensified. Keeping the headphones on, she said that the preschooler, who earlier in the session had angrily rebuked Sara for not protecting her, wanted to know how I felt about her protestations. I replied that I understood how upset she was and that I was comfortable with strong feelings. I said I hoped the preschooler would allow Sara to help her work through her feelings of anger.

Although her feeling of dread continued to intensify, I encouraged Sara to stay focused and to continue the auditory stimulation as I felt it would help her move through her fears more quickly. As she had learned during the preparatory phase of our work, I asked her to go to the most relaxed part of her body. Initially she said she was too frightened to do this, indicating again her fear of letting go of her self-protective tension, of letting her guard down. But then she said that as a result of our relaxation work she had come to realize that her relaxed body could act as a cradle for the frightened young child. She imagined holding this child in her arms and soon felt calmer, reporting that the child now knew that Sara loved her and would protect her. Clearly Sara had gained significant skills in affect management and self-soothing since the beginning of our work, and I felt she was progressing well.

Sara now reported a SUD of 0 for the previously angry preschool child and 6 for the cynical thirteen-year-old, who still did not trust adults. We agreed that this teenager would be the focus of our next session. To end the session we reviewed the affect management strategies that Sara could use if troubling thoughts or feelings from this session should arise during the coming week, including containment images, journaling, and her safe space. Sara said that she felt remarkably relaxed and calm at the end of this session in spite of the upsetting images and feelings to which she had been exposed, and she attributed her calm to the musical stimulation that had continued through most of the session.

Session 6: Reprocessing Feelings of Defectiveness

Returning two weeks later for her sixth session, Sara appeared even more relaxed than previously. She described a successful session with Laurel during which she was able to express, through her child ego states, her anger that Laurel had not referred her earlier for EMDR treatment to relieve the distress of her nightmares and traumatic memories. In childhood she would have been subjected to further abuse if she had voiced such feelings of discontent. With Laurel she was able to experience expressing anger and resentment and having those feelings accepted and validated by Laurel in a supportive and nondefensive manner. At the same time, she learned that relationships endure through conflict; both she and the therapeutic relationship survived her expression of genuine feelings. She found the act of giving voice to her feelings empowering and attributed her success in this to our work, which validated the existence and needs of her ego states.

Reflecting further on the previous session, Sara said that both the six-year-old who had been angry with Laurel and the thirteen-year-old now seemed less distressed since that session and the next session with Laurel. The thirteen-year-old now felt that at least three adults (Laurel, me, and Sara herself in her adult ego state) were trustworthy.

We returned to the target of our previous session, the image of Sara's father shouting at her angrily. Sara reported a shift in her feelings from feeling alone and unprotected to being able to provide self-protection.

The six-year-old and the thirteen-year-old reported an anxiety rating of 0 on the SUD Scale. In this session Sara chose visual rather than auditory stimulation, and I reinforced her feelings of internal security with some short sets of eye movements.

Sara asked to change her positive cognition from "I'm a protector" to "I'm a strong protector." Holding those words in her mind, she gave them a VOC rating of 5, and the six-year-old and thirteen-year-old ego states concurred. She said that the target image was beginning to fade. After more eye movements she gave the image a VOC rating of 7 and then reported that the image had disappeared entirely. We did several more sets of eye movements to enhance the positive cognition, and Sara confirmed that the VOC remained at a firm 7.

I asked Sara to scan her body and focus on the positive cognition "I'm a strong protector" while I did more eye movements. She reported that to her surprise her body felt warm and relaxed. I reinforced those comfortable sensations with several short sets of eye movements. Showing that she was truly internalizing the positive cognition, she said that she wanted us to work further on self-esteem and meeting her needs more effectively, including the needs of her internal family.

Sara was not yet finished working with the target image of her father. She expressed her resentment of her father's controlling and narcissistic personality: "He would never spend time with me just for fun or because I was worthy of his attention. He just wanted to impart his lofty, bullying rules." Referring to her school-age part she said, "No one ever met her needs. She would just have to shut up, stuff her feelings, and meet everyone else's needs."

With these memories Sara began to feel nauseous and couldn't breathe. She was able to relieve these feelings through deep breathing. She described an internal split between her younger and older parts. As she had grown older, Sara's father had intensified his verbal abuse. Her youngest ego states were unaware of the severe abuse reported by the older states. That caused the youngest states to doubt the older states' reports of her father's cruelty, setting up a conflict among them. This split was further intensified by Sara's lack of a sense of belonging in the family as a teenager. She felt awkward, an embarrassment to the family. She now felt sad and disgusted with herself. As she expressed those feelings, her stomach began to hurt and she said, "I'm garbage."

Sara now became entangled in the war among her ego states and became confused by the multiple conflicting messages she was receiving from them. One ego state said that her parents were going to abandon her because she was bad and an embarrassment. An older child pointed out that her parents needed to turn their anger and criticism on her and avoid addressing their own defects in order to preserve their dysfunctional union;

therefore her imperfections served to maintain the cohesion of the family. While recognizing that these perceptions of her ego states lacked validity in the present, she still professed to believing them emotionally. They were quite distressing to her, making her feel inadequate and childish. She made a series of self-disparaging remarks, reflecting the internalization by her child ego states of her parents' perception of her as defective.

I asked Sara what she would like to believe about herself now, as an adult. She said she wanted to believe that she was not defective, that she was okay, and that she was not responsible for her parents' troubled marriage. She wanted to achieve internal calm in spite of the disparate sets of beliefs held by her ego states; that is, she wanted to validate those beliefs initially while working to resolve them. The first step was to be able to tolerate the anxiety that they caused.

We established a new target: Sara's father shaking his finger at her menacingly while berating her for her shortcomings. We identified her negative cognition "I'm garbage." To the positive cognition "I'm okay" she gave a VOC rating of 4 out of 7. The feelings associated with the target image were anger, disgust, alienation, and sadness. Her SUD rating was 6, and she identified body sensations of tightness and soreness in her stomach.

Sara chose to return to using bilateral music at this point. As she projected the image of her father onto the imaginary movie screen she expressed discomfort with the closeness of the image, saying her child ego states felt anxious at that distance. I asked her what would help to see if she could take the initiative of making an adjustment to manage her anxiety. She decided to add more seats to the projection room so that the child ego states could sit farther from the screen.

Refocusing on the target image, Sara began to cry and said, "They were terrible parents. They thought life was hard and their job was to toughen us up at home so we could survive. They wanted to show us at home just how bad life can be. That's what they thought parenting was. That's ridiculous!" Sara stopped crying and her sadness changed to anger as she contemplated this bleak scenario. She continued, "They were so dysfunctional in their marriage. They had absolutely no parenting skills and they used me to make sure no one noticed how inept and crazy they were. They made it look like *I* was the defective one and the cause of that mess."

Sara now expressed a more realistic perception of herself as a child: "I wasn't bad. I was a good child, but I wasn't really allowed to be a child most of the time. I want to allow my parts to be children, the way we couldn't do with my parents." A playful image came into her mind of taking her ego states to the park, but then she began to cry again when that image made her realize how many important nurturing experiences she had missed out on. Her next thought, though, was that she could provide herself with that nurturing care now in adulthood while also providing it to her own children. "I wish I had had more caring parents," she said. "I'll take the child parts to the park when I go with my daughters and I'll include them in my relaxation every night."

Sara next contemplated telling her parents how angry she was about their abusive parenting style. She quickly rejected that idea as too frightening but realized she could achieve the same objective by confronting the target image of her father. After a long silence she said that she had told her father what a poor parent he had been and that she was a much better parent to her own children. When she next focused on the target image, it had changed. Instead of intimidating her verbally and physically, her father stood impotently in front of her looking very surprised and dazed, amazed that his daughter had the audacity to criticize him. He was no longer moving or speaking at all, but frozen in space. Sara seemed very satisfied with this image and began to laugh. She told me that "the spell was broken" because her father now looked so ridiculous and pathetic.

Sara now reported a SUD of 0 for the negative cognition "I'm garbage" and a VOC of 6 for the positive cognition "I'm okay"; in fact she upgraded that belief to "We're just fine!" which was a stronger positive cognition. I used a few sets of eye movements to enhance the new belief, and it rose to a rating of 7. To reinforce the positive cognition herself, Sara visualized writing a letter to her parents to tell them about her new beliefs about herself. She said she wouldn't mail the letter because "it would be a waste of time," indicating her understanding that the important transformation was taking place within herself and that validation from her parents was not necessary. Sara confirmed that her child ego states had participated in this transformation and were in agreement with her new positive cognitions. What was more, they all agreed that secrecy about her past abuse was no longer required and that she could share this experience with her husband and Laurel.

A body scan revealed Sara's feeling of physical well-being, and we ended the session with a deep relaxation exercise.

Session 7: Closure

Sara's happy and relaxed demeanor when she arrived for her final session was remarkably altered from the initial anxiety, confusion, and depression she manifested at the beginning of our work. During my vacation she had had two very productive sessions with Laurel that reinforced the work she had done with me. She reported that she was no longer experiencing nightmares or flashbacks. She was no longer anxious about her parenting skills and was confident that she could raise her children in a nurturing manner that would be significantly different from how her abusive parents had raised her. Her libido had returned and overall she was feeling more at ease. Laurel had noted these positive changes and was pleased with the effectiveness of Sara's EMDR and ego state work. They had agreed that Sara could end her work with me when she felt ready. In our consultation Laurel informed me that she had been researching ego state work and believed she would be able to continue working with Sara and her internal family.

In our seventh session Sara and I consulted her ego states about their readiness to terminate our work. It seemed that the internal family members were reassured by Laurel's newfound understanding of their existence and needs and her willingness to work with them and thus were in agreement to end their work with me. We agreed that Sara could return for further EMDR work if Laurel advised it.

We used this session for closure of our relationship. At Sara's request we both listened to the bilateral music that she had enjoyed in the sessions. She and her ego state system chose to say good-bye to me at their home base, the lakeside cabin in the mountains. There she communicated messages to me from her ego states. Several younger states wanted me to know that Sara was much more playful and fun to be with. The adolescent affirmed her acceptance and appreciation of me as a trustworthy adult but was glad I approved of her returning to work only with Laurel. Ego states that had formerly felt defective and inadequate were grateful to me for my acceptance of them and for restoring their self-acceptance. I told them how courageous they had been to make themselves known to me so that I could be of help to Sara.

At this point, Sara reported that all the child states had "gone back inside." She expressed that they were in her heart now, just like her own daughters.

In evaluating her experience with EMDR and ego state therapy, Sara said that her current emotional functioning was significantly better even than her status prior to the birth of her last child, that is, better than what she previously considered to be her normal, functional state. She said that our team approach to her treatment had provided her with a model that she and her husband could now apply to their teamwork as parents. Clearly her ego state system had been functioning as a conflicted and disunited group much like her family of origin. I pointed out to Sara that her internal family members were also now able to coexist peacefully as a team.

To end our final session we used eye movements to practice the sensory and visual relaxation strategies that Sara would continue to apply in her daily life to manage stress and affect.

CONCLUSION

Although it would have been impossible to deal with all of Sara's emotional difficulties in such a short course of integrated EMDR and ego state therapy, our seven sessions had a significant impact on Sara's presenting symptoms such that she was able to return to work effectively with her primary therapist after only seven of the ten sessions in our contract. Several factors coalesced to ensure that our work would be successful. The primary therapist realized that conventional treatment was not working with her client and that the client was regressing. The therapist was able to recognize her limitations in working with a trauma survivor with chronic PTSD and, being invested in her client's welfare, referred the client for specialized integrated EMDR and ego state therapy that she could not provide herself. Despite the worsening symptoms, the therapist had established a strong working relationship with the client; this relationship provided a secure basis that allowed the client to transition to a triadic treatment relationship. My assessment of the client's history and current symptoms revealed that she was an excellent candidate for EMDR and ego state work. Finally, the primary therapist and I were able to establish clear and effective parameters for our collaboration. The information provided by the primary therapist allowed me to formulate an effective short-term treatment plan.

The client herself brought several qualities and strengths to our work that resulted in positive resolution. She was highly motivated to work to be free of her symptoms. She was self-reflective and analytically minded and showed a great deal of curiosity about her psychological functioning. She was courageous in her willingness to try a new therapist and a new therapeutic approach.

Once our work began there were further signs in the client's response to the preparatory phase of our work that she could be assisted by EMDR. This phase consisted of training in stress and affect management and ego state work, during which the client learned to know, accept, and work with her internal family. The client showed increasing ability to master her anxiety and overwhelming feelings of instability. The EMDR work ahead aimed to effect major changes in the client's perceptions of past events, in her self-image as conveyed by her abusive parents, and in her present self-image. During the preparatory stage it was necessary to work directly with individual ego states to reassure them that the coming work did not pose a threat to their existence and well-being, that the client and I would support their right to existence and validate their needs. We worked to establish trust among the child ego states, the client in her adult ego state, and myself as the therapist who would be guiding the ego states through the work of revisiting their trauma. Additionally the internal system needed to learn that the dual treatment team would not become the negative parent figures that were so feared in the past. The collaborative therapy model provided ongoing reality testing by allowing the client to review her experiences with both of her therapists.

The client's increasing ability to tolerate strong affect and understanding of her internal ego state system signaled that she was ready to undertake the standard EMDR protocol. At this stage I was alert to negative sequelae but detected none; the client was subsequently able to proceed through the protocol to resolution of her symptoms. Our EMDR work allowed the client to reprocess powerful negative feelings and memories associated with childhood trauma and to transform negative cognitions about her lack of self-worth and safety into forceful new positive beliefs about her worth, her skills, her ability to function in her current adult roles as a mother, wife, and professional, and her ability to provide self-protection and self-soothing.

In effect the client was able to neutralize negative feelings associated with abusive parenting in childhood and learned to become a parent to her own internal family, resulting in greater confidence and skill in her adult relationships. The collaborative therapy model allowed the client to access specialized treatment that would not otherwise have been available to her and freed her from the limitations of childhood trauma.

REFERENCES

Bergmann, U., & Forgash, C. (1998, June). *Working successfully with apparent EMDR non-responders.* Workshop presented at the EMDR International Association Annual Conference, Baltimore.

Bergmann, U., & Forgash, C. (2000, June). *EMDR and ego state treatment of dissociation.* Workshop presented at the International Society for the Study of Dissociation Conference, San Antonio, TX.

Bradley, S. (1990). Nonphysician, psychotherapist-physician, pharmacotherapist: A new model for concurrent treatment. *Psychiatric Clinics of North America, 13*(2), 307–322.

Forgash, C. (1997). EMDR in a concurrent treatment mode. *The Clinician, 28*(2), 10, 17.

Forgash, C. (2005, May). *Deepening EMDR treatment effects across the diagnostic spectrum: Integrating EMDR and ego state work.* Two-day workshop presentation, New York. (Available on DVD from www.advancededucationalproductions.com)

Forgash, C., & Knipe, J. (2001, June). *Safety-focused EMDR/ego state treatment of dissociative disorders.* Workshop presented at the EMDR International Association Annual Conference, Austin, TX.

Goin, M. K. (2001). Practical psychotherapy: Split treatment: The psychotherapy role of the prescribing psychiatrist. *Psychiatric Services, 52,* 605–609.

Gold, S. (2000). *Not trauma alone.* Philadelphia: Brunner-Routledge.

Herman, J. L. (1992). *Trauma and recovery: The aftermath of violence—From domestic abuse to political terror.* New York: Basic Books.

Lovett, J. (1999). *Small wonders: Healing childhood trauma with EMDR*. New York: Free Press.

Lustig, S., Smrz, A., Sladen, P., Sellers, T. D., & Hellman, S. (2000). It takes a village: Caring for a traumatized art student. *Harvard Review of Psychiatry, 7*, 290–298.

Parnell, L. (2007). *A therapist's guide to EMDR*. New York: Norton.

Paulsen, S. (1995). EMDR and its cautious use in the dissociative disorders. *Dissociation, 8*(1), 32–44.

Phillips, M. (1993). The use of ego state therapy in the treatment of posttraumatic stress disorder. *American Journal of Clinical Hypnosis, 35*(4), 241–249.

Shapiro, F. (2001). *Eye movement desensitization and reprocessing: Basic principles, protocols, and procedures* (2nd ed.). New York: Guilford Press.

Shapiro, F., & Forrest, S. M. (1997). *EMDR: The breakthrough therapy for overcoming anxiety, stress, and trauma*. New York: Basic Books.

van der Kolk, B. A., & van der Hart, O. (1991). The intrusive past: The flexibility of memory and the engraving of trauma. *American Imago, 48*, 425–454.

Watkins, J. G., & Watkins, H. H. (1997). *Ego states: Theory and therapy*. New York: Norton.

Appendix

EMDR Training

EMDR International Association
5806 Mesa Drive, Suite 360
Austin, TX 78731
Tel: 512-451-5200
Toll-Free: 866–451–5200
E-mail: info@emdria.org
www.emdria.org

Listing of approved and independent EMDR trainers, training institutions, and universities.

EMDR Institute
PO Box 750
Watsonville, CA 95077
Tel: 831–761–1040
Fax: 831–761–1204
E-mail: inst@emdr.com
www.emdr.com

EMDRIA-approved U.S. and international trainings.

EMDR Humanitarian Assistance Programs (EMDR HAP)
PO Box 6505
Hamden, CT 06517
Tel: 203–288–4450
Fax: 203–288–4060
www.emdrhap.org

A nonprofit organization providing low-cost EMDR training to mental health agencies that serve poor, minority, and underserved populations in the United States. EMDR HAP also provides training and support to agencies and clinicians internationally to assist traumatized populations after disasters, and to support growth of national centers for EMDR practice around the globe.

Training in Trauma and Dissociation (ISST-D)

International Society for the Study of Trauma and Dissociation
8201 Greensboro Drive, Suite 300
McLean, VA 22102
Tel: 703–610–9037
E-mail: info@isst-d.org
www.isst-d.org

A nonprofit professional organization that works to educate mental health professionals through courses on the study and treatment of trauma and dissociative disorders. It supports the development of comprehensive, clinically effective resources and responses to trauma and dissociation.

Ego State Therapy and Advanced Specialty Workshops

Uri Bergmann, PhD
EMDRIA-approved consultant, trainer, and workshop provider
Traumatology, editorial board
Journal of EMDR Practice and Research, editorial board
Workshops:

- Treating Dissociation in the Spectrum of Personality Disorders
- The Neurobiology of EMDR: Recent Insights and Findings
- Trauma, a Natural Response to Unnatural Events: A Glimpse at Its Neurobiology

Contact: ubergmann@worldnet.att.net

Carol Forgash, LCSW, BCD
EMDRIA-approved consultant and workshop provider
Workshops:

- Deepening EMDR Treatment Effects Across the Trauma Spectrum: Integrating EMDR and Ego State Therapy in the Treatment of Complex Trauma and Dissociation (EMDRIA-approved distance-learning workshop, DVD)

- Advanced Techniques in Providing EMDR and Ego State Treatment to Dissociative Disordered Clients
- Disaster Work: Treating Survivors of Overwhelming Trauma
- Dissociation, Avoidance Issues, and Dental Health
- The Negative Impact on Physical Health: Addressing Dissociation and PTSD in Adult Sexual Abuse Survivors

Contact: cforgash@optonline.net
www.advancededucationalproductions.com

Jim Knipe, PhD
EMDRIA-approved consultant, trainer, and workshop provider
EMDR HAP Level II trainer
Workshops:

- EMDR and Dissociation
- The Use of the Adaptive Information Processing Model with Psychological Defenses ("EMDR Toolbox")

Contact: jsknipe44@earthlink.net

Barry K. Litt, MFT
EMDRIA-approved consultant and workshop provider
AAMFT-approved supervisor
Workshops:

- The Marriage of EMDR and Ego State Theory in Couples Therapy
- The Interior Life of the Family: Legacy, Loyalty, and Healing through EMDR

Contact: bklitt@gsinet.net

Michael C. Paterson, PhD, DClinPsych
Consultant clinical psychologist
EMDR Europe-approved consultant and trainer
Training and Workshops:

- EMDR Institute basic training, UK
- The Acquisition of Traumatic Memories: An Introduction to Ego State Therapy

Contact: paterson@trauma-stress.co.uk
www.trauma-stress.co.uk
www.emdr-training.org

Sandra Paulsen, PhD
EMDRIA-approved consultant and workshop provider
Workshop:

- Looking Through the Eyes: EMDR and Ego State Therapy Across the Dissociative Continuum

Contact: sandra@paulsenphd.com
www.bainbridgepsychology.com

Maggie Phillips, PhD
EMDRIA-certified therapist
Workshops:

- The Relationship Between Trauma and Chronic Pain
- Clinical Applications of Hypnosis and Ego State Therapy

Contact: mphillips@lmi.net
users.lmi.net/mphillips/workshops.html

Richard C. Schwartz, PhD
Training Institute: The Center for Self Leadership
Workshops:

- Internal Family Systems Model of Psychotherapy
- Basic and Advanced IFS Trainings
- Annual IFS Conference

www.selfleadership.org
Contact: info@selfleadership.org

Joanne H. Twombly, MSW, LICSW
Consultant, American Society for Clinical Hypnosis
EMDRIA consultant
Facilitator, EMDR Humanitarian Assistance Programs
Executive Council Director, International Society for the Study of Trauma and Dissociation
Workshops:

- Diagnosis and Treatment of Dissociative Disordered Clients
- Stabilization of Dissociative Disordered Clients
- Phase One Treatment
- What IFS Therapists Need to Know about Diagnosis and Treatment of Dissociative Disordered Clients
- Using EMDR with Dissociative Disordered Clients

Contact: jtwombly@rcn.com

Index